# ABORIGINAL ONTARIO

# ABORIGINAL ONTARIO

## HISTORICAL PERSPECTIVES ON THE FIRST NATIONS

edited by
## Edward S. Rogers and Donald B. Smith

A publication of the
Ontario Historical Studies Series
for the Government of Ontario
Published by Dundurn Press
Toronto • Oxford

This book has been published with the assistance of funds provided by the Government of Ontario through the Ministry of Culture, Tourism and Recreation.

The publisher wishes to acknowledge the generous assistance and ongoing support of the Canada Council, the Book Publishing Industry Development Program of the Department of Canadian Heritage, the Ontario Arts Council, and the Ontario Publishing Centre of the Ministry of Culture, Tourism and Recreation.

Care has been taken to trace the ownership of copyright material used in the text (including the illustrations). The editors and publisher welcome any information enabling them to rectify any reference or credit in subsequent editions.

*J. Kirk Howard, Publisher*

Printed and bound in Canada

Canadian Cataloguing in Publication Data

Main entry under title:

Aboriginal Ontario : historical perspectives on the First Nations

(Ontario historical studies series)
Includes bibliographical references and index.
ISBN 1-55002-209-1 (bound)
ISBN 1-55002-230-X (pbk.)
1. Native peoples – Ontario – History.* I. Rogers, Edward S. II. Smith, Donald B., 1946–  III. Series.

E78.05A26 1994     971.3'00497     C94-930936-2

| Dundurn Press Limited | Dundurn Distribution | Dundurn Press Limited |
|---|---|---|
| 2181 Queen Street East | 73 Lime Walk | 1823 Maryland Avenue |
| Suite 301 | Headington, Oxford | P.O. Box 1000 |
| Toronto, Canada | England | Niagara Falls, N.Y. |
| M4E 1E5 | 0X3 7AD | U.S.A. 14302-1000 |

*Dedicated to Cam Currie,*
*who died 14 March 1981, with only nine months to retirement*

Campbell "Cam" Currie was a fur trader for the Hudson's Bay Company at Big Beaverhouse Post in northwestern Ontario before he joined the Ontario Department of Lands and Forests – now the Ministry of Natural Resources – in the 1950s. Here Cam is shown seated, holding the *mide* pipe. Standing in the back to the right is Thomas Fidler, chief of the Sandy Lake band. On either side of Cam are the two councillors. This photo was taken by Ed Rogers inside the *mide* lodge at Sandy Lake, 15 July 1958.

# Contents

# Maps

# Tables

# The Ontario Historical Studies Series

For many years English Canadian historical writing has emphasized the emergence and the consolidation of the Canadian nation. This theme has been developed in uneasy awareness of the persistence and importance of regional interests and identities, but because of the central role of Ontario in the growth of Canada, Ontario has not been seen as a region. Almost unconsciously, historians have equated the province's history with that of the nation and have often depicted the interests of other regions as obstacles to Canada's unity and welfare.

The creation of the province of Ontario in 1867 was the visible embodiment of a formidable reality, the existence at the core of the new nation of a powerful if disjointed society whose traditions and characteristics differed in many respects from those of the other British North American colonies. The intervening century has not witnessed the assimilation of Ontario to the other regions in Canada; on the contrary, it has become a more clearly articulated entity. Within the formal geographical and institutional framework defined so assiduously by Ontario's political leaders, an increasingly intricate web of economic and social interests has been woven and shaped by the dynamic interplay between Toronto and its hinterland. The tension between a rapid adaptation to the processes of modernization and industrialization in modern Western society and a reluctance to modify or discard traditional attitudes and values has formed the character of this regional community. Not surprisingly, the Ontario outlook has been, and in some measure still is, a compound of aggressiveness, conservatism, and the conviction that its values should serve as the model for the rest of Canada.

From the outset, the objective of the Series' Board of Trustees* was to describe and analyse the historical development of Ontario as a distinct region within Canada. The Series includes biographies of several premiers and thematic studies on the growth of the provincial economy, educational institutions, labour, welfare, the Franco-Ontarians, the Native peoples, and the arts.

---

* The corporation known as the Ontario Historical Studies Series ceased to exist 31 August 1993. This volume was completed and approved for publication before that date.

Professor Edward S. Rogers initiated *Aboriginal Ontario*. Following Dr. Rogers's untimely death in 1988, Professor Donald Smith generously agreed to become co-editor and to collaborate with the Series' editors in preparing the manuscript for publication. The contributors cooperated fully with Dr. Smith in completing this task.

From the outset, Dr. Rogers and his colleagues sought to prepare a series of essays on the histories of the Native peoples or First Nations in the area now defined as Ontario. Thus, they avoided structural and static descriptions of the Native societies. They worked instead to describe the development of the several First Nations in the context of their own rich history and the impact of their ongoing encounters with European culture. They have shown that, despite unrelenting pressure to become assimilated, the Native peoples have preserved their sense of social and cultural identity.

*Aboriginal Ontario* is a sympathetic and scholarly account, based on the large and steadily growing body of sources. It recognizes the complexity and variety of the historical experience of the First Nations in Ontario. We hope that it will be useful to Native and non-Native scholars and students, and that it will stimulate new research and writing on past and contemporary Native issues in this province.

The editors and the Board of Trustees are very grateful to the late Professor Rogers, to Professor Smith, and to their contributors for undertaking this task. We wish to thank Dr. Mary Black Rogers most warmly for her thoughtful assistance in completing this work. We hope that this volume will be a worthy memorial to Edward Rogers, a distinguished scholar, whose understanding of and respect for the Native peoples was recognized generously by them. Edward Rogers is buried at Weagamow (Round) Lake, Ontario, in the cemetery of the North Caribou Lake people with whom he worked from 1958 until his death. In honour of their friendship with this remarkable individual they welcomed his burial amongst them.

Goldwin French
Peter Oliver
Jeanne Beck
J.M.S. Careless, Chairman of the Board of Trustees

Toronto
August 1993

# Contributors

**CHARLES A. BISHOP** teaches anthropology at the State University of New York in Oswego, New York.

**GORDON M. DAY** (1911–93) was with the Canadian Ethnology Service, Canadian Museum of Civilization.

**WILLIAM G. DEAN** is the director of the *Historical Atlas of Canada* in Toronto.

**CHARLES HAMORI-TOROK** taught anthropology at Trent University in Peterborough.

**CHARLES M. JOHNSTON** taught history at McMaster University.

**HARVEY McCUE** is director of education and chief executive officer, Nova Scotia Mi'kmaq Education Authority, Membertou, Nova Scotia.

**EDWARD S. ROGERS** (1923–88) was chief ethnologist at the Royal Ontario Museum.

**DONALD B. SMITH** teaches Canadian history at the University of Calgary.

**ROBERT J. SURTEES** teaches history at Nipissing University College in North Bay.

**J. GARTH TAYLOR** is with the Canadian Ethnology Service, Canadian Museum of Civilization.

**ELISABETH TOOKER** taught anthropology at Temple University, Philadelphia, Pennsylvania.

**BRUCE G. TRIGGER** teaches anthropology at McGill University.

**SALLY M. WEAVER** (1940–93) taught anthropology at the University of Waterloo.

**JAMES V. WRIGHT** is curator emeritus of the Archaeological Survey of Canada, Canadian Museum of Civilization.

Ed Rogers, a sketch by his friend, James Lumbers, at Weagamow (Round Lake), Northern Ontario, in 1973.

# Dr. Ed Rogers, My Friend

I first met Dr. Rogers at the opening of the new Canadian Indian Centre on Church Street in Toronto in 1963.

In the summer of 1969, Dr. Rogers asked me – along with Jim Turner, Al Bigwin, and several others whose names I no longer remember – to serve on a search committee to select a candidate from an anticipated flood of applicants for a position with the Royal Ontario Museum that entailed initiating and developing an "Indian program" from an "Indian perspective." The program would be offered by the museum's Education Department and would use the Ethnology Department's resources. When no candidate applied for the position after several months of advertising, the committee and Dr. Rogers asked me to serve on a interim basis until a candidate was found. Two and a half years later, without a single applicant having come forward, Dr. Rogers asked me to stay on permanently. However, the museum management was not as keen as he was to employ a non-specialist. When Dr. Rogers heard of their reluctance, he stormed the director's office with fire in his eye in the same spirit as he had stormed the enemy lines in Germany in the Second World War. Management agreed to my services.

When hiring was confirmed, I asked Dr. Rogers what he wanted me to do to make the program work. He said that he didn't know and that it was up to me to develop a program. Until I saw the textbooks that were available to teachers and students and examined the Ministry of Education guidelines, I followed no particular strategy to carry out an "Indian program" from an "Indian perspective." I was bothered by the fact that I had no specific objective and was not introducing anything new to the gallery talks. Compared to Dr. Rogers and his colleagues, who were productive, I could show nothing special for my efforts.

I was uneasy. From time to time Dr. Rogers would appear in the alcove, in the storage area that served as my office, to summon me to his office with dread words delivered in a grave tone and with equally grave looks: "I want to see you in my office ... now!"

On my way to his inner sanctum, I quaked as I examined my conscience for misdeeds committed. This was of course absurd, for I had done nothing that could be construed either as good or bad. I surmised that the real reason Dr. Rogers wanted to see me was for doing nothing. I found myself regretting having left the security and the nine years of seniority of service with the North York Board of Education to take on this uncertain position.

"Close the door!" That invitation only served to confirm my foreboding and I waited for the worst. The dark looks, the tone, and the pause were charged with presentiment. "A situation has arisen ... I need your advice."

It was only after I realized that this was the way of an intense, serious, and sincere person that my fear of Dr. Rogers subsided. Dr. Rogers sought my advice as well as that of others because he felt that his experience and academic training did not qualify him to interpret Native culture with the degree of accuracy that his principles and his sense of integrity demanded. Besides, there were none better qualified to interpret their own cultures than Native people themselves. He valued the advice of Tom Archibald, Tom Medicine, Willie Wilson, Gus Debossige, Jean Shawana, Flora Tobobondung, Tom Hill, Delia Opekokew, Mel Hill, Dick and Dan Pine more than he did that of academics. "We're here to serve the Natives," he often said, "and we have to listen."

And Dr. Rogers listened to anyone regardless of his or her cause or politics, and he listened to the unpleasant with the same attention he gave to the pleasant. Three members of the Canadian Branch of the American Indian Movement came into his office and castigated the museum, the Department of Ethnology, and anthropologists. For three hours Dr. Rogers listened. The delegation left at noon shaking hands with him as in friendship before they went out. In the same year a militant young woman took Dr. Rogers aside at a conference and denounced him as a pretentious do-gooder and for butting into the lives of Native people. Throughout the tirade Dr. Rogers said nary a word, difficult as this must have been for a man with his temper. Before the conference wound up, the young woman offered her hand in conciliation. It is doubtful that Dr. Rogers would have gained the trust and respect in Native communities that he did had he not respected and trusted the ideas and ways of others.

As I got to know Dr. Rogers better, I lost my fear of him. I now proposed that instead of artifacts I would use "Indian culture" as the focus of my talks. Dr. Rogers agreed, although I believe he was disappointed in my disregard of anthropology and artifacts. Now I felt sure enough of Dr. Rogers and confident enough in myself to try new directions and approaches. His willingness to listen to me and to allow me scope in my work was in keeping with his principles.

For years I felt, perhaps without reason, that I was indebted to Dr. Rogers for putting up with my lack of production and allowing me scope in my work, but after my fifth book, *Ojibway Ceremonies,* was published by McClelland & Stewart in 1982, I felt that I had earned my place on the staff of the museum on my merits. I invited Dr. Rogers to lunch and there proposed a toast: "To our association, Ed. I don't owe you a thing anymore." He looked at me quizzically and then replied, "I was wondering when you'd say that ... I'm glad."

As administrator and teacher, Dr. Rogers was demanding and tough, but it wasn't until a publisher sent me a raw manuscript for evaluation that I found that he also had a sense of fairness. When I asked him what to look for in a manuscript, he replied, "Look for the good however hard it may be to find," and then he added, "but above all be fair."

In the late 1970s a major expansion program for the Royal Ontario Museum was announced. There were to be new and enlarged galleries for every department. Dr. Rogers looked forward to the day when the new and expanded ethnology galleries would be opened to the public. He dreamed. He had always been addicted to work. Now with something to look forward to, he, Ken Lister, and Arnie Brownstone worked with even greater energy in the design and planning of the new galleries.

But times had changed. Curators no longer had the authority they formerly had to direct what exhibitions were to be mounted and when. After the Scott Report of 1976 recommended a restructuring of the museum's organization and systems and as succeeding administrations added further refinements and modifications, the institution became more and more bureaucratic, its bureaucracy finally being matched in complexity by its bureaucratic system. It was now agonizing to initiate and carry out plans, programs, and exhibitions. Despite the money, the service of consultants, and the time and energy expended upon the new designs, the first set of plans that Dr. Rogers and his team drafted was scuttled in the labyrinth of bureaucracy. For a man with a dream and accustomed to getting things done, the sabotage of his plans was a bitter disappointment.

But he started afresh. Again, and again. By the time he and his planning team had submitted their fifth revision of gallery designs, Dr. Rogers was dispirited and depressed. He was also ravaged by cancer.

The last time I saw Ed and Mary, his wife, at their home in Burlington, Ontario, he asked me, "Basil, when do you think our galleries will be open?"

I wish I could have said, "In two years" or some other projected time, but I couldn't. Instead, I replied, "Not for twenty years, if ever."

Ed looked at me with great sadness and resignation. The fire had gone out of his eyes. Before the winter was over, the life had gone out of my friend's body.

Basil Johnston

# *Preface*

DONALD B. SMITH

Long before the current resurgence of interest in Canada's Native peoples, Ed Rogers saw the importance of their contribution to our history. In the late 1970s he solicited the papers for this collection of essays on the history of the First Nations in Ontario. Unfortunately, this pioneer of Canadian ethnography died in 1988 before he had finished editing the volume. Appointed as the co-editor of the manuscript in 1989, I have completed Dr. Rogers's work. As editor I have kept the original format of the book and have made only one major addition, a short concluding chapter.

Ed Rogers was, with J.M.S. Careless, one of my two PhD thesis advisers in the early 1970s. To him I owe so much. It has been an honour to complete my adviser's, and friend's, unique contribution to our understanding of Aboriginal Ontario.

In addition to all the contributors, Ed Rogers wished to thank Kay Hipgrave, his secretary, for her help in the preparation of the manuscript. He also thanked Goldwin French, Peter Oliver, Jeanne Beck, and also Shirlee Ann Smith, John Leslie, David McNab, Ted Wilson, and Don Bourgeois; and in particular his wife, Mary Black Rogers. After his death Heather Duncan assisted with the typing of the final drafts. Michel Bouchard, Ken Lister, John Macfie, Brian Turner, and Roger Wheate helped with the photos. Marta Styk drew several special maps. Barbara Nair completed the index. At Dundurn Press we thank president Kirk Howard, editor Judith Turnbull, designer Andy Tong, and promotion manager Jeanne MacDonald. Donald Smith adds his gratitude to his mother, Jean Smith, for her hospitality on editorial trips to Toronto, and thanks his wife, Nancy Townshend, and his two sons, David and Peter, for allowing him to bring the manuscript on several family vacations.

University of Calgary
23 January 1994

# Introduction

EDWARD S. ROGERS and
DONALD B. SMITH

Formerly, ethnologists generally ignored the history of Canada's Aboriginal peoples, offering instead structural and static descriptions of "traditional" cultures as though the North American Indians had never experienced any change in their way of life. In the 1950s, however, a growing number of historians, ethnologists, and social scientists began to investigate the history of the First Nations in Ontario and Canada. Research utilizing historical and ethnological methodologies (and drawing as well on the insights of historical geographers, archaeologists, linguists, and biologists) has altered dramatically the non-Indian's perception of the Indian.[1]

So much remains to be done. To date, researchers have only just begun to probe the published and manuscript accounts about North American Aboriginal peoples. In addition, the usefulness of the First Nations' own traditions in deepening our understanding of the changes that have occurred in their culture is only now fully appreciated.[2] Yet, at the same time, the general reader needs an interim summary of the published information that already exists about the rich, varied, and complex history of North American Indians in Ontario. We hope that many others will add, in further books and publications, to our awareness of the First Nations' history.

Throughout this volume various words – Amerindian, Native, and Aboriginal – are used to designate the North American Indian population of Ontario and Canada. Recently, the population's favoured designation has become an English term used in the Royal Proclamation of 1763, in treaties, and in major American legal decisions – the word "nation." Today many Amerindians in Canada refer to themselves as "First Nations." According to the definition of the House of Commons Special Committee on Indian Self-Government (the Penner Commission) of 1983, "nation" means "a group of people with a common language, culture and history who identify with each other as belonging to a common political entity." The term "First Nation" appears in the title of this book and in the text. While no longer the preferred term, "Indian" does remain in regular use, even among the Aboriginal people themselves; hence it also appears.

A word about First Nations and European cultural interchange is also necessary. The authors of the following chapters sometimes write about "Indians" and "Europeans" as though each had remained a distinct entity throughout their years of contact. Although true in the sense that ethnic identities have been preserved, it must be kept in mind that the two peoples have influenced each other. In the process, new cultural configurations have emerged, and the Indians and the immigrants have become in a sense bi-cultural.

Cultural exchanges have taken place between the two peoples; genes have been mixed. Soon after the arrival of Europeans, a new group arose, the "half-breeds," also spoken of at various times as "mixed-bloods" or "country born." Today "Métis" is the official term, one that began to be used during the last century. It has now been enshrined in the Canada Act, 1982.

The chapters in this volume describe the historical events and changes that have occurred in the culture of the First Nations since the arrival of Europeans in what is now known as Ontario. Significantly, in spite of all the alterations in their original way of life, their descendants continue to maintain a distinct identity, one that, while not identical with that of pre-contact Indians, is surely not European.

At the outset it must be pointed out that the federal Indian Act applies only to "status" Indians. In Canada the federal government has, since Confederation, decided who would be legally recognized as Indians. According to the federal Indian Act, the term "Indian" refers to "a person who pursuant to the Act is registered as an Indian or who is entitled to be registered as an Indian." Neither culture nor ethnic origin serves as a necessary condition for an individual to become registered. Instead, only those individuals whom the Canadian government has enrolled through treaty, or who (if not covered by a treaty) have been duly registered, are recognized legally as Indians.

From the time of the enactment of the first Indian Act, in 1876, until 1985, a non-registered woman who married a registered male automatically gained legal Indian status. But a registered Indian woman who married a non-Indian lost hers. Consequently, many Indian women and their descendants became non-status Indians and were subsequently deleted from the rolls. Since 1985, however, these women and their children (and grandchildren) have been able to regain their Indian status.

A number of individuals who are not registered but who do have significant Native ancestry consider themselves either Métis or non-status Indians. These non-status Indians are those who, for one reason or another, have never been enrolled. In 1982 "Métis" gained equal status with "Indian" in the Constitution Act of 1867 (formerly the British North America [BNA] Act) as Aboriginal inhabitants of what has become Canada. Possibly there are as many Métis and non-status Indians residing within Ontario as treaty or registered Indians.[3]

Although the First Nations of Ontario have experienced many alterations in their way of life through contact with Europeans, these changes have taken place within the context of a rich and varied heritage, one the Indians possessed long before the arrival of aliens from across the Atlantic Ocean. They continue to perceive themselves as a distinct and distinctive people – whether under the name Indian or Native American; Cree, Ojibwa, or Mohawk; or, as the Ojibwa (and many others in their own speech) would say today, the *Anishinabeg*, "the people."

Most of the Native peoples of Ontario spoke, and many still do, a language in one of either the Algonquian (or Algonkian) or Iroquoian linguistic families. Until the eighteenth century members of the Siouan linguistic family may also have occupied the Boundary Waters region along the 49th parallel, separating present-day Minnesota from Ontario. The languages of these three linguistic families are mutually unintelligible. Within the respective language families, however, the separate languages can be close, which is the case for Cree and Ojibwa in the Algonquian linguistic family and, say Mohawk and Oneida in the Iroquoian.

The Algonquians originally resident in what is now Ontario include the Algonquin (or Algonkin), Nipissing, Ottawa (or Odawa), Cree, and Ojibwa. The Ojibwa carry one of several names that reflect historical developments and/or minor dialect differences. Chippewa, Saulteaux, Mississauga, and Ojibwa all refer to peoples speaking similar, if not identical, dialects. In this volume, Ojibwa is used throughout for all five, unless a variant occurs in a quotation. Other bands of Algonquians arrived in the region during the late eighteenth and early nineteenth centuries. These included Ottawa, Delaware, Potawatomi, and a few Shawnee and Nanticoke.

The Iroquoians comprise several groups. The original inhabitants, the Huron, Petun, and Neutral, became dispersed shortly after the middle of the seventeenth century. Somewhat later, a few Huron and their allies, now known as Wyandot, returned to the neighbourhood of modern Sarnia and Windsor. Others – Mohawk, Oneida, Tuscarora, Onondaga, Cayuga, Seneca, and a small number of Tutelo – came to reside in present-day Southern Ontario during the late eighteenth and early nineteenth centuries. Many still live in one of their five territories within the province.

For convenience of presentation, the province has been divided into two. Arbitrarily the Robinson-Huron, Robinson-Superior, Treaty No. 3, and Treaty

No. 9 areas have been chosen to represent Northern Ontario. The northern region lies roughly above a line running from North Bay to Lake of the Woods (extending north to James and Hudson bays) and contains (including all inland waters) over a million square kilometres. The southern section, below this line, is roughly one-quarter of the province.[4]

This volume describes the diverse historical events that have had an impact on the First Nations in Ontario and the cultural changes in their societies since they first encountered Europeans. Although cultural change has taken place continuously both before and after the arrival of Europeans, the moment when a particular change occurred generally went unrecorded. Accordingly, precise dating is often not possible; one must infer an approximate date or period. It must be added as well that, as a rule, only the invaders left accounts of what happened. Not until relatively recently have Amerindians committed their observations to paper. The contributors to this volume have done their best to interpret the records, both published and unpublished, left by the non-Indians, records often written from a highly partisan point of view.

It should be noted, too, that the non-Indian contributors to this volume do not necessarily perceive history in the same light as would Aboriginal persons.[5] A history of Aboriginal Ontario written by Amerindians would not have been so concerned with precise dates and chronological sequences. North American Indians have their own style of narration that often collapses time, in effect making it relatively unimportant. In the Ojibwa's case, for example, the verification of events occurs as follows: "I saw the event and therefore know"; "I was informed by those who witnessed the event"; "I was told stories of the past when no one now living was there to witness the event."

*Aboriginal Ontario* chronicles Indian-European relationships and the First Nations' changing ways of life from the sixteenth century, when the Europeans' presence was first beginning to be felt in northern North America, to the present. It divides the story into four sections: Part One, Background; Part Two, Southern Ontario, 1550–1945; Part Three, Northern Ontario, 1550–1945; and Part Four, Post–Second World War Years.

In chapter 1, Part One (Background), William G. Dean describes the natural environment when Europeans first arrived in what is now known as Ontario. In time their presence greatly changed the environment in ways that had an important impact on the First Nations. In chapter 2 archaeologist James V. Wright reviews the history of the former inhabitants of what is today Ontario, from their first appearance several millennia ago to the sixteenth century.

In chapter 3, Part Two (Southern Ontario, 1550–1945), Bruce G. Trigger outlines the experience of the Huron, Petun, and Neutral, who by the mid-seventeenth century had been captured, killed, or dispersed from their homes by members of the League of the Iroquois, then residing south of Lake Ontario in what is today the state of New York. The Iroquoians, routed from their homeland in Southern Ontario, farmed small plots of land and lived in villages. They proved relatively easy prey for the Iroquois warriors.

Many members of the League eventually migrated to Southern Ontario, where their descendants still live. Accordingly, it is important to know something of their history prior to their arrival in the province. Elisabeth Tooker, in chapter 5, provides this kind of information when she describes the League and its military activities, which for a time seriously threatened the French and their Indian allies living north of the Upper Great Lakes.

The fortunes of the Iroquois confederacy changed at the end of the American Revolution, when the Mohawk and other League members sought asylum in what is now Ontario. In chapter 8 Charles M. Johnston describes their movement to and settlement in the Grand River valley, where they established a viable farming community. Sally M. Weaver recounts their story to 1945, giving particular emphasis to the history of the Six Nations Confederacy Council, in chapters 9 and 10. The history of the other Iroquois groups – those belonging to the Akwesasne, Mohawks of the Bay of Quinte (Tyendinaga), and Wahta Mohawk (Gibson) communities, and the Onyota'a:ka (Oneida of the Thames) – is dealt with briefly by Charles Hamori-Torok in chapter 11.

The Algonquian-speaking inhabitants of what is now northeastern Ontario never felt the full impact of the Iroquois attacks as did the Huron, Petun, and Neutral. Following the dispersion of the Huron, Petun, and Neutral during the mid-seventeenth century, the Ojibwa gradually migrated southward to occupy the vacated lands. Other Algonquians, such as the Algonquin, Nipissing, and Ottawa, who had been dispersed from their ancestral territories by the once-powerful Iroquois, eventually returned to their homelands, a migration described by Bruce G. Trigger and Gordon M. Day in chapter 4. Some Algonquians, such as the Potawatomi, fled from the United States in the 1830s to escape its Indian policy and settled in what is now Ontario.

With the Treaty of Paris in 1763, the Algonquians of what is now Southern Ontario, as well as the Native people living in the borderlands near the Thirteen Colonies, came (in terms of European law) under British jurisdiction, a fundamental event that was marked by the Royal Proclamation of 1763. Little more than a decade after the settlement with France, however, the American Revolution challenged British rule in North America. One significant consequence was the exodus of Amerindian and white Loyalists into Ontario. To secure land for these settlers, the imperial government initiated a process whereby the Ojibwa surrendered most of their territory to the Crown

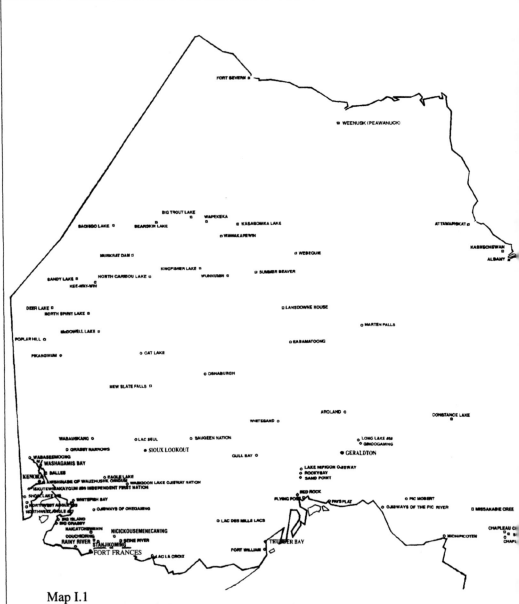

Map I.1
First Nations Communities in Northern Ontario
(showing Northern Ontario as it is defined in *Aboriginal Ontario;* northwestern
Ontario above, northeastern Ontario facing page)

From a map entitled "First Nations, Ontario," prepared by Indian and Northern Affairs Canada and the Ontario Native Affairs
Secretariat, 1991. Revised 1993

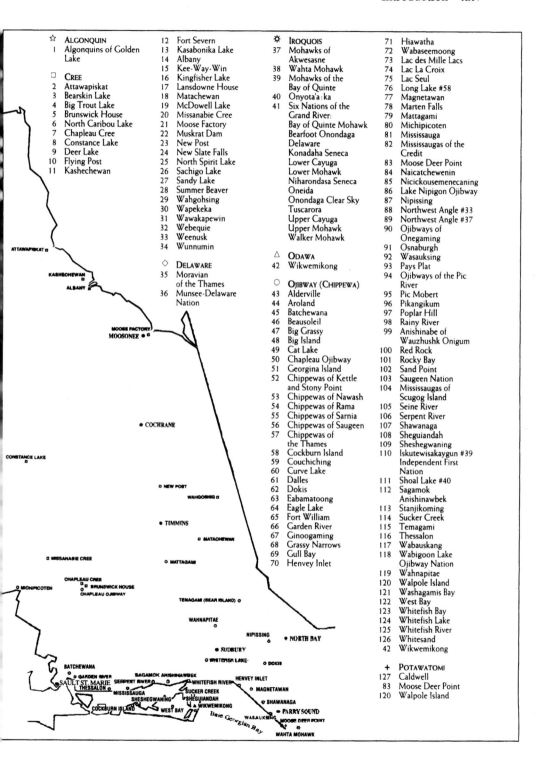

☆ ALGONQUIN
1 Algonquins of Golden Lake

□ CREE
2 Attawapiskat
3 Bearskin Lake
4 Big Trout Lake
5 Brunswick House
6 North Caribou Lake
7 Chapleau Cree
8 Constance Lake
9 Deer Lake
10 Flying Post
11 Kashechewan

12 Fort Severn
13 Kasabonika Lake
14 Albany
15 Kee-Way-Win
16 Kingfisher Lake
17 Lansdowne House
18 Matachewan
19 McDowell Lake
20 Missanabie Cree
21 Moose Factory
22 Muskrat Dam
23 New Post
24 New Slate Falls
25 North Spirit Lake
26 Sachigo Lake
27 Sandy Lake
28 Summer Beaver
29 Wahgohsing
30 Wapekeka
31 Wawakapewin
32 Webequie
33 Weenusk
34 Wunnumin

◇ DELAWARE
35 Moravian of the Thames
36 Munsee-Delaware Nation

✿ IROQUOIS
37 Mohawks of Akwesasne
38 Wahta Mohawk
39 Mohawks of the Bay of Quinte
40 Onyota'a:ka
41 Six Nations of the Grand River:
Bay of Quinte Mohawk
Bearfoot Onondaga
Delaware
Konadaha Seneca
Lower Cayuga
Lower Mohawk
Niharondasa Seneca
Oneida
Onondaga Clear Sky
Tuscarora
Upper Cayuga
Upper Mohawk
Walker Mohawk

△ ODAWA
42 Wikwemikong

○ OJIBWAY (CHIPPEWA)
43 Alderville
44 Aroland
45 Batchewana
46 Beausoleil
47 Big Grassy
48 Big Island
49 Cat Lake
50 Chapleau Ojibway
51 Georgina Island
52 Chippewas of Kettle and Stony Point
53 Chippewas of Nawash
54 Chippewas of Rama
55 Chippewas of Sarnia
56 Chippewas of Saugeen
57 Chippewas of the Thames
58 Cockburn Island
59 Couchiching
60 Curve Lake
61 Dalles
62 Dokis
63 Eabamatoong
64 Eagle Lake
65 Fort William
66 Garden River
67 Ginoogaming
68 Grassy Narrows
69 Gull Bay
70 Henvey Inlet

71 Hiawatha
72 Wabaseemoong
73 Lac des Mille Lacs
74 Lac La Croix
75 Lac Seul
76 Long Lake #58
77 Magnetawan
78 Marten Falls
79 Mattagami
80 Michipicoten
81 Mississauga
82 Mississaugas of the Credit
83 Moose Deer Point
84 Naicatchewenin
85 Nicickousemenecaning
86 Lake Nipigon Ojibway
87 Nipissing
88 Northwest Angle #33
89 Northwest Angle #37
90 Ojibways of Onegaming
91 Osnaburgh
92 Wasauksing
93 Pays Plat
94 Ojibways of the Pic River
95 Pic Mobert
96 Pikangikum
97 Poplar Hill
98 Rainy River
99 Anishinabe of Wauzhushk Onigum
100 Red Rock
101 Rocky Bay
102 Sand Point
103 Saugeen Nation
104 Mississaugas of Scugog Island
105 Seine River
106 Serpent River
107 Shawanaga
108 Sheguiandah
109 Sheshegwaning
110 Iskutewisakaygun #39 Independent First Nation
111 Shoal Lake #40
112 Sagamok Anishinawbek
113 Stanjikoming
114 Sucker Creek
115 Temagami
116 Thessalon
117 Wabauskang
118 Wabigoon Lake Ojibway Nation
119 Wahnapitae
120 Walpole Island
121 Washagamis Bay
122 West Bay
123 Whitefish Bay
124 Whitefish Lake
125 Whitefish River
126 Whitesand
42 Wikwemikong

+ POTAWATOMI
127 Caldwell
83 Moose Deer Point
120 Walpole Island

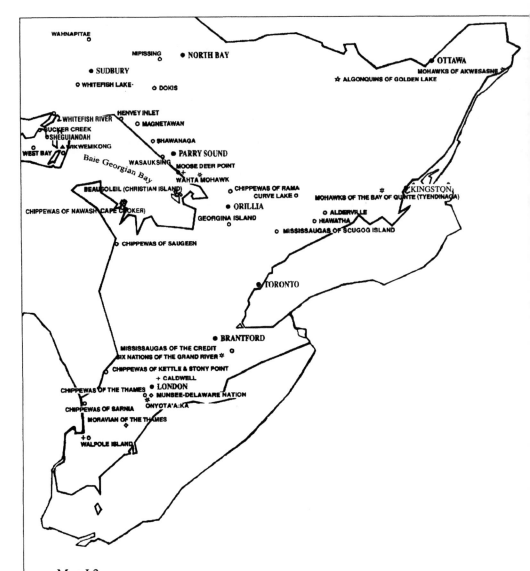

Map I.2
First Nations Communities in Southern Ontario
(showing Southern Ontario as it is defined in *Aboriginal Ontario*)

From a map entitled "First Nations, Ontario," prepared by Indian and Northern Affairs Canada and the Ontario
Native Affairs Secretariat, 1991. Revised 1993

in return for some form of compensation. Robert J. Surtees introduces these land surrenders, the first of which was made in 1764, in chapter 6. He concludes his account with the Williams Treaty, which was finally signed in 1923 after three decades of negotiations. As the Southern Algonquians, primarily the Ojibwa, ceded their lands, they became more and more confined to reserves, where they began to farm. To a degree, this compensated them for the partial loss of their former hunting, fishing, and gathering grounds. In chapter 7 Ed Rogers describes the transformation of many Algonquian hunters and fishers into Victorian farmers during the nineteenth century in Southern Ontario.

In Part Three (Northern Ontario, 1550–1945) the history and adaptations made by the Algonquian inhabitants – the Cree and Ojibwa – are presented. Charles A. Bishop outlines in chapter 12 what is known of the way of life and the changes that took place among these Northern Algonquians, particularly in northwestern Ontario, after the arrival of the fur traders. Unfortunately, the data at best are fragmentary and hence open to alternate interpretations. Bishop continues the story in chapter 13, in which he reviews the intense rivalry between the Hudson's Bay and the North West companies, a conflict that ended with their amalgamation in 1821. Ed Rogers takes up the story in chapter 14. The mid-nineteenth century proved a time of relative stability in the relations between the Amerindians and the traders in both northeastern and northwestern Ontario. Conditions changed, however, as the nineteenth century drew to a close, at which time an increasing number and variety of Euro-Canadians entered Northern Ontario. This disrupted the familiar pace of life that the Indians had experienced during the preceding decades, as J. Garth Taylor describes in chapter 15.

In the last half of the twentieth century, the First Nations in Northern and Southern Ontario have gradually come to resemble each other more than previously. The final part of this history considers the two groups as one. Following the Second World War, the Amerindians of Ontario entered a new age, one of increasingly rapid technological and social change. Harvey McCue in chapter 16, Part Four (Post–Second World War Years), describes these developments (to 1980). In a brief concluding chapter Donald Smith provides a short overview of 10 000 years of Aboriginal Ontario's history.

# *NOTES*

1    See, for example, B.G. Trigger, *Natives and Newcomers: Canada's "Heroic Age" Reconsidered* (Kingston and Montreal 1985), particularly chapters 2 and 3. See also B.G. Trigger, "Indians and Ontario History," *Ontario History* 74, no. 4 (1982): 246–57.

2    See, for example, G.R. Hamell, "Strawberries, Floating Islands and Rabbit Captains: Mythical Realities and European Contact in the Northeast during the Sixteenth and Seventeenth Centuries," *Journal of Canadian Studies* 21, no. 4 (1986/87): 72–94.

3    Canada, House of Commons, *Minutes of the Special Committee on Self-Government*, 12 and 20 October 1983 (Ottawa 1983), 12

4    Ontario has an area of 1 068 582 square kilometres, including 177 388 square kilometres of inland waters (Robert Bothwell and Norman Hillmer, "Ontario," in *The Canadian Encyclopedia*, 2d ed. [Edmonton 1988], 1567.

5    All the contributors to the volume, with the exception of Harvey McCue, are non-Indian.

# ABORIGINAL
# ONTARIO

# *Part One*
## *Background*

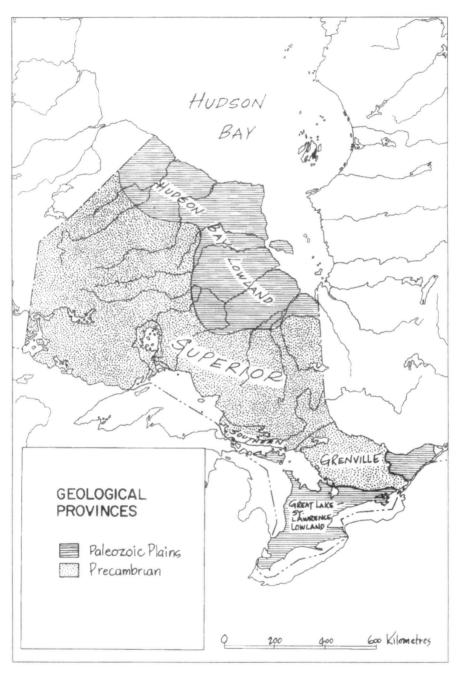

GEOLOGICAL
PROVINCES

Paleozoic Plains
Precambrian

HUDSON BAY

HUDSON BAY LOWLAND

SUPERIOR

SOUTHERN

GRENVILLE

GREAT LAKE ST LAWRENCE LOWLAND

0   200   400   600 Kilometres

Map 1.1
Geological Provinces of Ontario

# 1 *The Ontario Landscape, circa* A.D. *1600*

WILLIAM G. DEAN

Today there is no place where one can feel confident the landscape remains exactly as the first inhabitants saw it. No matter how remote, the most isolated places have not escaped being altered by people in some subtle way. Even without human interference, the landscape itself is never completely stable. Natural processes continually change existing vegetation, landforms, stream systems, soils, and animal life – in short the total ecosystem. Climatic variations, natural fires, and erosion are but three crucial elements among many involved in the alteration of the landscape; over the centuries such elements have affected in many ways, still little understood, the way of life of the Amerindians.

The landscape of Ontario circa A.D. 1600, that is, before the arrival of Europeans, was occupied by an indigenous population. Scattered and often living in isolated groups, the Amerindians made use of their environment and thus changed it. Those who lived in semi-permanent settlements cultivated maize and other crops in cleared areas of the forest that enclosed their villages; locally, therefore, they changed their surroundings. Indeed, an early French missionary, Gabriel Sagard, described Huronia, in present-day northern Simcoe County, as "a well cleared country bearing much excellent hay."[1] Others subsisted by hunting and trading up and down the river systems, and in all likelihood, except for causing the occasional forest fire, set intentionally or accidentally, they scarcely altered the primeval wilderness that was their home.

## Major Geographical Units

To gain some insight into the Ontario landscape at the beginning of the seventeenth century, one must turn to reports of explorers or travellers. Although they made no apparently conscious effort to do so, the earliest accounts of the land and resources distinguished the major geographical units within Ontario.

Early in the seventeenth century, for example, Champlain referred to the "pleasing character" of the land south of Georgian Bay and the "ill favoured" "bad country" to the north.[2] Captain Thomas James, in 1633, wrote of the bleak coasts of Hudson and James bays, "utterly barren of all goodness."[3] In 1822 the shrewd and imaginative Robert Gourlay prepared a map consisting of three areas: the peninsula between Lakes Huron, Erie, and Ontario and the Canadian Shield; the Canadian Shield; and the Hudson Bay Lowland. These are still recognized as the fundamental landscape regions of Ontario (see Map 1.1, page 2). The Amerindians who inhabited this vast area made their own accommodations to each region.

Territorially, Ontario encompasses over a million square kilometres, of which nearly 180 000 square kilometres are inland waters. This is roughly one-tenth (10.8 percent) of the total size of Canada. The south-north distance by air from Middle Island in Lake Erie, the most southerly place in Canada, to Fort Severn on the shores of Hudson Bay is over 1 770 kilometres. From the southeastern limit near Cornwall to the northwestern just beyond Kenora, the air distance is over 1 609 kilometres.

Despite the geographical immensity of Ontario, the physical variation in a general sense is relatively small. The comparative uniformity is reflected in the relatively small and gradual differences in elevation. Most of Ontario stands between 152 metres and 304 metres above sea level. Only along the shores of James and Hudson bays is sea level reached. Ogaidaki Mountain, Ontario's highest point, reaches 665 metres. This vast extent of country with so few impediments to mobility allowed the Indians, if they so desired, to travel long distances with comparative ease.

The physical characteristics of Ontario are most conveniently described in the context of Robert Gourlay's three broad regions: the Canadian Shield, the Southern Ontario Plains, and the Hudson Bay Lowland.

The Canadian Shield, exposed over much of Northern Ontario, has been for centuries the home of Algonquian-speaking Indians – hunters and fishers *par excellence*. It is a land of many lakes tied together by a network of streams and rivers that provided highways for the Native peoples both summer and winter. Thin acidic soils and short cool summers inhibited the raising of crops. Accordingly, the Amerindian inhabitants had little choice but to be hunters, fishers, and gatherers.

Across the Great Lakes–St. Lawrence Lowland, two steep escarpments of more resistant rocks rise sharply above intervening lowlands underlain by weaker rocks (see Map 1.2). Their steep limestone cliffs face the Shield; their backslopes dip gently to the southwest. Here on this lowland the horticultural Iroquoians made their home. Soil and climate, favourable for the raising of crops, allowed them to lead a sedentary existence.

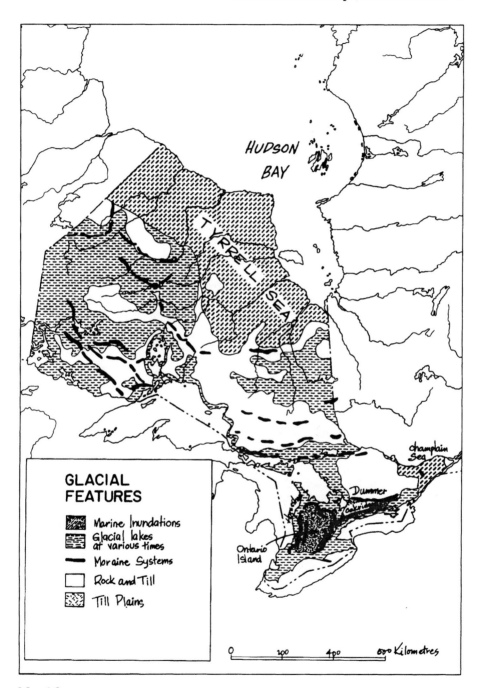

**Map 1.2**
**Glacial Features of Ontario**

The other plain, the Hudson Bay Lowlands of Northern Ontario, is completely different. Its surface is comprised largely of the floor deposits of the Tyrrell Sea, the early post-glacial forerunner of Hudson Bay. As the land rebounded from the weight of the ice sheet, this sea gradually fell in level to the present configuration of Hudson and James bays, forming flights of raised beaches, bars, and spits whose low profiles are the only relief on an otherwise flat plain of over 260 000 kilometres. Across the plain the major rivers flow in canal-like valleys; the only significant tree growth is found along these river banks. Muskeg and bog cover most of the plain, and the dominant sphagnum moss forms a kind of organic terrain, controlling local drainage and vegetation patterns.[4] Within these lowlands only a few Algonquians eked out a meagre existence.

**Retreat of the Glaciers**

The massive glaciers of the last two million years of Earth's history – the Pleistocene Ice Ages – had profound effects on the Ontario landscape, especially the last, "Wisconsinan" ice advance. This reached its maximum limits well south of Ontario approximately 18 000 years ago. It wasted away from the Great Lakes area beginning about 14 000 years ago and disappeared from Northern Ontario between 8 000 and 9 000 years ago. The Wisconsinan ice sculptured the details of the Ontario landscape and produced the network of waterways and the gentle terrain that later became the home of the Iroquoians and Algonquians.

Of particular significance both to the appearance and human settlement of Ontario were the landforms resulting from the rise and fall of the Great Lakes. As the Wisconsinan ice sheet melted, large and small melt-water lakes gradually evolved into the modern Great Lakes over a period of some 13 000 years. Various recognizably independent lakes successively occupied each of the present lake basins.[5] Between 13 000 and 11 000 years ago, Lake Whittlesey and then Lake Warren filled the Erie Basin, Lake Iroquois the Ontario Basin, and Lake Algonquin the Huron–Georgian Bay basins. At their highest levels, all extended many kilometres inland from present lake shores. In turn, all gave rise to a lake-bevelled terrain, often clay floored, bordered by discontinuous, usually sandy shore structures. Along the beaches left by these bodies of water, evidence of early humans has been recovered. Other large pre-glacial lakes later in time profoundly affected the landscape of Northern Ontario. Successive high- and low-level stages of Lakes Barlow, Ojibway, and Antevs in northeastern Ontario produced the extensive clay belts of the area.[6] A similar succession of fluctuating lake levels occurred in northwestern Ontario where Lake Agassiz flooded eastwards from central Manitoba, virtually to

Lake Nipigon during some phases.[7] Similarly, when some 11 500 years ago the Champlain Sea flooded the St. Lawrence Lowlands, salt water from the Tyrrell Sea inundated the Hudson Bay Lowland.[8] Not until the water receded and the flora and fauna had become re-established were the Aboriginal peoples able to occupy these areas. With the draining of the great glacial lakes, Ontario came to look very much as it does in thickly forested places today.

## Ontario's Climate

Most of Ontario's territory is truly northern, yet its southernmost peninsula juts as far south as the latitude of Florence in Italy and the northern boundary of California in the United States. Thus, climatically, this land ranges from an Arctic climate along the shores of Hudson Bay to the climate of temperate southern regions along the shores of Lakes Erie and Ontario. (See Map 1.3, page 8.)

The Great Lakes moderate to some degree Ontario's climate of extremes. They retard the warming of the surrounding land in spring and early summer because the water remains cool. They also extend the autumn season by retaining their summer warmth. In all seasons, the lakes are an important source of moisture, providing much of Southern Ontario with unusually uniform precipitation throughout the year. (See Map 1.4, page 9.) Because of these favourable climatic conditions, the Native peoples of the southern parts could engage in horticulture.

The coolest climatic period in the historic era is known as the "Little Ice Age." Authorities differ on its precise dates, but there is no doubt its major effects were felt between A.D. 1430 and A.D. 1850. Except for a brief warm spell between 1635 and 1650, the whole period between 1600 and 1730 was one of severe cold. The nadir of post-glacial low temperatures was reached between 1665 and 1685.[9] Much warmer weather has been experienced in the twentieth century.

Although there were undoubtedly episodes of equable weather, the overall climate of the 1600s was certainly harsher than it is today. Average temperatures ranged from one to three degrees Fahrenheit lower, which meant slightly shorter, cooler summers. Precipitation, too, was different. Droughts, for instance, have been calculated as having occurred two to three times every ten years, some severe enough to produce crop failures and famine among the Huron.[10] Midsummer frosts were then not uncommon. In 1600 ninety-day frost-free periods were probable, still a long enough growing period for most of the crops cultivated by Native peoples. It was, however, only in Southern Ontario that climate[11] and soils amenable to their agriculture existed. The northern or Boreal climates and soils were unsuited to agriculture.

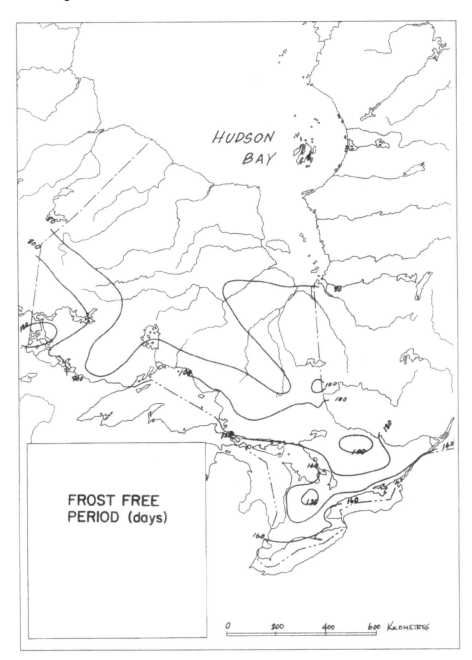

Map 1.3
Frost-Free Period (Days) in Ontario

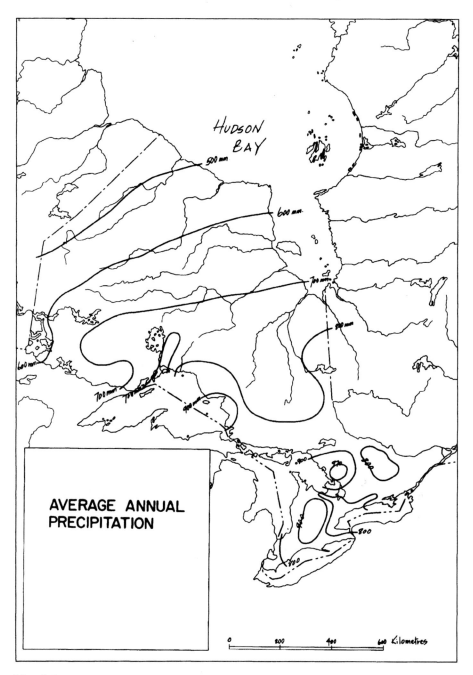

Map 1.4
Average Annual Precipitation in Ontario

Boreal climates are harshly cold, having mean annual temperatures at or below freezing. Ontario's tiny fragment of the Arctic extends in a narrow band along the south shore of Hudson Bay and northwestern James Bay, a treeless, open tundra. This frigid band of land was likely not inhabited by Amerindians until the arrival of European traders.

## Vegetation

Before it was stripped and forever altered by European farmers, lumbermen, and others, most of Ontario's vegetation consisted of relatively dense forest interspersed with open park-like woodland. Today, Ontario includes the remnants of what were once three major distinctive forest regions: the Southern Broadleaf Forest, the Southeastern Mixed Forest, and the Boreal Forest.[12] (See Map 1.5.) The Native peoples accommodated their lifestyle to their local environments.

### Southern Broadleaf Forest

Extending inland varying distances from the shores of Lakes Huron, Erie, and Ontario, from Goderich to Belleville, the Southern Broadleaf Forest is a continuation of the widespread deciduous forests of the eastern United States. It probably reaches this particular northern limit because of the moderating influences of Lakes Erie and Ontario. In composition it has many similarities with the Great Lakes–St. Lawrence Forest in that prevalent trees are sugar and red maple, beech, black cherry, ironwood, basswood, white ash, and red and white oak. Also present are white elm, shagbark, hickory, and butternut. Within various combinations of these, however, are scattered other broad-leaved trees such as the tulip tree, paw-paw, Kentucky coffee-tree, wild crab, flowering dogwood, chestnut, black gum sassafras, hickory, and black and pin oak, which reach their northern limits here. In addition, black walnut, sycamore and swamp white oak are mainly confined to this region. Vast open oak woodlands, in some places containing prairie grasses, formerly covered the extensive sand plains of the region. Conifers are comparatively few, being represented only by white pine, tamarack, white and red cedar, red juniper, and hemlock.[13] There are also many southern species of shrubs and herbs. The Indians used many of these trees and plants in one way or another. Furthermore, in this area the Amerindians could and did engage in horticulture.

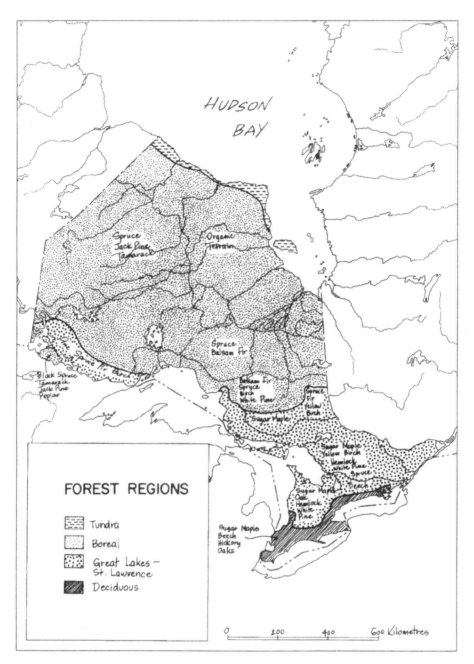

FOREST REGIONS

Tundra
Boreal
Great Lakes – St. Lawrence
Deciduous

Map 1.5
Forest Regions of Ontario

*Southeastern Mixed Forest*

The predominantly mixed broad-leaved and coniferous forests bordering the Great Lakes and the St. Lawrence River vary in their composition.[14] Four representative sections embody the transition between the Broadleaf Forest in the south, and the Boreal Forest to the north.

The Huron-Ontario section forms the northern limit of the Broadleaf Forest and extends from Lake Huron and Georgian Bay to the eastern end of Lake Ontario. It covers the higher ground of the Niagara Escarpment as well, including Manitoulin Island. Long settled and logged, little of the original forest exists today. Its northern fringe coincides with the Precambrian rocks of the Shield and is also the northern limit of sycamore and black walnut. Within it, too, are the southern limits of some species, such as jack pine. The raising of corn by Indians also reached its most northward extension in this section. Sugar maple, beech, and hemlock form a dominant tree association. Along with these are other species such as basswood, elm, white and red ash, yellow birch, red maple, and red, white and burr oak. Locally in river bottoms or swampy tracts stand blue beech, silver maple, slippery and rock elm, black ash, and eastern white cedar. The most prevalent conifers are eastern white pine and balsam fir.

Immediately to the north, in the Muskoka area, lies the Georgian Bay section, with an extension that covers the remainder of the Shield in Southern Ontario, from the middle Ottawa River to the Thousand Islands. A mixed forest, but containing fewer species than the southern section described above, it is dominated by sugar maple, beech, basswood, yellow birch, eastern hemlock, eastern white pine, red maple, and white ash on the upland surfaces. Dryer sandy stretches are commonly the site of white spruce, which replaces the red and white pine more common towards the Ottawa valley. Over thin soils and on the highest ground, species more representative of the Boreal Forest persist. These are white and black spruce, with balsam fir, scrubby stands of jack pine, trembling aspen, red oak, and white birch. The latter attained their maximum growth here, providing the Amerindians with bark in such large pieces that canoes could be easily constructed. Swampy areas support red maple, black ash, and eastern white cedar.

In the upland tract north of Lake Nipissing in the Lake Temagami area lies a spectacular transition zone where eastern white pine, white spruce, and white birch form the typical association. Another association is a mixture of birch, pine, and spruce with trembling and largetooth aspens and balsam fir. Red pine and jack pine tend to dominate on dry ridges or patches of sandy or rocky soils. Tolerant hardwoods, such as sugar maple and yellow birch, are peppered throughout. In lowlands and poorly drained areas, black spruce, tamarack, and white cedar prevail.

Finally, the Quetico section, stretching from Thunder Bay to the Lake of the Woods, was once overgrown with eastern red and white pine but, following logging and intensive fires, is now covered with Boreal Forest species. In this area pure and mixed stands of jack pine intermingle with stands of large-tooth and trembling aspen, white birch, balsam fir, and white and black spruce. The fir/white spruce/birch association is extensive on drier sites, while in low-lying areas a spruce/fir mixture is seen. Scattered in some parts are yellow birch, sugar maple, basswood, Manitoba maple, hop-hornbeam, and red and burr oak. Wetter sites contain white elm, black ash, red maple, and eastern white cedar. Some typically Boreal bogs contain black spruce and tamarack.[15]

## Boreal Forest

Black and white spruce, balsam fir, jack pine, larch, and several hardy broad-leaved trees, such as trembling aspen, balsam poplar, and mountain ash, dominate the remarkably uniform Boreal Forest formation. Their growth in various associations almost entirely reflects drainage. On better-drained uplands and along river banks mixed forest stands of white spruce, black spruce, balsam fir, aspen, and balsam poplar, with some white birch, dominate. On higher drier sites, on burned-over rocky soils or well-drained sand, jack pine grows in almost pure stands, frequently in association with mountain ash. Where drainage is poor, black spruce, interspersed with larch on wet sphagnum- and feather moss–covered floors, completely dominates. As drainage diminishes, such areas revert to muskeg, or open stunted stands among bogs and fens. Changes in the forest continue to occur as one proceeds northward. With increasingly rigorous climatic and soil conditions, the dense spruce and fir forest gives way to an open lichen woodland that then merges into the treeless tundra.

Along the forest's wide southern transition zone stands an admixture of southern species on better-drained sites; these occur as scattered individuals or in isolated patches. Of these species sugar maple and yellow birch are most common, although white elm, eastern white cedar, and black ash extend further north along river banks. Eastern white pine, red pine, and eastern hemlock reach their northernmost limits near the south shores of Lake Abitibi. Species of willow and speckled alder frequently form dense thickets, especially along river banks and in poorly drained areas.

An important element in the Boreal vegetation is the relative abundance of berry-bearing shrubs. Such plants as the blueberry, high bush cranberry, low bush cranberry, crowberry, strawberry, and mountain ash are widely dispersed. Like those of many other floral species, the fruits of these shrubs were often gathered by the Amerindians. During the winter easily stored blueberries were sometimes a major source of nutrition.

In the past as today, forest fires, most often caused by lightning, yearly burnt stretches of the resinous Boreal Forest, in some years devastating enormous tracts. Regeneration in such areas is unusually slow, reflecting the low-energy environment of short growing seasons. Of the first invaders of newly burned forest, fireweed predominates. Within a few years blueberries and other shrubs begin to replace the fireweed, an association that provides food for bear, hare, and moose, all animals the Amerindians depended upon. In turn these plants are replaced by aspen and birch, fast-growing trees that provide nourishment for that all-important animal, the beaver. The shade of the birch and aspen encourages the slower-maturing conifers to develop. The latter, spruce and fir, in time grow to dominate the landscape; at this point a mature forest again covers the land, now the habitat of only a few animals, for example, marten and squirrel.

Forest fires repeatedly initiate new cycles of vegetative growth. Thus, they have been of extreme importance to the Indians of the Boreal Forest, since the mature forest of dense conifer stands offered little in the way of foods or raw materials of use to them. New growth invading the devastated areas provided food for a greater variety of the animals and birds they hunted.[16]

In the Hudson Bay Lowlands the flat topography and poor drainage give rise to an area of open "subarctic" vegetation. Only along the elevated river banks (levees) are there fairly dense narrow stands of Boreal mixed-forest growth, increasingly interrupted further northwards by pure stands of black spruce. Back from the rivers below the levees lie immense stretches of muskeg, bog, and string bog dominated by sphagnum mosses. The tree species on such terrain are black spruce and larch, often in patches but also growing as stunted, distorted individuals among the bogs. Willows and speckled alders are other species found in the lowlands. As the coast is neared, trees and shrubs practically disappear. Despite their desolate appearance, these extensive plains of "little sticks" produce lichens, herbs, and mosses, and reportedly were once the abode of large herds of caribou.[17]

The Indians depended on the forests, whether mature or second growth, for food, raw materials, and spiritual inspiration. Trees provided the materials to make their homes, cache racks, smoke lodges, snowshoe frames, canoes, toboggans, ladles and spoons, cradle-boards, weapons, and mortars and pestles. The vegetation provided foods, such as wild rice, maple sugar, nuts, and berries, as well as many medicines. The Indians of Ontario used about 400 plant species in one way or another.[18]

Although there may not have been large-scale natural changes in Ontario's forest cover during the last several centuries, white pine, for example, has increased in abundance in Southern Ontario over the past five to six hundred years. Whether this was a response to the Little Ice Age or to the Indian clearance of tracts in the original forest is under debate. That certain types of grasses also increased in amount over the same time strengthens the case for Amerindian-induced changes.[19] Moreover, historical geographer Conrad Heidenreich deduced that "since the Huron created changes in the original forest through selective cutting and large-scale clearing, the forest during Huron times was by no means the mature forest ... Young stands of the dominant species and grassland (Champlain's and Sagard's 'meadows' and 'fields') occupied the areas of preferred soils which had been repeatedly cleared and abandoned in past times." He continues: "It is quite likely that few of the tree stands in the preferred agricultural areas were allowed to mature beyond ten to fifteen years. The Huron had to occupy forested land, not only because the forest revitalized the soil and they did not have the tools to cope with grasslands; but also because they needed wood for burning and village construction."[20]

## Animal Life

The Indians utilized Ontario's fauna as fully as they did its flora. Most species – from the mosquito to the moose – were in one way or another vital for food, clothing, shelter, containers, and tools, or played a prominent role in Native religion and mythology. The myriad of creatures belonging to the animal kingdom exist in an almost endless variety of plant-dependent or predatory-prey relationships. These animals intermix with the plants to form a series of enormously complex interdependent biotic or life systems. These interactions, called eco-systems, are ultimately dependent on solar energy and available moisture. A detailed discussion of such systems is beyond the scope of this chapter; instead, the focus is on the major mammals, prey and predator, that were a life-giving necessity to the Indians.[21]

In Ontario's strip of tundra not only are Boreal animals found, notably some of the shrews, timber wolf, and most of the important fur-bearers – beaver, mink, otter, and snowshoe or varying hare – but also true denizens of the Arctic, like the arctic fox, lemming mouse, polar bear, and visitors of varying frequency such as certain arctic marine mammals – walrus, several seals, and the white whale. Large herds of barren-ground caribou migrated from the northwest eastward along the coast of Hudson Bay to summer near Cape Henrietta Maria. In the summer they provided food and hides to the Amerindians. By the beginning of the nineteenth century, however, the barren-ground caribou's numbers had been drastically reduced. It has been suggested that they have now totally disappeared from Northern Ontario, replaced by woodland caribou from the south.[22]

Waterfowl, especially Canada geese and waveys, migrated northward each spring in vast numbers, many to remain and nest in the area. Then each fall innumerable flocks migrated southward. To the Amerindians, waterfowl, like caribou, were a major source of food. After the arrival of the Europeans, each spring and fall many families of neighbouring, or Home Guard, Indians assembled about the Hudson's Bay Company (HBC) posts located on the shores of Hudson and James bays to kill waterfowl for the traders. Waterfowl that might be killed during the summer along the treeless coast included arctic loon, pintail, American widgeon, greater scaup, bufflehead, old-squaw, common eider, king eider, and surf scoter, all providing sustenance. Also caught during the summer were sandhill cranes. During the winter the snowy owl arrived, as well as, quite often, immense numbers of ptarmigan, the latter providing food for Indian and trader alike.[23]

At the other geographical extreme, a number of species inhabited the Broadleaf Forest, which did not range northward from that zone. These included the common opossum, short-tailed shrew, the eastern mole, and the pine mouse. The cougar or mountain lion and bobcat were found here and also somewhat to the north in the mixed forest. Of particular importance to the Indians was the turkey, a wild bird exterminated in Southern Ontario by the end of the nineteenth century. The multitudinous passenger pigeon by 1914 had suffered the same fate as the turkey, but during its existence it was an abundant source of food for the Indians.[24] The passenger pigeon, however, was not restricted to the Broadleaf Forest but ranged as far north as Hudson Bay, if the fur trader James Isham's observations are correctly interpreted.[25] Atlantic salmon were once profuse in Lake Ontario, each fall ascending the streams entering the lake, at which time they were easily caught by the Amerindians.

While the Boreal and Southeastern Mixed forests were distinctive in vegetation, the fauna of the two regions were very similar and many of the species nourished the inhabitants. Big game, woodland caribou and moose, ranged throughout, although by the first half of the nineteenth century their numbers were greatly reduced. A variety of causes, such as over-hunting, forest fires, disease, and climatic conditions, no doubt led to this. When big game became scarce, the Amerindians depended more than ever on fish and hare. Even when present, moose and caribou were difficult to secure unless the snow covering the ground was over two-thirds of a metre in depth.

Although white-tailed deer occurred, their northern range fluctuated greatly over time. Wapiti, commonly known as elk (extinct in Ontario since the mid-1800s), black bear, timber wolf, lynx, and wolverine roamed widely. Other inhabitants included the porcupine (which sometimes ventured south into the Broadleaf Forest), raccoon, woodchuck, skunk, chipmunk, squirrel, shrew, mice, vole, and several species of bats. The varying hare was at times of extreme importance to the Indians for both food and clothing. Every seven to ten years these creatures became extraordinarily numerous, but then suddenly almost vanished from the country and were scarcely seen for several years.

Reptiles and amphibians were ubiquitous, but were most numerous in Southern Ontario.[26] Here, along the rocky escarpments, slithered the timber rattler and massasauga. Only the eastern garter snake wriggled northwards into the mixed forest. Turtles, salamanders, and frogs crept and leapt, but although they were enjoyed by some as food (frog's legs were especially favoured), they were of significance to the Amerindians largely for their mythological associations.[27]

The Natives caught a variety of fish.[28] It should be pointed out that several species, when not overexploited, can grow to extremely large sizes. This is the case for sturgeon (one weighing 140 kilograms was caught at Batchawana Island, Lake Superior, in 1922)[29] and lake trout (one estimated to have weighed 31 kilograms was taken in North Caribou Lake around 1960).[30] Considering that such large fish were the equivalent of from one to three caribou, their importance as a supply of food cannot be overlooked. Other species of fish taken provided satisfactory amounts of food because of their abundance rather than their size. These included white fish (the *attikameg* or "caribou of the water" of the Algonquians, especially abundant in the St. Mary's River, Sault Ste. Marie), several species of suckers, tullibee, goldeye, walleye, bass, perch, ling, and pike.

Insects were a fauna of another sort, inedible but troublesome during the summer months. Of most nuisance were mosquitoes, black flies, sand flies, and moose and deer flies. The many other insects that inhabited Ontario were not of direct concern to the Amerindians. They did, however, affect people indirectly by attacking various species of flora and fauna.

Some creatures great and small initiated long-lasting modifications to the vegetation and hence to the total landscape. Epidemics of spruce-budworm, certain bark-beetles, or tent-caterpillar, for example, exerted heavy pressures on the whole system through the temporary decimation of specific tree species; dead and dying, these species became especially susceptible to forest fires. Large mammals also had a deleterious effect on vegetation growth and reproduction. Some, through their browsing, interrupted natural succession; others ate or trampled a large proportion of the seed crop. The most effective mammalian landscape modifier was, of course, the beaver. This ever-busy

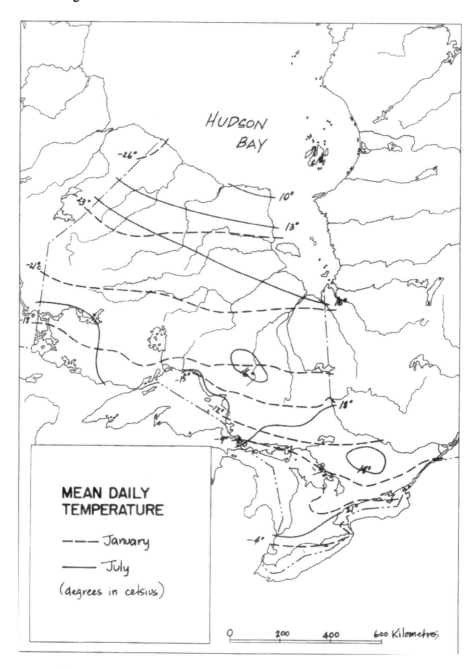

Map 1.6
Mean Daily Temperature in Ontario

symbol of industry not only destroyed certain tree species, but also modified drainage systems and flooded large tracts of land.

To the Amerindians, wherever they lived, and Europeans alike, the dominating feature of the landscape was the forest. For those who lived in the Boreal Forest, game animals and fish were far from numerous and the winters long and often extremely cold. Nevertheless, there was sufficient food and shelter for the adept. In summer, travel was easy, and swift birchbark canoes easily conveyed the inhabitants from one food source to another; in winter, snowshoes gave access to vast stretches of land where food might be found.

Southern Ontario in 1600, on the other hand, especially in the summer, was undoubtedly a hospitable place. (See Map 1.6.) Climatically somewhat like the present, comparatively long summers of pleasant weather cheered the spirit and were suitable for many crops native to the region. Extensive tracts of easily workable sandy loams originating from glacial action could be readily cleared of forest cover for both settlement and agriculture. Moreover, game animals, birds, and fish were widely available.

Thus, the forests, the climate, the landforms, and the fauna in their varied combinations throughout Ontario contributed to the varied lifestyles of the Amerindians. These nature-oriented lifestyles altered drastically with the arrival of Europeans.

## NOTES

1   G.M. Wrong, ed., *The Long Journey to the Country of the Hurons by Father Gabriel Sagard* (Toronto 1939), 90

2   H.P. Biggar, ed., *The Works of Samuel de Champlain*, 6 vols. (Toronto 1929), 3:37–42

3   T. James, *The Dangerous Voyage of Captain James ...* , 2d rev. ed. (London 1740), 33

4   W.G. Dean, "Physiography and vegetation of the Albany River Map Area, Northern Ontario" (PhD thesis, McGill University, 1959), 330

5   R.J.W. Douglas, ed., *Geology and Economic Minerals of Canada* (Ottawa 1976), 714

6   W.G. Dean, F. Helleiner, H. Morisset, and M. Villeneuve, *Le Bouclier Canadien des Clay Belts/Canadian Shield Clay Belts* (Montréal 1972), 3

7   S.G. Zoltai, "Eastern Outlets of Lake Agassiz," in W.J. Mayer-Oakes, ed., *Life, Land and Water* (Winnipeg 1967), 107

8   Douglas, *Geology and Economic Minerals of Canada*, 724

9   R.L. Dansgaard, "One Thousand Centuries of Climatic Record from Camp Century on the Greenland Ice Sheet," *Science* 166 (1966): 379

10  C.E. Heidenreich, *Huronia: A History and Geography of the Huron Indians, 1600–1650* (Toronto 1971)

11  F.K. Hare and M.K. Thomas, *Climate Canada* (Toronto 1974), 117, 129–34

12  Canada, Energy, Mines and Resources, *The National Atlas of Canada,* 4th ed., rev. (Ottawa 1974), 45–6

13  W.W. Judd and J.M. Speirs, eds., *A Naturalist's Guide to Ontario* (Toronto 1964), 24–5

14  J.S. Rowe, *Forest Regions of Canada* (Ottawa 1972), 93

15  Shan Walshe, *Plants of Quetico and the Ontario Shield* (Toronto 1980)

16  Ross W. Wein and David A. MacLean, eds., "The Role of Fire in Northern Circumpolar Ecosystems," *Scope* 18 (1983)

17  John Richardson, *Fauna Boreali-Americana or the Zoology of the Northern Parts of British North America* (London 1829), 250; G. Williams, ed., *Andrew Graham's Observations on Hudson's Bay 1767–91* (London 1964), 6

18  See Charlotte Erichsen-Brown, *Use of Plants for the Past 500 Years* (Aurora, Ont. 1979); and Richard Asa Yarnell, *Aboriginal Relationships between Culture and Plant Life in the Upper Great Lakes Region,* Anthropological Papers, Museum of Anthropology, University of Michigan, no. 23 (Ann Arbor 1964).

19  I. Bowman, *The Draper Site: White Pine Succession on an Abandoned Late Prehistoric Iroquoian Maize Field* (Toronto 1974); M. Boyko, "The Fossil Pollen Record of European and Indian Man in Southern Ontario," *Archaeological Notes* 73, no. 1 (February 1973)

20  Heidenreich, *Huronia,* 63

21  A.W.F. Banfield, *The Mammals of Canada* (Toronto 1974)

22  Randolph L. Peterson, *The Mammals of Eastern Canada* (Toronto 1966), 333

23  W. Earl Godfrey, *The Birds of Canada,* Bulletin 203, National Museum of Canada (Ottawa 1966)

24  M. Kapches, "The Middleport Pattern in Ontario Iroquoian Prehistory" (PhD thesis, University of Toronto, 1981), 64; A.W. Schorger, *The Passenger Pigeon: Its Natural History and Extinction* (Norman 1973), 133–40

25  E.E. Rich, ed., *James Isham's Observations on Hudson's Bay, 1743* (Toronto 1949), 125

26  E.B.S. Logier, *The Reptiles of Ontario* (Toronto 1939); E.B.S. Logier, *The Frogs, Toads and Salamanders of Eastern Canada* (Toronto 1952); E.B.S. Logier, *The Snakes of Ontario* (Toronto 1958)

27  Kapches, "The Middleport Pattern," 149

28  W.B. Scott and E.J. Crossman, *Freshwater Fishes of Canada,* Bulletin 184, Fisheries Research Board of Canada (Ottawa 1973)

29  N. Robert Payne, "A Century of Commercial Fishing Administration in Ontario," *Ontario Fish and Wildlife Review* 6, nos. 1–2 (1967): 9

30  Edward S. Rogers and Mary B. Black, "Subsistence Strategy in the Fish and Hare Period, Northern Ontario: The Weagamow Ojibwa, 1880–1920," *Journal of Anthropological Research* 32, no. 1 (Spring 1976): 1–43

# 2 Before European Contact

JAMES V. WRIGHT

A great deal of cultural change has occurred in what is now the province of Ontario over the last 11 000 years. To present a general picture, it has been necessary to make the complex appear simple, to present the poorly known as well known, and to favour one interpretation when, in fact, several conflicting interpretations exist. Most archaeologists, however, will be in essential agreement with the major themes as presented here.

Archaeologists attempt to reconstruct human events and developments that took place prior to written records. Nearly 400 years ago Samuel de Champlain made many important observations concerning the Huron with whom he wintered in 1615–16, but he did not comment on where the Huron originally came from, how they learned to plant corn, beans, and squash, or when they first began smoking tobacco. The when, where, what, how, and why of the past are the questions that archaeology, for the most part, must answer. Consequently, archaeologists have developed a wide range of field and laboratory techniques that assist in the reconstruction of past cultures.

The vast bulk of material studied consists of such things as broken tools and discarded food bones. In a very real sense, archaeologists are glorified collectors and analysts of early human beings' garbage. Unfortunately, most of the cultures that archaeologists attempt to reconstruct disappeared a long time ago. You have only to look around the room in which you are now reading and exclude everything except glass, china, brick, and a few other imperishable objects to have an idea of how little the archaeologists of the future will have to work with in terms of our own culture. Despite these limitations, sufficient information does survive to permit the archaeologist to at least partially decipher the past. Different cultures made distinct stone and bone tools, built their houses, and buried their dead in various ways. Some hunted and others farmed, some made pottery vessels and others did not. These similarities and differences allow the archaeologist to identify various culture groups and to trace their development through time.

During the actual process of establishing cultural sequences, the archaeologists often begin with the period of post-European contact and then successively look back in time. Native villages, recorded by early European explorers and missionaries, are located and their identification confirmed by the presence of European trade goods and other evidence. The archaeologists then compare the artifacts of pottery, stone, and bone associated with the European metal tools and glass beads with those of a nearby site not containing European artifacts. If the comparisons are close, the investigators then assume that the pre-contact site was occupied by the ancestors of the people who lived in the post-contact site. The archaeologists then compare the artifacts and other evidence from the pre-contact village with other similar villages. On the assumption that the degree of similarity reflects a relationship in time, it is possible to extend a series of site relationships down through time, with the identified post-European contact sites as a starting point. The archaeologists establish this sequence of sites to represent the development of the Native peoples identified by the written European sources. This approach allows for more meaningful cultural reconstructions, as it incorporates the use of early European and present-day studies of Native peoples. Such cultural information could not possibly be provided by the limited remains recovered from pre-contact sites.

The archaeologist must be a jack of all trades. One must know sufficient geology to be able to distinguish human work from that of nature, to identify varieties of stone, and to interpret the manner of soil deposition and modification. An adequate knowledge of biology permits the accurate identification and interpretation of the animal and plant remains recovered from sites. The archaeologist must also know some chemistry, physics, mathematics, and a range of other disciplines in order to re-create the past from the fragmented and vague evidence left behind by human beings.

## The Northern and Southern Regions of Ontario and the Archaeological Periods

The early history of the North American Indians who occupied what is now Ontario can best be understood if the province is divided into a northern and a southern region. (See Map 2.1.) Most of the northern region lies within the Canadian Shield and has predominantly coniferous forest, whereas the southern region has predominantly hardwood forest.

The southern region always supported a far greater population than the northern; the same situation persists today, as is demonstrated by modern population densities. Local culture groups that interacted with each other and

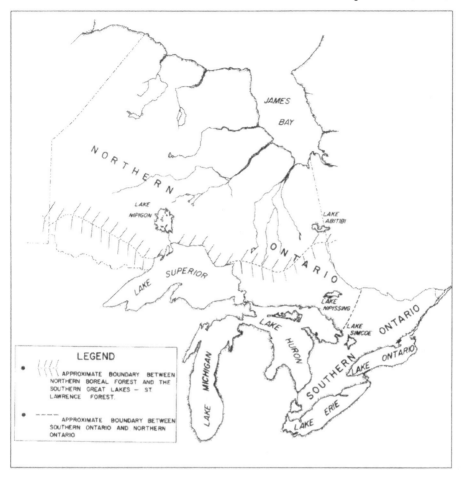

Map 2.1
Northern and Southern Regions of Ontario
From J.V. Wright, *Ontario Prehistory: An Eleven-Thousand-Year Archaeological Outline* (Ottawa: National Museum of Man 1972), 6. Map by D.W. Laverie. Reproduced with the permission of the Canadian Museum of Civilization

with those from outside areas in a highly complex fashion developed in the south. On the other hand, a high degree of cultural similarity that allows certain general interpretations to be drawn from relatively limited archaeological data arose in the north. The available evidence suggests that these two regions have been distinct and different from earliest times. Certainly, cultural interactions and contacts took place along a broad span of the somewhat ill-defined boundary between the two areas, but such events apparently had relatively little impact on the two respective populations.

Archaeologists separate Ontario's last 11 000 years of pre-European contact history into four distinct periods: the Palaeo-Indian (9000 B.C.–5000 B.C.); the Archaic (5000 B.C.–1000 B.C.); the Initial Woodland (1000 B.C.–A.D. 1000); and the Terminal Woodland (A.D. 1000 to European contact). This last period ended shortly after the appearance of Europeans who provided written records on the indigenous people.

### The Palaeo-Indian Period (9000 B.C.–5000 B.C.)

Archaeologists have given the earliest inhabitants of Ontario the archaeological name "Clovis." Clovis culture spread across North America east of the Rocky Mountains and extended as far south as Central America. It is believed that ancestors of these people crossed from Asia into North America at a time when a broad land bridge in the area that is now the Bering Strait joined the two continents. The similarity of their archaeological remains over an enormous area suggests that they must have spread quite rapidly throughout North America. In Ontario these people were probably caribou hunters, although it is possible that they occasionally stalked the now extinct mammoth and mastodon. Their distinctive dart heads have been found only in Southern Ontario, since the continental glacier still covered Northern Ontario. Recently, archaeologists have found campsites of these early hunters along the old beach lines of Lake Algonquian – an ancient glacial lake that covered a large area of Southern Ontario and is now dry land. (See Map 2.2.)

The Plano culture followed that of Clovis, evolving from an early Clovis base, and appears to have developed mainly on the Plains, entering Northern Ontario from the west and, to some extent, from the southwest. These people, too, hunted big game. Archaeologists have found a number of Plano culture quarry sites along the coasts of Lakes Superior and Huron where suitable stone such as taconite and quartzite were fashioned into tools. Some of these sites, originally located on an ancient shoreline, are now as much as ten kilometres inland and nearly sixty metres above the level of Lake Superior. To discover Palaeo-Indian sites, an archaeologist must know something about the local geological events that altered lake levels and land surfaces.

Typical tools of both Clovis and Plano culture include distinctive dart heads used for killing game, knives for butchering and other tasks, scrapers for shaping tools of wood and bone and for preparing hides, and small engraving tools for delicate carving work. Reconstructing these early hunters' way of life from the few stone tools that have survived is a difficult task. From our knowledge of the climate at this early period we can assume that the Palaeo-Indians wore tailored skin clothing and built some form of shelter from the elements. Their religious beliefs were probably closely tied to the

Map 2.2
The Palaeo-Indian Period
From J.V. Wright, *Ontario Prehistory: An Eleven-Thousand-Year Archaeological Outline* (Ottawa: National Museum of Man 1972), 10. Map by D.W. Laverie. Reproduced with the permission of the Canadian Museum of Civilization

successful hunt upon which their survival depended. For much of the year they hunted in small family groups; these groups would periodically gather into a larger grouping or band during a favourable period in their hunting cycle, such as the annual caribou migration.

Palaeo-Indian cultures did not cease to exist; they simply altered to meet new conditions. Various Archaic groups developed out of Clovis culture in eastern North America. In the west the Plano culture developed into a number of cultures that archaeologists have assigned to the Archaic period.

*The Archaic Period (5000 B.C.–1000 B.C.)*

Two quite different Archaic cultures occupied Ontario. In Northern Ontario the Shield Archaic culture appears to have developed out of the preceding Plano culture and to have followed a very similar way of life. Archaeologists chose the name "Shield Archaic" because sites of a similar kind have been found throughout much of the Canadian Shield, from Labrador to northern Manitoba and into the central Keewatin District of the Northwest Territories. Dietary staples probably included caribou and fish, supplemented by bear, beaver, hare, and waterfowl. This statement, however, is largely conjectural, since little bone has survived the acid soils of the north. To judge from the location of sites along waterways and on islands, the Shield people must have possessed some form of watercraft, probably the birchbark canoe. For mobility in deep snow they likely produced snowshoes. Towards the end of this period, the bow and arrow weapon system appears to have been adopted from Palaeo-Eskimo peoples on the Labrador coast. In short, their way of life appears similar to that recorded for the northern Algonquian-speaking peoples at the moment of direct European contact. Most likely the Shield people were the ancestors of the historic Ojibwa, Cree, Algonquin, and Montagnais. (See Map 2.3.)

A people who possessed a distinctively different culture from their Shield Archaic neighbours to the north occupied the hardwood forests of Southern Ontario. Archaeologists have named this group the "Laurentian Archaic." They hunted deer, elk, bear, and beaver with the aid of dogs and also supplemented their diet with smaller game, fish, shellfish, berries, and other wild plant foods. In addition to chipped-stone dart heads, knives, and scrapers, they manufactured polished-stone axes and adzes for wood working, ground-slate darts, lances, and knives; they also produced a wide variety of bone items, such as barbed fish harpoons, chisels, fish-hooks, awls, needles, beads, and combs. Through trade with the Shield Archaic people, they obtained native copper from Lake Superior. They fashioned the copper into dart heads, awls, needles, bracelets, beads, adzes, and many other necessary or ornamental objects.

From the evidence found in excavated Laurentian Archaic cemeteries in adjacent Quebec and New York, archaeologists know that the people were of robust build. To a minor degree they suffered from accidental bone fractures, arthritis, and some tooth loss through gum disease. Death by violence is occasionally evident in the form of skull fractures, projectile points lodged in bones or the chest cavity, and signs of beheading. There is even one recorded instance from a New York site of unsuccessful surgery to remove the tip of a dart head lodged in a human forehead.

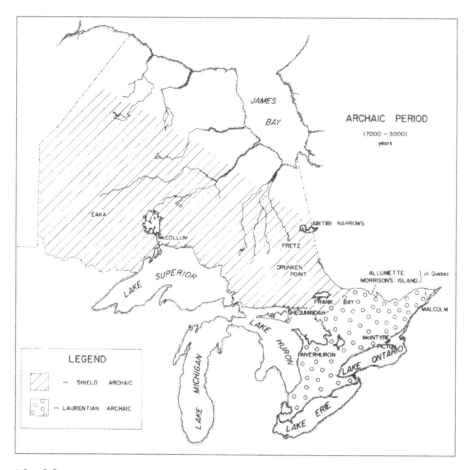

Map 2.3
The Archaic Period
From J.V. Wright, *Ontario Prehistory: An Eleven-Thousand-Year Archaeological Outline* (Ottawa: National Museum of Man 1972), 22. Map by D.W. Laverie. Reproduced with the permission of the Canadian Museum of Civilization

The Laurentian Archaic people participated in a wide-ranging trade network. They obtained conch shells made into ornaments and shell beads from the Atlantic coast, copper from Lake Superior, and exotic flints from widely dispersed locales. These items almost certainly arrived in Southern Ontario as a result of many individual hand-to-hand transactions rather than through actual trading parties traversing enormous areas of North America.

Archaeologists know little about the houses of the Laurentian Archaic people. The sites dug by archaeologists are summer camps and the Laurentian Archaic people's flimsy structures have left no trace. There is also evidence that 5 000 years ago the warmer climate that then prevailed would have resulted in an extra month of summer, thereby even further reducing the need for substantial houses. In the late fall, when the individual families dispersed to their winter hunting grounds, they likely built more solid structures. Such winter sites, however, would have been very small and extremely difficult for the archaeologist to find many thousand years after their abandonment.

*The Woodland Period (1000 B.C.–European Contact Period)*

The Woodland period begins with the first appearance of pottery vessels in Ontario sites. No major cultural changes appear to have taken place other than the introduction of this single item. Pottery, which is durable and frequently abundant (one pottery vessel will break into many pieces), provides the archaeologist with a convenient means of separating Woodland sites, which yield ceramics, from Archaic and earlier sites, where no ceramics are found. Considerable evidence now exists to suggest that the preceding Laurentian and Shield Archaic peoples adopted pottery and were thereby transformed, for the archaeologists' convenience, into Woodland people. Pottery vessels were made in the southeastern United States as early as 2000 B.C. By 1000 B.C. the knowledge of how to manufacture pottery had spread north into portions of Southern Ontario.

Far more is known about the Woodland period than about the preceding Archaic and Palaeo-Indian periods. This is not only because there are more sites, owing to what appears to be an increase in population, but also because the passage of time has had less effect upon the archaeological remains. To handle the much-increased body of information, archaeologists have divided the Woodland period into an Initial and a Terminal Woodland period. (See Map 2.4.) The people of the Initial Woodland period include those Archaic peoples who first adopted pottery between 1000 B.C. and 700 B.C. and their descendants up to approximately A.D. 1000. The cultures of the Terminal Woodland period can be traced to post-contact peoples such as the Cree and Huron. As archaeological research progresses, scholars will certainly push the Terminal Woodland period further back in time and adjust accordingly the artificial separating point of A.D. 1000 between the Initial and Terminal Woodland periods.

**The Initial Woodland Period (1000 B.C.–A.D. 1000).** Archaeologists have identified five major Initial Woodland cultures in Ontario: the Meadowood, Point Peninsula, Saugeen, and Princess Point cultures of Southern Ontario and adjacent Quebec and New York State; and the Laurel culture of Northern Ontario and neighbouring provinces and states.

Map 2.4
The Initial Woodland Period
From J.V. Wright, *Ontario Prehistory: An Eleven-Thousand-Year Archaeological Outline* (Ottawa: National Museum of Man 1972), 38. Map by D.W. Laverie. Reproduced with the permission of the Canadian Museum of Civilization

From their main homeland in Quebec and New York, Meadowood people appear to have occupied only the margins of Southern Ontario. Their distinctive pottery vessels are found throughout much of Southern Ontario but generally in association with the Point Peninsula and Saugeen cultures. What little is known of the Meadowood people comes from sites in Quebec and New York, particularly from accidentally discovered cemeteries. The burial ceremonialism of the late Archaic period was continued and elaborated upon, with cremation of the dead becoming quite common. Graves were often richly provided with goods manufactured from stone and copper and particularly with large numbers of carefully flaked triangular flint blades, which appear to have been manufactured with the single purpose of placing them with the dead. Natural minerals such as hematite, limonite, and graphite, presumably used for painting the body and other objects, commonly occur in the graves. Meadowood culture flourished between 1000 and 500 B.C. and then eventually changed or was absorbed into Point Peninsula culture.

The Point Peninsula culture occupied Southern Ontario from present-day Toronto eastward into Quebec and New York for a period of roughly 1 000 years, from 700 B.C. to A.D. 700. Archaeologists have investigated a number of village sites as well as cemeteries of the Point Peninsula people. Most are small campsites but a few cover many hectares; these latter must have been used seasonally for many years by successive generations of Point Peninsula people, as well as by earlier and later populations. Such sites usually have some rich seasonal food resource, such as spring sturgeon runs, that attracted people to the same spot for thousands of years.

In their seasonal cycle of activities the Point Peninsula people continued to occupy the same sites as their Archaic ancestors. Internal change, of course, did occur and is seen in the manner they made tools and other practices. No other major changes followed, and one has the impression of small groups of hunters following the interminable rounds necessary for survival.

Roughly 2 000 years ago, however, outside ideas about burial practices reached the Point Peninsula people. These practices, associated with religion, came from the Hopewell culture of the Ohio area via what is now New York State. The most dramatic feature adopted from the south was the construction of earth burial mounds. The stone implements in the graves from this period are frequently made from flint originating in Ohio, Pennsylvania, and eastern New York. The earlier Archaic period trading patterns – marine shells from both the Gulf of Mexico and the Atlantic coast to the east and native copper from Lake Superior – were maintained. (See Map 2.5.) Items made from Ohio pipestone and Ontario silver (from Cobalt) appear in the graves. Ohio valley items such as copper ear spools, stone platform pipes, worked wolf and bear skull parts (probably portions of headdresses), and copper panpipes also appear for the first time. Certainly the most impressive expression of the new burial practices is to be seen in the sixty-metre-long "Serpent Mound" at Rice Lake, southeast of Peterborough. Sites similar to Rice Lake's Serpent Mound are relatively few in number and are restricted to the St. Lawrence valley and southern edges of the province.

The Saugeen culture shared Southern Ontario with the Point Peninsula culture but occupied the region between Lake Huron and Lake Erie to the west of Toronto. The culture of these people was, in most respects, quite simi-

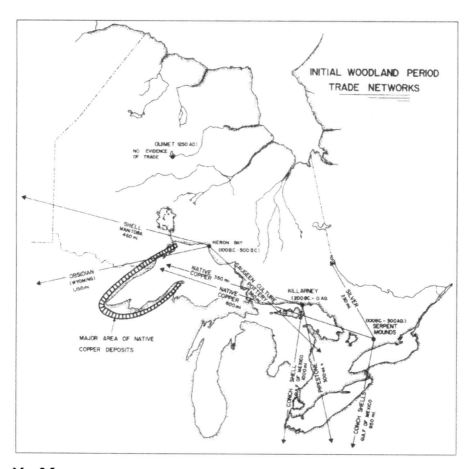

Map 2.5
The Initial Woodland Period Trade Networks
From J.V. Wright, *Ontario Prehistory: An Eleven-Thousand-Year Archaeological Outline* (Ottawa: National Museum of Man 1972), 49. Map by D.W. Laverie. Reproduced with the permission of the Canadian Museum of Civilization

lar to that of the Point Peninsula people. Differences between the two cultures appear to be the result of their slightly different Archaic ancestry as well as their different geographic locations.

Most Saugeen culture village and camp sites discovered to date are found along rapids or at the mouths of rivers and creeks emptying into Lakes Huron and Erie. Discarded food bones from these sites are predominantly of fish that spawn in rivers from spring to early summer. Such sites must represent one segment of the seasonal rounds of the Saugeen people, when individual families gathered at a favourite fishing location during the spring and formed a

larger community. Perhaps marriages were contracted and various other ceremonies, involving the population as a whole, were carried out at this time.
The villages may have been occupied throughout the summer and into the
fall. Certainly for the first time substantial rectangular house structures with
hearths and pits can be recognized from the moulds left in the soil by the
house wall and interior posts. Apparently with the coming of winter the
inhabitants abandoned these villages and individual families travelled to their
winter hunting territories. Such a move was necessary, for in the absence of
stored foods such as corn large numbers of people could not find enough food
in the area during the winter months; they were forced to scatter across the
country in small family groups.

Although the development of Saugeen culture out of an earlier Archaic
population around 700 B.C. is well documented, its eventual fate is not. It may
have, in a manner yet unknown, developed into the Princess Point culture.

The Princess Point culture occupied the north shore of Lake Erie and the
western end of Lake Ontario between A.D. 500 and A.D. 1000. Relatively little
is known about the Princess Point culture; the sites are small and often located
in the river-valley flats, where they became buried under the sediments deposited during spring floods. But evidence exists that the Princess Point people were
the first to adopt corn agriculture in Ontario. Archaeological research in
Ontario is only now beginning to concentrate on what happened when mobile
hunting peoples accepted corn and were transformed into sedentary farmers.

All of the cultivated plants used by the Native peoples of Canada had
been domesticated far to the south and only gradually penetrated into the
north. Corn was domesticated in northern Mexico about 5 000 years ago but
did not enter Ontario, through the Windsor and Niagara areas, until A.D. 500.
It took time for the various plants to adapt to the shorter growing season and
more rigorous climate as they spread northward. Also, the various domesticated plants did not move as a group. Some form of tobacco had probably
entered eastern Canada as long ago as 1 000 years before corn. Beans, on the
other hand, did not appear until nearly 900 years after the adoption of corn.

While the preceding events were occurring in Southern Ontario, the
Laurel culture dominated in Northern Ontario as well as in western Quebec,
central Manitoba, Saskatchewan, and northern Minnesota, from approximately 700 B.C. to A.D. 1000. This widespread culture represents the preceding
Shield Archaic but with the addition of pottery. From the Point Peninsula and
Saugeen cultures of Southern Ontario the northerners probably obtained their
knowledge of ceramics.

Stone scraping tools for working hides, wood, and bone dominate the
Laurel culture tool kit, although arrowheads, lances, knives, hammerstones,
and net-sinkers are common. Bone tools consist of awls, harpoons, beaver-

incisor knives, snowshoe-netting needles, and pottery markers. The copper items include beads, bangles, awls, parts of composite fish-hooks, and chisels. Nothing, of course, remains of the wooden, bark, and leather goods that probably represented the most common and elaborate items in the material culture of these people.

The hunters of the northern forests did not live in complete isolation from the outside world. Materials from the Meadowood and Saugeen cultures have been found in Laurel sites, and vice versa. In the west, between Lake Superior and the Manitoba border, particularly along the Rainy River, the Laurel people constructed numerous burial mounds. These mounds, the largest pre-contact structures in all of Ontario, can be over thirty-five metres in diameter and over eight metres high. No doubt the mound ceremonialism of the Laurel people derived from the Hopewell culture of southern Minnesota.

**The Terminal Woodland Period (A.D. 1000–European Contact).** This period includes three major cultural groups: the Ontario Iroquois from Southern Ontario, who gave rise to the historic Huron, Petun, Neutral, and Erie; the St. Lawrence Iroquois, a distinctive population encountered by Jacques Cartier in 1535 but who had disappeared by the time Samuel de Champlain returned to the same area in 1603; and, from Northern Ontario, the pre–European contact groups that gave rise to the historic Algonquian-speaking people – the Cree, Ojibwa, and Algonquin. (See Map 2.6, page 34.)

**The Ontario Iroquois**

Although the information available for the Ontario Iroquois exceeds that for any other pre-contact group in Ontario, gaps do exist in our knowledge. The archaeological information indicates that for some time prior to A.D. 900 and up to A.D. 1300, two related populations in Southern Ontario practised corn agriculture, supplementing this activity with hunting and fishing. To the east the Pickering culture arose out of the preceding Point Peninsula culture. To the west the Glen Meyer culture, which descended directly from the Princess Point culture, developed.

Archaeologists can describe these two cultures in some detail. The location of palisaded villages on easily defended hillocks indicates that armed hostilities occurred. The presence of longhouses (as opposed to small, one-family houses) reveals that a number of different families lived in each dwelling. A burial pattern is in evidence that will lead to the large pits containing the remains of many people, typical of a later period. In short, a whole series of cultural practices in both the Glen Meyer and Pickering cultures foreshadowed the historic Iroquoian culture.

Map 2.6
The Terminal Woodland Period
From J.V. Wright, *Ontario Prehistory: An Eleven-Thousand-Year Archaeological Outline* (Ottawa: National Museum of Man 1972), 65. Map by D.W. Laverie. Reproduced with the permission of the Canadian Museum of Civilization

At approximately A.D. 1300 a portion of the Pickering population expand-ed to the southwest and conquered the Glen Meyer people. This major event resulted in a relatively uniform culture in Southern Ontario that also over-lapped into southwestern New York State. From this common base the his-toric Huron, Petun, Neutral, and Erie gradually developed.

The archaeological record reveals significant events: sunflower seeds, used mainly for their oil, appear in the garbage dumps by A.D. 1300; beans and squash become a common occurrence by A.D. 1400; evidence of captive warrior sacrifice and ritualistic cannibalism appears at A.D. 1300 and reaches a peak shortly after A.D. 1500; tobacco smoking in pipes becomes a common practice by A.D. 1350; and village sites become larger and more abundant after A.D. 1400.

The regional developments that terminated in the historic Ontario Iroquois can be recognized as having occurred as early as A.D. 1400. The Neutral eventually occupied the region around the west end of Lake Ontario, while the Erie dwelt near the southeast shore of Lake Erie in what is now New York State. A large number of villages gradually moved up the rivers draining into the north shore of Lake Ontario, and their people joined a related population near the south end of Georgian Bay. These groups became the historic Huron and Petun.

Close contact between the Ontario Iroquois and the Europeans began in 1615 when the Récollets and then later (1626) the Jesuits began missionary work among the Huron and, to a lesser extent, the Petun. Also, Samuel de Champlain became involved in the wars of the various Algonquian- and Iroquoian-speaking peoples. A close relationship between the French and the Huron-Petun developed, as is outlined in the following chapter.

### The St. Lawrence Iroquois

In 1535 Jacques Cartier visited the village of Hochelaga on the present site of the city of Montreal. Yet, less than seventy-five years later, Champlain found Hochelaga and related villages along the St. Lawrence River abandoned. The disappearance of the St. Lawrence Iroquoians is discussed in the next chapter, by Bruce G. Trigger.

The St. Lawrence Iroquois lived in large, stoutly defended villages. They farmed the surrounding land, growing corn, beans, squash, sunflowers, and tobacco. Some of their villages contained as many as forty longhouses, which could have sheltered close to 2 000 people. Archaeologists have located numerous St. Lawrence Iroquois sites in eastern Ontario and adjacent New York State near the St. Lawrence River. From the evidence it can be tentatively suggested that, out of a regional expression of Point Peninsula culture, the St. Lawrence Iroquois developed in the upper St. Lawrence River valley.

### The Algonquians

It would be very convenient if we could refer to the northern Algonquian-speakers who occupied what is now Ontario as Algonquin, Ojibwa, and Cree. These names, however, refer to groups of small, independent bands of hunters who were loosely related through marriage and clan affiliation and, more generally, through language and way of life. Tribal names equivalent to those used in describing the Iroquoian-speaking people of Southern Ontario cannot be applied to the Algonquian-speakers of Ontario. Despite this difficulty, sufficient archaeological evidence exists to suggest that there were three major areas of Algonquian development in Northern Ontario.

## The Eastern Area

The eastern area of Algonquian cultural development extended northward to Lake Abitibi and westward to the northeast shore of Lake Superior; on the east it was adjacent to land occupied by the Huron, Petun, and St. Lawrence Iroquois. Although the stone and bone tools of the Eastern Algonquians and Huron-Petun differed, their pottery and pipe styles were similar or identical. Indeed, portions of the Eastern Algonquians appear to have shared the same ceramic tradition with their Iroquoian neighbours from as early as A.D. 800. In addition to the Iroquoian-style pottery, however, these people also made pottery very similar in style to that made by related people in northern Michigan and Wisconsin. The mixture of pottery styles appears to be characteristic of the Northern Algonquians. There is a reason for this. Because there would have been a limited number of marriageable women within the small bands, men would frequently obtain their wives from other areas. Imagine, for example, that there were three brothers living on a site near Manitoulin Island who required wives at the same time but who could find no marriageable women in their small, local community. If one man obtained a wife from Lake Nipissing, the second a wife from northern Wisconsin, and the remaining brother a spouse from the west end of Lake Superior, their three Algonquian-speaking wives would eventually be sitting together at the same site making completely different kinds of pottery vessels.

Certain of the eastern Algonquians adopted corn agriculture from their Iroquoian-speaking neighbours, but only in a limited fashion. They planted in the spring, abandoned the crop during the summer, and harvested whatever had survived the ravages of raccoons, birds, and insects, in the fall.

## The Western Area

The western area of Algonquian cultural development involved a region running from Lake Superior, to the height of land separating the Hudson Bay drainage from the Great Lakes drainage, to southern Manitoba and the northern edge of Minnesota. In this region the dominant pottery style developed out of the preceding Laurel pottery of the Initial Woodland period. The western-area Algonquians also retained the Laurel cultural practice of constructing earth burial mounds. As was the case with the Laurel mounds, these later mounds are restricted to a narrow band along the Ontario and Minnesota border and extend eastward to the western end of Lake Superior and westward into Manitoba.

The stone tools of the Western Algonquians resemble those of the Eastern Algonquians. The western group, however, had readier access to the native copper deposits of Lake Superior, and as a result, copper awls, beads, bangles, and knives are relatively common. Stone smoking pipes, which appear as early as A.D. 950, are shaped in a typical western style that has no relation to the pipe complex of the Iroquoian peoples to the east. In the rare instances where bone survives the acid northern soils, tools such as harpoons, beaver-incisor knives, and awls are common and bone refuse consists mainly of fish and big game such as caribou and moose. As was the case with the Eastern Algonquians, a number of Western Algonquian sites containing European (French and English) trade goods have been excavated. The contact period is thus ushered in.

*The Northern Area*

The northern area of Algonquian cultural development centred basically in north-central Saskatchewan and Manitoba, but it also extended into adjacent Northern Ontario. The little that is currently known of the Northern Algonquians of Ontario suggests that these people are fundamentally the same as the Western Algonquians, except for their development of a distinctive kind of pottery.

If one ignored the pottery and considered only the stone and bone tools, the eastern, western, and northern Algonquian areas would be regarded as part of a large, general archaeological complex. This impression is supported by the occurrence in the same area of rock paintings and boulder constructions, both of which probably served some religious function. The different pottery traditions have, however, been useful in dividing the enormous area of Northern Ontario into the three geographic regions outlined above.

With the coming of Europeans and written records, the story of the Native peoples of Ontario passes from archaeological history to documentary history. It should be pointed out, however, that for more than 97 percent of the time that humans have occupied this province the First Nations were in sole possession.

ADDENDUM: The preceding brief essay on the pre-European history of the Native peoples of Ontario was originally published in a slightly different form in 1981 as *Ontario Prehistory*, volume 45 of Canada's Visual History series. Each volume in this series, a cooperative venture of the Canadian Museum of Civilization (then the National Museum of Man) and the National Film Board of Canada, includes 35 mm illustrative transparencies and a section on suggested classroom activities. The series is intended as an aid to the teaching of Canadian history. The essay, therefore, is both brief and simplified, with many aspects of the archaeology of Ontario excluded. It is republished here by permission of the Canadian Museum of Civilization and the National Film Board.

For those readers requiring more detailed information, it is recommended that the following sources be consulted:

1 *Historical Atlas of Canada*, vol. 1: *From the Beginning to 1800*. R. Cole Harris (editor) and Geoffrey J. Matthews (cartographer/designer). Toronto, University of Toronto Press, 1987, 198 pp. Available in French as well as English. The introductory text, together with the plates and their associated texts, places the archaeological record of Ontario within a national framework, but two specific Ontario plates dealing with the Palaeo-Indian period of 8600 B.C. and Iroquoian agricultural settlement are also considered.

2 *The Archaeology of Southern Ontario to A.D. 1650*. Chris J. Ellis and Neal Ferris (editors). Occasional Publication of the London Chapter, Ontario Archaeological Society, no. 5, 1990, 570 pp. This well-illustrated work represents a major synthesis of the archaeology of Southern Ontario and should be consulted for its content and extensive bibliography.

3 Unfortunately a detailed synthesis for Northern Ontario similar to the above is not yet available, but readers can consult brief syntheses such as "Prehistory of Northern Ontario" by K.C.A. Dawson, Thunder Bay Historical Museum, 1983, 40 pp.; *Ontario Prehistory: An Eleven-Thousand-Year Archaeological Outline* by J.V. Wright (Ottawa: National Museum of Man, 1972), 120 pp., available in French as well as English; and the references in "A History of Archaeology in Northern Ontario to 1983 with Bibliographic Contributions" by K.C.A. Dawson, *Ontario Archaeology* 42 (1984): 65 pp. A large number of archaeological reports are also available from the Ontario Ministry of Culture, Tourism and Recreation.

As a final note, it is probably appropriate to observe that archaeological evidence, by its very nature, tends to be very impersonal. The chipped-stone dart head picked up from a ploughed field in Southern Ontario, for example, could be described as a Brewerton Side-Notched projectile point type dating between 1500 and 2500 B.C., the period of Laurentian Archaic cultural development. The possibility that the same dart head had been used by a courageous hunter to slay an aggressive bear threatening a party of women and children on a berry-picking expedition can be determined no more than if the same dart head had been used against an enemy, had been provided as a gift to a spirit power, or had simply been lost. Such elements of humanity as those of the preceding speculations have disappeared forever, but all of the material evidence studied by archaeologists are the products of human beings. The archaeologists must continue to remind themselves that the study of such objects has the single purpose of increasing our understanding of past people. The blood and tissue of what once was have been replaced by the dust of time. While the dust still has a story to tell, it is most definitely an incomplete and dry version of the original human experience.

*Part Two*

*Southern Ontario, 1550–1945*

# 3 The Original Iroquoians: Huron, Petun, and Neutral

BRUCE G. TRIGGER

In the mid-sixteenth century an estimated 65 000 Iroquoian-speaking people – Huron, Petun, and Neutral – inhabited the area now known as Southern Ontario.[1] The various groups that later formed the Huron or Wendat confederacy were scattered in many individual villages and village clusters along the north shore of Lake Ontario, in the Trent valley, and throughout modern Simcoe County. They probably numbered 25 000 people. Since the Petun (or Tionontati) of the seventeenth century do not appear to have lived very long in their historic homeland (situated between Nottawasaga Bay and the Niagara Escarpment) and were closely allied to the Huron in speech and culture, it seems likely that they too originated in the triangle of settlement north of Lake Ontario.[2] They numbered perhaps 7 000. Farther south, the earlier Iroquoian settlements lying west of the Grand River valley had already been abandoned and the ancestors of the various tribes of the Neutral confederacy lived in the present-day Hamilton area and the Niagara Peninsula. Even more numerous than the Huron, they numbered, say, 30 000 to 35 000.

The status of tribal confederacies in the middle of the sixteenth century is obscure. The Huron later claimed that the two founding nations or tribes of their confederacy, the Attignawantan and the Attigneenongnahac, formed their alliance about A.D. 1450 and that the two other nations, the Tahontaenrat and the Arendahronon, only became part of the confederacy at the beginning of the seventeenth century.[3] Various smaller groups were joining these nations as late as the 1630s. At least one anthropologist has expressed doubts that any Indian confederacy predates the start of the fur trade. T.J.C. Brasser views confederacies as the responses of inland groups to problems of gaining reliable access to supplies of European goods.[4]

## Iroquoian Culture

The Huron-Petun and Neutral languages were closely related to each other within the Iroquoian language family. The linguistic status of the St. Lawrence Iroquoians, whom Jacques Cartier had encountered in the sixteenth century, is less clear, but they seem to have spoken a language or languages that were more closely related to Ontario Iroquoian than to the languages of the Five Nations Iroquois.[5] The Ontario Iroquoian groups each had distinctive traits, but they shared a general pattern of life already well established by the beginning of the sixteenth century. They lived in villages that were located near light, easily worked soil and sometimes numbered 1 500 or more inhabitants. The cultivation by women of corn, beans, and squash produced up to 80 percent of the food that was eaten. Apart from the dog, the Iroquoians kept no

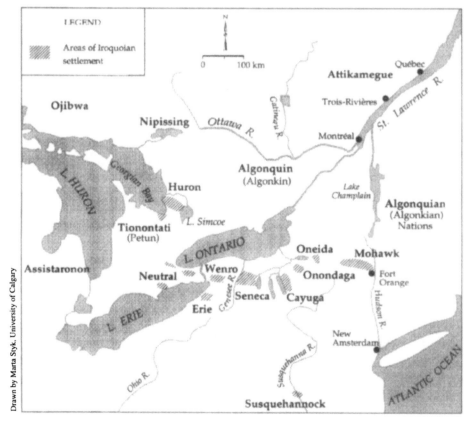

Map 3.1
Areas of Iroquoian Settlement in 1630s, Early 1640s

Canadian Museum of Civilization, J10162

Model of Huron village based on historical and archaeological information.

domestic animals. As they did not practise crop rotation, their fields had a declining fertility. The increasing distance that villagers had to go to obtain firewood compelled them to relocate their villages every ten to thirty years. The Neutral lived in an area particularly rich in game. They appear to have depended more upon hunting than did the Huron. Their villages may have been also on average somewhat smaller than Huron ones.[6] Most Iroquoian women and children remained in or near the villages on a year-round basis. Men tended to reside in the villages only over the winter; during the rest of the year many of them dispersed in small groups to hunt, fish, trade, and wage war. Some Neutral men also may have left their villages to hunt (or perhaps to wage war) for extended periods during the winter.[7]

This pattern of economic activities encouraged the development of matrilocal residence patterns. A woman and her daughters, or a number of sisters or cousins related through the female line, together with their husbands and children, lived in a single longhouse. This extended family constituted the basic unit of cooperation for the production and sharing of food and other necessities. A number of these extended families who lived in a single village and believed themselves to be related matrilineally constituted a clan segment. Each of these units, named after a particular animal or bird, had its own chiefs (one for peace and one for war). Clan members were forbidden by rules of incest to marry one another. One or more clan segments constituted a village, and adjacent villages a nation. The nation might average as many as 5 000 members. There were also village and national councils made up of clan-segment chiefs. The recognition of a close affinity among members of clan segments named after the same animal or bird reinforced the solidarity of the group, and ultimately of the confederacy. Clans that bore the same name were further grouped to form three phratries, or larger groups, which cooperated for ritual purposes.

The Iroquoians valued self-reliance. Every person prized his or her independence and resented being given orders; hence chiefs, having to rely on public opinion to support general policy, had to consider the wishes of their people carefully before proposing a particular course of action. Kin groups were responsible for protecting and avenging their members. Murder or injury had to be atoned for with heavy payments and expressions of condolence if blood feuds were to be avoided. Among groups not united by kinship or trading links, warfare was rationalized as a continuous process of blood feud. War and its associated rituals were also valued as a means to achieve individual male prestige. It further provided male prisoners, who frequently were tortured to death as a sacrifice to the sun, the patron spirit of war and natural fertility.

Before European contact, intertribal trade generally consisted of small amounts of luxury items, such as marine shell beads and native copper; however, as early as A.D. 1000, in northern Simcoe County, a trade in utilitarian items seems to have developed across the southern margin of the Precambrian Shield. The Iroquoians traded with the Nipissing and other groups who lived around the shores of Georgian Bay, exchanging corn, fish nets, and tobacco from present-day Southern Ontario for furs, dried fish, and meat.[8] The heads of particular clans or families generally controlled individual trade routes. In return for presents they allowed other traders to use them. All traders were forbidden to cross the territory of other nations without obtaining, also in return for presents, prior permission from local chiefs. Most intertribal trade was between specific trading partners who adopted each other as ritual kinsmen and often exchanged children as tokens of trust and goodwill. While the value of goods was related to scarcity and traders sought good value for their wares, the Indians avoided haggling over the price of individual items. Arguments about prices were phrased in terms of friendship and alliance rather than in terms of economic considerations.

The Iroquoians believed that no community member should go hungry or lack necessities while others had more than they needed. The principal motive for accumulating surplus food stuffs and obtaining rare goods from other groups was to be able to give them away to fellow tribesmen. Chiefs and their kinsmen strove particularly hard to accumulate goods so that their clan could win approval and influence by giving them away. The Iroquoians strongly disapproved of stinginess, a trait that could lead to accusations of witchcraft. Prestige was derived from giving away property.

The Iroquoians viewed most aspects of nature, such as the sun, moon, rivers, lightning, and disease, as animate and therefore responsive to human behaviour and entreaty. They also attributed souls to man-made objects, such as nets. They sought to invoke these forces through ritual and to win their support or avert their anger. They employed charms to bring luck in hunting, fishing, and related activities, and performed rituals to ensure the successful growth of crops and the increase of wild plants. Much ritual was concerned with curing disease and alleviating psychological distress.[9] The Iroquoians valued feasts and gift-giving as protection against witchcraft. They employed shamans as part-time specialists to deal with the spirit world. Ritual curing societies, the membership of which cut across clan and even national boundaries, assisted these people of power. Although the Iroquoians had no priests or formal creeds, religion permeated every aspect of their lives.

Among the most important Iroquoian rituals were those associated with the burial of the dead. The Huron kept the bodies of their dead relatives in village cemeteries until they relocated their villages, when they reburied their bones in a common ossuary or bone pit. The Feast of the Dead, the ritual associated with this reburial, gradually grew more elaborate. The Huron invited friendly neighbouring groups and trading partners to participate in the lavish exchanges of presents that became a major feature of this ritual. This collective tribute to the dead, whose memory each family loved and honoured, promoted goodwill and cooperation among the disparate segments of villages, nations, and allied groups.

## The Proto-historic Period (1550–1615)

This period lasted from 1550, when European goods first arrived in the Great Lakes area, until 1615, when European travellers first recorded their impressions of the Ontario Iroquoians. In the first half of the sixteenth century, small amounts of European goods apparently appeared in Iroquoian sites in what is now Ontario and New York State, most of it probably originally obtained from European fishermen who traded for furs along the lower St. Lawrence and the coasts of the present-day Maritime provinces.[10] Rumours about Jacques Cartier's exploration of the St. Lawrence River and about the European settlements that he and Jean-François de La Rocque, Sieur de Roberval, attempted to establish near what is now Quebec City between 1541 and 1543 must have reached the Ontario Iroquoians. The arrogance of the French and their kidnapping of Indians led the St. Lawrence Iroquoians to close the St. Lawrence River above Tadoussac to European visitors after 1543, although they continued to trade with them farther down-river.[11]

After 1550 Basque whalers and other Europeans traded at Tadoussac with some regularity. By 1580 professional fur traders started to send ships to the St. Lawrence and soon began to seek a monopoly over the fur trade there. The increasing popularity of beaver hats led to a new emphasis on beaver pelts.[12]

The small amount of European goods that reached the Iroquoians living in the Trent River valley and near the north shore of Lake Ontario at first may have come by way of the St. Lawrence Iroquoians. The Huron already living in what is now Simcoe County obtained European goods from the Nipissing and Algonquin. These goods reached the Algonquin along a trade route that ran from Tadoussac across central Quebec to the upper part of the Ottawa valley. This route duplicated that by which, according to Cartier's reports, native copper from the Upper Great Lakes had reached the St. Lawrence valley in the 1530s.

The Five Nations Iroquois in the interior of present-day New York State probably felt considerably threatened by their lack of access to iron axes and metal arrowheads.[13] They may have been the Amerindian group who attacked and dispersed the remaining St. Lawrence Iroquoians towards the end of the sixteenth century. Certainly it was the Mohawk and not the Huron who raided the St. Lawrence valley in the first decade of the seventeenth century and who contended with the Montagnais (Innu) and Algonquin for control of that region.[14] If so, this is the first recorded case of an Iroquoian group attacking and dispersing its neighbours in order to gain a more secure access to European goods. The St. Lawrence Iroquoians around present-day Montreal and Quebec City also appear to have been the first Iroquoians who were dispersed as a result of intertribal conflicts arising from the fur trade.

Archaeological finds indicate that large numbers of St. Lawrence Iroquoian refugees went to live among various Iroquoian groups in the Trent valley and still farther west. Historical evidence suggests that other St. Lawrence Iroquoians who were attacked by the Mohawk found refuge among the Algonquin and the Abenaki.[15] After the dispersal of St. Lawrence Iroquoians, increasing amounts of European goods continued to reach the Huron by way of the Algonquin and Nipissing, who traded these goods principally in return for cornmeal, fish nets, and tobacco. These traders visited the Huron both by way of Lake Nipissing and Georgian Bay and up the St. Lawrence River and the Trent valley until the Iroquois attacks finally closed the Trent valley route as an artery of trade late in the sixteenth century.[16] After that time all European goods reached the Huron by way of Georgian Bay.

The Arendahronon and the Tahontaenrat joined the Huron confederacy around the end of the sixteenth century. About the same time, all of the Huron nations settled in the northern half of today's Simcoe County. This location, at the southeastern corner of Georgian Bay, was as close as their horticultural economy would permit them to live to the remaining dependable source of European goods. At the same time, the Huron began to trade large quantities of European goods to the Petun and Neutral. This expanded trade apparently stimulated a growing demand among the Ontario Iroquoians for luxury goods obtained from Native people to the south. These items included fancy furs, marine shells, shell beads, and gourd storage vessels. The Huron's direct contacts with the Susquehannock or Andaste, an Iroquoian-speaking people who lived south of the Iroquois in the Susquehanna valley, probably began about this time. The Susquehannock were important suppliers of beads made from marine shells. By 1615 the Huron and the Susquehannock had concluded an alliance against their common enemy, the Iroquois.

The Neutral's hunting territories along the north shore of Lake Erie contained many swampy areas rich with beaver colonies. Favourably located, they could easily trade with many neighbouring Iroquoian groups – the Erie, Susquehannock, Seneca, Petun, and Huron; this may explain the origin of their celebrated neutrality in the Huron-Iroquois rivalry. Later the Neutral probably also obtained European goods from both the Huron and the Iroquois in return for furs. In general, such goods seem to be more abundant in Neutral sites of the seventeenth century than in Huron ones.[17]

The war between the Huron and the Iroquois predated direct European contact. Prior to 1609 the Huron's possession of European goods may have provided the Seneca with a motive for raiding them. This may have marked the first step in the transformation of the confrontations among the Iroquoian tribes of the interior from largely ritual hostilities into economically motivated warfare. The initial impact of the fur trade apparently stimulated broader political alliances among the Iroquoians, such as the expansion and consolidation of the Huron, Iroquois, and perhaps Neutral confederacies, as well as more intensive and wide-ranging intertribal contacts of both a friendly and a hostile nature throughout the Lower Great Lakes region.

## Early Contact with the French (1615–1634)

With the upper St. Lawrence River blockaded by the Mohawk and Oneida, the Neutral, poor canoeists themselves, did not seek to trade directly with the French. Early in the seventeenth century, however, the Huron became interested in establishing a direct trading relationship with the French so that they might obtain European goods in larger quantities and at cheaper prices. The Algonquin opposed this, as they wished to continue profiting from their exclusive role as middlemen in trade between the Huron and the French. Yet, as the Mohawk and Oneida began to attack the Algonquin more fiercely in an effort to steal vital European goods from them, the Algonquin were compelled to seek military support. They sought this from the Huron; they were already trading European goods with them in return for furs and corn-meal, and some Algonquin groups wintered among them.

The French traders at Tadoussac soon realized that this expanding coalition of northern tribes could increase the volume of high-quality beaver pelts that were reaching them from the interior. They sought to lower the prices that they had to pay for furs by eliminating the Montagnais and Algonquin middlemen. In 1608 Samuel de Champlain built a fortified trading post at Quebec, the first step in freeing the St. Lawrence valley from Iroquois attack and turning it into a major artery of trade. In 1609 Champlain accompanied his Montagnais and Algonquin allies in battle against the Iroquois, and the following year they defeated a party of about a hundred Mohawk warriors near the mouth of the Richelieu River. As a result of this defeat, the Mohawk ceased raiding the St. Lawrence valley for over twenty years, until 1633. The Iroquois found it safer and easier to obtain European goods from the Dutch traders who had begun to frequent the Hudson River valley after Henry Hudson had explored the river in 1609.

A party of Arendahronon warriors became the first Huron to make direct contact with the French. An Algonquin chief named Iroquet, who had wintered in the Huron country, invited them to join Champlain's expedition against the Iroquois in 1609. Two years later the council chiefs of the Huron confederacy secretly sent a valuable present to Champlain and stated that the Huron wished to conclude a trading alliance with the French that would be independent of the French alliance with the Algonquin. Their envoys promised to help Champlain reach the Huron country if the French concluded such a treaty.

In 1615 the Algonquin finally gave the Huron the right of passage through their territory. Too few in number and too dependent on Huron corn, they could not deny the Huron the use of the Ottawa River, an action that probably would have led to war between them. Henceforth, the Algonquin had to be satisfied with the tolls that intertribal law required the Huron to pay them for rights of passage through their territory. They continued, however, to try to undermine good relations between the Huron and the French by spreading rumours and fomenting various unpleasant incidents.

By the 1620s armed Frenchmen who travelled to and from the Huron country with Huron traders had compelled the Oneida to abandon their attacks on the Ottawa valley. The French also protected the Huron from intimidation by the Algonquin. The historical geographer Conrad Heidenreich has argued that the Huron's main reason for seeking an alliance with Champlain was to enjoy French military support against the Iroquois rather than to be able to trade with them.[18] Yet, apart from their utilitarian value and ritual signifi-

Battle of Lake Champlain, 30 July 1609 – from Champlain's *Voyages* of 1613.
Champlain and two French musketeers and the Huron are in combat with the Iroquois.
On the right is shown the Iroquois' temporary camp in which they have spent the
night. The canoes that look like French riverboats as well as the Indians' nudity and
erroneous hairstyles weaken the picture's credibility. The engraver freely borrowed
the hammocks and palm trees from illustrations of Latin America.

cance, French trade goods were essential for maintaining the network of aboriginal alliances by means of which the Huron protected themselves against
the Iroquois.

The terms of the French-Huron alliance recognized Atironta, the principal
council chief of the Arendahronon, as their special friend and ally. The
Arendahronon had been the first Huron nation to make direct contact with the
French. In return the Huron chief agreed to share with the chiefs of the various nations and clan segments that made up the Huron confederacy his right
to trade with the French. This distribution of authority, which allowed the
chiefs to acquire wealth through their control of trade with the French, reinforced rather than altered traditional Huron social and political organization.
Effective control of much of this trade seems to have fallen into the hands of
the Attignawantan, the most numerous nation of the Huron confederacy.

After 1615 groups of Huron traders travelled to the St. Lawrence valley
each summer by way of Lake Nipissing and the Ottawa River. They supplied
the French with ten to twelve thousand beaver skins each year. By 1630 they
obtained all of these skins in trade, having exhausted the beaver population of

their own hunting territories.[19] The Huron obtained many skins through the exchange of corn, fish nets, tobacco, and European goods with the Nipissing, who in turn bartered for furs as far north as James Bay each summer, and with the Algonquian-speaking Indians, who traded west into the Lakes Michigan and Superior regions. Huron traders also exchanged corn for furs with the Algonquin in the Ottawa valley. By preventing both the Petun and the Neutral from concluding a trading relationship with the French, the Huron expanded their trading of European goods with these groups, receiving in return tobacco and luxury goods from the south, as well as furs.

Although it required considerable extra effort, the fur trade brought additional wealth to all of the Iroquoian societies of Southern Ontario. Iron knives permitted easier and more elaborate bone carving (which produced a wide variety of tools), while the metal from many worn-out kettles could be reworked, using techniques that had formerly been applied to scarce native copper. The Huron also modified iron tools to adapt them for the uses they now made of them.[20] Ritualism grew more elaborate in the wealthier and expanded societies of Southern Ontario. Among the Huron, large amounts of European goods were interred or given away at major festivals to validate the status of the givers. The ossuaries of pre-contact times, which contained only a few goods, contrast with the richly endowed ones of the contact period. No evidence exists that the new wealth succeeded in undermining the emphasis on sharing and redistribution that was part of traditional Iroquoian culture or that it undermined the existing social code. Its main impact was to make a simple way of life more dramatic. It allowed the Ontario Iroquoians to realize a potential for development that was inherent in their culture but that otherwise might not have been realized.

On account of the large Ontario Iroquoian population and its relative isolation from the Europeans (the Huron had to transport goods hundreds of kilometres inland from the French trading stations along routes that required frequent portages), the influx of European goods did not undermine most Native crafts. The Huron continued to regard cloth as a luxury, and glass beads remained few in number and highly valued. The Huron did not carry alcoholic beverages inland and generally avoided them. Metal kettles were favoured for travelling and as prestige items at feasts and celebrations; yet the production of clay cooking pots continued. As they were able to transport only a limited amount of goods, the Huron traded mainly for iron knives, axes, and other cutting tools that allowed them to work more quickly. The Huron also valued metal arrowheads, which they either bought from the French or made out of worn-out kettles. These could penetrate the traditional wooden armour worn by both the Huron and the Iroquois. During this period warfare between the Huron and the Iroquois remained traditional in its conceptualization and objectives, and both sides were relatively evenly balanced in their strengths. On account of the metal arrowheads, however, set battles tended to be replaced by hit-and-run encounters.[21]

Only a small number of Europeans visited the Ontario Iroquoians prior to 1634. Most of them were employed by the trading company to live among the Huron and encourage them to bring their furs to the St. Lawrence each year. Étienne Brûlé, the most famous, appears to have arrived in the Huron country in 1610, and he lived there (apart from short absences) until 1633. In that year Brûlé was murdered by some Huron traders who suspected him of trying to persuade the Seneca to trade with the French.

Many early visitors learned to speak the Huron language and adapted themselves in varying degrees to the Huron way of life. The Huron allowed the traders to visit the Petun and Neutral to trade furs on their own account, so long as they did not winter among these peoples or attempt to persuade them to conclude an alliance with the French. A few missionaries, mostly Récollets and after 1626 also Jesuits, lived among the Huron. They spent most of their time trying to master the Huron language. One did more. The Récollet priest Joseph de La Roche Daillon infuriated the Huron by attempting in 1626 to conclude an alliance between the French and the Neutral. This action earned him the Huron's enmity.

**The Jesuit Mission Period (1634–1650)**

Following a brief period during which the English held Quebec, the Jesuits in 1634 renewed their mission to the Huron. They sought to convert the entire Huron confederacy to Christianity as a first step in the conversion of all the peoples of the region. Unlike the Récollets, they worked only to alter the Huron way of life in ways that would make it conform with Christian standards of morality. The Jesuits realized that if they were to work safely and effectively among the Huron, the Huron must accept them as part of their trading alliance with the French. The Society of Jesus also used their influence in government circles in France to have the French traders, of whose conduct they disapproved, withdrawn from the Huron country and replaced by the Jesuits' own lay employees.

The Jesuits' return to the Huron country coincided with the beginning of a series of epidemics that continued until 1640 and culminated in a violent smallpox outbreak. As the Native people had little immunity to these diseases, the epidemics reduced the population of the Ontario Iroquoians and of the neighbouring hunting peoples by about half. The Five Nations Iroquois were also stricken at this time and probably suffered losses of about equal magnitude. Anthropologist William Fenton has suggested that less than a century earlier epidemics perhaps played a role in the dispersal of the St. Lawrence Iroquoians.[22] Between 1616 and 1619 disease devastated the Indians from Maine to Cape Cod. Less serious outbreaks of what may have been European-introduced illnesses were reported for the Ottawa valley in 1611 and 1623–24. Yet recent studies of archaeological evidence suggest that neither the Huron and Petun nor the Mohawk themselves experienced any major declines in population prior to the 1630s. It is, however, quite possible that less lethal epidemics of European diseases had reached these groups at an earlier period.[23]

The epidemics of the 1630s hit children and old people more than any other group in the Huron population. Since technological and political skills, as well as ritual information, tended to be a prerogative of older men and women, the surviving Ontario Iroquoians must have found themselves more reliant on European goods. The death of so many elders deprived them of much of their experienced leadership at a time when they most needed it. By the late 1630s, the Huron felt so dependent on European goods that they believed they would be ruined if two successive years elapsed without their traders visiting the St. Lawrence.[24] The ratio of population to political offices also declined, altering these offices' meaning and making their validation in terms of clan productivity more difficult. The epidemics left the Huron far more vulnerable to the Jesuits' pressure to convert to Christianity.

At first, the Huron viewed the Jesuits as members of a ritual curing society that employed baptism as its curing ritual. The Jesuits' claim that the souls of those who were baptized would go to heaven, and thus not be able to join those of relatives and friends in the traditional Huron "villages of souls," troubled the Indians. This claim corresponded with the Iroquoian belief that the souls of people who had died in different ways experienced different fates after death. Some Huron sought baptism so that their souls might join those of relatives who had permitted themselves to be baptized in the hope that this might cure them. Others refused baptism so that their souls might join those of relatives who had died without being baptized. Later the Huron suspected the Jesuits of being sorcerers who spread the epidemics to destroy the Huron and their neighbours. In Huron eyes, the apparent unwillingness of the Jesuits to cure them confirmed this accusation. During the epidemics they could observe that, in contrast to themselves, the French either remained healthy or quickly recovered. The Huron did not slay the Jesuits as sorcerers , however, being convinced the French would cease trading with them if they did so. Yet, in 1641, a Jesuit winter mission to the Neutral so angered the Huron that they compelled the Jesuits to abandon their missions to the Neutral and Petun for an interval of several years.

By the 1630s the Five Nations Iroquois had grown sufficiently reliant on European goods that their own hunting territories no longer yielded enough pelts to supply their wants. In 1633 they resumed their raids on the St. Lawrence valley. They robbed furs and European goods from the Algonquin, Montagnais, and Abenaki, and also encroached on the hunting territories of these groups. Around 1640, first the New England colonists and then the Dutch began to sell large numbers of muskets to their Native trading partners. This allowed the Mohawk, and to a lesser degree the other nations of the Iroquois confederacy, to wage war more effectively. Yet to pay for these guns and for the powder and shot needed to operate them, the Iroquois had to obtain still more furs.

In the early 1640s the Neutral, although they did not have guns, took advantage of their iron hatchets and metal-tipped arrows to wage a particularly ferocious and destructive war against the Algonquian-speaking peoples of what is now southeastern Michigan. The Neutral apparently wanted to gain control of the rich beaver grounds in the vicinity of Lake St. Clair. Slightly earlier, either the Neutral or the Seneca had dispersed the Wenro, an Iroquoian nation living in western New York State whose territory embraced swampy areas rich in beaver.[25] The Huron obtained more pelts by expanding their trade with the northern hunting peoples. Thus, in various ways, a number of Iroquoian peoples worked to increase their supply of beaver pelts at this time.

By the early 1640s the three western nations of the Iroquois confederacy – the Onondaga, Cayuga, and Seneca – felt as pressed as the Mohawk and Oneida to obtain more furs. But unlike the Mohawk and Oneida, they were not in a convenient location to raid hunting peoples such as the Montagnais and Algonquin. All of their neighbours were Iroquoian-speaking horticulturists like themselves. Yet, by 1642, the Western Iroquois had destroyed an Arendahronon village after plundering it of the trade goods and furs that the Huron had collected there. Within a short time, the Seneca, Cayuga, and Onondaga seem to have made it their policy to plunder and destroy more and more villages until they had dispersed the Huron. Then they would be free to raid the hunting peoples of what is now central Ontario, as was the practice of the Mohawk and Oneida, who had already raided the Algonquin. To accomplish this task, the Seneca enlisted the Mohawk's help. The Mohawk, who had more guns than did the other members of the Iroquois confederacy, wanted to join in a war that would provide them with larger quantities of Huron furs than they had ever obtained before. All of the Iroquois nations also sought captives whom they could adopt to make up for their heavy losses sustained through epidemics.[26]

In 1639 the Jesuits established Sainte Marie, a fortified, agriculturally self-sufficient mission centre on the banks of the Wye River. The priests transported pigs, calves, and even a cannon inland from Quebec to equip this mission, which became a sizable, all-male European settlement in the heart of the Huron confederacy.[27] After 1640 the Jesuits succeeded in converting over a hundred Huron each year, and by 1646 the practising Huron Christian community numbered about 500. To achieve this, the Jesuits employed a variety of different approaches. They consciously strove to impress the Huron with the technological superiority of the French and with their own superior knowledge, including their ability to predict eclipses. In trading, the French treated converts with more respect than non-Christians and paid them higher prices for their furs. When the French began to sell muskets to the Huron in 1641, they sold them only to trustworthy and tested converts. These actions encouraged the baptism of many Huron traders and warriors. The number of converts rapidly increased, particularly in the large towns of Ossossané and Teanaostaiaé.

Huron Christians praying.
From Bressani's map of New France, 1657, *Novae Franciae Accurata Delineatio,* National Archives of Canada

The Jesuits forbade their converts to attend any functions where traditional rituals were practised. This made it impossible for Christian Huron to participate in most public activities of their communities, including feasts, curing rituals, and burial rites. Christians also refused to fight alongside non-Christians, even though both faced a common enemy. In the opinion of most Huron, such antisocial behaviour was a form of witchcraft that threatened the well-being of their communities. By the winter of 1648–49 the Christians had become the majority in the town of Ossossané. While they had been allowed to behave as they wished when they were in a minority, the rules changed once they became a majority. Now in Ossassané, the Jesuits had their converts deny non-Christians the right to practise their religion in the community.

Not surprisingly, the late 1640s saw the development of a traditionalist faction among the Huron that opposed the spread of Christianity. The more radical members of this faction called for the Jesuits' expulsion from the Huron country, as well as the exile of all Indians who refused to renounce Christian teachings. They advocated ending their thirty-three-year-old trading alliance with the French. In the place of the French alliance, they proposed peace and a trading pact with the Iroquois.

The radicals among the anti-Christian party found enough support to begin the negotiation of a peace treaty with the Onondaga. However, when a group of chiefs killed a young Frenchman who worked for the Jesuits and then demanded the expulsion of the Jesuits and their converts, they found themselves outnumbered by an alliance of Christians and those traditionalists reluctant to make peace with the Iroquois.

The development of new factions for and against the French, and for and against Christianity, further divided the Huron. These factions were all the more dangerous because some of them corresponded roughly with national divisions. The Attignawantan, the most favourably disposed towards Christianity, had suffered the least from the Iroquois and opposed making peace with them. The Arendahronon, the least disposed towards accepting Christianity and the most favourably inclined towards making peace with the Iroquois, already had many of their people living as captives in Iroquois villages.[28]

Although the Huron Christians looked to the Jesuits to protect their villages, Jesuit help proved ineffectual beyond the confines of the fathers' mission headquarters at Sainte Marie. By 1647 the Ahrendahronon had been compelled to abandon their settlements near Lake Simcoe. The following year the Iroquois attacked and destroyed two large Attigneenongnahac villages. In the spring of 1649, a war party of over a thousand Seneca and Mohawk destroyed at least two more Huron settlements. At this point, the Huron ceased trying to resist and abandoned their remaining villages.

After the collapse of the Huron confederacy, many Huron died of starvation or exposure. Several thousand more either were taken prisoner by the Iroquois or joined them voluntarily. Those who freely travelled to the Five Nations country included many whose relatives had already been captured and adopted by the Iroquois. A large number of Huron attempted to regroup on Gahoendoe (now Christian Island), an island in Georgian Bay close to the Huron country, but after a winter of starvation, sickness, and harassment by the Iroquois, the survivors were forced to disband. About 600 Christians followed the Jesuits to Quebec, where their descendants continue to live and are known as the Huron of Lorette or Wendaké. Others who escaped the Iroquois and survived continued as best they could. One whole nation, the Tahontaenrat, moved south to join the Neutral and eventually the Seneca, while smaller groups of refugees sought shelter among the Petun, Neutral, and Erie, as well as among their Algonquian-speaking trading partners to the north.

To prevent the Petun from serving as the nucleus around which the Huron refugees might attempt to revive their settlements, the Iroquois attacked them in the winter of 1649–50. They pillaged and burned the village of Etharita, where they no doubt seized many furs. Following this defeat, the poorly armed Petun dispersed. Many of them fled to the northwest accompanied by Huron refugees.

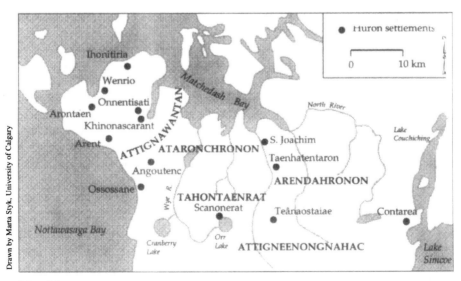

Map 3.2
The Country of the Huron, between 1639 and 1648
(showing the location of some of the major Huron settlements)

The Iroquois next attacked the Neutral. Their villages, like those of the Huron, offered the prospect of captives and rich booty, while their dispersal opened up new hunting territory to the Seneca, as well as a new route (through Michigan) along which the Iroquois could raid the hunting tribes of the Upper Great Lakes. Already, in 1647, the Seneca had pillaged one Neutral village on the pretext that the Neutral had allowed an Iroquois warrior to be killed by his Huron pursuers in sight of that village. Now the Iroquois also feared that the Huron refugees might draw the Neutral into a trading alliance with the French. In spite of some successful resistance, the Iroquois dispersed the Neutral, who lacked guns, in 1651. Some 800 fled westward. They gathered on the western shore of Lake Huron in 1652–53 and were reported to be planning to move farther west the next spring. Other groups appear to have fled south. None of these groups retained their identity, nor is there any further record of their activities. Following the dispersal of the Neutral, most of present-day Southern Ontario remained unpopulated for more than fifty years, during which time the area served as a vast hunting territory for the Iroquois.

### Without a Home (1650–1780)

After 1650 remnant groups of Ontario Iroquoians were widely dispersed in the region of the Upper Great Lakes. Their story becomes closely intermeshed with that of the Algonquian-speaking Indians whom the seventeenth-century French termed "Ottawa." The history of the Ottawa is reviewed in chapter 4.

In the late seventeenth century, the Petun-Huron sought to find a remedy for their small numbers by playing French off against English and one Native people against another. These tactics earned them the mistrust of everybody with whom they had dealings. In particular, their relations with the Great Lakes Algonquian-speaking Indians became progressively more strained in the latter part of the seventeenth century. Yet the behaviour of the Petun-Huron also ensured that no one in the region could afford to take them for granted as political and economic conditions changed. On occasion they even won the grudging admiration of their victims, including the French.[29] Chief Kondiaronk, whose activities were first recorded in 1682, was particularly adept at keeping the French and Iroquois at war with one another. He did this because he feared that if the French and Iroquois were not at war, the Iroquois would be free to harass the Petun-Huron and other peoples of the Upper Great Lakes region. Kondiaronk skilfully exploited his own amicable contacts with both the French and the Iroquois to foment incidents that sabotaged their efforts at reconciliation.[30] In particular, he played a major role in disrupting Governor Jacques-René de Brisay de Denonville's peace talks with the Iroquois in 1688.

Following the Treaty of Ryswick, which in 1697 established peace between France and England and ended active British support for the Iroquois war effort, the Five Nations negotiated a lasting peace with the French that was ratified at Montreal in the summer of 1701. That summer, Antoine de Lamothe Cadillac established the small French colony of Pontchartrain at what is now Detroit on the west side of the Detroit River. The French established this settlement to keep English traders out of the Upper Great Lakes area. Despite Jesuit opposition and the reluctance of some Indians to move, the Petun-Huron were persuaded to resettle at Detroit. Their chiefs sought to have their men enrolled as a regular paid company of French troops to police the other Aboriginal peoples of the region. The French refused this offer because they feared having these Indians acquire the discipline of regular European soldiers.[31]

The Petun-Huron, who continued to live in their traditional longhouses during the eighteenth century, established their first village near Fort Pontchartrain. There they had some trouble with their more numerous Algonquian-speaking allies, the Potawatomi, Ottawa, and Ojibwa, who also founded their villages nearby. In 1742 the Petun-Huron established new villages around the Jesuit mission on Bois Blanc (now Bob-lo) Island, near the mouth of the Detroit River. In 1748 they were relocated near a new mission station at La Pointe de Montréal, opposite Detroit, where they were placed under closer French supervision. Father Pierre Potier, who was a missionary to the Petun-Huron in this region from 1744 until his death in 1781, recorded much valuable information about the Petun-Huron language at this time.[32] Later, increasing European settlement in the Windsor area caused many Petun-Huron to relocate farther south along the Canard River.

After they moved to Detroit, the Petun-Huron also began to hunt, and some to settle, south of Lake Erie, in the vicinity of the Sandusky and Maumee rivers. Although by this time the Petun-Huron had lost all memory of their specific national identities, clan and phratry membership continued to play a vital role in their social and political activities. According to anthropologist James Clifton,[33] more conservative senior Petun-Huron chiefs, including the three phratry leaders and the chiefs of the deer clan, received special patronage from the French. They continued to live in the north and to support the French. Less-favoured chiefs tended to encourage the movement to Ohio, where they could often trade at more favourable rates with independent traders from the colony of Pennsylvania. There the Huron-Petun also interacted with the Miami who were moving into the region from the west, the Iroquois and Delaware from the east, and the Shawnee from the southeast.

In 1747 Nicolas Orontony, a Petun-Huron chief of the Turtle clan, was probably induced by fear of retaliation for his people's murder of some

French traders to try to form a league of peoples that sought to destroy the French posts in the western Great Lakes region. When the French learned of his plans and military reinforcements were sent to Detroit, Orontony burned his fortified village at Sandusky and retreated to the Ohio valley, where he died around 1750, likely during an epidemic.

As a result of their territorial expansion, the Petun-Huron were able to lay claim to a large part of present-day Ohio as well as to land in the extreme southwestern part of Ontario. Their alliances with both the French and the English strengthened this claim, which was recognized by other Indian groups. Although few in number, the Petun-Huron exercised the right to light the council fire at intertribal gatherings in Ohio. In this fashion, they acquired a more secure position for themselves in the disrupted tribal mosaic of the western Great Lakes.

## Epilogue

It was about the time that the Petun-Huron first began to trade with Pennsylvanians that the Pennsylvanians began to refer to them, especially those living south of Lake Erie, as the "Wyandot" (a corruption of Wendat, a term of self-reference that prior to 1650 had been restricted to the tribes of the Huron confederacy).[34]

The Wyandot, perhaps in part fearing the expansion of English settlement west of the Appalachians, generally supported the French during the Seven Years' War. They also initially backed Pontiac in his unsuccessful effort to expel the British from the Upper Great Lakes in 1763. Following General Anthony Wayne's defeat of the local Indians at the Battle of Fallen Timbers in 1794, the Wyandot were forced to cede land to the United States government. The Treaty of Greenville, signed in 1795, was the first of several cessions in which the Wyandot surrendered their territory and reservations in the eastern United States. In 1843 all the Wyandot living in the American midwest were resettled in Wyandotte County, Kansas. Those who wished were declared to be United States citizens in 1855, but in 1867 the American government restored tribal status and granted the Wyandot a small tract in the northeastern corner of Oklahoma. Their descendants live there to the present. In spite of prolonged exposure to missionaries, these Wyandot kept the knowledge of Iroquoian religious beliefs and rituals, as well as of the Petun-Huron language, alive into the twentieth century.[35]

At the end of the eighteenth century, European settlement increased in the area near present-day Windsor, Ontario. In 1790 the British deputy superintendent of Indian affairs acquired title to all Wyandot land in the area, except for the Old Huron Mission site, opposite Detroit, and the larger Huron (or

Anderdon) Reserve on the Canard River. The Old Huron Mission site was wholly ceded to the Crown in 1800. In 1836 the Huron Reserve was also ceded and sold, except for 7 770 acres that were conveyed to the Wyandot. During the early 1840s, many Wyandot moved to the United States to join their kinsmen in their removal to Kansas. In 1876 the remaining Wyandot applied for enfranchisement under the terms of the Indian Act. In 1880–81 the forty-one remaining heads of families were enfranchised and their reserve divided in severalty. In 1907 J.N.B. Hewitt claimed that the Anderdon band was now entirely scattered, "with the possible exception of a very few persons."[36] Nevertheless, in 1911, when Marius Barbeau visited the "Wyandots of Amherstburg" in his search for Wyandot myths, tales, and traditions, he recorded important information from Miss Mary McKee, a seventy-three-year-old member of the Bear clan.[37] He noted, however, that only two or three

National Gallery of Canada, Ottawa, 15305

Huron Indians leaving their residence near Amherstburg, Upper Canada, on a hunting excursion. Painted between 1825 and 1834 by the Canadian artist William Bent Berczy (1791–1873).

other Indians still spoke Wyandot and that they had little interest in their traditional culture. The descendants of the Anderdon band continue to live in the Windsor area. The traditional names of Warrow, Splitlog, Gibb, and White are found in local telephone directories, and a "Green Corn" picnic has been held on Grosse Isle on the Detroit River each summer in recent years.[38]

## NOTES

1  All but the final section of this paper is based heavily on Bruce G. Trigger, *The Children of Aataentsic: A History of the Huron People to 1660* (Montreal 1976). The latter work should be consulted for the detailed documentation of many arguments. The interpretation of the proto-historic period has been altered somewhat to take account of material presented in Peter G. Ramsden, *A Refinement of Some Aspects of Huron Ceramic Analysis*, Archaeological Survey of Canada, Mercury series, no. 63 (Ottawa 1977).

2  C.E. Heidenreich, *Huronia: A History and Geography of the Huron Indians, 1600–1650* (Toronto 1971), map 22

3  Reuben G. Thwaites, ed., *The Jesuit Relations and Allied Documents,* 73 vols. (Cleveland 1896–1901; reprint, New York 1959), 16:227–9

4  T.J.C. Brasser, "Group Identification along a Moving Frontier," *Verhandlungen des XXXVIII Internationalen Amerikanistenkongresses* (Munich 1971), band 2, 261–5

5  Floyd G. Lounsbury, "Iroquoian Languages," in *Handbook of North American Indians*, vol. 15: *Northeast,* ed. Bruce G. Trigger (Washington, D.C. 1978), 334–43

6  Bruce G. Trigger, "Settlement as an Aspect of Iroquoian Adaptation at the Time of Contact," *American Anthropologist* 65 (1963): 86–101

7  Thwaites, *The Jesuit Relations*, 21:207–11

8  Bruce G. Trigger, "The Historic Location of the Hurons," *Ontario History* 54 (1962): 137–48

9  A.F.C. Wallace, "Dreams and the Wishes of the Soul: A Type of Psychoanalytic Theory among the Seventeenth Century Iroquois," *American Anthropologist* 60 (1958): 234–48

10  C.F. Wray and H.L. Schoff, "A Preliminary Report on the Seneca Sequence in Western New York, 1550–1687," *Pennsylvania Archaeologist* 23, no. 2 (1953): 53–63; Ramsden, *A Refinement*. For an alternative view of the coastal sources of European trade goods, see James W. Bradley, *Evolution of the Onondaga Iroquois: Accommodating Change, 1500–1655* (Syracuse 1987). The primacy of the St. Lawrence is reaffirmed by William R. Fitzgerald, "Chronology to Cultural Process: Lower Great Lakes Archaeology, 1500–1650" (PhD dissertation, McGill University, 1990).

11  Richard Hakluyt, *The Principall Navigations, Voiages and Discoveries of the English Nation*, facsimile edited by D.B. Quinn and R.A. Skelton (Cambridge 1965), 723

12  Harold A. Innis, *The Fur Trade in Canada* (Toronto 1956), 12–14; S. de L. Barkham, "A Note on the Strait of Belle Isle during the Period of Basque Contact with Indians and Inuit," *Études Inuit Studies* 4, nos. 1–2 (1980): 51–8

13   H.P. Biggar, ed., *The Works of Samuel de Champlain*, 6 vols. (Toronto 1929), 2:96

14   Bruce G. Trigger, "Hochelaga: History and Ethnohistory," in J.F. Pendergast and B.G. Trigger, eds., *Cartier's Hochelaga and the Dawson Site* (Montreal 1972), 1–108

15   Thwaites, *The Jesuit Relations*, 22:215

16   Trigger, *The Children of Aataentsic*, 233–4

17   William C. Noble, "The Neutral Indians," in W.E. Engelbrecht and D.K. Grayson, eds., *Essays in Northeastern Anthropology in Memory of Marian E. White* (Rindge 1978), 152–64

18   Conrad E. Heidenreich, "History of the St. Lawrence – Great Lakes Area to A.D. 1650," in C.J. Ellis and N. Ferris, *The Archaeology of Southern Ontario to A.D. 1650* (London, Ont. 1990), 490

19   Gabriel Sagard, *Histoire du Canada* (Paris 1866), 585

20   Charles Garrad, "Iron Trade Knives on Historic Petun Sites," *Ontario Archaeology* 13 (1969): 3–15

21   K.F. Otterbein, "Why the Iroquois Won: An Analysis of Iroquois Military Tactics," *Ethnohistory* 11 (1964): 56–63

22   William N. Fenton, "Problems Arising from the Historic Northeastern Position of the Iroquois," *Smithsonian Miscellaneous Collections* 100 (1940): 175

23   Biggar, *The Works of Samuel de Champlain*, 2:207; G.M. Wrong, ed., *The Long Journey to the Country of the Hurons by Father Gabriel Sagard* (Toronto 1939), 263. For population trends, see Dean R. Snow and William A. Starna, "Sixteenth-Century Depopulation: A View from the Mohawk Valley," *American Anthropologist* 91 (1989): 142–9; and Gary Warrick, "A Population History of the Huron-Petun, A.D. 900–1650" (PhD dissertation, McGill University, 1990).

24   Thwaites, *The Jesuit Relations*, 13:215–17

25   Marian E. White, "Neutral and Wenro," in *Handbook of North American Indians*, vol. 15: *Northeast*, ed. Bruce G. Trigger (Washington, D.C. 1978), 407–11

26   Daniel K. Richter, "War and Culture: The Iroquois Experience," *William and Mary Quarterly* 40 (1983): 528–59; Heidenreich, "History of the St. Lawrence–Great Lakes Area," 491

27   Kenneth E. Kidd, *The Excavation of Ste. Marie I* (Toronto 1949); W. Jury and E.M. Jury, *Sainte-Marie among the Hurons* (Toronto 1954)

28   Bruce G. Trigger, "The French Presence in Huronia: The Structure of Franco-Huron Relations in the First Half of the Seventeenth Century," *Canadian Historical Review* 49 (1968): 107–41

29   E.H. Blair, ed., *The Indian Tribes of the Upper Mississippi Valley and Region of the Great Lakes*, 2 vols. (Cleveland 1911–12), 2:44–5

30   William N. Fenton, "Kondiaronk," in *Dictionary of Canadian Biography*, vol. 2: *1701–1740* (Toronto 1969), 320–3

31   James A. Clifton, "Hurons of the West: Migrations and Adaptations of the Ontario Iroquoians, 1650–1704," *Research Report*, Canadian Ethnology Service (Ottawa 1977). For a general account of Petun-Huron relations, see the relevant sections of Richard White, *The Middle Ground: Indians, Empires, and Republics in the Great Lakes Region, 1650–1815* (New York 1991).

32   Pierre Potier, "Elementa grammaticae huronicae" and "Radices huronicae," in A. Fraser, ed., *Fifteenth Report of the Bureau of Archives for the Province of Ontario for the Years 1918–1919* (Toronto 1920), 1–455

33 James A. Clifton, "The Re-emergent Wyandot: A Study in Ethnogenesis on the Detroit River Borderland, 1747," in *Papers from the Western District Conference,* ed. K.G. Pryke and L.L. Kulisek (Windsor 1983), 10–15

34 Elisabeth Tooker, "Wyandot," in *Handbook of North American Indians*, vol. 15: *Northeast*, ed. Bruce G. Trigger (Washington, D.C. 1978), 398–406; Clifton, "The Re-emergent Wyandot"

35 Marius Barbeau, *Huron and Wyandot Mythology*, Memoir 80, Geological Survey of Canada (Ottawa 1915); Marius Barbeau, *Huron-Wyandot Traditional Narratives in Translations and Native Texts*, National Museum of Canada, Bulletin 165 (Ottawa 1960)

36 J.N.B. Hewitt, "Huron," in Frederick Webb Hodge, ed., *Handbook of American Indians North of Mexico*, 2 vols. (Washington, D.C. 1907, 1910), 1:591

37 Barbeau, *Huron and Wyandot Mythology*, xi

38 Charles Garrad, personal communication

# 4 Southern Algonquian Middlemen: Algonquin, Nipissing, and Ottawa, 1550–1780

## BRUCE G. TRIGGER and GORDON M. DAY

Early in the seventeenth century European visitors identified the Native inhabitants of what is now southeastern and central Ontario as the Algonquin (Algonkin), Nipissing, and Ottawa. At this time these groups were already actively participating in the fur trade. All three groups, as well as the Ojibwa, who lived farther west than the first Amerindians termed "Ottawa," have been described as speaking a single Algonquian (Algonkian) language within which neighbouring dialects were mutually intelligible.[1] The Cree, who lived to the north of them, and the Montagnais (Innu), who lived to the east, spoke less closely related Algonquian languages. The Algonquian languages were not related in any way to the Iroquoian ones, used by the Huron, Petun, and Neutral of Ontario and the Iroquois to the south.

### Geographical Distribution

The Nipissing around the lake bearing the same name may have been a single large band with about 800 members, although Father Henri Nouvel spoke of them as consisting of four bands.[2] The Algonquin and Ottawa, broader Aboriginal groupings, included a number of such bands. Generally speaking, the French termed the Algonquian-speaking Indians in the Ottawa valley "Algonquin," and those Algonquians who came from the area west of Lake Nipissing "Ottawa."

Each Algonquian-speaking band had its own name, hunting territory, and one or more chiefs. The chiefs had no coercive power at their disposal, except for public opinion. Yet they played an important role in regulating the internal affairs of their bands and acted as spokespersons in dealing with other groups.

Qualified candidates within particular family lines inherited such offices. Although care was taken to avoid conflicts among bands belonging to the same nation or tribe, each band freely managed its own affairs. Solidarity at the tribal level was based on a cultural affinity and also, no doubt, on patterns of intermarriage.

Algonquin hunting territories probably stretched from the Ottawa valley to as far east in Quebec as the St. Maurice River. After the disappearance of the St. Lawrence Iroquoians, sometime in the second half of the sixteenth century, the Algonquin laid claim to the adjacent lowlands lying south of the St. Lawrence River.[3] In 1620 a mixed group of Algonquin and Montagnais inhabited a village at Trois-Rivières and grew corn there.[4] Because of fear of Iroquois attacks, however, the Algonquin generally avoided settlement in the St. Lawrence valley in the early seventeenth century. At that time most of them lived in the Ottawa valley. As Mohawk and Oneida war parties sometimes penetrated the lower Ottawa valley, the Algonquin usually located their summer camps in secluded places along tributaries of the Ottawa River. Farther north, where Iroquois raiding parties did not penetrate, the Kichesipirini (or Big River People), the most powerful and the richest Algonquin band, lived on Morrison Island. The principal chief of this band of skilled traders was known by the hereditary name "Tessouat."

The Nipissing lived to the west of the Algonquin around Lake Nipissing. The extent of their hunting territory is unknown. A number of Ottawa bands lived south of Nottawasaga Bay in Georgian Bay, and west of the Petun, though apparently they did not extend as far west as the Bruce Peninsula, which they may have used only as a hunting territory.[5] The Jesuit missionaries identified the "Outaouan" band as living on Manitoulin Island and a number of others as inhabiting the east and north shores of Georgian Bay.

## Traditional Culture

Unlike the Iroquoian-speaking peoples, the Algonquin, Nipissing, and Ottawa depended primarily on hunting, fishing, and collecting wild plant foods. Yet they differed from Algonquian-speaking peoples living farther north in that they regularly planted corn. Nevertheless, the poor soil and the dangerously short growing season throughout most of the region they inhabited made agriculture quite marginal. These groups represented the northernmost extension of native food production in eastern North America.

Like other northern hunting peoples, the Algonquin and Nipissing dispersed in small hunting parties to survive the winter. These groups usually consisted of a man and his sons or of several brothers, together with their dependents. During the summer, the hunting parties belonging to a particular band (or portion of a band) assembled by a lake or river to catch fish and grow corn.

The Ottawa groups who lived west of the Petun relied more on horticulture. Each of these Ottawa bands may have lived in villages inhabited year-round by women, children, and old men. During the summer, Ottawa groups composed of both sexes moved from such villages to hunt, fish, and dry blueberries. During the winter, male hunting parties travelled for long periods and brought meat back to their communities in processed, usually smoke-dried, form.[6]

In the first half of the seventeenth century, groups of Algonquin and Nipissing wintered near Huron villages, where they traded deer and beaver skins for cornmeal, wampum, and fish nets. Other bands that did not live in the Huron country bartered for corn with the Huron. The Ottawa who resided west of the Petun appear to have had similar relations with them. These exchanges provided a more secure food supply for the Algonquians during the lean winter months and possibly allowed them to increase in numbers beyond what their own economy would have supported. Archaeological evidence exists of close relations between the Huron and the Nipissing dating back several centuries prior to European contact.[7]

The material culture and world view of the Algonquin, Nipissing, and Ottawa in the early seventeenth century closely resembled those of neighbouring hunting peoples (see also chapters 7, 12, and 13). All of them used birchbark canoes, snowshoes, toboggans, and birchbark containers. There was a limited amount of polygamy, dependent on a man's economic capacity. They recognized numerous supernatural beings, most of which were related to animal or natural forces. They believed in the power of shamans, people who had special powers to call on spirit beings to mediate for the ordinary people with the supernatural forces. The Nipissing were renowned for their shamanism.

The Algonquin covered the graves of prominent persons with a painted wooden structure shaped like a ridged roof. The graves had a wooden pole at one end representing the deceased. The Ottawa disposed of the dead by inhumation, scaffold burial, and cremation.

Tattooing of the body and face painting were as common among the Ottawa as among the Petun. Ottawa men wore their hair cut short and upright in front, hence earning the name Cheveux-relevés (high hairs) that the French first gave them. They also pierced their nasal septums and earlobes and placed stone, copper, and shell ornaments in them.

These same three groups shared a variety of traits with the Iroquoian-speaking peoples who lived in the warmer and more fertile regions to the south. They erected barrel-vaulted multi-family houses that looked like a shorter version of the Huron longhouse. Archaeological evidence indicates that houses of this sort in the Upper Great Lakes region long antedate the

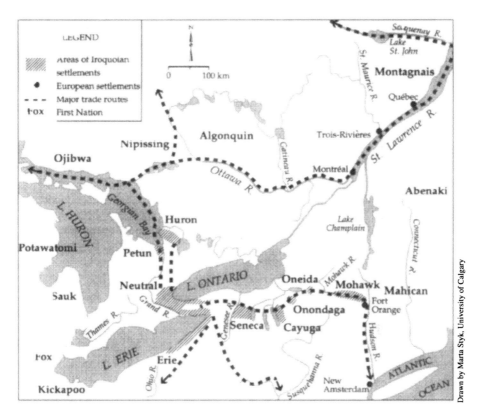

Map 4.1
The St. Lawrence Lowlands, c. 1640
Adapted from Bruce G. Trigger, *Natives and Newcomers* (Kingston and Montreal: McGill-Queen's University Press 1985), 228

development of the larger Iroquoian longhouse.[8] Like the Huron but unlike the Montagnais, the Algonquin used nets to fish through the ice.[9]

The formalities observed at Algonquin feasts and councils were similar to those of the Huron culture. The Algonquin, Nipissing, and Ottawa engaged in the torture of prisoners and ritual cannibalism. The Nipissing and Ottawa also practised their own version of the Huron Feast of the Dead. At these ceremonies the Algonquians installed new chiefs and transferred the names of the illustrious dead to living persons.

## History to 1650

By the early seventeenth century the Algonquin, on account of their location, momentarily monopolized the movement of European trade goods into the interior. They, and to a lesser extent the Nipissing and Ottawa, profited from the shipment of furs from the Upper Great Lakes region to the St. Lawrence valley. Before 1612 Nipissing traders had begun to travel as far north as James Bay each summer, exchanging Huron corn and European goods for furs that ultimately made their way to French traders on the St. Lawrence. A decade later, according to the early-seventeenth-century Récollet Gabriel Sagard, the Ottawa operated similar routes, from Georgian Bay westward into the vicinity of Lakes Michigan and Superior. The Huron represented the most serious long-term challenge to the Algonquin's control of the fur trade.

*Algonquin*

Following the St. Lawrence Iroquoians' dispersal, the Algonquin and neighbouring Montagnais both found themselves at war with the Mohawk, who raided the St. Lawrence valley, probably in an attempt to gain access to the Europeans who now regularly visited Tadoussac. This conflict apparently began about 1570.[10] The Montagnais, within whose territory Tadoussac was located, allowed a number of Algonquin to trade directly with the French. In their desire to retain a monopoly over trade with the French, they offered this privilege only to the Algonquin, whose military aid they needed to oppose the Mohawk. On account of the danger of attack by the Iroquois, the Algonquin apparently came to Tadoussac by way of the lakes and rivers of central Quebec, following the same route along which native copper had been transported from Lake Superior to Tadoussac in the 1530s.

The amount of European goods reaching the Algonquin gradually increased. Basque whalers apparently began to trade for furs at Tadoussac regularly around 1550. By 1581 they made sufficient profits that professional French traders began to send ships there.

European goods reached the Huron with some regularity beginning around 1580. These probably came to the Huron country by way of Lake Nipissing.[11] By the late sixteenth century the Algonquin exchanged European goods for cornmeal with the Huron. Some began to winter in the Huron country, as their Nipissing neighbours had done for some time.

At Tadoussac French traders, seeking to increase their intake of furs, encouraged the Montagnais and Algonquin from 1602 onward to drive the Mohawk hunters and raiders from the St. Lawrence valley. They wanted the river opened as a main artery of trade. They also wanted to establish, as soon as possible, more direct trading links with nations living farther inland, whence they hoped to obtain large quantities of prime pelts at cheaper prices.

In 1609 Champlain fought the Iroquois alongside his Indian allies. The following year they inflicted such severe injuries on a large Mohawk war party that the Mohawk (who soon afterwards were able to obtain European goods from Dutch traders along the Hudson River) temporarily abandoned their raids on the St. Lawrence. By 1610 the French travelled up the St. Lawrence River to trade with the Algonquin on their own territory. Champlain sent young Frenchmen to winter with the Algonquin and learn their language. Thus, while the Montagnais retained control of the lucrative trade reaching the St. Lawrence along the Saguenay River, they were bypassed as intermediaries between the French and the Algonquin.

In the spring of 1609 the Algonquin had invited the Huron to join Champlain in a planned foray against the Mohawk. As a result of this initial encounter, the French and Huron wanted to forge a direct trading link. The Algonquin, however, though they needed the corn, furs, and military aid of the numerically superior Huron, also wished to protect their role as middlemen between the French and the inland nations around the Great Lakes. This they were unable to do. Because they needed military support from the Huron against the Iroquois, the Algonquin had to be satisfied with the customary tolls that they collected from the Huron traders in return for granting them safe passage through their territory. Once the Huron traded directly with the French, they became the chief suppliers of European goods as well as corn to the Nipissing and Ottawa. In exchange for their corn, they also sought furs rather than trade goods from the Algonquin, thus consolidating their position as the great traders of the Upper Great Lakes.

The Algonquin deeply resented the loss of their middleman position, but their efforts to intimidate individual parties of Huron traders were discouraged by the armed Frenchmen who travelled to and from the Huron country with these parties. French traders and priests who lived among the Huron and Nipissing also worked to expose rumours spread by the Algonquin to discourage these nations from proceeding to Quebec or Trois-Rivières. A common rumour was that no trade goods had arrived from France that year.[12]

The Algonquin also sought to enhance their bargaining position with the French by playing the French off against their Dutch rivals at Fort Orange, near modern Albany. In 1634 the Kichesipirini in the Ottawa valley, then on particularly bad terms with the French, concluded a separate peace treaty with the Mohawk. Yet, when Oumasasikweie, one of the Kichesipirini headmen, and some companions attempted to cross the Mohawk country to trade at Fort Orange, the Mohawk killed them. They did not wish their Dutch allies to establish trading relations with the fur-rich northern tribes.[13]

Between 1634 and 1640 the Algonquin suffered from the same series of epidemics that afflicted the Nipissing, Ottawa, Huron, and other Indian peoples. These culminated in the devastating smallpox epidemic of 1639. It is impossible to determine if apparently less serious outbreaks of disease among the Algonquin in 1611 and 1623–24 were also of European origin.[14] The combined effect of the epidemics of the 1630s reduced the Native population by more than half. As among the Huron, this produced many social problems, especially as the losses included a disproportionately large number of old people, who possessed special technological, political, and ritual skills, and also of young people. The relative immunity of the French gave rise to suspicions that they were bewitching the Native people. The Algonquin exploited the mistrust to undermine good relations between the French and the Huron.

By 1640 the hunting territories in present-day New York State no longer supplied enough furs for trade to satisfy the Iroquois' growing appetite for European goods. The Mohawk and Oneida who lived nearest to the Ottawa and St. Lawrence valleys sought to obtain more furs by encroaching on the Algonquin's hunting territories. They also seized pelts and trade goods from the Algonquin, either when the Algonquin were in their winter hunting camps or when they were on their way to or from French trading posts. The war that followed the murder of Oumasasikweie of the Kichesipirini band soon turned into a life-and-death struggle in which the Iroquois' superiority in firearms gradually gave them the upper hand. The Kichesipirini sought refuge in times of crisis in the French settlements along the St. Lawrence. While the Jesuit mission at Sillery attracted some Algonquin after it was established in 1637, Montreal and Trois-Rivières were the principal refuges. Although the Algonquin retained their proud and independent reputation, their increasing insecurity coincided with the conversion of some of their chiefs, such as Tessouat of the Kichesipirini. The French baptized him with great solemnity at Montreal in 1643, but ardour for the new faith later seems to have wavered.[15]

The conversion of many of the Algonquin who sought refuge reflects their growing need for French protection and the increasingly unequal nature of their alliance with the newcomers. In 1646 the Mohawk succeeded in killing Simon Piskaret, a famous Algonquin warrior, and they captured two hunting parties near Trois-Rivières. The Algonquin sought aid from the Montagnais, Nipissing, and other Algonquian-speaking groups, but because these alliances were poorly coordinated, little good came of them.[16] In 1650 the Mohawk launched a general offensive against the Indians of present-day southern and central Quebec, carrying their raids as far east as Lac St. Jean and the Tadoussac area. These raids caused the Algonquin to abandon the Ottawa valley between about 1650 and 1675.

*Nipissing*

Although the Huron trade route to the St. Lawrence also crossed Nipissing territory, the Nipissing, unlike the Algonquin, remained on consistently good terms with the Huron, maintaining a friendship that apparently long antedated the fur trade. By the 1620s they were travelling down the Ottawa River to trade with the French at Trois-Rivières, although they did not do this as regularly or with the same enthusiasm as did their Algonquin neighbours. The Récollet priest Guillaume Poulain wintered with the Nipissing in 1621–22. Between 1620 and 1633 Jean Nicollet lived among them, encouraging them to trade with the French each year. As a result of his long stay, the Frenchman was reported to pass for a Nipissing, having his own cabin and household in their village, fishing and trading for himself, and taking part in tribal councils.[17] Jesuits worked among the Nipissing in the 1640s.[18]

Huron corn became so vital to the Nipissing subsistence economy and to their northern trade that they allowed the Huron to act as their intermediaries in much of their trade with the French. The Nipissing may also have relied on the Huron to supply many of their European goods because they feared that unless they had the Huron as allies, the more numerous Algonquin might interfere too much with their trading expeditions along the Ottawa River. Every year as the Huron traders passed through the Nipissing country on their way home from the St. Lawrence, the Nipissing exchanged furs for European goods with them. While they wintered in the Huron country, the Nipissing traded other furs they had collected and fish for corn and still more European goods. Between 1634 and 1640 the Nipissing suffered as much from European diseases as did the Algonquin.

In 1649 the Iroquois combined to decimate and disperse the Huron confederacy and the neighbouring Petun. The scattering of these groups meant that the Algonquian-speaking peoples of what is now central Ontario were cut off from the supplies of corn on which they had become reliant. The dispersal also permitted Iroquois raiders to travel north with impunity to invade the northern peoples' hunting territories and to rob them of their furs. The three western Iroquois nations – the Onondaga, Cayuga, and Seneca – now obtained furs in central Ontario in the same way that the Mohawk and Oneida had for years from the Algonquin and Montagnais. Eventually, the Nipissing joined the other Native groups from central and southwestern Ontario in their retreat westward, away from the Iroquois raiders.

*Ottawa*

The Ottawa entered written history in 1615, when Champlain encountered a large group of them gathering blueberries near the mouth of the French River.[19] Unlike the Nipissing and Algonquin, the Ottawa never travelled to the St. Lawrence River to trade prior to 1650. Instead, they obtained European goods from the Huron and other groups who did. They then traded these items for corn and furs from the Petun and Neutral, with whom they were on good terms. They also carried European goods westward into the vicinity of Lakes Michigan and Superior, where they exchanged them for furs, shell beads, pigments, and perhaps native copper. The scarcity of European goods in this western area probably gave them a higher exchange value, which compensated the Ottawa for the cost of acquiring these goods from other tribes. The Ottawa were renowned for their skill as traders.[20]

## History, 1650–1710

By the early 1650s, Iroquois attacks had dispersed the Native peoples of present-day Southern Ontario and turned the region into a large hunting territory. The Iroquois now maintained a tenuous hold over this area. The Algonquian-speaking peoples who had not perished as a result of these disruptions or in the preceding epidemics found themselves either prisoners of the Iroquois (who generally killed Algonquian men)[21] or in exile in the northeast and northwest.

### Algonquin

Very little is known about the Algonquin's dispersal. Some retreated as far east as the Lac St. Jean region, where they still lived in 1710. Others joined the Jesuit mission at Sillery, near Quebec, where most of them perished in an epidemic in 1676. Others remained near Trois-Rivières until about 1820, when the last fourteen families moved to Lake of Two Mountains (Kanesatake or Oka). Some joined the Sulpician Mission of the Mountain, which was founded at Montreal in 1677. In 1704 a separate Algonquin mission was founded at Sainte-Anne-du-bout-de-l'île (Sainte Anne de Bellevue), and in 1721 a new mission was established at Lake of Two Mountains, where the priests brought all the Algonquin in the vicinity of Montreal together with Nipissing and Iroquois. Additional Algonquin joined this mission in 1747. Ten years later the Algonquin lived there in houses built of squared timbers, but in a settlement separate from those of the Nipissing and Iroquois. Each of these three groups also had its own council house. The Algonquin trapped each winter in the upper part of the Ottawa valley, which they still regarded as belonging to them.

As early as 1715 the Algonquin participated in the clandestine fur trade that flourished between Canada and Albany until the outbreak of the Seven Years' War in 1755. They remained, however, faithful allies of the French. In 1684, the Algonquin at Trois-Rivières had accompanied Governor Joseph-Antoine Le Febvre de La Barre to his disastrous council with the Iroquois at Anse de la Famine (near Oswego, New York). They fought alongside the

French at the Plains of Abraham in 1759. Early in the eighteenth century they ceded their claims to land lying south of the St. Lawrence River to the Abenaki and Sokoki, who had settled at Bécancour and along the St. Francis River as refugees from the encroachments of the New Englanders. The Algonquin continued to claim territory extending east to the Sainte-Anne-de-la-Pérade River and north to the vicinity of Coucoucache.[22] Sometime in the mid-eighteenth century the Algonquin of Two Mountains became members of the so-called Seven Nations of Canada, a confederacy of French mission Indians.

### Nipissing

By 1661 the Nipissing had retreated as far west as Lake Nipigon. From this base they continued to trade with the Cree who lived in the vicinity of James Bay. In 1657 and 1660 Nipissing traders visited Trois-Rivières by canoeing on an interior water route. In the summer of 1664 about sixty Nipissing reached Montreal by travelling down the Ottawa River, although they faced repeated Iroquois ambushes. In 1667 Father Claude Allouez visited the Nipissing at Lake Nipigon. He encountered families who professed to be Christian, although they had not seen a missionary for almost twenty years. After the French and Iroquois made peace in 1667, many Nipissing returned to their former homeland, where the Iroquois attempted to trade with them. Jesuit and Sulpician missionaries who sought to convert and keep them in the French alliance also visited them.

The Iroquois attacked the Nipissing who remained in the west between 1677 and 1680 during the Iroquois' war with the Illinois Indians. About this time, Father Pierre Bailloquet established a mission centred at Michili-mackinac for the western Nipissing. Like the Algonquin, the Nipissing remained firm allies of the French.

Following the French-Iroquois peace treaty of 1701, the Sulpicians gathered their Nipissing converts at Baie d'Urfé and later at Île aux Tourtes, where they constructed a fort and mission house. By 1735 they had transferred all of the residents of their missions in the Montreal area to Lake of Two Mountains, where the Nipissing lived adjacent to, but separate from, the Algonquin. In 1742 additional Nipissing, who probably came from the west, joined this mission. In 1748, however, smallpox again reduced the population. During the Seven Years' War, the Nipissing fought alongside the French at Oswego, Fort William Henry, and behind enemy lines. After the British conquest of Canada, Sir William Johnson, the British Indian superintendent, estimated that the Nipissing had only forty warriors. They became loyal allies of the British and fought for them in the War of 1812.

*Ottawa*

After the scattering of the neighbouring Huron and Petun in 1649, the Ottawa also retreated westward to escape from the attacks of the Iroquois. Some of them settled around the Straits of Mackinac, others made their way (with a substantial number of Huron and Petun) to Green Bay, Wisconsin, where for a number of years they defended themselves against Iroquois attacks. Others settled in various parts of Michigan. In the late 1650s some groups made their way farther west, eventually arriving at Chequamegon Bay, on the south shore of Lake Superior in 1660. Three Ottawa bands had established their villages there by 1666. Three years later there were five Algonquian-speaking villages, although some of these may have belonged to other Algonquian groups.

In the west both the Petun-Huron and the Ottawa continued to need fresh supplies of European goods. Three canoes arrived at Trois-Rivières in 1653 carrying Indians representing various refugee groups from the Upper Great Lakes. They announced that the following year more men from these groups would bring many beaver pelts to Trois-Rivières. To fight their enemies they needed guns and ammunition. The next year about 120 Indian traders travelled down the Ottawa River. Some were Huron and Petun; the rest Ottawa. The Huron, the fewest in number, led the Petun and Ottawa to trade with the French for the first time. Médard Chouart des Groseilliers and another Frenchman accompanied these Indians home so that they might trade with their people and also explore the Upper Great Lakes region. Two years later they returned to the St. Lawrence accompanied by 250 Native traders, mostly Ottawa. For several decades the Ottawa dominated the French trade with the Upper Great Lakes Indians, much as the Huron had prior to 1650. On account of Ottawa predominance in the trade, the French often called the whole of the Upper Great Lakes region the Ottawa Country, a vague term that made no differentiation among the various nations that lived there.

In the late 1650s the Petun-Huron and Ottawa were encroaching on the lands of the Dakota, a Siouan-speaking group. The Dakota succeeded in pushing back the Ottawa, who had reached the Mississippi River. The immediate cause of this conflict appears to have been the arrogant treatment of the Dakota by the Petun-Huron allies of the Ottawa. The Petun-Huron had tried to reduce the Dakota to the status of clients and gain control of their upper Mississippi valley hunting territories. Reluctantly the Ottawa were drawn into the growing warfare between the Petun-Huron and the Dakota. The campaign of 1670 resulted in a serious defeat for the Petun-Huron and Ottawa coalition. In the spring of 1671 the Ottawa at Chequamegon, fearing Dakota reprisals and finding their position intolerable, took advantage of peace between the French and the Iroquois to return east. Many of them went to live on

Manitoulin Island; other Ottawa lived for a few years at Green Bay, on Lake Michigan; while a number of partially converted Ottawa lived at Sault Ste. Marie until 1676, when they moved to the mission of Saint Ignace at Michilimackinac, near the Petun-Huron who had moved there directly from Chequamegon in 1671.

After 1660 the Jesuits established further missions among the Ottawa in the Upper Great Lakes. Few of the Indians accepted Christianity, but the missions helped to maintain links between the French and their Native trading partners. French traders also began to penetrate the Ottawa territory in increasing numbers. Beginning with René-Robert Cavelier de La Salle's expedition in 1679, the French established trading posts at key locations, such as Sault Ste. Marie and Michilimackinac. This eliminated the need for Indian groups to travel to Montreal, and hence the Ottawa's control of the fur trade was gradually undermined.

In 1685 English and Iroquois traders, travelling by way of Lake Erie, reached Michilimackinac for the first time. They sought to recruit the Petun-Huron as their trading partners. This led to a serious rift between the Petun-Huron and Ottawa at Michilimackinac; their relationship, although close, had never been without its tensions. As a result, the Petun-Huron and Ottawa villages, formerly separated by a single palisade, moved apart. The Ottawa, however, were no less tempted than the Petun-Huron by the possibility of trading with the English. A few years later the Ottawa chief, Little Root, conspired to eliminate the French settlements in the Upper Great Lakes region; the Petun-Huron refused to support him in this endeavour.

At the beginning of the eighteenth century, Ottawa from Michilimackinac settled near Fort Pontchartrain, which the French trader Antoine de Lamothe Cadillac had established on the Detroit River in an effort to keep traders from the English colonies out of the Upper Great Lakes. In 1706 violent quarrels arose as a result of Ottawa suspicions that the Miami and Petun-Huron, also at Detroit, planned to plunder their settlement. These conflicts led to scores of killings and threatened the whole system of French alliances in the Great Lakes. Nevertheless, many Ottawa continued to live in the vicinity of Detroit, alongside Petun-Huron, Potawatomi, and Ojibwa. Some Ottawa retired to Manitoulin Island for a time after 1712, following conflicts with the Fox and Mascouten, other Algonquian-speaking groups. A number of Ottawa had settled at Saginaw Bay, Michigan, by at least 1712, and near the St. Joseph River in western Michigan by 1730. The Michilimackinac bands moved to Arbre Croche (now Cross Village, Michigan) in 1742.

The Ottawa generally sided with the French in their colonial wars and were on good terms with the Ojibwa, Potawatomi, and Menominee, all closely related Algonquian-speaking groups. Nevertheless, during the 1740s, one of the Ottawa villages at Detroit apparently cooperated with Orontony, a Petun-Huron chief who worked to drive the French from their forts in the Upper Great Lakes region. Mikinak, who was described as the "great chief of the Ottawa," apparently sympathized with Orontony, while Kinousaki, another Ottawa chief at Detroit, remained friendly with the French. The crisis ended when French troop reinforcements reached Detroit in 1747 and the French halved the price of trade goods. Some Ottawa groups, however, preferred to trade with the English and followed the example of the Petun-Huron by establishing villages on the Maumee and Cuyahoga rivers in Ohio during the 1740s. As French and English penetration of the western Great Lakes region increased, competition between these rival European nations became more intense. Native groups, already thrown together in various novel combinations as a result of the fur trade, now had to make increasingly uncomfortable and extreme choices in an effort to maintain themselves.

Many Ottawa switched alliances after the British gained control of New France. Considerable resentment arose, however, concerning the failure of the British to give presents to their Indian allies as the French had done. The Indians also feared encroachment on their lands. The Ottawa chief Pontiac, who followed the example of previous Indian leaders who had sought to eliminate European influence in the western Great Lakes region, led the hostile faction. In 1762 he formed a pan-Indian coalition of Ottawa, Potawatomi, Ojibwa, and Petun-Huron, which aimed to attack and wipe out all the British forts in the area. The Indians captured many forts, but Pontiac's own plans were revealed. Consequently, he failed to capture Detroit either by surprise attack or by siege in the summer of 1763. The anticipated French aid did not materialize. In 1766 Pontiac was forced to conclude a treaty of peace and friendship with the British. Factionalism weakened the chief's resistance, with the Arbre Croche Ottawa, in particular, tending to favour the British. After the war, many pro-French Ottawa retreated to the Miami River, in Ohio, and to the south shore of Lake Michigan. The Grand River valley in western Michigan developed into an important centre of Ottawa settlement.

## Conclusion

Soon after 1650 the Iroquois drove from their ancestral homelands the majority of the Southern Algonquians who had been middlemen in the early years of the fur trade. By 1750 the French settled most of the Nipissing and Algonquin at Lake of Two Mountains near Montreal, on what was an early form of Indian reserve. Nevertheless, the Nipissing and Algonquin continued to hunt during the winter in the upper part of the Ottawa valley. Scattered in many parts of the western Great Lakes, the Ottawa's fortunes became intertwined with those of other displaced and refugee groups; these peoples inhabited a land the Europeans had as yet occupied only thinly with their forts and trading posts. By the late eighteenth century, however, land cessions laid the basis for a flood of settlement by non-Indians.

# *NOTES*

1   Ives Goddard, "Central Algonquian Languages," in *Handbook of North American Indians*, vol. 15: *Northeast*, ed. Bruce G. Trigger (Washington, D.C. 1978), 583; Carl F. Vogelin and E.W. Vogelin, "Linguistic Considerations of Northeastern North America," in Frederick Johnson, ed., *Man in Northeastern North America* (Andover 1946), 181–2
2   Reuben G. Thwaites ed., *The Jesuit Relations and Allied Documents*, 73 vols. (Cleveland 1896–1901; reprint, New York 1959), 62:201
3   Gordon M. Day, "The Identity of the Sokokis," *Ethnohistory* 12 (1965): 237–49
4   Gabriel Sagard, *Histoire du Canada* (Paris 1866), 846
5   Charles Garrad, "Did Champlain Visit the Bruce Peninsula? An Examination of a Myth," *Ontario History* 62 (1970): 235–9
6   James E. Fitting and Charles E. Cleland, "Late Prehistoric Settlement Patterns in the Upper Great Lakes," *Ethnohistory* 16 (1969): 289–302
7   Frank Ridley, "The Frank Bay Site, Lake Nipissing, Ontario," *American Antiquity* 20 (1954): 40–50
8   Bruce G. Trigger, *The Children of Aataentsic: A History of the Huron People to 1660* (Montreal 1976), 113–17
9   Thwaites, *The Jesuit Relations*, 9:11
10  H.P. Biggar, ed., *The Works of Samuel de Champlain* (Toronto 1929), 5:78
11  Trigger, *The Children of Aataentsic*, 233–45
12  George M. Wrong, ed., *The Long Journey to the Country of the Hurons* (Toronto 1939), 266
13  Bruce G. Trigger, "The Mohawk-Mahican War (1624–1628): The Establishment of a Pattern," *Canadian Historical Review* 52 (1971): 276–86
14  Biggar, *The Works of Samuel de Champlain*, 2:207; Wrong, *The Long Journey*, 263
15  Elsie McLeod Jury, "Tessouat," in *Dictionary of Canadian Biography*, vol. 1: *1000-1700* (Toronto 1966), 640–1
16  Nicolas Perrot, *Mémoire sur les moeurs, coustumes et relligion des sauvages de l'Amérique septentrionale* (Leipzig et Paris 1864), 109–10
17  Thwaites, *The Jesuit Relations*, 9:215–17, 23:275–7
18  Ibid., 21:239–49
19  Biggar, *The Works of Samuel de Champlain*, 3:43–5
20  Sagard, *Histoire du Canada*, 192
21  Thwaites, *The Jesuit Relations*, 27:287
22  National Archives of Canada (NA), C series, I.J. Duchesnay, "Letter to Lieutenant-Colonel Couper" (1829), 268:529–32

An old Amerindian trail in the territory of the Seneca, near Conesus Lake in New York State.

# 5 *The Five (Later Six) Nations Confederacy, 1550–1784*

## ELISABETH TOOKER

## Introduction

The Iroquois who today constitute some 20 percent of the Indian population of Ontario are descendants of those who moved to the region after the American Revolution. By so doing they continued their old alliance with England as well as their involvement in the affairs of the region north of Lakes Ontario and Erie.[1]

The homeland of the five nations of the Iroquois confederacy (Mohawk, Oneida, Onondaga, Cayuga, and Seneca) comprised the region from the Mohawk River to the Genesee River in what is now New York State. At the time of the first visits by Europeans, the Mohawk had three principal villages, all located in the middle of the Mohawk valley. The Oneida had one such village, situated south of Oneida Lake near Oneida Creek. The Onondaga had two, one large and one small, in the region between Cazenovia and Onondaga Creek, a territory southeast of the present city of Syracuse. The Cayuga occupied three major villages, at the northern end of Cayuga Lake; the Seneca, four – two large and two small – in the region between Canandaigua Lake and the Genesee River.

The available evidence indicates that each nation had long lived in these areas, although they relocated their villages, as did the Ontario Iroquoians, when the land suitable for farming became exhausted and the firewood nearby became scarce. Accessibility to water and abundance of fertile land were important factors in choosing a new location for the village.

Each nation had its own hunting territory, extending south from the location of their principal villages to the height of land near the present New York–Pennsylvania line, and north to Lake Ontario and the St. Lawrence valley. Beyond these lands lay the regions into which the warriors ventured to trade and wage war. The number of men available for such activities was estimated by observers in 1660 as approximately 2 150. Of these warriors, 400 were Mohawk, 150 Oneida, 300 Onondaga, 300 Cayuga, and 1 000 Seneca.

It is not known when these five nations united to form the Iroquois confederacy. The Iroquois state that the League of the Iroquois was founded sometime before the European arrival, but how long before remains uncertain. Such data as are available suggest, however, that the League was established sometime between 1450 and 1600.

According to the traditional Iroquois account of the founding of the League, two men, Deganawida and Hiawatha, went among the then warring five nations to end the feuding and institute the confederation.[2] The "Great Peace" they established, however, was only a peace between the Five Nations, not among the other Indian nations with whom the Iroquois were often at war.

**Politics of the League**

Archaeological evidence indicates that the Iroquois participated in the fur trade long before Europeans actually entered Iroquoia. Then, when the Dutch established Fort Orange (later Albany) and the French settled on the St. Lawrence in the seventeenth century, the Iroquois found themselves in a peculiarly advantageous position. They held the Mohawk River valley, which with the St. Lawrence River was one of the two gateways to the Great Lakes. To the west the headwaters of the Ohio provided routes to the middle of the continent. Living on the edge of the easternmost of the Great Lakes, they also had access to this great system of inland lakes. To the north they could easily reach the St. Lawrence, the other gateway to the western furs. To the south rose the headwaters of the Susquehanna and the Delaware, which flowed to a point midway down the Atlantic Coast.

Their geographic location permitted the Iroquois, so skilled politically, to rise to power in the northeast. Trading with the Dutch, but unwilling to be subject to them, the Five Nations also dealt with the French on the St. Lawrence, playing off the Dutch (and later the English at Albany) against the French.

The Iroquois sought to increase the number of furs coming to Albany and to decrease those traded by other Indians to the French on the St. Lawrence. To further this end, the Iroquois carried out raids along the St. Lawrence River, seeking to prevent fur-carrying fleets of Algonquian canoes from reaching the French fur trading posts at Montreal, Trois-Rivières, and Quebec. They also worked to prevent the participation of other Iroquoians in this trade – most notably the Huron, the most important trading partners of the French – by attacking their fleets of canoes and sometimes their villages. The Dutch (and later the English) in the seventeenth century encouraged the Iroquois to bring their furs to Albany. They left the Iroquois to deal with other Indians as they saw fit.

The various relationships of the Iroquois confederacy with the Dutch, English, and French had an effect on those among the Five Nations themselves. No one Iroquois nation wished to be dominated by another. Thus, the four western nations, sometimes called the Upper Iroquois, reluctant to have the Mohawk, with their proximity to Albany and control over the Mohawk River, gain the upper hand, on occasion sought alliances with the French to prevent Mohawk domination. The Western Seneca, closest to the French presence in the Upper Great Lakes, on occasion allied themselves with French interests to a greater extent than did other Iroquois groups, including even the Eastern Seneca.

Despite these differences, the Five Nations' ultimate strength lay with the League. The Mohawk needed the Upper Iroquois and their access to the west, and in turn the Upper Iroquois required access to Albany. The Five Nations likened their League to a longhouse – with the Seneca characterized as Keepers of the Western Door and the Mohawk as Keepers of the Eastern Door – for, by this route, furs passed from west to east in exchange for European manufactured goods, which flowed in the opposite direction.

At their League councils the Iroquois discussed matters of common concern. Decisions required unanimity. As the council had no police power, only by consensus could they enact any policy. The council sought merely to reach agreement on those issues that threatened to break apart the alliance between themselves; they did not attempt to agree on a single course of action. Often it proved to the advantage of the Iroquois to leave the nations and groups within them to take advantage of whatever opportunities presented themselves.

## Organization

The great accomplishment of Deganawida and Hiawatha was to bring the leading chiefs of the five Iroquois nations together in council. To perpetuate the council, the Iroquois turned to their ancient traditions. By Iroquois custom, personal names are owned by specific clans. When a child is born, he or she is given one of the names belonging to the clan that is not then in use, that is, a name that once belonged to someone who has since given it up for another name or to someone who has died. Since Iroquois clans are matrilineal, the child receives a name belonging to his or her mother's clan. When this name is changed on the attainment of adulthood or on other occasions, the new name taken also is one belonging to the mother's (and the individual's) clan. Certain of these names have come to be associated with particular positions. Consequently, the person obtaining the name also assumes the role with which it is associated.

Successors to the chiefs on the original council were chosen in accordance with this practice. When one of these chiefs died, his successor received his name, and since the name belonged to the clan, he was of the same clan. The "clan mother," the woman recognized as the senior woman in the clan, chose the successor. Ideally she reached her decision in consultation with other women of the clan. If the man so selected proved unsatisfactory, the name he had received could be taken away from him and a new chief chosen.

The five Iroquois nations were not equally represented on the League council. Nine names, and hence nine positions on the council, belonged to the Mohawk, nine to the Oneida, fourteen to the Onondaga, ten to the Cayuga, and only eight to the Seneca, who were by far the largest in population. Each nation, however, did not need to be represented equally or in accordance with size, since all decisions required a consensus, which proved an often lengthy procedure.

The Onondaga, the most centrally located of the Five Nations, were the "firekeepers" of the League. Meetings of the council were held in their principal village. The Onondaga were also the keepers of the League's wampum, its record keepers. Custom specified the usual order in which the nations would address the matter at hand, as well as how the chiefs of each nation should consult among themselves.

In time, wampum (cylindrical beads made of shell) came to be the Iroquois' most valuable commodity, and hence the customary gift in treaty negotiations. (By Iroquois custom all important statements, including those made in treaty negotiations, should be accompanied by a gift.) Made into wampum belts, the design of purple and white beads served as a mnemonic device to recall both the details of the treaty at which it was given and the nature of the agreement reached.

The Iroquois also used wampum in a number of other contexts. It might be buried with the deceased. The wampum accompanying a call to council signified the truth of the invitation. Wampum served, too, as compensation for murder. If a man killed another, his family tried to smooth over the antagonism by giving gifts to the murdered man's family. But if that family deemed the gifts insufficient, they were free to kill a member of the murderer's family. The same principle applied with respect to the murder of a member of one nation by a member of another: the murderer's nation attempted by gifts to restore good relations with the murdered person's nation. As such gifts could be wampum, the League, anxious to keep the peace among the Five Nations, established the number of strings of wampum required to compensate for the murder of a member of one of the Iroquois nations by a member of another.

## Iroquois Rise to Power

The year 1609 marked the Iroquois' first contact with the two European groups that so influenced their affairs in the following decades: the French and the Dutch. In that same year Champlain joined some Montagnais and Algonquin on an expedition against the Iroquois, and Henry Hudson sailed up the river that came to bear his name, opening the way for the Dutch to establish the fur trade in that valley. In succeeding years, the proximity of the French on the St. Lawrence and the Dutch on the Hudson allowed the Iroquois direct access to European goods.

As the fur trade developed, Iroquois reliance on European trade goods grew. To gain control over their access to the Dutch trading post on the Hudson, the Mohawk attacked the Mahican in 1624. This war ended three years later with the Mahican's defeat. Meanwhile, the French had entered into an alliance with the Huron (see chapter 3).

By 1640 the number of beaver in Iroquoia had been greatly depleted, and the Five Nations' attacks against Native groups on the Ottawa River and in the St. Lawrence valley increased in frequency. Equipped with guns from the Dutch traders, they gained the upper hand in a series of attacks on Huron villages that ended in 1649, when the Huron dispersed, abandoning their country. Shortly afterward, the Iroquois defeated the Petun and then the Neutral.

After these victories, the Iroquois pressed their advantage. They raided extensively in the north and for a few years succeeded in preventing furs from reaching the French posts on the St. Lawrence. But when the Upper Iroquois war with the Erie Indians to the west intensified, they decided in 1653 to make peace with the French. The Mohawk, however, opposed the peace. They complained that by avoiding them and going instead to the Onondaga, the French had entered the longhouse (of the Iroquois League) by the chimney.

Despite Mohawk objections, Father Simon Le Moyne visited the Onondaga in the summer of 1654 to explore the possibility of establishing a Roman Catholic mission among them. In the spring of 1656 French Jesuits, some soldiers, and a number of other Frenchmen built a mission near Onondaga Lake, between four and five "leagues" from the principal Onondaga village. Called Ste. Marie after the chief mission station in Huronia, it served as a base for Jesuit visits to the villages of the Upper Iroquois. But the mission proved short-lived. Abetted by the Mohawk, the antagonism of the

Upper Iroquois towards the French increased after the Iroquois defeated the Erie in 1657. Learning that the Onondaga planned to destroy the mission, the French abandoned it during the night of 30 March 1658.

A faction at Onondaga, however, continued to support the French. In 1661 they invited the French to return to Onondaga and Le Moyne went to spend the winter there. The following year the Iroquois planned further overtures, but a false report of thousands of soldiers being sent from France for the purpose of destroying the Iroquois put an end to the invitation. In the spring of 1664 an Iroquois embassy led by Onondaga did leave to seek peace with the French. The peace party, however, abandoned its mission after the Algonquin attacked it. Those not taken prisoner or killed, fled.

The transfer of New York to England in 1664 had little effect on Mohawk trade relations. Albany remained a Dutch town in both population and language, and the Mohawk continued to deal with Dutch traders there. The other Iroquois nations, however, were not so anxious to maintain close trading ties with Albany, partly because of their perennial fear of Mohawk domination of the trade and partly because they were still engaged in an inconclusive war with the Susquehannock, a war that did not involve the Mohawk. Ever reluctant to fight on two fronts, the Upper Iroquois wished to be left free to pursue the Susquehannock war in the south without being threatened by the French in the north. To attain these ends, they made peace with the French in 1665. The Mohawk did not.

To humble the Mohawk, the French sent an expedition against them in the winter of 1665–66. The expedition failed to find the Mohawk villages, arriving near modern Schenectady instead; then, tricked into an ambush by some Mohawk, it was forced to retreat. This first expedition's failure led in the fall of 1666 to the dispatch of a second, which burned the Mohawk villages and corn supplies. The following year the Mohawk (along with the other Iroquois) concluded a peace treaty with the French at Quebec.

This peace made the Jesuits' return to Iroquoia possible. By the end of 1668 they had established missions among all five Iroquois nations. At the same time the Sulpicians established a mission among those Cayuga who had settled on the northeastern shore of Lake Ontario, on the Bay of Quinté, to escape Susquehannock harassment. The peace also facilitated increased French exploration in the west and the establishment of Jesuit missions in the Upper Great Lakes region. The French also built several new forts to draw trade away from Albany. In 1673 they constructed Fort Frontenac at Cataraqui (now Kingston, Ontario) to control travel down the St. Lawrence, and a few years later established a temporary fort and trading post at Niagara to control the route between Lake Erie and Lake Ontario.

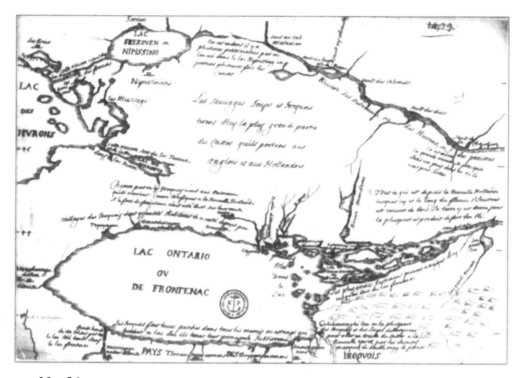

Map 5.1
An Early French Map Showing the Iroquois Villages on the North Shore of Lake
Ontario, c. 1680
National Archives of Canada, National Map Collection, Recueil 67 (Ancien 1044B), no. 47, Ph/902-[1680]

The peace of 1667 also led a number of Iroquois, many of them Mohawk, to settle permanently near Montreal. Two such settlements were established. The first was initially located on the south side of the St. Lawrence at La Prairie but was moved upriver in 1676 to the Sault St. Louis (Lachine Rapids); those living there became known as the Iroquois of the Sault. This village's Indian name – Caughnawaga, or Kahnawake – means "at the rapids." Relocated several times in succeeding years, it reached its present location in 1716. The other settlement was near Mount Royal at Montreal, and for this reason the group became known as the Iroquois of the Mountain. Subsequently these Indians, many of them Mohawk, moved to the Sault au Récollet on the northeastern shore of the Island of Montreal, and then to the Lake of Two Mountains (Kanesatake). From there, a century and a half later, a contingent of Mohawk migrated to Muskoka, Ontario, where their descendants, the Wahta Mohawk, still reside today, near Bala.

The rapprochement between French and Iroquois deteriorated after the Iroquois defeated the Susquehannock. In the late 1670s the Jesuits living among the Iroquois faced increasing hostility. The elimination of the Susquehannock as a power in the region also enabled the Iroquois to extend their influence to the south and west. The Oneida, Onondaga, and Cayuga began to hunt and to plunder furs along the borders of Maryland and Virginia. The Seneca and Cayuga did likewise in the west, where their attacks against the allies of the French, the Illinois, again brought them into conflict with the French.

## The Decline of Iroquois Power

As French-Iroquois relations became increasingly strained, the Jesuits closed their missions among the Five Nations, leaving only one at Onondaga. Some military action seemed necessary. In 1684 the French, fearful that the Iroquois (particularly the Seneca) would extend their control beyond the Illinois country to Michilimackinac, the most important French trading centre in the Upper Great Lakes region, planned an attack against them. The La Barre expedition, however, did not even reach Iroquois country. It only resulted in a council with the Iroquois that accomplished little.

In 1687, assisted this time by the Ottawa, Ojibwa, Fox, Huron-Petun, and others, the French mounted another expedition against the Seneca – the Iroquois nation most active in the west. The Seneca ambushed the expedition before it reached their large eastern village. But as the Iroquois so often did when outnumbered, the Seneca abandoned and burned the village, leaving to the French only the solace of destroying their cornfields and other Seneca villages. The Seneca warriors continued their raids along the St. Lawrence.

Although the Iroquois appeared ready for peace with the French, in 1689 the outbreak of war between France and England prevented it. The Iroquois' attacks on settlements in the St. Lawrence valley persisted, bringing the Iroquois of the Sault (Kahnawake) and the Iroquois of the Mountain (Kanesatake) into the conflict – on the side of the French. Early in 1693 they joined a French expedition against their relatives still residing in the Mohawk valley and contributed to the destruction of many Mohawk villages. The following spring furs from the west again reached the St. Lawrence. In spite of this apparent success, the Iroquois continued to threaten the French, who undertook an expedition in 1696 against the Onondaga and Oneida. The French burned their villages and destroyed their corn. The Ojibwa, furthermore, occupied their hunting grounds north of Lakes Ontario and Erie.

Although the conflict between France and Britain ended in 1697, peace was only made between the Iroquois and the French in 1701, at a council held in Montreal. At the same time, the Iroquois sent another delegation to Albany to affirm their alliance with England. This treaty and rapprochement with the French left the Iroquois free to pursue their role in the fur trade. The Iroquois still held the balance of power in the area, and for their part, the French secretly welcomed some Iroquois aggression against their Algonquian allies because it kept these Indians in the French alliance.

The peace established with the French freed the Iroquois from fear of attack in their homelands. As a result, they no longer palisaded their villages and the villagers built their houses at a little distance from each other, abandoning the larger longhouses in favour of dispersed neighbourhood clusters of houses. The houses themselves also changed. The average house now served as a home for far fewer nuclear families than had been the case in the seventeenth century. Greater quantities of European goods now came into use, and

Ontario Provincial Museum, Archaeological Report for 1904, 57

Depiction of the Ojibwa defeat of the Iroquois. Around 1900 Mesaquab (Jonathan Yorke), an Ojibwa from the Rama Reserve, Lake Simcoe, made this representation of a rock painting that once stood on Quarry Point, Lake Couchiching. As it was "some years since the rock fell into the water," he relied exclusively on his own memory. The design was made for the lid of a birchbark box. The Ontario Provincial Museum's *Archaeological Report for 1904* states: "The design is said to represent two Ojibwa warriors after the last great battle fought with the Iroquois, the central figure being a Mohawk, or Canienga. Mesaquab asserts that the Ojibwas, coming from the north, occupied the territory forsaken by their enemies."

as the century progressed, the Iroquois grew more European-introduced fruits and vegetables.

In the conflict between England and France that broke out again in 1702 and lasted until 1713, the Iroquois in New York maintained a partial neutrality. For the most part, the French and English preferred this arrangement. Both wanted the fur trade to continue, including the contraband trade between Albany and Montreal in which the Kahnawake Iroquois (Iroquois of the Sault) played an important role by exchanging surplus French furs for English goods.

As the French had enlisted Iroquois on the St. Lawrence to participate in their raids against the settlers of New England, so too did the English work to draw the Iroquois in New York into the war. Most notable was the command visit of the so-called Four Indian Kings to England in 1710. The English intended the visit to impress the New York Iroquois with their power. They wanted the Iroquois to strengthen their alliance with England. In London the four Indians were fêted, had an audience with the Queen (of whom they requested missionaries), had their portraits painted, and were written about by literary figures. After their visit and in part as a result of it, the English began the construction of a fort in Mohawk country west of Albany. Called Fort Hunter, they completed it in 1712, the year before the war ended.

National Archives of Canada, c-92419

Portrait of the Iroquois chief Sa Ga Yeath Qua Pieth Tow (baptized Brant), one of the four Amerindian leaders to visit England in 1710. John Verelst (c. 1648–1734) painted the portrait.

Fort Hunter secured the Mohawk valley for the English, and not long after it had been built, English settlers entered the valley. Their numbers increased during the 1720s, a decade that also witnessed the establishment of other settlements in and near Iroquoia. The French once again built a fort at Niagara in an effort to control and attract trade passing between Lake Erie and Lake Ontario. Shortly after, the English built a fortified trading post at Oswego near the other end of Lake Ontario to attract Indians there; from this point, goods could be easily taken by water to Albany. The French countered by building a small trading post at what later became Toronto, hoping to attract the trade of those who had been using this route to go to Oswego.

In the same period, various southern Indians came under the New York Iroquois' protection. Among them were the Tuscarora, who began leaving North Carolina about 1712 to settle in Pennsylvania. Shortly thereafter some Tuscarora moved further north, settled in Iroquoia, and about 1722 were adopted into the League of the Iroquois as the sixth nation of the confederacy. The Five Nations, however, only admitted them as a "junior" member of the League. They left the organization of the League unchanged and did not expand the list of names of League chiefs to include any Tuscarora chiefs.

The confederacy tried to keep its neutrality in the next round of French-English conflict, between 1744 and 1748. The English, however, induced some Iroquois to take up arms against the French. Again the Iroquois near Montreal fought for New France.

At the war's end in 1748 the French made increased efforts to gain influence over additional numbers of Iroquois. In 1749 Abbé François Picquet, a Sulpician missionary, began a settlement on the St. Lawrence at Oswegatchie (now Ogdensburg, New York) and induced a number of Iroquois, particularly pro-French Onondaga, to move there. A fort was built at a narrow part of the channel to regulate trade on the river and to protect Fort Frontenac and the upper St. Lawrence from the British. At about the same time, Iroquois from Kahnawake founded St. Regis (Akwesasne), a move that strengthened French control of the upper St. Lawrence.

On their part, the English renewed missionary activity among the Mohawk and made missionary visits to some Oneida and Tuscarora settlements. Moravian missionaries from Pennsylvania also made tours of varying lengths to the lands of the Iroquois. But of probably greater importance was the increased influence of William, later Sir William, Johnson. He had come to live in the Mohawk valley in 1738 and shortly after had begun buying land there, becoming one of the most prominent settlers. He also became involved in trade with the Indians and, in time, was recognized as the most influential British colonist among the Iroquois.

The confederacy attempted to remain neutral in the Seven Years' War, the new French-English conflict that broke out in North America in 1754. The French took Fort Oswego in 1756, but after two years of combat English fortunes changed. They took back Oswego in 1758 and seized Fort Frontenac, gaining control of Lake Ontario, and the following year they took Fort Niagara. The French also lost Quebec, New France's capital, in 1759. A year later the French surrendered New France to the English. The English victory annoyed many of the western Indians (Algonquians for the most part) who had long been allied to, and had long traded with, the French. In 1763, the year the treaty ending the war was signed, a number of them, under the leadership of Chief Pontiac in the Detroit area, tried to drive the English out. That same year the Western Seneca attacked the English in the Niagara area. These attempts to expel the English failed.

The English victory, which meant the transfer of New France to England, had at least two profound consequences for the Iroquois. First, it ended the Iroquois' position as middlemen between Albany and the western Indians; these people could now trade directly with the English. Second, the removal of the French to the north led to settlers' increased interest in western lands. The Crown attempted to forestall conflict between settlers and Indians by forbidding, in the Royal Proclamation of 1763, with limited success, settlements west of a line drawn along the crest of the Appalachians.

## The League Is Divided

The defeat of New France eventually contributed to a movement by the Thirteen Colonies for independence from Britain. No longer did they need British armed assistance against the northern enemy. When the American Revolution broke out in 1775, the Iroquois were not in agreement among themselves as to the best course of action. Some wished to side with the English, others with the revolutionaries, but the majority preferred to remain neutral. There was agreement neither between nor within nations. Being unable to agree, the Iroquois "covered" the League's council fire of 1777, leaving each nation to pursue its own course of action.

Not unexpectedly, given their long and close association with the English, many Mohawk who still resided in the Mohawk valley eventually joined the British side. The most noted was the Mohawk war chief Joseph Brant, who with other Mohawk went to Fort Niagara. Often in conjunction with English soldiers, the Iroquois at Fort Niagara raided the frontier settlements of the seceding colonists. Those Mohawk who remained in their homeland did not escape the war's ravages. The most devastating came in 1777, when some Oneida and revolutionaries attacked and plundered their settlements. A number of these Mohawk fled, eventually making their way to Montreal, where they established a settlement near Lachine.

Of all the Iroquois, the Oneida were the most sympathetic to the revolutionaries – probably as a result of the influence among them of the New England missionary Samuel Kirkland. The Onondaga, Cayuga, and Seneca, on the other hand, were more inclined to the British, although no consensus existed. The Iroquois faction, however, which fought under Joseph Brant for England, convinced General George Washington of the necessity to mount an expedition under generals John Sullivan and James Clinton into Iroquois country in 1779. In the face of the invading army, the Onondaga, Cayuga, and Seneca abandoned their villages, which the American army then burned. The American attack transformed these neutral Indians into active British allies. Many fled to Niagara, joining those Iroquois already there. The increased numbers strained the resources of the resident British but added to their military strength, for many refugees joined the raiding parties dispatched from Niagara against the Americans.

The Treaty of Paris ended the war in 1783. Those Mohawk who, under the leadership of Captain John Deserontyon, had settled at Lachine near Montreal took up land given them at the Bay of Quinte (Tyendinaga). The Mohawk under Captain Joseph Brant settled on land awarded to them by the Crown along the Grand River west of Lake Ontario. With Brant went a number of Cayuga, some Onondaga and Tuscarora, and a few Seneca. Other Cayuga and Onondaga chose to reside with the Seneca at Buffalo Creek, New York. Still other Cayuga and Onondaga decided to remain in their old homelands, as did the Oneida. Some Cayuga who had remained in New York State moved to the Grand River after all their lands in New York State had been sold. Still later, a number of Oneida left New York State and took up residence on land they had bought near London, Ontario. Thus, the Iroquois continue to be a presence in the region they once more fully dominated in the mid-seventeenth century.

# NOTES

1   The data contained in this paper are largely collated from material contained in *Handbook of North American Indians*, vol. 15: *Northeast*, ed. Bruce G. Trigger (Washington, D.C. 1978), principally the articles "The League of the Iroquois: Its History, Politics, and Ritual," "Mohawk," "Onondaga," "Cayuga," and "Seneca."

2   The name of Hiawatha was later appropriated by Henry Wadsworth Longfellow for his epic poem. The poem has nothing to do with the founder of the League of the Iroquois.

# 6 Land Cessions, 1763–1830

ROBERT J. SURTEES

The Amerindians remained undisturbed in their ownership of the northern shores of Lakes Ontario and Erie until the late eighteenth century. Then, in the space of forty years, thousands of newcomers arrived in two waves, not to trade but, rather more ominously, to colonize. The first invasion occurred during, and shortly after, the American Revolutionary War. By 1812 the Native peoples found themselves pushed away from large sections of their waterfront lands on the upper St. Lawrence River, Lake Ontario, the Niagara River, Lake Erie, and the Detroit River. The second influx, this time into the interior, followed the War of 1812. To provide land for the settlers, British officials made a series of treaties with the resident Indians.

During their long tenure in Canada the French had restricted settlement to the St. Lawrence and Richelieu river valleys. At the time of the conquest the westernmost seigniory lay slightly west of the junction of the Ottawa and St. Lawrence rivers near Montreal. The French had established trading posts in the Great Lakes area, at Fort Frontenac (at present-day Kingston, 1673), Michilimackinac (1681), Detroit (1701), Niagara (1725), La Présentation or Oswegatchie (Ogdensburg, New York, 1749), and St. Régis (1758). Apart from using the relatively small parcels of land around their forts, however, the French made no encroachments on Indian lands. After the British conquest of New France in 1760, the British did.

## British Amerindian Policy: The Royal Proclamation of 1763

The Thirteen Colonies each developed their own individual Amerindian policies. The colonies – and also the Hudson's Bay Company in the extreme north – entered into a variety of arrangements with the Indians of their respective regions. Essentially, the colonies made a payment, usually in the form of trade goods, in return for a specific tract. In an attempt to standardize Indian policy and prevent hostilities on the frontier, the imperial government in 1755 took control of the management of all Indian affairs within British North America. A special proclamation issued by King George III in October 1763 outlined the new imperial policies. Generally referred to as the Royal Proclamation of 1763, this document dealt with a variety of subjects, including the boundaries of the new colonies and their constitutions. Fully one-third of this document dealt with Amerindians and their lands.

Two distinct schools of thought exist concerning the nature and the significance of the Royal Proclamation. The first argues that the document represents a Magna Carta for Canadian Indians. In the proclamation the British government formally recognized what we now know as Aboriginal rights. In issuing the proclamation, the British Crown asserted its sovereignty over this vast region, but concurrently it declared the land to be in the possession of the Indian peoples who occupied it. It also forbade non-Indians to enter the region, and ordered any who had already done so to leave. In a final attempt to avoid confusion, the document also denied individuals the right of purchasing any portion of the Indian Territory.

A second interpretation concedes the proclamation's short-term, but not its long-term, importance. The group endorsing this viewpoint argues that the proclamation was a temporary – indeed emergency – measure designed merely to deal with circumstances peculiar to the day: the recent violence and extremes of the Pontiac War. To maintain a peaceful frontier, the British authorities required all fur traders travelling to the Indian Territory to secure a licence to do so and to restrict their activities to the sites of British military posts in the interior, such as Oswegatchie, Niagara, Detroit, and Michilimackinac.

Perhaps the best interim summary that can be made at the present would be that the Magna Carta school has exaggerated the proclamation's importance, while the second has underemphasized it. All of this being said, one must accept the proclamation's lasting impact on the administration of both British and Canadian Indian policy. The Royal Proclamation established the procedures, followed for over two centuries after 1763, for Amerindian land surrenders.

The proclamation stipulated that henceforth only the Crown could purchase lands in the Indian Territory. It could accomplish this through formal and public councils held between representatives of both the Crown and the particular Native peoples whose lands were involved. Having acquired the desired lands through formal purchase, the Crown could then redistribute them, by sale or grant, to settlers.

The proclamation was designed to prevent the purchase by private individuals of ill-defined or overlapping parcels of land. It made illegal as well the acquisition of land through the unscrupulous methods frequently employed before 1763, such as the heavy distribution of liquor during the negotiations. The Royal Proclamation certainly recognized Aboriginal proprietorship, but at the same time it provided a means by which that right could be formally alienated.

In 1763 the British faced two problems regarding the Indian Territory around the Great Lakes. First, the Appalachian highlands did not extend into the newly acquired colony of Canada, and thus did not provide a natural barrier as it did at the western end of the other American colonies. Secondly, the French had never formally recognized any Aboriginal rights of ownership to the lands in the St. Lawrence River valley, where they had established their settlements. The French claimed that they held that region by right of discovery and occupation. To include the region of French settlement in the St. Lawrence River valley as part of the Indian Territory would place the rights of the current landowners in jeopardy. That area, therefore, received the same treatment as the settled regions of the Anglo-American colonies in the south – British officials exempted it.

The Royal Proclamation, therefore, created a zone of exemption for the St. Lawrence valley. British officials drew a line from the south shore of Lake Nipissing in a southeasterly direction to a point on the St. Lawrence River at the 45th parallel of latitude. From that point the line ran in an easterly direction until it crossed the Appalachians. It also ran from the same point on the south shore of Lake Nipissing in a northeasterly direction to Lake St. John, and from there in an easterly direction to the coast of Labrador. (See Map 6.1.) This area, essentially the St. Lawrence valley, became the Province of Quebec.

### The Location of Amerindian Communities in Ontario in the 1770s and 1780s

Several Amerindian groups occupied present-day Ontario in the 1770s and 1780s. Two Iroquois communities claimed the upper St. Lawrence River lands: the Mohawk at the mouth of the St. Regis River, where they formed a permanent settlement known as Akwesasne; and the Onondaga at La Présentation at the mouth of the Oswegatchie River.

The Mississauga (as the settlers called the Ojibwa along the north shore of Lake Ontario and in the Trent River valley) lived immediately to the west. Around 1700 they had expelled the Iroquois from their hunting territories so recently acquired from the Huron, Petun, and Neutral half a century earlier. The Ojibwa, termed "Chippewa" by the first settlers (following American usage), resided around Lake Simcoe, the Bruce Peninsula, and Matchedash

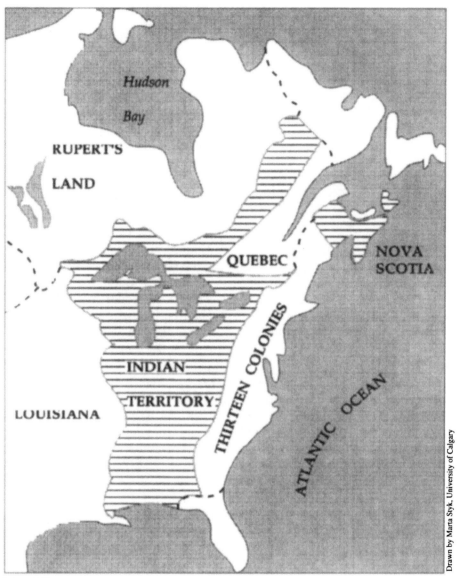

Map 6.1
Eastern North America after the Royal Proclamation of 1763

"Canise of Great Sail," a sketch of a Lake Simcoe Ojibwa chief, completed in the mid-1790s by Mrs. John Graves Simcoe, the wife of the first governor of Upper Canada.

Bay, and much of the Thames River valley (although at its lower end they were joined by the Potawatomi and Wyandot). The northern Ojibwa occupied the shores of Lakes Huron and Superior. The Ottawa (Odawa), a group closely related to the Ojibwa, claimed Manitoulin Island, often referred to as "the Island of the Ottawas." North of the Ojibwa dwelt the Cree, a fellow Algonquian-speaking nation.

In 1774 the British altered the boundaries of the Province of Quebec to include the lands of the Ohio country. For Native peoples in what is now Ontario, these changes had no immediate effect – nor did the first two land cessions enacted under the provisions of the Royal Proclamation of 1763.

Sir William Johnson, who had been appointed superintendent general of Indian affairs in 1763, concluded the Treaty of Fort Stanwix in 1768. This agreement with the Six Nations Confederacy led to an expansion of the European line of settlement in Pennsylvania and New York by as much as fifty kilometres. The British wanted additional lands for settlers who, regardless of the prevailing regulations, continued to migrate westward. None of the territory involved in this transaction lay within the bounds of what is now Ontario, although a portion of a much smaller purchase at Niagara in 1764 did.

The Seneca, the most westerly of the Six Nations, claimed the east bank of the Niagara River. During the summer of Pontiac's resistance, the portage route around Niagara Falls formed a vital link in the route to supply Detroit. In the summer of 1763 supply caravans suffered some harassment from the Seneca. There the Seneca struck one of the severest blows of the war, ambushing a supply caravan at a point known as the Devil's Hole, about six kilometres downstream from the falls.[1] The deaths of over seventy British soldiers and their officers made clear the urgent need for British control of the portage around the great falls of Niagara. Once reinforcements arrived, the British constructed several blockhouses along the fifteen-kilometre passage.

Short of food supplies, the Seneca made peace in 1764. Under great pressure from Sir William Johnson,[2] the Seneca surrendered to the British a strip of land, six and a half kilometres in depth on the east side and (although the Mississauga claimed the Niagara Peninsula) three kilometres deep on the west side of the Niagara River.[3] The arrangement served the double purpose of securing the route around the falls for the British and of punishing the Seneca for their support of the French during the Seven Years' War and at the Devil's Hole massacre. (The British only addressed the Mississauga claim to the west bank of the Niagara River seventeen years later, in 1781.)

## The First Invasion of Newcomers

The outbreak of the American Revolution in 1775 led, within three years, to an influx of refugees around Fort Niagara. As early as 1778 the Niagara region received the first Amerindian and British Loyalists. The number of these early British Americans who made their way to the Niagara region was not large, but they did require care and management. The more substantial numbers of Indian allies who sought the protection of the Niagara military post also required assistance.

During the American Revolution the confederacy had split apart, with many Oneida and Tuscarora backing the Americans, and the other four nations, the British[4] (see chapter 5). Many of those Mohawk, Onondaga, Cayuga, and Seneca who had chosen to support the British found their positions untenable in their traditional homelands. This was especially true of the Mohawk, whose lands on the Mohawk River lay closest to the rebels. A group of some 200 Mohawk, led by Chief John Deserontyon, sought refuge near Lachine near Montreal, and remained there until the end of the war. A much larger number followed the war chief Joseph Brant to the Niagara frontier. This group, when joined by other Iroquois allies, grew at one point to a total of 5 000 people, including warriors and their families.[5] While the number varied, depending on the season and the current wartime conditions, it remained consistently large, always in excess of 2 000.

About two-thirds of the Iroquois refugees at Niagara were dependent women, children, and elderly men. Their need of provisions placed an enormous strain on the fort's resources. To feed them, Frederick Haldimand, the newly arrived governor of Quebec, considered (as early as 1778) the possibility of establishing an agricultural settlement near the fort.[6]

The British dealt with the Mississauga land claim in a special council with them on 9 May 1781. In return for 300 suits of clothing the Mississauga sold to the Crown a strip of land, six and a half kilometres deep along the full length of the west bank of the Niagara River from Lake Erie to Lake Ontario.[7]

(See Map 6.2.) Concurrently, British agents negotiated with the Ojibwa at the junction of Lakes Michigan and Superior for the sale of the island of Michilimackinac, concluding the sale on 12 May 1781. For £5 000 worth of goods the Ojibwa ceded the island formally to the Crown. The island, however, lay on the American side of the boundary established by the Treaty of Paris of 1783, which ended the first Anglo-American war.

The success of the American rebels created a vastly altered political and military situation in North America, one that resulted in the dispersal of roughly one out of twenty-five inhabitants of the newly independent Thirteen Colonies. The number of Loyalist refugees who sought British protection increased after the British defeat at Yorktown in 1781, and grew even larger after the signing of the Articles of Peace in 1783. The Loyalists moved to England, the West Indies, Nova Scotia, and the Province of Quebec. Those who fled to the western portion of the Province of Quebec (to become the colony of Upper Canada in 1791) formed the smallest group, but these 5 000 or so newcomers had a significant effect on Indian lands.

The Amerindian situation troubled Governor Haldimand. The boundaries allocated to the new American republic by the Treaty of Paris included the traditional homeland of the Six Nations. Yet the Indians and their lands had received no mention in the treaty. The Indians felt abandoned by the British, and they expressed their displeasure to the point that Haldimand feared that the Iroquois might direct their wrath against the incoming white Loyalists.

Haldimand consequently directed the Indian agents to be generous in the distribution of supplies, rations, and presents to Britain's Indian allies. Secondly, contrary to the terms of the peace treaty, he held on to the Great Lakes posts of Oswegatchie, Niagara, Detroit, and Michilimackinac, all located south of the Great Lakes on the "American" side. Known collectively as the "western posts," these military centres gave Britain influence south of the Great Lakes. Britain's continued occupation showed that the Crown had not abandoned its Indian allies. Using as a pretext the American failure to protect the property of the Loyalists – also a breach of the treaty – the British occupied these forts for thirteen years until, in accordance with Jay's Treaty of 1796, they turned them over to the United States. Finally, again in an effort to ease Indian anger, Haldimand welcomed all of the Crown's Indian allies who felt compelled to leave their former lands and move to what remained of British North America.

Governor Haldimand knew that the New York Mohawk would migrate: the small group under John Deserontyon and the larger force under Joseph Brant. Neither contingent felt comfortable about returning to the Mohawk valley, and no one suggested that they attach themselves to the existing Iroquois settlements at Kanesatake (Oka or Lake of Two Mountains), Akwesasne

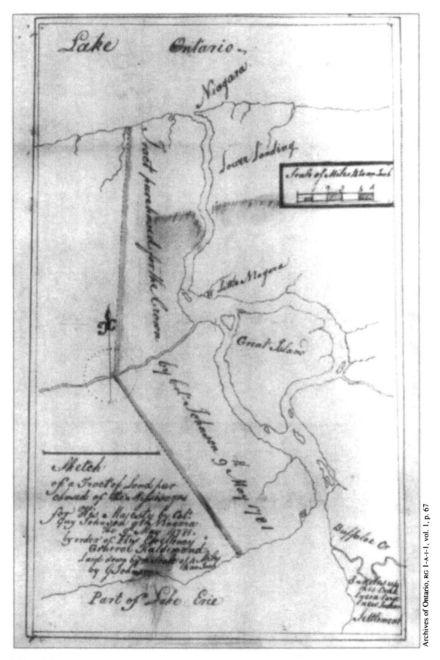

Map 6.2
The First Land Surrender by the Mississauga, 9 May 1781
(entire tract purchased for 300 suits of clothing)

A spokesperson's use of wampum in addressing the British. For the Amerindian, the record was the wampum; for the European, the written document.

An engraving from a painting by Benjamin West, from William Smith, *An Historical Account of the Expedition Against the Ohio Indians* (Philadelphia 1766)

National Archives of Canada, c-1511

A southeast view of Cataraqui (Kingston), painted by James Peachey in August 1785.

(St. Régis), or Kahnawake (Caughnawaga). In fact, the British did not wish to assemble their allies in one large, powerful Iroquois community.

At first both Deserontyon and Brant agreed to locate their respective groups on the northeastern shore of Lake Ontario, opposite the Quinte Peninsula. Then Brant changed his mind. In response to charges from the Seneca that by moving to the north shore of the lake he would be abandoning his fellow Iroquois, the Mohawk war chief declared his preference for lands in the Grand River valley, just west of Lake Ontario.[8]

### The Land Cessions by the Mississauga in the 1780s

There then followed, in 1783 and 1784, two sets of land-cession agreements between the Crown and the Indians of the upper St. Lawrence River and the northern shore of Lake Ontario. The first consisted of three agreements with the Mississauga. At the eastern end of Lake Ontario, Sir John Johnson, who had recently replaced his cousin, Colonel Guy Johnson, as chief superintendent of Indian affairs, approached the Quinte Mississauga. As Johnson had other pressing duties, the task of actually negotiating the final arrangements fell to Captain William Redford Crawford, a young officer who had been seconded to the Indian branch during the recent war. Crawford assembled a number of the Mississauga chiefs at Carleton Island at the eastern end of Lake Ontario in October 1783. Also present at this council were some Onondaga chiefs, probably from Oswegatchie, and an old chief named Mynas from Kanesatake. Unfortunately neither the council's proceedings nor the final written agreement (which apparently was made at the time) have survived.[9]

On 9 October 1783 Crawford reported that in return for clothing for all families, guns for those who had none, some powder and ball, twelve laced hats, and red cloth sufficient for twelve coats, the Mississauga chiefs agreed to sell all the lands "from Toniato or Onagara River to a river in the Bay of Quinte within eight leagues of the bottom of the ... Bay including all the islands, extending back from the lake so far as a man can travel in a day."[10] In addition, Chief Mynas agreed to sell land to which he had personal claims. Two additional agreements were apparently made in October 1783 and subsequently confirmed by further dealings with chiefs who had not been present at the time. One involved the shoreline from the Trent to the Gananoque River, purchased from the Mississauga (see Map 6.3, No. 3); the second (the land claimed by Chief Mynas – Map 6.3, No. 4) included the St. Lawrence River shore from the Gananoque River to the Toniato River, which is actually a small stream, now named Jones Creek, near present Brockville. From the lands obtained, Haldimand carved one full township, later known as Tyendinaga, to give to the Mohawk who moved there with Chief Deserontyon in 1784. (No. 25 on Map 6.3 shows that much of this reserve was later sold in 1820 and 1835.)

In the meantime, British agents also negotiated with the Mississauga at the western end of Lake Ontario to secure lands in the Grand River valley for Joseph Brant and his nearly 2 000 followers. The Quinte Mississauga had initially expressed concern about the arrival of the Mohawk, fearing that they might be so numerous that the land would not support everyone. That fear was allayed somewhat when it was learned that only the Deseronto group would be moving to the region. No such fears were expressed in council at the other end of the lake. Indeed, Chief Pokquan, the principal Mississauga speaker, told Colonel Butler that the Mississauga considered themselves and the Six Nations to be "one and the same people" and welcomed their coming.[11]

The Mississauga at the western end of Lake Ontario sold the Grand River lands as well as another huge tract to the British. The entire cession included the Niagara Peninsula, lands close to the head of Lake Ontario, and the north shore of Lake Erie as far west as the mouth of Cat Fish Creek (see Map 6.3, No. 6, page 104). The purchase cost the British £1 180 worth of trade goods.[12] From this enormous tract of over one million hectares, the British carved out a tract to run nearly ten kilometres deep on each side of the Grand River from

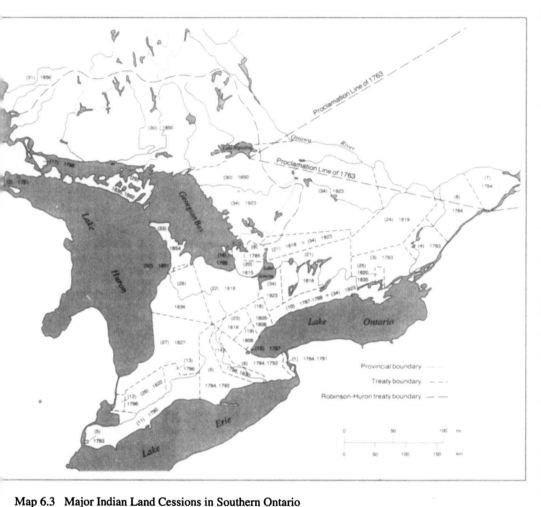

Map 6.3   Major Indian Land Cessions in Southern Ontario
(1) Niagara Purchase; (2) Island of Michilimackinac; (3) Crawford Purchase I; (4) Crawford
Purchase II; (5) Indian Officers Lands; (6) Between the Lakes Purchase; (7) St. Régis Purchase; (8)
Oswegatchie Purchase; (9) Collins Purchase; (10) Johnson-Butler Purchase; (11) McKee Purchase;
(12) Sombra Township; (13) London Township; (14) Grand River; (15) Joseph Brant's Land; (16)
Penetanguishene Peninsula; (17) St. Joseph Island; (18) Toronto Purchase; (19) Head of the Lake
Purchase; (20) Lake Simcoe Purchase; (21) Rice Lake Purchase; (22) Lake Simcoe-Nottawasaga
Purchase; (23) Ajetance Purchase; (24) Rideau Purchase; (25) Tyendinaga; (26) Long Woods
Purchase; (27) Huron Tract Purchase; (28) Bond Head–Saugeen Treaty; (29) Bond Head–Manitoulin
Treaty and Manitoulin Island Treaty; (30) Robinson-Huron Treaty; (31) Robinson-Superior Treaty;
(32) Indian Strip Sale; (33) Saugeen Surrenders; (34) Williams Treaties (based on Robert J. Surtees,
"Indian Land Cessions in Ontario, 1763–1862: The Evolution of a System" [PhD thesis, Carleton
University, 1982]).

its mouth to its source, and awarded it to the Six Nations and others who followed Joseph Brant (No. 14). A confirming document in 1792 later made the actual limits of this grant more definite.

### Discussions with the Akwesasne Mohawk and Oswegatchie-Iroquois in the 1780s and 1790s

These three agreements provided sufficient land to accommodate both the Loyalists and the Indian allies of the British, but from a military point of view, it was necessary that these lands be joined to the existing settlements just west of Montreal. The British now extinguished the claims of the Onondaga of Oswegatchie and the Mohawk of St. Régis (Akwesasne) to the north bank of the St. Lawrence River.

During the Seven Years' War a number of Mohawk from Kahnawake (Caughnawaga) had settled at the junction of what is now the Quebec–Ontario–New York State border. The French called the new mission St. Régis, but the Indians named their settlement Akwesasne. The French civil and military authorities, pleased to have another loyal Amerindian outpost as a buffer against the English colonies, approved the move from Kahnawake. Father Gordon, the leader of the new mission, apparently received a promise from Governor Vaudreuil for "a Grant of any Spot or Tract of Land he might pitch upon that were unceded Lands on the St. Lawrence above the Sault St. Louis [Kahnawake]," but the war ended before the governor honoured his promise.[13] Following the surrender of New France, Gordon appealed to Col. Daniel Claus, the Montreal-based British Indian agent. He requested that the Jesuits be given a grant of lands on both sides of the St. Lawrence River from the Raisin River to the Long Sault, to a depth of six leagues. Claus managed "to put him off,"[14] however. No grant followed at that time.

When it became evident that the St. Lawrence lands might be required for the Loyalists, Governor Haldimand dealt with the claim of the Iroquois at St. Régis (see Map 6.3, No. 7). Once he had learned that no grant had been made from Claus's office, he had a thorough search undertaken of the French records at Quebec, but it failed to turn up any deed or grant from the previous regime. Haldimand thus concluded that as this region lay to the east, it lay within the region exempted from the Royal Proclamation (as did the St. Lawrence valley). In short, the Iroquois had no title to the lands they claimed between the Long Sault and the Raisin River.

The Mohawk, however, continued to press their claims to lands on the British side, although their accounts on occasion contradicted each other. They told Claus, for example, that a grant had been duly made to them but that Father Gordon had simply refused to show it to them. On another occasion they claimed that the record of the grant had been destroyed in a fire.[15]

Sir John Johnson visited their village on the south shore of the St. Lawrence in March 1783. In that session, and in a subsequent meeting with Colonel Campbell of the Indian Department, the Akwesasne Mohawk claimed that Sir William Johnson had promised them the land. In mid-April Haldimand conceded that the village lands on the south shore should be theirs, and subsequently he accorded the site to them, "as an indulgence, during the King's pleasure."[16] Later he also set aside a small reserve on the north shore, approximately opposite their village, but this tract was, like the concession of the village lands, to be considered as an indulgence, not as a right. The reserve (for which the band received a written title) came to be called the Nutfield Tract. It ran four kilometres along the shore between the townships of Cornwall and Charlottenburgh. It remained in the band's possession until 1847, when the band sold it to the Crown.[17]

The Oswegatchie Iroquois occupied both sides of the St. Lawrence shoreline west of Akwesasne. Their territory, from the Long Sault to Toniato River, clearly lay within the Indian Territory (Map 6.3, No. 8). This band, like the other Iroquois mission settlements in Canada (Lake of Two Mountains, St. Régis, and Caughnawaga), had been enticed to relocate by French missionaries after they established the mission of La Présentation at the mouth of the Oswegatchie River in 1748. By 1751 nearly 400 families of Onondaga, with some Cayuga and Oneida,[18] had settled in villages on the north shore of the river, near the fort. The settlements grew rapidly for a time, attracting perhaps half of the Onondaga nation in the years before the Seven Years' War. By moving to Oswegatchie these Iroquois had allied themselves with the French. After the defeat of New France in 1760, the population did decline, but eight years later it still numbered about 500.[19] During the American Revolution the Oswegatchies supported the British.

Following the war, the Oswegatchies continued to occupy their villages near present-day Johnstown on the north shore of the St. Lawrence River. Colonel Campbell met them in 1784, intending to acquire their lands for the Loyalist settlements. After lengthy consideration they agreed to let the British have "the Front of the Water" to "give lands to the troops."[20] As the British at the time (to 1796) still retained the fort at Oswegatchie (Ogdensburg, New York), they were able to convince the Onondaga to move their principal settlements to the south shore. From the government officials' viewpoint, this agreement now opened up the waterfront on the north shore of the St. Lawrence River. The Indians of Oswegatchie believed otherwise. When a government surveyor attempted to survey Marlborough Township in the back country on the Canadian side, the Iroquois advised him that he was trespassing on Indian land.[21]

In 1796 Jay's Treaty gave Oswegatchie to the Americans. Although the Oswegatchies' village on the south shore was clearly a permanent settlement, New York State simply removed the villagers from their lands in about 1806. Some went back to Onondaga country or elsewhere. Others moved to Akwesasne.[22] Their dispersal allowed the British to ignore the Oswegatchies' claims to lands on the Canadian side.

The Crawford purchases, as well as those from the St. Régis Mohawk and the Oswegatchie Onondaga, secured for Loyalist settlement a virtually unbroken accession of land on the north shore of the St. Lawrence River. Regrettably, these transactions are poorly documented, as is another early cession, the Collins purchase of 1785 (Map 6.3, No. 9).

### The Collins Purchase of 1785

In 1785 John Collins investigated the route from the mouth of the Humber River, known as the "Toronto Carrying Place," to Lake Simcoe as a possible alternate means of communication with the interior. From the scant evidence that survives, the surveyor apparently made a provisional agreement to purchase a portion of the route.[23] No copy of the actual surrender document has been found, however, and the descriptions of the territory involved are vague.

According to J.B. Rousseau,[24] the French Canadian interpreter who accompanied the expedition, Captain Crawford and John Collins met the Ojibwa of Lac La Clie (Lake Simcoe) in August 1785. That meeting, said Rousseau, resulted in the purchase of "one mile on each side of the foot path from the Narrows at Lake Simcoe to Matchedash Bay with three miles and a half square at each end" of the road, as well as one mile on each side of the Severn River. Thirty years later another land cession described its own territorial limits (see Map 6.3, No. 20) and, in doing so, declared that part of its limits corresponded to the limits of a parcel of land "said to have been made in the year one thousand seven hundred and eighty-five."[25] Collins's memorandum of this journey noted that the agreement also permitted the Crown to build "roads through the Mississauga Country." For this concession no payment had been made or even requested; the chiefs, according to Collins, had simply declared that their people were very poor, that they desired some clothing, and that they left it to "their good father" to determine the amount to be paid.

Irregularities abound in this transaction. No formal cession document exists; the description of the tract is vague; and, it seems, the British made no payment. Yet the Crown's claim to the area has never been questioned. In 1794–95 Lieutenant-Governor Simcoe discussed the matter with the Lake Simcoe Ojibwa when consulting with them regarding the purchase of the

Penetanguishene harbour lands (Map 6.3, No. 16). The agreement, concluded at Penetang in 1798, called for the payment of £101 and the surrender to the Crown of the tip of the Penetanguishene Peninsula. In the process of arranging this surrender, the bands concerned assured Simcoe that the sum now paid included payment for lands taken in the Collins purchase of 1785.

### The Invalid Surrenders of 1787–1788

The large tract on the north shore of Lake Ontario between the Trent and Etobicoke rivers, reaching back from Lake Ontario to Lake Simcoe, constitutes another area surrendered without proper regard for the provisions of the Royal Proclamation of 1763. In 1787 and 1788 senior officials of the Indian Department, including Sir John Johnson and Col. John Butler, met with Indian bands at both the Carrying Place on the Bay of Quinte and Toronto. As a result of these meetings, both Johnson and Lord Dorchester (who replaced Haldimand as governor of Quebec in 1784) believed that they had successfully obtained, and paid for, the large portion of land on the north shore of Lake Ontario (Map 6.3, Nos. 10, 21, and 34). The document which supposedly formalized the transaction, however, omitted a description of the area surrendered. Instead it contained a blank section into which the descriptions were apparently, after the fact, to have been inserted.

After Simcoe brought the irregularities to Lord Dorchester's attention in 1794, the governor declared the document invalid. Concerns about a claim were temporarily allayed by the fact that the Ojibwa of Lake Simcoe assured the British they considered the lands south of that lake to have been sold. Yet, according to the procedures outlined in the proclamation, the lands legally remained unsurrendered. The matter lay dormant for over a century, until, in 1916, an inquiry revealed that the land between Lake Simcoe and the north shore of Lake Ontario remained unceded. At that time the Ontario government also sought to extinguish the Amerindian title to the western Ottawa valley. Subsequently, the provincial government quickly arranged for a set of three cessions – known as the Williams treaties (they were named after the man who negotiated them) – that formally brought to the Crown, in 1923, the region Sir John Johnson had first attempted to secure in 1787–88.[26]

### Land Cessions in Southwestern Ontario in the 1790s

In southwestern Upper Canada, settlement proceeded more slowly than in the southeast. Governor Haldimand's decision to retain the western posts meant the British remained in control of Detroit. As a result, the inhabitants felt no need to seek immediate refuge in British territory on the opposite side of the

Detroit River. Some movement did occur, however, as occasional Loyalists or individuals moved into the Thames River valley or to the northwestern shore of Lake Erie. Technically they violated the Royal Proclamation by moving into this unceded territory.

In May 1790 Alexander McKee, a leading agent in the Indian Department, convened a formal council at Detroit with twenty-seven chiefs of the "Ottawa, Chippewa, Potowatomie and Huron Nations of Detroit"[27] to arrange for a formal cession of Aboriginal lands. McKee had been instructed to purchase all the shoreline between Long Point on Lake Erie and the Chenal Ecarté River (presently called the Snye), which empties into the St. Clair River.[28] The chiefs proved cooperative. They agreed to dispose of the eastern tract for a payment of £1 200 and the retention of two specific parcels of land – the Huron Reserve and the Huron Church Reserve – on the east bank of the Detroit River. The surrendered land also included the territory between the Thames River and Lake Erie (Map 6.3, No. 11).

Most likely the chiefs accepted the sale because they resided for the most part on the west bank of the Detroit River and beyond, and thus they felt little need to retain the ceded eastern region. Secondly, as they faced the possibility of an American invasion of their territory, they probably wanted to strengthen their friendship with the British.

The American invasion did come. In the first two invasions (the first, in 1790, led by General Harmar; the second, in 1791, by General St. Clair), the western Indians successfully defeated the American armies. A third major expedition, led by General Wayne, moved against the western tribes in 1794. This time the Americans scattered the Indians at the Battle of Fallen Timbers. The following year they imposed the Treaty of Greenville, forcing the Amerindians to cede two-thirds of present-day Ohio.

Anxious to avoid a second Anglo-American war, the British did not assist their Indian allies in their fight with the Americans. Consequently, the western nations openly questioned their British alliance, particularly as the British agreed (by Jay's Treaty in 1796) to vacate the western posts immediately.

Once again the British offered to provide lands in British North America for those bands, dissatisfied with the Treaty of Greenville, wishing to relocate in British territory. Britain immediately relocated its garrisons, moving those at Detroit, Niagara, and Oswegatchie to Fort Malden (Amherstburg), Fort Erie, and Prescott, respectively. The British met no difficulty in occupying these lands, as they had already purchased them from their Indian owners. The move from Michilimackinac (often called Mackinac Island) to St. Joseph Island, a post on Lake Huron, however, required a formal purchase.

To secure lands for those estimated 3 000 Indians who might come to Canada,[29] Lord Dorchester sent Alexander McKee to buy lands from the

Ojibwa of the Chenal Ecarté region. In August 1796 McKee explained to the chiefs at the Chenal Ecarté that the king wanted the land "for the use of his Indian children and you yourselves [the Ojibwa] will be as welcome as any others to come and live thereon."[30] The Ojibwa agreed to the surrender, for which they received £800 in goods. For a variety of reasons, however, the anticipated migrations to the area did not take place. Subsequently the British simply opened this newly acquired area (later named Sombra Township) to white settlement (Map 6.3, No. 12).

Concurrently, McKee engaged in negotiations with the Ojibwa for a township at the forks of the Thames River (Map 6.3, No. 13). Governor Simcoe wished to establish Upper Canada's capital at the forks, as it could be more easily defended than either York or Niagara. A provisional agreement for that tract was secured in September 1795 and confirmed in September 1796.[31] The Crown obtained a tract of over thirty square kilometres at the forks of the Thames in exchange for £1 200 worth of goods. Named London, the site never did become the capital of the province, but the Ojibwa nonetheless lost the land.

## Miscellaneous Cessions in the 1790s

During the American Revolutionary War, the Mohawk war chief Joseph Brant and his family had performed considerable military services for the British. As a reward, the Indian Department recommended that Brant receive a section of land for his own use.[32] When he chose a tract at the head of Lake Ontario (present Burlington), Simcoe issued the necessary instructions for a purchase to be made from the Mississauga at the head of the lake (Map 6.3, No. 15). The provisional agreement, made in 1795, stipulated a payment of £100 in goods; it was confirmed two years later.[33]

The British made two other small land purchases immediately after the signing of Jay's Treaty, confirmed in 1795 and executed in 1796. If England wished to maintain a strong presence on Lake Huron, it would have to secure a new location for the garrison that now must leave Michilimackinac. Governor Simcoe believed the best possible site was the Penetanguishene Peninsula, which could be reinforced and supplied by way of the Toronto portage route, as well as by means of the St. Clair River from Lake Erie. Subsequently, the British completed the purchase of the tip of the peninsula in 1798 (Map 6.3, No. 16). In the meantime, Lord Dorchester, the commander-in-chief, had chosen St. Joseph Island, at the western end of Lake Huron, as the site for the new post. He moved the Michilimackinac garrison there in the summer of 1796. The British purchased the island from the Ojibwa (Map 6.3, No. 17) in 1798, in return for £1 200.[34]

In the late 1790s Britain failed to secure immediately the "Mississauga Tract." In 1797 Peter Russell, who had replaced Simcoe, announced the executive council's wish to purchase the Mississauga's remaining land between York and the Head of the Lake (present-day Hamilton). Russell also wanted to settle a group of French royalists, refugees from the French Revolution, there.[35] But the Mississauga at the western end of Lake Ontario had recently appointed Joseph Brant as their agent in land matters. At his urging, they insisted on receiving a payment which the government considered excessively high. No arrangement could be made. The British tried again in 1805 after Brant's influence had waned among the Mississauga.

In the late 1790s concerns arose again regarding the Johnson-Butler agreement of 1787, particularly regarding that portion of it on which the town of York stood. Since York was the seat of government, Peter Hunter, the new lieutenant-governor, called for a new deed for that land. A further cession followed.

William Claus, the deputy superintendent of Indian affairs, had little difficulty with regard to the York region when he met with the Mississauga at the Credit River on 31 July 1805. The Mississauga readily agreed that Sir John had purchased that land in 1787. They recalled their reservation of the fishery at the mouth of the Etobicoke River as their only condition to the sale. Claus now prepared a formal surrender document describing the areas as consisting of over 100 000 hectares in and around the town of York.

The Mississauga Tract at the head of the lake was not as easily surrendered. When the Mississauga encountered Claus the next day, on 1 August, they agreed to sell the tract but imposed conditions. First, they wished to retain small pockets of land and the fisheries at the mouths of the Credit River, Sixteen Mile (Oakville) Creek, and Twelve Mile (Bronte) Creek. Secondly, the Indians pointed out that a small parcel they had previously sold to the Tuscarora and a sugar bush they had given to Mrs. Brant belonged to their new owners. Thirdly, they wished to retain the shoreline to a depth of "two or three chains" for the "whole length of the [Burlington] Beach." Chief Quinipeno also complained that contrary to assurances made to them by Col. John Butler at Fort Niagara, the settlers had harassed them and driven them off the shoreline of lands previously sold in the 1780s.[36]

The next day Claus worked hard to obtain a compromise. The Mississauga obtained goods to a value of £1 000 and the right to retain their fishery sites. The Crown would pay the Tuscarora one ox, the Tuscarora Indians' previous payment for the parcel of land obtained from the Mississauga, which now reverted to the Crown. The Indians asked that the Crown confirm Mrs. Brant's ownership of the sugar bush. They agreed to trust the king to protect them in their use of Burlington beach. This provisional agreement was executed a year later after the goods were distributed. The Crown thus obtained another 35 000 hectares of land.[37]

Five years later, the Crown sought another large piece of land. Leading partners in the North West Company had complained of "vexatious interference" from American customs officers along the route to the west via Lake Ontario, the Niagara River, Lake Erie, and the Detroit River. By using the Toronto Carrying Place, the company could avoid American customs officials, but the new route would require the construction of a road from Lake Simcoe to Penetanguishene, a distance of forty-five kilometres. This, in turn, required the purchase of yet another tract from the Lake Simcoe Ojibwa. Lieutenant-Governor Gore approved the plan. It would assist both the Nor'westers and the government, which would secure an alternate route to the Upper Great Lakes in the event of a second Anglo-American war. By 1811 war had become a definite possibility. In June 1811 Claus reached an agreement with the Lake Simcoe Ojibwa, but before the government made the payment of £4 000 in goods, the War of 1812 broke out.[38] Not until the war's conclusion in 1815 could this agreement be completed (Map 6.3, No. 20).

These early agreements were concluded with remarkable ease. The angry Indian frontier of the American experience, with its thousands of American and Native casualties, was not repeated north of the Great Lakes. Three factors explain this phenomenon. First, it is unlikely that the Indians of Ontario understood fully the implications of the land-sale agreements, as their

National Archives of Canada, c-40137

York, 1804: a painting by Elisabeth Frances Hale.

communal approach to land use varied so much from the Europeans' attitudes. Secondly, the newcomers had been relatively few in number in the interior of Upper Canada. For many Native groups in the back country, intensive contact with settlers only came after the War of 1812. Indeed, because the arduous task of clearing forested land proceeded slowly, even the bands who had sold the shoreline continued to use portions of it. Thirdly, the Indians of Ontario possibly looked upon the land cessions as a means to acquire substantial quantities of trade goods for what appeared to be a small price.

All of these agreements obtained before the War of 1812 were relatively simple arrangements. The Crown made a single, one-time payment in goods in return for a specific portion of territory. The evidence suggests that as time passed the Indians learned from their mistakes. The negotiations for the Mississauga Tract in 1805, in particular, indicate that the Mississauga had acquired a better understanding of the true meaning of the agreements.

### The Second Invasion of Newcomers

The second settler invasion of Upper Canada occurred immediately after the War of 1812. From 1815 to 1824 the non-Aboriginal population doubled, from 75 000 to 150 000, mainly as a result of heavy immigration from Britain. To accommodate the newcomers, the government concluded six major land-cession agreements that brought nearly three million more hectares into its hands.

The relative importance of the Indians as a military and political force in Southern Ontario declined in the post-war years. Demography helps to explain this change. Although the Native population in Upper Canada remained stable at about 8 000, the settlers had increased to nearly half a million by 1840. The weakening of the Natives' link with Amerindian groups south of the Great Lakes also contributed to their demise as a political force. Until Tecumseh's death in 1813 at the Battle of Moraviantown, the Indians north of the Great Lakes had a close relationship with the Western Confederacy of Indians, centred in the American northwest. Following the War of 1812, however, the Americans who had broken Tecumseh's pan-Indian confederacy, imposed on the western tribes a series of treaties that forced them to move from the Detroit region. As a consequence, Indian groups in Upper Canada were isolated from their relatives on the American side.

In this period of reduced Amerindian strength after the War of 1812, Britain altered its treaty terms. Henceforth the bands would receive a small annual payment, in perpetuity, rather than a considerably larger, but one-time only, payment. This annuity system was designed to save money. After purchasing land from the Indians, the government would then sell it to settlers whose interest payments on their purchases were expected to cover the cost of the annuity paid to the band. In this fashion, the colonists, not the British tax-payers, would pay. The system began in 1818, and while it did not work quite as neatly as planned, it has continued ever since.

The new annuity system also had the incidental advantage of being a negotiating tool in councils with the Indians. The Crown's agents could argue that by giving up their lands, the bands obtained an income that would contin-ue to assist them forever. It was a powerful point when made to bands border-ing on destitution. Yet, although the relative status of the Indians had declined, they had become more wary than before. They now demanded bet-ter terms. They requested that the retention of reserved land and the entrench-ment of hunting and fishing rights be stated in the agreements. In the treaties made after 1850 these became normal conditions.

The cessions after 1815 involved lands well behind the original waterfront settlements. Indians in the hunting regions in the interior of the province now experienced repeated encroachments by settlers, as well as intrusions by the British government, anxious to secure alternative transportation routes through the province in the event of another war with the United States. The British had discovered the value of the Rideau waterway system, between the St. Lawrence and Ottawa rivers, and the Trent River–Kawartha Lakes system, which offered passage from the Bay of Quinte to Georgian Bay. To secure these areas, the British approached the Mississauga of Rice Lake and those of the Rideau River. After determining that the two bands would be amenable, and having secured Treasury approval, British Indian agents made the purchas-es. They did so with some urgency, as settlers had begun to enter the region.

On 5 November 1818 William Claus negotiated for the Kawartha Lakes region (Map 6.4, No. 20) in a council with the Rice Lake Mississauga at Smith's Creek (Port Hope). There he introduced the new payment plan, stress-ing its advantages by declaring that the king "does not mean to do as formerly to pay you at once, but as long as any of you remain on Earth to give you Cloathing in payment every year."[39] The reply of Chief Buckquaquet revealed the vulnerable state of the Rice Lake Mississauga:

> Father: You see me here, I am to be pitied, I have no old men to instruct me. I am the head Chief, but a young man. You must pity me, all the old people have gone to the other world. My hands are naked, I cannot speak as our Ancestors were used to.
>
> Father: If I was to refuse what our Father has requested, our Women and Children would be more to be pitied. From our lands we receive scarcely any-thing and if your words are true we will get more by parting with them, than by keeping them – our hunting is destroyed and we must throw ourselves on the compassion of our Great Father the King.

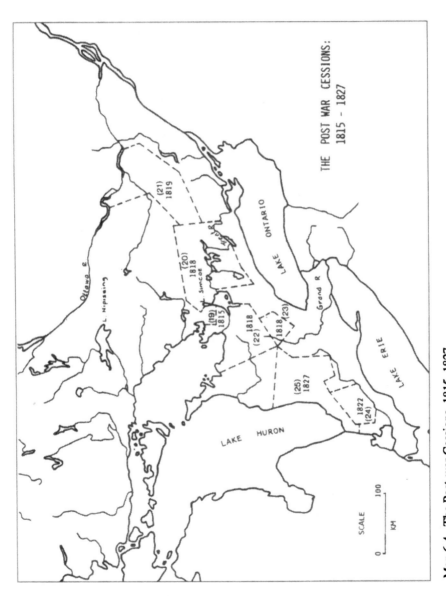

Map 6.4   The Post-war Cessions, 1815–1827

From R. Surtees, *Indian Land Surrenders in Ontario, 1763–1867* (Ottawa 1984), 69

Father: Our young People & Chief have always thought of not refusing our Father any request he makes to us, and therefore do what he wishes.[40]

Buckquaquet also expressed the hope that his people would be allowed to continue hunting and fishing where they could still find game, that the settlers who came would not mistreat them, and that the islands would be reserved for the Indians for farming. Claus replied that the rivers and forests remained open to all and that the Mississauga had an equal right to them. He made no promise regarding the islands but did say he was sure the governor would accede to that wish. The written agreement did not mention either the islands or the right to continue hunting and fishing.[41] It simply stated the size of the annuity (£740 per year) and provided a description of the surrendered tract north of Rice Lake, estimated to contain nearly one million hectares of land. The annuity provided each man, woman, and child with ten dollars yearly.

Late the following spring, the veteran Indian agent John Ferguson dealt for the tract of land behind Tweed and Perth (Map 6.4, No. 21). At a council held on 31 May 1819, Ferguson met with the approximately 250 Mississauga of the Bay of Quinte and Kingston areas who claimed the area included in the intended purchase. The Algonquin who lived in the Ottawa valley, a portion of which was included in the surrender, were not invited. The Rideau Purchase Tract, as it was known, was enormous – one million hectares. The Mississauga agreed to sell it for an annuity of £642 10 s.[42] The government calculated this sum at the rate of two and a half pounds per person. The Treasury approved the provisional agreement, but because of delays in making some of the annuity payments, it only signed the confirmatory surrender six years later, on 26 April 1825.[43] At that time the per capita annuity was officially stated to be two and a half pounds, and the number of persons receiving payment could be no greater than 257 (that being the number claiming ownership of the land at the time of the agreement).

The government also desired complete access along the Toronto Carrying Place to Lake Huron. Purchases in 1785, 1798, and 1815 had already secured the bulk of the lands between Lake Simcoe and Lake Huron (Georgian Bay). In 1816–17 the government at first considered acquiring only the portion of the portage route between Kempenfelt and Nottawasaga bays,[44] yet this would leave the Nottawasaga River, an important line of communication, still largely in the Ojibwa's possession.

Probably the knowledge that the Indians would sell land determined the government's decision to request an even greater tract.[45] When William Claus met the assembled Ojibwa in council on 17 October 1818,[46] he asked for over half a million hectares to the west and south of Lake Simcoe,[47] an enormous tract (Map 6.4, No. 22). At the council, Claus observed that while the ultimate intention was to settle the region, it would be "many years after both of us and most of your people will have left the world before any settlement" would "come near to your villages." At present the land lay idle, he said, and the Ojibwa received no benefit from it. By selling it to the king, they could use it as they always had and still annually receive clothing, in addition to the usual presents the king distributed. "Consider," he said, "whether it is not better to get some covering for yourselves, your wives and children than letting it lay idle."[48]

Chief Yellowhead, who had led the delegation of Ojibwa chiefs at the earlier surrender in 1815, replied that they could "not withold a compliance with the subject of your request." The government agreed to pay an annuity of £1 200 currency in goods.[49] The method for distributing the annual payment would presumably be the chiefs' responsibility. The refinement of a "per capita" designation would come in the agreements of 1819.

Yellowhead did not, apparently, mention hunting or fishing. He did, however, ask that a doctor be encouraged to live in the area and tend to the medical needs of his people. Claus replied that his words would "be faithfully communicated" to the governor, "who I have no doubt will attend your wishes." This consideration was not mentioned in the formal agreement for the land surrenders, but it can be said to have been honoured inasmuch as doctors were subsequently stationed at the Penetanguishene naval base and were later attached to the Indian establishment at Coldwater.

After Claus had arranged in 1818 for the purchase in the Lake Simcoe area, he sought to acquire the remainder of the Mississauga Tract, the quarter of a million hectares that lay north of the lakefront surrender in 1806 (Map 6.4, No. 23). This area belonged to the Credit River Mississauga, who had in the agreement of 1806 retained for their exclusive use three small pieces of land at the mouths of the Credit River, Sixteen Mile Creek, and Twelve Mile Creek, as well as their inland territory. This band had subsequently found itself under steady pressure from settlers because of its location between the provincial capital of York and the Head of the Lake (present-day Hamilton). Despite government proclamations and the efforts of Indian Department officials to protect them, the Credit River Mississauga suffered encroachments on their lands and fisheries. They found themselves the victim of disease and substance abuse. Over a thirty-year period, epidemics of smallpox and other diseases had helped to reduce the number of Mississauga at the western end of Lake Ontario by half, from over 500 to barely 200.[50] In addition, advancing settlement had driven game from their hunting areas.

Their debilitated state was evident when William Claus met them at a council at the Credit River in late October 1818.[51] After the customary greetings, Claus remarked that the band appeared to him to be "thin and miserable" and deriving no benefit from their land, which was "lying dead." To help them, the king proposed buying their land and in return giving them "goods yearly to cover" their "Women and Children" in addition to the regular annual presents. Ajetance, who had become chief of the Credit River band in 1810, delivered the Mississauga's response the following day. As Claus requested, he agreed to the surrender but asked that his band be allowed to retain their land at the mouth of the Credit River, adding that "it is but small and we will not have it long; it is all we have to live upon." Claus agreed. By the terms of the agreement, the Mississauga of the Credit received goods to the value of £522 10 s. annually.[52] They also retained their three small reserves at the river mouths, although both the Sixteen and Twelve Mile Creek reserves would be sold in 1820.

In the western portion of the province, the Indians along the Thames River between London and Chatham were first approached by John Askin, the superintendent of Indian affairs at Amherstburg. In October 1818 Askin met the chiefs of the Ojibwa bands of the Chenal Ecarté, the St. Clair River, Bear Creek, the Sable River, and the Thames River.[53] He advised them that the king wished to purchase all of their lands on the Thames River and on Lake Huron just north of the Sable River and extending inland as far as the Grand River tract (Map 6.4, Nos. 24 and 25), and asked the chiefs "to state on what terms they would dispose of the said Tract."

After deliberation, Chief Chawne replied for the assembled chiefs. They agreed to sell and left it to Governor Maitland of Upper Canada to assess the land's value. Payment was to be made annually for fifty years. This payment, they said, was to be above and beyond the annual presents; furthermore, part of the new annuity was to be used to furnish them with a blacksmith and a farm instructor, to be stationed near their reserves. The blacksmith would service their axes, traps, and guns; the farmer would instruct them "in the art of Husbandry." They stipulated that six small reserves should be set aside for them at specific designated sites.

As a result of Askin's exploratory mission, the government decided to purchase this enormous area through two separate agreements.[54] The section known as the Long Woods (Map 6.4, No. 24), extending on the north bank of the Thames River between the Delaware village in London Township and the Moravian village in Oxford Township, interested the government the most. The Ojibwa owners met Askin in early 1819.[55] In the provisional agreement that grew out of that council, the Ojibwa chiefs agreed to sell the prescribed tract of land, estimated at 210 000 hectares, for an annuity of £600 currency, half of which was to be paid in specie and the other half in goods.[56] The agreement for the Long Woods area also called for two reserves for the

Ojibwa. It reserved about 6 000 hectares on "the northerly shore of the Thames River, nearly opposite the Township of Southwold." A second reserve was described as "two miles square distant about four miles above the rapids near the source of Big Bear Creek where the Indians have their improvements."[57] The sketch of the proposed purchase sent to Askin before the agreement was made showed both reserves.[58]

At the end of March the Ojibwa of the Chenal Ecarté, the Ausable River, and the St. Clair River, having been sent for some weeks earlier, met Askin at Amherstburg to discuss the sale of the remainder of the lands desired by the government. Known as the Huron Tract (Map 6.4, No. 25) and containing over one million hectares, this area was sold by its owners for an annuity of £1 375 currency, half to be paid in specie and half in goods.[59] The reserved areas (named the previous October) were duly made by this agreement of 30 March 1819 and shown on the sketch of the proposed surrender.

Neither of these two agreements was executed, however, as objections were raised regarding the proposal to make payment in cash.[60] As a result, new agreements had to be drawn up and the Indians asked to approve the proposed changes. This was done, but with some difficulty, and during the several years required to complete the purchase agreements they changed considerably. The Long Woods annuity was altered to provide a per capita payment of £2 10 s. to a maximum of 240 persons, that being the number of persons who claimed and inhabited the area at the time of the original surrender.[61] In view of the arrangements that had been made for the Rideau Tract and the Rice Lake surrenders, this alteration is easy to understand. More difficult to comprehend, however, is the omission of the two reservations mentioned in the original Long Woods agreement. And more difficult still, while the original reserve set aside for the Ojibwa in Caradoc Township did continue to be recognized as Indian land (indeed a portion of it remains as such today), the planned reserve on Bear Creek seems never to have been established.

The Huron Tract, the second of the two agreements Askin sought, took longer to settle. Initially, Maitland saw no urgency about completing the purchase, since other land had become available to the government. After John Galt's scheme to form the Canada Company took shape, however, the question of the Huron Tract became more important, for nearly half a million hectares was to be given to the company from Indian territory.[62] Finally, on 25 April 1825, a second agreement for the Huron Tract was made with the Chippewa of the Chenal Ecarté, the St. Clair River, and the Ausable River. It provided for the four reserves called for in 1818 and 1819, two below the St. Clair River rapids, a third at Kettle Point, and a fourth at the mouth of the Ausable River, the latter two both on Lake Huron.[63] These four parcels of land totalled nearly 10 000 hectares, which was no more (or less) than called for at the council of 1818. For their lands, the several bands received an annuity of £1 100, to be divided equally among the 460 persons said to inhabit the tract in 1825.[64] This sum was £275 less than the sum stipulated in the provisional agreement of 1819.

The new agreement also provided that should the total population decline by half, the annuity would be reduced by the same amount and would continue to be reduced in like amounts if the population further declined. No provision was made to increase the annuity in the event of a population increase. Clearly, no one anticipated that the Amerindian population would increase, as it was commonly believed that the race would become extinct.[65] The final agreement actually came two years later, on 10 July 1827, at which time the 1825 arrangement was confirmed.[66]

One area of Indian land in the western and London districts stayed unceded – the tract of land known as Walpole Island. This large island at the outlet of the St. Clair River into Lake St. Clair was not included in any of the land cessions of 1790, 1796, 1819, or 1825. To this day it remains unceded Amerindian land, nearly two centuries after the extensive land-cession agreements of the early nineteenth century in what is now Southern Ontario.

## NOTES

1   Donald Braider, *The Niagara* (New York 1972), 130–7
2   Anthony F.C. Wallace, *The Death and Rebirth of the Seneca* (New York 1972), 115–16
3   National Archives of Canada (NA), B107, Haldimand Papers, 151–2, Guy Johnson to Haldimand, 21 August 1780
4   Barbara Graymont, *The Iroquois in the American Revolution* (Syracuse 1971)
5   "United Empire Loyalists," Niagara Historical Society Publications No. 37 (Niagara-on-the-Lake, Ont. 1925), 11–12
6   E.A. Cruickshank, ed., "Records of Niagara 1778–1783," Niagara Historical Society Publications No. 38 (Niagara-on-the-Lake, Ont. 1927), 7
7   Robert J. Surtees, "Indian Land Cessions in Ontario, 1763–1862: The Evolution of a System" (PhD thesis, Carleton University, 1982), 38–50
8   Ibid., 50–67
9   Ibid., 58–9
10  NA, B158, 314, Crawford to Haldimand, 9 October 1783
11  C.M. Johnston, ed., *The Valley of the Six Nations* (Toronto 1965), 47
12  Ibid., 44–5
13  NA, B114, 307–8, D. Claus, "Memorandum of what I can recollect relative to the settlement of St. Régis," 11 March 1784
14  Ibid.
15  NA, B115, Johnson to Haldimand, 11 March 1784
16  Archives of Ontario (AO), RG 1, A-1-7, box 8

17  Surtees, "Indian Land Cessions," 72–5
18  A good account of this band can be found in H. Blau, J. Campisi, and E. Tooker, "Onondaga," in *Handbook of North American Indians*, vol. 15: *Northeast*, ed. Bruce G. Trigger (Washington, D.C. 1978), 494–5.
19  Ibid.
20  AO, Simcoe Papers, MU2790, envelope #39, Council of Indians of Oswegatchie to Simcoe, 2 February 1795
21  Surtees, "Indian Land Cessions," 77–8
22  Ibid.
23  John Collins, "Memorandum on Indian Purchase," in F.B. Murray, ed., *Muskoka and Haliburton* (Toronto 1963), 97
24  J.B. Rousseau, "Severn River Purchase Certified," in F.B. Murray, ed., *Muskoka and Haliburton* (Toronto 1963)
25  Canada, *Indian Treaties and Surrenders from 1690–1890* (2 vols., Ottawa 1891; reprint, 3 vols., Toronto 1971), 3:196–7 (henceforth *Treaties and Surrenders*)
26  A more detailed discussion of this very unorthodox set of negotiations and apparent agreements can be found in Surtees, "Indian Land Cessions," 86–113.
27  *Treaties and Surrenders*, 1:1
28  Ontario, *Third Report of the Bureau of Archives for the Province of Ontario, 1905* (Toronto 1906), 6
29  McKee to Chew, 24 October 1795, in E.A. Cruikshank, ed., *The Correspondence of Lieut. Governor John Graves Simcoe, with Allied Documents*, 5 vols. (Toronto 1923–30), 4:42
30  "Minutes of a Council with the Chippewas and Ottawas," Chenal Ecarté, 30 August 1796, in E.A. Cruikshank and A.F. Hunter, eds., *Correspondence of the Honourable Peter Russell*, 3 vols. (Toronto 1932–36), 1:34–5
31  *Treaties and Surrenders*, 1:19
32  NA, RG 10, vol. 9, 8929, Simcoe to McKee, 10 May 1795
33  *Treaties and Surrenders*, 1:8–9
34  Surtees, "Indian Land Cessions in Ontario," 102–3
35  Ibid., 116–26
36  NA, RG 10, 1, 294–8, "Meeting with the Mississaugas at the River Credit"
37  *Treaties and Surrenders*, 1:36–40
38  Surtees, "Indian Land Cessions," 174–80
39  "Minutes of a Council held at Smith's Creek, ... the 5th of November, 1818," in judgment in the Supreme Court of Ontario, Court of Appeal, *The Queen* v. *Taylor and Williams*, 16 October 1981, 4–6
40  Ibid.
41  *Treaties and Surrenders*, 1:48–9
42  Ibid., 2:62–3
43  Ibid., 1:63–5
44  NA, RG 8, vol. 261, 130, Claus to Addison, 30 March 1817
45  Ibid.
46  NA, Claus Papers, vol. 11, 101–4, "Minutes of an Indian Council held ... the 17th October, 1818, with ... the Chippewa Nation"
47  *Treaties and Surrenders*, 1:47
48  "Minutes of an Indian Council held ... the 17th October 1818
49  *Treaties and Surrenders*, 1:47

50  Donald B. Smith, *Sacred Feathers: The Reverend Peter Jones (Kahkewaquonaby) and the Mississauga Indians* (Toronto 1987), 39

51  NA, Claus Papers, vol. 11, 110–12, "Minutes of the Proceedings of a Council at the River au Credit on the 27th, 28th and 29th October, 1818"

52  *Treaties and Surrenders*, 1:47–8

53  NA, Claus Papers, 11:95–6, "Minutes of a Council at Amherstburg, the 16th October, 1818"

54  NA, Claus Papers, 11:95, Askin to Claus, 19 February 1819

55  Ibid., Askin to Claus, 3 March 1819

56  *Treaties and Surrenders*, 1:49

57  Ibid., 50

58  NA, Claus Papers, 11:137, sketch of proposed purchase

59  NA, Claus Papers, 11:187–90, "Articles of a Provisional Agreement entered into on the 30th day of March, 1819"

60  NA, RG 8, 263:104–5, Claus to Hillier, 7 August 1820

61  *Treaties and Surrenders*, 1:59

62  Lillian Gates, *Land Policies of Upper Canada* (Toronto 1965), 205

63  *Treaties and Surrenders*, 1:65–7

64  Ibid., 66

65  Basil Hall, *Travels in North America in the Years 1827 and 1828*, 3 vols. (Edinburgh 1829), 1:257; NA, MG 29, A8, vol. 80, Sandford Fleming Papers, Diary, entry for 28 June 1845; John Richardson, "A Trip to Walpole Island and Port Sarnia," *The Literary Garland* (Montreal January 1849), reprinted in A.H.U. Colquhoun, ed. *Tecumseh and Richardson* (Toronto 1924), 70–1; Samuel Strickland, *Twenty-Seven Years in Canada West*, 2 vols. (London 1853; facsimile, Edmonton 1970), 2:68

66  *Treaties and Surrenders*, 1:71–5

# 7 The Algonquian Farmers of Southern Ontario, 1830–1945

EDWARD S. ROGERS

During the 1830s and 1840s, several thousand Algonquian-speaking Indians living in the United States immigrated to Upper Canada. The United States government passed the Indian Removal Act in 1830, permitting it to relocate eastern American Indians. Accordingly, that government pressed Amerindian groups to sign treaties with provisions stating that their communities must migrate to the prairie country west of the Mississippi River. This clause generated great dissatisfaction. Many Amerindians south of the Great Lakes refused to leave and remained in what became the states of Indiana, Michigan, Wisconsin, and Illinois. But pressures for their removal mounted. In 1837 the U.S. government informed the Indians that no further annuities would be given until they complied with the terms of the treaties.[1] By moving north they could remain in the Great Lakes area.

The British policy of giving gifts to its North American Indian allies also encouraged Indians to settle in Canada.[2] For many years the Crown annually provided the "Western Tribes," as the British Indian Department called the Amerindians of the Upper Great Lakes, with gifts. Until 1828 the British had used Drummond Island as the northern distribution point. In 1829 the location was shifted to neighbouring St. Joseph Island. From 1830 to 1835 they made the distribution at Penetanguishene on Georgian Bay. Beginning in 1836 the British ended the distribution at Amherstburg, the southern point, and at Penetanguishene, in favour of one central location, Manitowaning on Manitoulin Island. Here the Western Indians assembled each summer to receive their gifts. In 1836 nearly 2 700 Indians arrived and received presents.[3] A year later 3 700 Ottawa, Ojibwa, Potawatomi, Winnibago, and Menominee came from the United States.[4] Anxious to end this continued expenditure, the British officials announced in 1837 that the distribution of presents to Indians who continued to reside in the United States would soon cease.[5] A second notice in 1841 stated that unless the "Visiting," or American, Indians settled permanently on the British side of the border by 1843, they would lose their eligibility.[6] After 1843 only "Resident" Indians, those who lived permanently within British territory, received presents.[7]

The fact that many Algonquians living south of the Great Lakes had relatives in Upper Canada also encouraged migration, as did the similarity of Upper Canada's natural environment to their former homeland. Finally, many American Indians regarded the British as fairer in their Indian policies than the Americans.

Many Algonquians (with the Potawatomi apparently in the majority) made their way into Upper Canada.[8] The population estimates of these arrivals vary somewhat. One authority, for instance, believes that some 2 000 to 3 000 Potawatomi arrived from Wisconsin, Michigan, and Indiana between

National Archives of Canada, c-114384

"Two Ottawa Chiefs who with others lately came down from Michillimackinac Lake Huron to have a talk with their great Father, the King or his representative." They are wearing clothing of trade cloth and trade-silver ornaments. Watercolour (1813–20) by Sir Joshua Jebb.

1837 and 1849.[9] Another has estimated that the different groups of Indians who moved into Upper Canada in this period (including the Potawatomi) numbered no more than 1 500 to 4 000.[10] During the next four decades, roughly from 1840 to 1880, the immigrant Potawatomi slowly became settled on existing reserves in present-day Southern Ontario. Walpole Island at the northern end of Lake St. Clair became an early refuge.[11]

Information regarding the movements and final destinations of the Ottawa (or Odawa) is somewhat less precise than the data for the Potawatomi. Nevertheless, it is known that in 1836, when some Ottawa signed a treaty with the U.S. government for their remaining lands in Michigan's lower peninsula, a large number of them, particularly the Roman Catholic converts, migrated to Manitoulin Island.[12] Apparently, some had preceded them, for five or six families of Ottawa already resided at Wikwemikong and had one to two hectares of land under cultivation.[13]

Andrew Blackbird, an Ottawa who acted as interpreter for the U.S. government, claimed that more than half of all his people in the United States had, by 1840, immigrated to Canada.[14] Further negotiations with the U.S. government to alienate land and dissolve their tribal governments induced more Ottawa to leave Michigan for Manitoulin Island and Georgian Bay in 1855.[15] The Ottawa primarily settled on Manitoulin and Walpole islands. As some of the Potawatomi had, others found their way to reserves on Georgian Bay, such as Cape Croker, Christian Island, and Moose Deer Point, and to Rama on Lake Simcoe. By the late 1870s, a few had moved to Parry Island and most likely to other locations in Southern Ontario.[16]

The international border meant little to a group like the Ottawa, who had lived on both sides of the Great Lakes at the time of first European contact. In the mid-seventeenth century the Iroquois raids had forced them to migrate. Now, like the Ojibwa (called Mississauga on the north shore of Lake Ontario by the British settlers), who had expelled the Iroquois around 1700, the Ottawa returned to their former homeland.

In the mid-seventeenth century the Iroquois had also dispersed many Nipissing as well as the Algonquin who at the time of European contact had resided in Southern Ontario (see chapter 4). Some returned, however, to settle in the summers at Lake of Two Mountains (Kanesatake or Oka) and to use their hunting territories in the St. Lawrence valley. As early as 1807, some Algonquin settled at Golden Lake in the western Ottawa valley, their community gaining reserve status in 1870. Although the Algonquin claimed land west of the Ottawa River, it was the Ojibwa[17] who in 1923, after years of litigation and protests, signed the Williams Treaty (see chapter 6).[18]

### The Government and the Church Impose Their Will

Government officials and Christian missionaries in the nineteenth century strongly believed that the Indians must become "civilized." Once government officials moved the Native people onto reserves, they were convinced that they would soon become Christian farmers like their Euro-Canadian neighbours. To assist the Indians in farming, the Indian Department built them houses and supplied equipment, seeds, and stock.

The Wesleyan Methodists, the Anglicans, the Baptists, the Roman Catholics, and the Moravians had, in many ways, a more immediate impact upon the Aboriginal way of life than the Indian Department officials. They lived with their converts and with those they wished to add to the fold.[19] Furthermore, some of the missionaries were of Native ancestry, a fact which no doubt assisted them when dealing with their people.

The missionaries experienced many setbacks, but in time they made nominal converts of many Algonquians.[20] The churches considered conversion to Christianity, a "British" education, and the adoption of farming together formed an integral whole that, when imposed upon the Indians, would render them "civilized." The converts attended church services, held family prayers and Bible readings, and participated in camp meetings. Yet a number of Algonquians maintained their traditional religion, and even the "converted" did not necessarily abandon their former belief system.

The Methodists began to proselytize during the mid-1820s, their first convert being Kahkewaquonaby ("Sacred Feathers"), or in English, Peter Jones, a twenty-one-year-old Mississauga of mixed ancestry. Raised to the age of fourteen among his Mississauga mother's people, he had then lived with his non-Native father and his family until he was twenty-one. Bilingual and bicultural, he became the Methodists' spokesperson. As a Native Methodist preacher he helped to recruit

Sacred Feathers, or the Reverend Peter Jones. This engraving appears as the frontispiece of Jones's *History of the Ojebway Indians* (London 1861). It would have been drawn about the time of his second British tour, 1837–38.

a number of talented Ojibwa converts as preachers, interpreters, and school-teachers, people such as John Sunday, Catherine Sunegoo Sutton, Peter Jacobs, Henry Steinhauer, George Henry, George Copway, and Allen Salt.[21]

Although some of these individuals (Jones and Salt, for example) had one white parent, they stressed their Native ancestry. Peter Jones was the most important Native missionary in Upper Canada for over more than a quarter of a century. With the assistance of the Methodists and funding from the Indian Department, obtained from the sale of their lands as well as from their annuities, the Mississauga Christians built a model village at the Credit River twenty kilometres west of York (Toronto) in 1826. The Methodists established other mission stations, which led the Upper Canadian government to establish several government-sponsored agricultural villages. Until his death in 1856 Jones acted as a religious leader and, at the same time, as a chief of his people. He and his band moved in 1847 to the Six Nations Reserve on the Grand River, where they acquired land at what they termed "New Credit," where they live to this day.[22]

Guided by Jones and others, the Methodists extended their mission westward. In 1832 John Sunday visited Sault Ste. Marie, and shortly thereafter Methodist missionaries commenced work on Manitoulin Island. Peter Jacobs undertook missionary work in what is now northwestern Ontario and Manitoba, but he later returned and settled at Rama on Lake Simcoe.[23] Allen Salt also laboured in what is now northwestern Ontario, but in 1883 he returned to minister to the people of Parry Island on Georgian Bay. Three years later the band appointed him secretary-interpreter. He remained at Parry Island until his death in 1911.[24]

Although not as active among the Indians of present-day Southern Ontario as the Methodists,[25] some Anglican clergy did become involved. The Reverend William McMurray ministered to the Ojibwa about Sault Ste. Marie from 1832 to 1839. The year after his arrival, he married Charlotte Johnston,[26] of Ojibwa and Irish descent and a sister of the wife of Henry Schoolcraft, the United States' Indian agent at Sault Ste. Marie, Michigan.[27] In 1838 an Anglican missionary arrived at Manitowaning; in 1841 one was appointed to serve the Indians living on Walpole Island.[28]

The emigration of Roman Catholic Ottawa from Michigan to Manitoulin Island in the 1830s established that faith there, just before the Methodist missionary outreach weakened in the early 1840s. Roman Catholicism has since become the dominant Christian denomination among the Indians living on Manitoulin Island and on the north shore of Lake Huron. By 1836 a Roman Catholic missionary lived amongst them and a chapel had been built. In the 1840s Jesuit missionaries arrived to serve the Manitoulin mission and the Indians about Amherstburg and Beausoleil Island in Georgian Bay.[29]

The Methodists' greatest rivals in Indian mission work in the 1830s and 1840s were the Roman Catholics. This watercolour by William George Richardson Hind shows a Catholic religious service on the north shore of the St. Lawrence River, 1861.

During the mid-nineteenth century the fur traders remained a strong presence on Georgian Bay. In the 1830s and 1840s Penetanguishene continued to be an important fur trade centre. The Hudson's Bay Company dominated the trade farther north, having a number of posts in operation, such as those at Timiskaming, Matagami, Michipicoten, La Cloche, and Sault Ste. Marie. The company, however, faced opposition from a growing number of freetraders.[30]

## Settlements and Schools for the Algonquians

By the mid-1830s many of the Algonquians in southern Upper Canada lived in permanent farming settlements. Governor Sir Francis Bond Head, however, judged the civilization policy a failure and advocated the migration of the Indians from present-day Southern Ontario to Manitoulin Island, in imitation of the Americans' removal program. In 1836 Head persuaded the Ottawa and Ojibwa living on Manitoulin to allow Indians living elsewhere to move to the island.[31] He selected the Saugeen Indians living south of the Bruce Peninsula for eviction and settlement.[32] That same year he approached the Delaware who had come to Upper Canada from the United States in the 1790s. He induced them to give up fifteen square kilometres of their land, granted to them some four decades earlier, in exchange for an annuity.[33] A year later, in response to Head's actions, approximately 150 Delaware left Moraviantown and Muncey, not for Manitoulin Island but for Kansas.[34]

After Head's recall to England in 1838, the colonial authorities allowed the Algonquians of Upper Canada to remain in their existing communities. Nevertheless, the Upper Canadian politicians continued to press the Indians to give up more unceded and reserve lands. In 1850 the Ojibwa along the north shore of Lake Huron and about Georgian Bay signed the Robinson-Huron Treaty, which became a model for the later numbered treaties such as Treaties No. 3 and No. 9 (by which most of Northern Ontario was ceded to the Crown). The Robinson-Superior Treaty, for lands north of Lake Superior, followed that same year.[35] In 1854 and 1857 the Indians of the Bruce Peninsula surrendered much of their remaining unceded land.[36] Finally, in 1862, Manitoulin Island was officially surrendered to the Crown with the exception of the most easterly portion.[37]

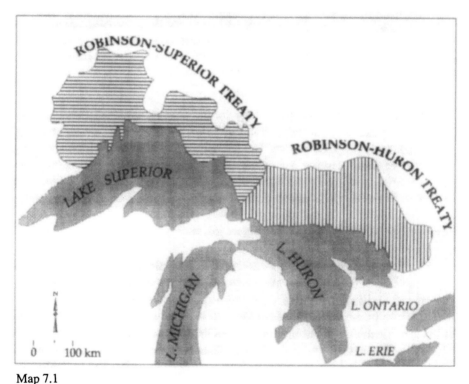

Map 7.1
Area of the Robinson Treaties, 1850
Drawn by Marta Styk, University of Calgary; adapted from "Area of the Robinson Treaties, 1850," in R. Surtees, *The Robinson Treaties, Treaty Research Report* (Ottawa 1986), 49

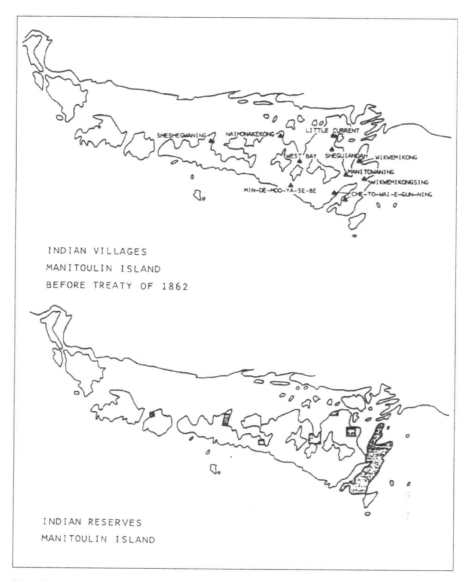

INDIAN VILLAGES
MANITOULIN ISLAND
BEFORE TREATY OF 1862

SHESHEGWANING   NAIMONAKEKONG   LITTLE CURRENT
WEST BAY   SHEGUIANDAH   WIKWEMIKONG
MANITOWANING
MIN-DE-MOO-YA-SE-BE   WIKWEMIKONGSING
CHE-TO-WAI-E-GUN-NING

INDIAN RESERVES
MANITOULIN ISLAND

Map 7.2
Indian Villages and Reserves, Manitoulin Island
From R. Surtees, *Indian Land Surrenders in Ontario, 1763–1867* (Ottawa 1984), 107

Although the Amerindians might retain the right to hunt, trap, and fish on Crown land, the amount of Crown land continually diminished as settlers bought land for farms. On their new properties the newcomers cut down the forest and fenced in the cleared lands. Even when game remained, an Indian who hunted on private property could be charged with trespass.

Between 1820 and 1845, at certain locations, the Algonquians by necessity cleared land, built homes, and raised a few crops. As the Indians became settled in villages, the churches established schools for the children. In 1826 the Methodists began at the Credit River settlement one of the first schools among the Algonquians of Upper Canada.[38] During the 1830s and 1840s the Methodists, Anglicans, and Roman Catholics established schools at their mission stations throughout southern Upper Canada. Schools for Indian children resident within any organized county or township came under the Common School Act of 1824, by which they could obtain provincial grants (after Confederation in 1867 the Indian schools became the sole responsibility of the government of Canada).[39]

Peter Jones in 1844 petitioned the government on behalf of the Credit River Indians to establish manual labour schools, where students would remain in residence for the entire year to receive religious as well as specific job training. The Methodists established two such residential schools in the late 1840s, one at Munceytown, near London (the Mount Elgin School), and the second at Alderville, near Rice Lake. The Anglicans had operated a school at Brantford, the Mohawk Institute, since the 1830s. In 1874 the Anglicans also built an industrial school at Garden River. After it burned down shortly after its completion, the government set up the Shingwak Home for Indian boys and the Wawanosh Home for Indian girls in neighbouring Sault Ste. Marie.

With financial help from the government, the churches in the late nineteenth century established additional schools for Indian children, usually day schools. By 1884 seventy-five day schools and six Indian residential schools existed in the province. Attendance, however, fell short of 100 percent. From time to time band councils tried to remedy the situation, no doubt at the urging of government and missionary officials. In 1891, for example, the Parry Island Band Council passed a resolution fining parents fifty cents a month for each of their children not in school. On occasion band councils appointed truant officers, but apparently they had little success. Similarly, strapping for misconduct was detrimental to school attendance, for, with the support of their parents, students refused to attend.[40]

## Seeking Survival: Furs and Farms

In spite of the influx of immigrants and the destruction of large sections of Upper Canada's forests, the Algonquians secured much of their food through hunting, fishing, and gathering.[41] This was especially true of those living in the more remote areas of Southern Ontario.[42]

Big game – moose, deer, and bear – was at times important, but to what extent is difficult, if not impossible, to determine. Deer, no doubt, supplied the most meat of the three species. As the land was opened for cultivation, more forage became available for deer and accordingly they increased in numbers. In the 1840s Peter Jones wrote: "I have known some good hunters in one day kill ten or fifteen deer, and have heard of others killing as many as twenty."[43] Moose, on the other hand, were now deprived of their appropriate habitat, and they decreased in numbers. Bear, although never as numerous as deer, were a welcome addition to the larder, as each animal possessed large amounts of bear fat, relished by the Algonquians.

Smaller game such as grouse, waterfowl, hare, and rabbit supplied some food at certain times of the year. Until their extinction in the late nineteenth century, passenger pigeons were an important food source. Beaver supplied both food and furs. The Indians sought other fur-bearing animals primarily for their pelts.

Hereditary hunting and trapping territories had apparently come into existence by the late eighteenth century.[44] Most likely the Algonquians considered as private property only the fur-bearing animals secured from these areas, whose pelts they sold to Euro-Canadians. Animals, if taken for home consumption, were no doubt free to all. Each Ojibwa group had its particular section of country which its members visited each year to secure food and furs. Important areas were the Credit, the Thames, and the Moira river valleys and the lands adjacent to the lakes between Lake Simcoe and the Bay of Quinte.[45] By 1860, however, the newcomers controlled these areas. Farther north, the Indians continued their old subsistence and fur-trapping activities until at least the end of the century, with specified areas claimed by each hunting group. The Lake Simcoe (Rama Reserve) and Parry Island Indians hunted in the Parry Sound–Muskoka districts, where each family possessed its own territory.[46]

From the mid-nineteenth century onward the Algonquians possessed various items of store-bought hunting and trapping equipment. While guns became the principal weapon for hunting big game and waterfowl, at what date they became common is not known.[47] When hunting deer during the fall, a number of men cooperated together to pursue the deer with dogs[48] or to build a drift fence.[49] Although the Ontario government enacted legislation in 1892 that restricted the hunting of deer to the first two weeks of November,

Indians killed deer at other times of the year as necessity dictated and the opportunity presented itself. Under the terms of their treaties, the Indians argued that they retained the right to hunt on unoccupied Crown lands and on their reserves. For securing smaller game, they utilized snares, deadfalls, and steel traps.[50] They used iron-headed, single-barbed spears to take muskrat in the late winter.[51]

Although hunting and trapping supplied a considerable amount of food, fishing was probably a more reliable food source for the greater part of each year.[52] Fish populations did not fluctuate greatly in number, and quantities could be preserved for future use. The Parry Island Indians, for instance, salted and stored trout in large barrels. Fish prepared in this manner could be eaten safely until the following May.[53] The Indians near Sault Ste. Marie had access to the abundant whitefish fishery in the St. Mary's River. Here they lived summer and winter on whitefish.[54] Lake Simcoe had an abundance of whitefish, trout, and bass. On the north shore of Lakes Ontario and Erie, the Algonquians fished in the same areas that they used for hunting.[55]

Fishing equipment consisted of several different items – the gill net, used extensively, the hook and line,[56] and at Sault Ste. Marie the dipnet for taking whitefish from the St. Mary's River.[57] The Amerindians occasionally employed a form of harpoon to take fish,[58] and they commonly speared them. The spear shaft might be ten to thirteen metres in length.[59] The spearhead was of iron, sometimes of trident form; at other times it was two-pronged.[60] During the summer and fall before freeze-up, the Indians speared fish at night from canoes. They used a jacklight, which originally consisted of birchbark placed in a cleft stick and set on fire, to attract the fish.[61] Later, they added an iron basket, mounted on the bow of the canoe, in which they placed and then ignited pine knots. In this century they substituted flashlights and electric lights. Although jacklight fishing became illegal, the practice continued for a time.

Once the ice became thick enough to support a human's weight, the Indians undertook "peep hole" fishing. Both men and women engaged in this winter activity. First the individual cut through the ice with an iron chisel, making an opening oval in shape and about half a metre wide on the surface, then gradually enlarging it. Once the hole was prepared, the Indian erected a small tent above it. Those fishing remained in their enclosures for three or four days until they had caught enough fish to make it worthwhile to return home. The Indians used a small wooden lure in the form of a minnow, stained blue,[62] to attract carnivorous fish. Once within range, the Indian attempted to spear the fish. Occasionally, in addition to pike and trout they might spear a sturgeon.[63]

Peep-hole fishing continued into the twentieth century. Although the government outlawed it, individuals fished in this manner practically under

National Archives of Canada, c-114501

Ojibwa fishing at the Sault Ste. Marie rapids, using a dipnet. A painting by William Armstrong, 1869.

Royal Ontario Museum, 910.1.10

*Spearing Salmon by Torchlight,* by Paul Kane. Although Kane's painting is of the Menominee Indians on the Fox River in present-day Wisconsin (in 1846), it could easily have been painted around the 1830s or early 1840s during the spring or fall salmon runs on the Credit River. The Mississauga used the same fishing technique as their fellow Algonquians of the Upper Great Lakes.

the noses of the game wardens. They constructed spears with a detachable head of three hardened steel points forming a trident. The shaft would be left concealed at the fishing site, the head, however, could easily be hidden. Seeing no long spear handle in evidence, the warden assumed that only a hook and line was used. On their arrival at the site, the men and women, out of the warden's sight, could easily assemble their spears and fish in their time-honoured manner. Trout were the principal species taken. Those who caught them often sold the larger ones in neighbouring communities for fifty cents for each half-kilo. They used the pike they speared for home consumption.

Gathering wild plants provided another source of food. Wild rice and maple sap were perhaps the two most important crops,[64] although the Indians also gathered berries (especially blueberries) whenever and wherever possible. The harvesting of wild rice occurred on Rice Lake, the western shore of Lake Ontario, and the Bay of Quinte. Among the Indians of Chemong Lake near Peterborough, and no doubt elsewhere, each family had its own sugar bush and a common occupation of the women each spring was the preparation of maple sugar.[65]

Equipment for collecting crops was minimal. Probably the Amerindians used ricing sticks for gathering wild rice[66] and a wooden scoop for collecting cranberries. At Parry Island the band council eventually outlawed the use of the scoop, as it damaged the cranberry bushes.[67] The Indians, however, needed more equipment for collecting and processing maple sap. The workers used cedar spiles to tap the maple trees for their syrup, which was collected in birch-bark containers and then transported to the sugar house on a stone boat pulled by a horse. Here, the syrup was stored in large elm or basswood troughs, each about a metre long, to await boiling down in large brass or iron kettles. The Indians stored the prepared sugar in birchbark boxes approximately 45 to 120 centimetres long and 30 centimetres high. Before the sugar hardened, the workers poured it into wooden moulds that they had carved in various designs.[68]

The Algonquians' means of transportation varied according to the seasons. In summer the Indians traditionally used birchbark canoes, from roughly 5 to 10 metres in length and up to 1.2 metres in width. They continued to build them into the early twentieth century.[69] For emergencies, the Indians constructed elm-bark canoes.[70] Eventually, however, the destruction of the mature forests in Southern Ontario deprived them of the large birch trees that provided the bark to cover their canoes. Other means of water transport now came into use. Dugout canoes began to be built towards the end of the last century in the Georgian Bay area[71] and earlier farther south.[72] As the people became more sedentary, such craft became more useful. Dugout canoes, constructed in about two weeks, were made either of pine or of basswood. The canoe builders hollowed out the hull by scraping, aided by

*Indian Sugar Camp,* engraving by J.C. McRae of a watercolour by Seth Eastman.
The women usually left for the maple sugar groves during the final muskrat hunt in
the spring.
From Henry Schoolcraft, *Historical and Statistical Information Respecting the History, Condition and Prospects of
the Indian Tribes of the United States,* 6 vols. (Philadelphia: Lippincott, Grambo & Co. 1851–57), 2:58

the use of fire. Dugouts were large enough to carry two or three people and a
few supplies.[73]

Rowboats in turn replaced dugouts. In the Georgian Bay area, sailboats,
in addition to rowboats, came into common use. They were from approximately five to seven metres long and were two-masted with a jib. Although
the Algonquians used cedar in much of the construction, they employed hardwood for the ribs. They utilized the inner bark of basswood to manufacture
rope and to make the rigging. The workers applied pine gum to seal any
cracks. The use of sailboats declined during the early twentieth century.[74]

Water travel decreased after the construction of roads. Although the government extended colonization roads northward during the 1840s and 1850s,[75]
highways remained few in number until after the First World War. With the
arrival of the car in the early twentieth century,[76] the Indians further adjusted
their modes of transportation. They gradually acquired cars, but in the meantime they used horses and wagons.

Sleds, toboggans, and snowshoes continued in widespread use, even after
the roads were built. The snowshoe style was that typical of the Ojibwa[77] and

others of the area – rounded in front and pointed at the rear, with two cross-bars. The frame was ash, with the lacings prepared from deer hide, cut spirally starting from the outer edge to obtain a long continuous thong. To lace the snowshoes, they used a wooden or bone needle, pointed at both ends and with a hole in the centre. The frames might be painted various colours and tassels of coloured yarn attached as ornamentation. A market developed for birchbark canoes and snowshoes for recreational use among the non-Native population.

Although the Indians continued hunting, trapping, and fishing, the imposition of game laws in the late nineteenth century made it more difficult for them to do so.[78] The continuing reduction in the amount of lands available to Indians curtailed hunting and fishing. As this occurred, the Indian Department and the missionaries exerted further pressure on the Algonquians to adopt agriculture. They provided instruction and gifts of farming tools.

The most critical obstacle to the transition from Indian hunter-gatherer to Indian farmer lay in the perception of the land. Although for over 200 years Europeans had attempted to erode the Indians' traditional beliefs and values, especially spiritual ones, many in the nineteenth century retained the old perception of the relationship between people and the land. Peter Jones, for instance, could write of the Indian elders in the mid-nineteenth century: "They suppose that all animals, fowls, fish, trees, stones, etc., are endowed with immortal spirits, and that they possess super-natural power to punish any who may dare to despise or make any unnecessary waste of them."[79]

Yet, in spite of the obstacles, a number of Algonquians did become farmers. The success of the Credit River "experiment" in the 1820s promoted further experiments. By 1829 Indian superintendents, such as Thomas Anderson, promoted agriculture among their Native charges.[80] The Indian Department purchased farm equipment and livestock for the Indians and hired farm instructors to demonstrate and teach agriculture. The desire to farm increased the need for additional fertile land. The village sites on Snake Island and at Balsam Lake, for example, were eventually abandoned in a search for land that had the potential to support farming. New settlements were established on Georgina Island and at Lake Scugog respectively.

The Algonquians raised a variety of crops. Indian corn was an important source of food, since ground corn formed one of the main dishes. The Parry Island Indians made bread and a gruel from dried corn ground very fine with a mortar and pestle. In making corn bread, they wrapped the ground corn in cornhusks and buried these in hot coals to bake.[81] Beans were another important crop; others included peas, potatoes, and, in time, squash, carrots, cucumbers, rhubarb, and turnips. The Indians raised wheat and timothy hay for the cattle, and oats and some wheat for the horses. In addition, each family might have an orchard, primarily of apple trees. From the apples, they made cider.[82]

Initially, and for some time after the adoption of farming, the Indians on some reserves worked with only hoes and spades. In time, the Algonquians acquired oxen and later horses as draft animals to pull ploughs, hayrakes, and harrows.[83] The Algonquians could make none of these items themselves and, accordingly, purchased their farm equipment from local merchants or obtained it from the Indian Department.

The Algonquian farmers kept some livestock – oxen, cattle, sheep, hogs, and horses, plus chickens, turkeys, geese, and ducks. From the livestock, the Indians obtained meat, dairy products, leather, and animal power for doing work in their fields. Geese assisted in the gardening by eating the weeds.[84]

As the Algonquians took up farming, buildings became more numerous, varied, and permanent. Dwellings at first consisted of log cabins. As early as 1827, the Mississauga of the Credit, about 200 individuals, occupied twenty substantial log homes.[85] As the Algonquians obtained permanent houses, they bought, or modelled on those of the settlers, more and more of their household furnishings. Yet, they continued to make some of their former handicrafts – splint baskets, birchbark boxes, wooden spoons, mortars, and cradle-boards.

From Egerton Ryerson, "The Story of My Life" (Toronto 1883), 59

*Indian Village at the River Credit in 1827 – Winter.* The houses were dressed log cottages with two rooms, like the type the settlers built as a second home after five to ten years on their farms. Two families occupied these houses, each family having its own room.

The Algonquian farmers now required other structures, such as squared-timber barns and sheds and root cellars for the storage of root crops during the winter. As missionary activities increased, the communities constructed churches and schoolhouses, and for government business, they built council halls.

Nevertheless, as long as the Algonquians travelled frequently in search of country game and furs, they made traditional lodge-type dwellings that could be quickly erected and easily moved.[86] Perhaps the most common of these was the conical lodge, but dome-shaped and ridge-pole lodges[87] were used as well, each covered with birchbark, sometimes cedar bark,[88] rush mats,[89] and/or canvas. Trappers might erect a conical lodge covered with evergreen boughs and floored with cedar boughs,[90] such as the artist Paul Kane painted near Sault Ste. Marie in 1845. Canvas tents eventually replaced the traditional portable lodges.

As the Algonquians adopted farming, their annual cycle of activities changed. In early spring, however, the collecting of maple sap remained the principal task. Occasionally, they sold some of the maple syrup and sugar to local merchants, but the Indians kept most for home use. At the same time, some trapping of muskrat and beaver might be undertaken in the neighbourhood of the sugar bush. Trapping was continued on into May after the sugaring had come to an end. When the ice left the lakes and bays, waterfowl returning from the south formed a welcome addition to the diet. The Indians

Royal Ontario Museum, 912.1.9

Ojibwa lodges near Sault Ste. Marie, 1845: a painting by Paul Kane.

then set gill nets to take a variety of fish, such as pickerel and whitefish. Later during June and July, sturgeon would be speared.

Once spring trapping and the gathering of maple sap ended, the people farmed. Those who had moved to the sugar bush, and the men who had gone any distance to their traplines, returned home. By now the ground had thawed and they could ready it for planting. Once the communities had planted their crops, the people engaged in other activities except when the gardens needed weeding. Fishing was not neglected, and throughout the summer and into the fall, the Algonquians collected a great variety of berries, such as strawberries, raspberries, blueberries, blackberries, and cranberries, the last being harvested in September. In the fall the harvesting of the crops and the collecting of the wild rice took place. In October (after the harvest) the Indians took trout with spear and jacklight, by trolling, and with hook and line. Some hunting might be undertaken for deer and ducks. At the same time, the Algonquians trapped mink and otter.

During the winter months, the Indians' workload decreased somewhat. Nevertheless, they had to take care of their livestock, clean and repair their farm equipment, and, of course, cut large quantities of firewood for heating and cooking. They also did some trapping. In the nineteenth century the

James Jerome Hill Reference Library, St. Paul, Minnesota

*Gathering Wild Rice,* a watercolour by Seth Eastman. Each family had the right to collect wild rice from a particular locality. One person guided the canoe, while others beat the kernels free.

Cornelius Krieghoff's painting of an
Amerindian woman with her handicrafts
for sale, in the 1830s.
Royal Ontario Museum, 977.314.1

Algonquians carved axe handles, pike poles, brooms and wooden bowls, ladles and shovels, which they sold in nearby towns, using the money to pay for the forthcoming Christmas festivities. The Algonquians celebrated Christmas with a large feast. They had another feast at New Year's, when they also held a dance.

Early in the new year, the women spent some of their time making craft items, such as quill boxes, splint baskets, and moccasins for the summer tourist trade. The communities did some trapping, hunting, and fishing during mid-winter. As winter drew to a close, the Indians made preparations to collect maple sap, the activity that signalled the end of another yearly round.[91]

## Southern Algonquian Social Systems

The Algonquians of Southern Ontario's social organization became modified in the mid-nineteenth century. Although the nuclear family had always been an important and basic Algonquian social unit, the adoption of farming strengthened its hold. Each family became, theoretically, independent of all others, residing on its own farmland, occupying its own house, and raising its own food. A household might consist of the husband, wife, and children as well as one or more dependents, such as an elderly parent. As polygamy was no longer practised, the couple was monogamous.[92]

Even in the most Christianized of the Ojibwa families at the Credit River, such as that of Peter Jones, the children continued to receive Indian names.[93] The parent would ask an elder to bestow a name upon the infant. If the elder accepted the honour, he or she became the child's godparent. The name chosen was usually that of some noted ancestor or was derived from some natural feature or event, occurrence at birth, or personal characteristic.[94] It could be given at a feast. Individuals might change their name during their lifetime.[95]

The Algonquians loved children and always indulged them during the early years of their lives. But as the children grew older, the Algonquians introduced subtle means of ensuring their obedience. As soon as the children could help the adults in their daily tasks, their parents expected them to do so. Girls, because of the nature of the work expected of them, might start assisting in household duties at a younger age than the boys, who aided their fathers in farm work, hunting, trapping, and fishing. In addition to helping at home, children attended school if one existed in the community. Some children might be sent away to a residential school.

On reaching puberty, boys and girls in the nineteenth century, even in a number of Christian families, underwent a vision quest. Originally, the young person left the group and fasted for ten days in some secluded spot, such as on the top of a high hill or upon a special platform erected in a tree. With the development of village life, the youth might be sequestered in the attic of the sponsor's home. If successful, the individual received a vision in which a spirit appeared, one who became the youth's guardian for life.[96]

Usually not long after their son had undertaken the vision quest, his parents arranged for his marriage. They contacted the parents of one of the local girls whom they considered suitable. If the girl's parents agreed, the couple would generally consent. A church wedding marked the occasion. After the ceremony, the community offered the young couple gifts such as livestock and built them a log house.

A well-defined distribution of labour existed between the sexes throughout their adult life. Although the division did not need to be rigidly adhered to, the men generally hunted, trapped fur-bearing animals, and did the wood working, whereas the women undertook the household tasks of cooking, sewing, and the working of hides. Both men and women, either individually or jointly, went fishing, gathered berries and maple sap, and tended to the farm work. Old age brought increased respect and a lessening of the labours imposed upon those of younger age. The elders could indulge their grandchildren, especially in recounting the legends of their people. These entertaining stories instructed the young people in the ways of their ancestors and on the proper way for them to behave.

When a death occurred, the community mourned its loss. The corpse was prepared for burial and a coffin constructed. Usually, a Christian burial service was performed, at the church and/or cemetery. Christian converts placed a cross or headstone at each grave and erected a picket fence about the plot. Some families continued the tradition of erecting a grave house over the burial.[97] Here, individuals might make offerings to the spirit of the deceased.

A number of nuclear families, each forming a household, made up a settlement. In the mid-nineteenth century more and more Algonquian families came to reside in settlements, really clusters of several or more houses and associated farm buildings, one or more churches, schoolhouses, and a council

The non-Christian Indians' form of burial. Seen here are graves at Munceytown. The non-Christian Indians believed that the soul lingered around the body for some time before taking its departure. Before placing the body within the coffin, the relatives of the deceased would bore several holes at the head of the coffin. They believed that this would permit the soul to go in and out at pleasure.
From Peter Jones, *History of the Ojebway Indians* (London 1861), opposite 99

An Indian Christian burial ground, at the Lower Village, Parry Island, Georgian Bay, 1890.

National Archives of Canada, PA-68316

hall. Adjacent to each homestead lay the orchards, pastures, and garden plots in which the Indians grew various crops. Overshadowing the cleared fields stood the primeval forest. Openings here and there might contain productive berrying grounds.

A web of kinship connections linked households together. On various occasions, these groups cooperated with one another. During the spring when the Indians prepared maple sugar, several related families often resided together in the sugar bush and prepared the sugar together. At other times, several families assisted each other in farm tasks that required more hands than a single household could muster.

The families that comprised a settlement frequently intermarried with each other, as other Native communities often were separated from them by considerable distance. In the mid-nineteenth century, and no doubt for some time thereafter, marriage between cross-cousins (father's sister's children and mother's sister's children) was a preferred practice, but missionary opposition probably reduced the incidence of such unions. Clan mates, however, could not wed. Clans among the Algonquians in Southern Ontario, whether a post-contact development or not, apparently at this time had no other function than to regulate marriage. Ojibwa clans had such designations as "Caribou,"

The Credit River Methodist Mission. Peter Jones's wife, Eliza Field Jones, made this sketch shortly after her arrival at the Credit Mission in the fall of 1833. The Credit River Mississauga used the building on the left as both a school and a council house. The building to the right is the church. On the top of the flagpole is a small house for martens to nest in, their presence being considered a good omen.
From Egerton Ryerson, *"The Story of My Life"* (Toronto 1883), opposite 72

"Beaver," "Otter," "Eagle," "Crane," "Birchbark," and "White Oak," and were patrilineal, the children taking the clan affiliation of their father.[98]

The Algonquians of Southern Ontario in the late nineteenth and early twentieth centuries held feasts, dances, and sporting events at various times of the year. Some of the feasts and dances had a spiritual component. Feasts occurred at Thanksgiving, Hallowe'en, Christmas, the New Year, the 6th of January, and on Easter Monday,[99] the most important occurring at Christmas and the New Year. On these occasions the Indians often performed a concert, sang songs, and made speeches. The speaker might recount legends of the past.

The elders organized the feasts, with the oldest in charge. The master of ceremonies made a speech and said grace; then everyone ate. After the meal, the women cleaned up and each man lit his pipe and told a story. Sometimes feasts were family affairs and held at home. Others were community functions held in the community hall.

Those who attended the feasts and dances wore their best clothes, which were based upon the current Euro-Canadian styles. Nevertheless, clothing styles did depend to some extent on the proximity to settlements, as well as on the individual's acceptance of the larger society's ways.[100]

Metropolitan Toronto Reference Library. T14386

Titus Hibbert Ware completed this sketch of Ojibwa at Coldwater, north of Lake Simcoe, in 1844. The Ojibwa men adjusted to the settlers' style of clothing more easily than did the women, but they still wore moccasins and colourful sashes around their waists in the mid-nineteenth century.

Some individuals wove certain items of traditional dress, such as deerskin leggings and jacket, each having the appropriate fringes. These practices continued much later in the north, into the twentieth century. Many individuals wore deerskin moccasins, especially when snowshoeing. Moccasins for special occasions were sometimes decorated with beadwork or embroidery. The Algonquians wore costumes that symbolized their Indian ethnic identity for special events such as official meetings with government representatives.

Clothing to express one's Indianness often mixed Native and European traditions, further modified by innovations conceived by the individual. The Algonquians in Southern Ontario, for instance, later in the nineteenth century added a feather headdress based on those worn by the Plains Indians. They also, on occasion, decorated their top hats with feathers and carried a pipe-tomahawk and fire bag.

The Algonquians usually decorated their jackets and leggings, whether made of cloth or hide, with beaded floral designs. Beading became, in time, the most popular decorative technique, replacing silk embroidery and quill work. The women prepared the deer hides, then sewed the material using three-cornered needles and (for thread) the sinew from the deer's back. Frequently they attached deer hoofs to costumes to produce a rattling sound.[101]

National Archives of Canada, PA-125840

The Algonquians performed dances among themselves and for Euro-Canadian audiences, and on occasion troupes from Upper Canada travelled as far as Europe. Maungwudaus, one of the most celebrated showmen, performed with his troupe before the King of France. The Indians' repertoire included the "*wabeno*," "shoe," "pipe," and "war" dances. To accompany the dances, the troupe drummed and sang.

The Algonquians had games for all ages. Children enjoyed the cup and pin game and horseshoes. The women played a ball game of their own. Each had a short pole about one metre long. With her pole the player propelled two hide balls joined together by a short piece of thong. Each ball was filled

Maungwudaus (George Henry), a daguerreotype probably taken around 1850. Originally from the Credit River, Maungwudaus had a very successful stage career in the late 1840s and early 1850s.

King Louis Philippe of France, his queen, and the Belgian royal family are introduced to Maungwudaus and his troupe in the park at St. Cloud Palace just outside Paris.
Drawing by George Catlin from his *Catlin's Notes of Eight Years Travels and Residdence in Europe, with his North American Indian Collection,* 3d ed. (London 1848), vol. 2, pl. 19, opposite 288

with sand and decorated with a fringe along the sewn edges. The women, organized into two teams, competed for possession of the balls and attempted to convey them to their opponents' goal at the opposite end of the field. Since the late nineteenth century, the Indians have played both softball and baseball. Often the reserve teams competed with teams from surrounding settlements.[102]

Although the Algonquians certainly could manage their own affairs, the government of Canada thought otherwise. The government's ultimate goal became the total assimilation of the Amerindians into the larger society. In 1876 it consolidated the legislation relating to Indians into the "Indian Act." A central principle of the legislation lay in its enfranchisement provisions, procedures by which an Indian could cease to be a member of an Indian nation and become a full citizen of Canada, giving up his or her separate Indian legal status (see chapters 9 and 10).

In 1884 Parliament added a section to the Indian Act that spelled out the form of government each settlement or "band" in eastern Canada should follow. Each was to elect a chief and one or more councillors (based on their community's population) every two or three years. The government intended to impose a democratic European-style form of government upon the Indians and to do away with the old political structures. The Indian Act stipulated that the chief and councillors of each settlement would be responsible to the local superintendent of Indian affairs.

Numbering the Indians at Wikwemikong, Manitoulin Island, 16 August 1856. A drawing by William Armstrong. Chief Assiginack is shown naming the Indians to Captain Ironsides, the Indian superintendent. They stand in front of Ironsides's office (in the frame building to the right). Indian homes appear on the left, and in the background one can view the Roman Catholic church.

By the twentieth century, the elective system prevailed, and where it did, band officials earned a salary. In addition to the elected officials, there might be one or more messengers appointed by the chief to assist him in his various duties. The band paid them an annual salary of from five to fifteen dollars. The messengers gathered provisions from the residents of the settlement for the sick, widows, and families unable to support themselves, and as well, they collected money to pay for funerals. The council appointed a secretary-treasurer and police, if needed, to assist the council in its work. It hired other salaried officials such as school trustees, forest bailiffs, truant officers, and school caretakers as required. The band paid for everything out of its own funds, derived from the monies received from the sale of timber and the fees band residents paid for the right to cut and sell cordwood.[103]

The chief, councillors, and all concerned residents met, as a rule, once a month in the council hall or, if none existed, in the schoolhouse. Council meetings might deal with a wide range of topics: from land allocation to resource management, from treaty concerns to the admittance of new members, from feasts to funerals.[104] Each settlement might also have an unofficial leader, who made suggestions, gave advice, and led in certain affairs, most prominently in religious ceremonies.[105]

New Credit election poster, 1896. Dr. Peter E. Jones, a medical doctor who trained at Queen's University, was one of the first status Indians in Canada (if not the first) to become an Indian agent. He was a son of the Reverend Peter Jones.

Above the local level of band government, the various Southern Ontario Algonquian settlements formed an association known as the Grand Council or General Council. The associated bands met periodically in one of the member's communities, sometimes on their own initiative, at other times at the instigation of government officials. To solemnize council meetings in the mid-nineteenth century, the Algonquians displayed their wampum belts,[106] recited the story each depicted, and smoked the traditional and sacred stone pipes.[107] The Grand Council concerned itself with the federal government's administration of Indian policy. The council petitioned the government regarding various grievances, such as treaty rights.[108]

Although as a rule the Indians pursued peaceful means to rectify wrongs committed by (or perceived to have been caused by) the invading Euro-Canadians, overt aggression sometimes erupted. In the mid-nineteenth century, trouble occurred at Mica Bay in 1849 and on Manitoulin Island during 1862–63.[109] In the case of Mica Bay, mining companies had begun operations in an unceded area. In reaction, the Ojibwa seized the property of the Quebec and Lake Superior Mining Company in an attempt to force government intervention on their behalf. The Mica Bay incident drew attention to the government's neglect of its responsibilities under the Royal Proclamation of 1763, with its provisions for the proper purchase of Indian lands. Subsequently, the government negotiated the Robinson Huron and Superior treaties in 1850.[110]

Great Grand Indian Council, Curve Lake, Ontario, 15 September 1926.

Similarly, the Indians of Wikwemikong would not surrender the east end of Manitoulin Island in the early 1860s and continued to claim exclusive fishing rights to the coastal waters. When non-Natives attempted to force an end to the dispute, violence erupted.

## Spiritual Sources – Mostly Traditional

In the mid-nineteenth century Christian missionaries actively worked among the Indians with remarkable outward success. The converted Indians, as well as the curious among the non-converts, often attended the summer camp meetings. Some took a more active role in church affairs, and as previously mentioned in this chapter, several became ordained Protestant ministers. Churches representing one or more Christian denominations were built in many Native communities. The Indians participated in baptisms, marriage rituals, burial services, and other Christian ceremonials. Yet, in spite of their best efforts, the Christian missionaries did not eradicate all traditional religious beliefs and practices. Rather, many went underground. The Indians generally withheld knowledge of their religious activities, as they did not want their old ceremonies (which many fervently believed in) ridiculed, laughed at, or condemned; they had too often experienced this sort of reaction from the newcomers.

In the mid- and late nineteenth century the Algonquians politely listened to the missionaries but did not necessarily accept all they said. Certain of the Christian teachings had for untold centuries been a part of the Indians' religion; other aspects of Christianity seemed absurd from the Native point of view. The Algonquians, for instance, did not believe in proselytizing and thought it strange that the Euro-Canadians wanted to force everyone to believe in one god of their own creation. On the other hand, the Amerindians respected the right of every individual to believe and pray in the manner he or she thought right. Nevertheless, by the early twentieth century, the Algonquians of Southern Ontario had become nominal Christians, few being classified as "pagan."

Traditionally the Algonquians believed that many of the animate and inanimate objects that existed in the world around them contained a spirit or spiritual force. They also believed that other spirits inhabited the universe as well.[111] Spirits included such beings as the Thunders; Windigo, a man-eating giant; Mishi-pishew, the Great Lynx; and the Memegwesi, little men who lived inside cliffs and paddled stone canoes.[112] The Indian, therefore, was not alone in the world. The spirit world often controlled many of the Indian's actions.

The Algonquians interacted with the spirit world in a variety of ways. Traditionally they made the appropriate sacrifices or offerings – a white[113] or a black dog, birds, or tobacco[114] – to the spirits. They also sought to establish a personal contact with the supernatural world through the vision quest, described earlier in this chapter. Youths undertook vision quests, but they could be undertaken as well at other times in life. Spirits also came to an individual in his or her dreams. At such times they gave counsel and advice. Through the instructions of the spirits, an individual acquired the necessary knowledge whereby he or she could prepare a personal medicine bag. The bag was made of an animal skin or woven of fibres, and in it were kept the ritual medicines designated by the spirits.[115]

Through the vision quest and by means of dreams, individuals acquired power as a result of their contact with the supernatural world. This power could be used in a variety of ways for both good and evil. Those individuals, men and women alike, who received more power than others specialized in one or more of such rituals as the Shaking Tent ceremony. Four or more specialized roles existed, each performed by a distinct religious leader.[116] Through these intermediaries, the average person could obtain communion with the spirit world.

One class of religious leaders included those who had received the appropriate power to perform the Shaking Tent ritual. The tent consisted of six or eight poles erected vertically in the ground in a circle about a metre or so in diameter. A wooden hoop encircled the poles near the top. Sometimes there was a second hoop farther down. This framework was covered, with the exception of the top, with either birchbark, hide, or canvas or a combination of these materials.[117] The tent was constructed prior to each performance, which could be held only at night. When evening fell, the Shaking Tent diviner entered the prepared structure and called upon the spirits to assist him. Generally, if not always, the individual in need of help arranged for the ceremony for which he or she had paid a fee. By means of the performance, lost objects or missing persons could be located or an enemy eliminated.[118]

The Ojibwa of Southern Ontario also practised the *wabeno* ceremony, known as the "morning dance." The performance, conducted by a member of another distinct class of religious leaders, had deep significance and was held each spring. First, the organizers made a dance floor by removing the branches of a tall tree and clearing the surrounding ground of saplings, brush, and debris. The participants had to fast beforehand and cleanse themselves thoroughly. The performance was held at dawn – although some contended that the participants danced all night – at which time those who had gathered began to dance around the tree to the accompaniment of a special drum. The *wabeno* leader, an elder male, acted as the drummer and led the dance. The children preceded the young adults, with the elders coming last. As a dancer passed the tree, he or she, at a signal from the drummer, touched the trunk.

The dance continued until all had performed this act. They held the *wabeno* ceremony to thank the "Great Spirit" for help rendered during the course of the past year. At the same time, the participants requested continued assistance in the year to follow, abundant farm yields, and a bountiful supply of meat and fish. The dance ended about midday, and all joined in a feast, the principal dish being bear's meat, with beaver meat and fish as well. For "butter" the Algonquians used sturgeon oil.[119]

The Midewiwin, a society of men and women who had received supernatural powers to cure the sick, apparently existed among some Algonquian communities in Southern Ontario. Information about the society in this area, however, remains fragmentary and sparse. It is not known whether or not the society was exactly the same in Southern Ontario as elsewhere. The anthropologist Diamond Jenness described the Midewiwin lodge as a large rectangular enclosure with stakes and brush for the walls and without a roof.[120]

Similarly, little is known about the ritual significance of the poles with carved faces near their tops erected in some Algonquian villages, or about the White Dog feast.[121] No doubt these rites were directed to the spirits, as were various sacrifices made with tobacco, birds, and white and black dogs.[122]

In addition to the Midewiwin society members who healed the sick, other individuals specialized in particular cures. Certain men and women had the power and knowledge to prescribe various herbal medicines,[123] while others practised the art of bloodletting. To perform bloodletting, the practitioner had a lancet,[124] the tip of a cow horn (with which to draw the blood once the cut had been made), and a small container with the medicines to be applied to the cut. Other healers withdrew (with the aid of a bone tube) the "substance" causing the illness. They applied one end of the tube to the patient's afflicted area. By sucking on the other end, the healer drew out into his or her mouth the foreign objects that had caused the sickness.[125]

## The Settlers Close In

By 1900 Euro-Canadians had settled throughout Southern Ontario. Farmers had cleared much of the land, lumbermen had cut over large tracts of forests, and railroads linked together the growing urban centres and towns of the hinterland.[126] No longer could the Indians move freely or flee to areas beyond the newcomers' influence. The great majority had no choice but to remain on their reserves and obey, at least outwardly, Indian Affairs personnel and the Christian missionaries. Under the pressures exerted by the newcomers, the Algonquians became enmeshed within the fabric of two cultural traditions, that of their ancestors and that of the new arrivals from across the Atlantic. In the years to come, they reached their own accommodation with the newcomers.[127]

## The First World War

After Canada entered the First World War in 1914, many Amerindians, including a number of Algonquians from Southern Ontario, made a valuable contribution. Out of 20 000 treaty Indians in Ontario, over 1 000 enlisted, of whom nearly 600 were Algonquians from the southern half of the province. As a result, a number of Southern Ontario Indian communities had very few of their able-bodied men at home during the war years.

Once overseas, many of the Algonquian soldiers became renowned sharpshooters. Accounts of the number of kills by Cpl. Francis Pegahmagabow of Parry Island vary, to as high as 378. Johnson Paudash of Rice Lake and the brothers Samson and Peter Comego of Alderville, near Rice Lake, also became noted sharpshooters.[128]

The Amerindians at home contributed to the war effort. Many gave freely to the Canadian Patriotic, Red Cross, and other war funds. Each band raised varying amounts, ranging from $25 to $1 000. In all, the Indians of Southern Ontario contributed approximately $9 000. The women of the Saugeen Reserve on Lake Huron also formed a branch of the Red Cross Society and sent overseas various items needed by the troops. No doubt other Indian communities did likewise. As the war went into its second, then third, then fourth year, the need for greater quantities of food arose. Subsequently, the Indians on the reserves increased production, even bringing back under cultivation lands that had for a time lain idle.[129]

Although the war disrupted their lives, it brought little obvious change to the Indian communities. Farming methods remained essentially the same. Horses and oxen continued to supply the operating power. The Indians grew the same crops. They still lived in squared-timber and frame houses, and wore clothing similar to that worn by their Euro-Canadian neighbours. At home they made their own tools and utensils as they had since time immemorial. The Algonquians went regularly to church and the children

Francis Pegahmagabow, Ojibwa, on a visit to Ottawa, 1945.

Canadian Museum of Civilization, 95292-3

Archives of Ontario, Acc. 9164 s15159

A group of soldiers, many of them Ontario Native people, before going overseas in the First World War. Photo taken in the North Bay area.

attended elementary school, usually on the reserve. They appeared completely integrated within the dominant society, but in reality many traditional attitudes and beliefs remained and they honoured their old spiritual beliefs.

By the early twentieth century fewer Algonquians lived in Southern Ontario than at any time since the arrival of the Europeans. The death rate so exceeded the birth rate that some Euro-Canadians believed that within a couple of decades the Indians would vanish biologically, and that the survivors would disappear culturally through intermarriage and assimilation into the larger society.

Increasing amounts of medical aid and other forms of assistance, however, helped to arrest declining numbers and slowly reversed the trend. The Indian population began to increase in the thirties. In 1934 approximately 30 500 registered Indians lived in Ontario. Twenty years later the total number had risen to 35 000.[130]

The First World War accelerated the pace of change for the Algonquians. The experiences that so many of the men, individually and collectively, had off the reserve as members of the Canadian armed forces proved a powerful catalyst for change. Those who returned had been introduced to many novel experiences, not the least of which was, for a moment, to be treated as equals

Amerindian houses, Wikwemikong, Manitoulin Island, 1916.

Ojibwa family, Chemung (Curve) Lake, Kawartha Lakes, 1910.

and not as "children" and wards of the state. For the returning veterans in particular the world was no longer to be confined within those boundaries that marked off the reserves. Henceforth, greater interaction and association with non-Indians occurred.

## The Interwar Years

Although farming continued in many Amerindian communities, it declined in importance after 1920.[131] The farmland on most Southern Ontario reserves was submarginal and unsuited for mechanized farming. On the more fortunate reserves the Indians lacked the necessary funds to secure the additional farm machinery needed to compete successfully in commercial farming.

The "allotment" or "location" system also hindered the development of profitable farming. Eventually, the continual subdividing of land among family members made the farms too small. On the other hand, an individual could acquire the allotments of others, thereby making farming profitable for himself but depriving others of the opportunity. Each reserve had too little farmland to meet the needs of an expanding population and of mechanized agriculture.[132]

The automobile also inhibited farming. Wherever roads were built to connect the reserve settlements with surrounding communities, the Indians wanted cars. They could purchase cars through the sale of their livestock, but once they had parted with their cattle, they could obtain no replacements. Indian Affairs disapproved of these transactions and was not prepared to subsidize the purchase of cars.[133]

The pull of the city also helps to explain the decline of Indian agriculture in Southern Ontario. Greater employment opportunities in nearby communities and urban centres attracted more and more individuals. Improved transportation made such work possible. If employment was nearby, individuals could commute daily; if further away, they could still return home on weekends.

Although farming continued to decline in the 1920s and 1930s, the Department of Indian Affairs, still operating in the mind-set of a different era, continued to promote agriculture among the Indians. Federal administrators at headquarters in Ottawa misunderstood the new realities of life on the reserve. What the Indians needed in the 1920s and 1930s was an increase in the Department of Indian Affairs' aid and assistance.[134] Although welfare or relief payments for Indians throughout Canada reached a peak in 1937–38 and dropped only slightly during the fiscal year 1938–39, the per capita cost for Indians in Ontario was only $4.68.[135]

The Indians did not become dependent on welfare in the 1930s. Some migrated to urban centres to make a living, and those who remained at home found seasonal employment in the lumber camps, on the railroads, as commercial fishermen, as domestics, in the mines, and in other forms of employment.[136] At Dokis Reserve on the French River, for example, the band leased its timber rights but with the stipulation that Indians be hired.[137] In addition to seasonal jobs and welfare, many of the Native people obtained a certain amount of their food from the land by hunting, fishing, and gardening.

Throughout the first half of the twentieth century, the federal government largely neglected Amerindians. Indian Affairs officials, of course, pursued their policy of assimilation of the Indians into the dominant society, but with little government funding behind them. The Department of Indian Affairs made education compulsory in 1920 for all Indian children between the ages of seven and fifteen, which increased enrolment. But the limited amount of funding given to the Indian school system, as well as student resentment of its assimilationist aims, led to limited academic success. Very few Algonquians in Southern Ontario continued on to secondary school.[138]

The educational system included local reserve schools as well as the church-run residential schools. Basil Johnston, an Ojibwa from Cape Croker, has written an entertaining account of his school days in the 1940s at the Jesuit-run residential school at Spanish, on the north shore of Lake Huron. Although the discipline at the school was harsh, students had their own means of getting back at the administrators.[139]

The family still remained the principal means of teaching the children about the world around them. In the early twentieth century, however, the extended family no longer served as the strong social unit that it had been in the nineteenth century. As the nuclear family became more autonomous, children often did not have the opportunity for intimate contact with their elders. Many parents believed that their children should find their rightful place in Canadian society, which meant that the knowledge of the elders was not stressed.

The Algonquians of Southern Ontario rarely performed their traditional ceremonies in the 1920s and 1930s. When they did so, it was out of the sight of the Euro-Canadians. The Native people attended church and outwardly conformed to Christian doctrines, yet many still opposed the total assimilation advocated by the government of Canada and the Christian churches.

In the Native communities, the residents, particularly the younger school-educated Indians who had knowledge of English and the ways of the dominant society, began to demand better treatment. They wanted to retain their special status and be provided for adequately under the Indian Act and the treaties. They believed that such assistance was just compensation for what their ancestors had lost. The negotiations preceding the signing of the Williams Treaty of 1923 (see chapter 6) reflected this new attitude.

For over fifty years some Ojibwa had contended that their ancestors had never ceded a large portion of Southern Ontario. The territory in question extended between Lake Ontario and Lake Nipissing and included many square kilometres of rich farm and forested land. The area was said to have been the hunting grounds of the ancestors of the claimants who represented seven Ojibwa communities – Christian Island, Georgina Island, Rama, Mud (Curve) Lake, Rice Lake, Alnwick (Alderville), and Scugog. Since the 1860s individuals from these reserves had repeatedly petitioned the government to rectify this oversight. Finally, the government acceded to the Ojibwa's request and in 1923 made a settlement. For half a million dollars (to be divided among the bands) and a per capita payment of $25, Ontario believed it had acquired title to this land.[140] In the negotiation process, however, both the federal and Ontario governments had overlooked the claims of the Algonquin of the Ottawa valley to the eastern section of the disputed territory. This omission surfaced in the 1970s when the Algonquin again brought forward their claim to their lands in the Ottawa valley.[141]

The Department of Indian Affairs' response to the Ojibwa's tactics in the Williams negotiations indicated its determination to complete the Indians' assimilation into the dominant society.[142] The department was furious that the Ojibwa had hired their own lawyers to present their case. In 1927 Parliament amended the Indian Act to make it, in effect, an offence to pursue land claims without departmental permission. The amendment forbade Native people to raise money without permission to investigate any of their claims against the government.[143] Until the 1930s Parliament continually increased the powers of the superintendent general of Indian affairs. The Second World War, however,[144] resulted in significant changes in the relationship between the Native people, the government, and Canadian society.

## The Second World War

The Southern Algonquians contributed as much to the Second World War as they had to the First. Again many enlisted in support of the Canadian war effort, and this time Native women also joined the ranks. Ontario, of all the provinces, contributed the greatest number to the total of 3 000 status Indians who enlisted in the Canadian armed forces. A total of 1 324 men and 32 women signed up.[145] Ontario Indians were represented in the Canadian Army in every rank, from private to brigadier-general (Milton Martin of the Six Nations).[146] Many Indians from across the province served with distinction in the European theatre, and their exploits earned several medals and military distinctions. Not so fortunate were the many families who lost sons, husbands, brothers, and fathers during the fighting. An extraordinary example of the sacrifices made by one Ontario Indian family has been recorded for the Cape Croker Reserve. John McLeod first served in the First World War, and in the Second he enlisted in the Veteran Guards. His six sons and one daughter entered the forces. Two sons were killed in action and two were wounded overseas.[147]

Again, contact with the non-Indian world intensified. Overseas many experienced a racial equality they had not known at home. Max King, a Mississauga from New Credit, wrote from his base in Britain: "They [the local British] are really swell, working-class people and in their distress they show a spirit which we never find in Canada."[148] A number of Canadian Indian soldiers returned to Canada with British war brides. Through marriage with treaty Indians these women secured all the rights and privileges of registered Indians. In fact, in the eyes of the law, they (like all those under the Indian Act) ceased to be citizens and became wards of the Crown. They could not vote in provincial or federal elections, serve on a jury, or drink alcohol in a public place.[149]

For those who stayed at home, opportunities for city work multiplied through the need for a greatly expanded labour force. The war effort needed hundreds of thousands of male and female workers for the munitions factories and related war industries.[150] At the end of the war, Native servicemen and women returned to a colonial existence on their reserves, ruled as they were under the rigid, dictatorial Indian Act. New voices would soon be heard. Native peoples called for their recognition as the original inhabitants of this land. A new generation of Algonquians, familiar with the dominant culture, fought in the decades to follow for their rightful place in society and for compensation for past grievances.

# NOTES

1   James A. Clifton, *A Place of Refuge for All Time: Migration of the American Potawatomi into Upper Canada 1830–1850* (Ottawa 1975), 32

2   Anon., *Report on the Affairs of the Indians in Canada Laid before the Legislative Assembly 20th March 1845* (8 Victoria Appendix EEE A 1844–45), 34

3   Ibid., 35

4   Anna Brown Jameson, *Winter Studies and Summer Rambles in Canada*, 3 vols. (London 1838), 3:268

5   Ibid., 3:279–82

6   See Clifton, *A Place of Refuge*, 36

7   Paul Kane, *Wanderings of an Artist among the Indians of North America* (Toronto 1925), 7, 10–11

8   I. McCoy, *History of Baptist Missions* (Washington, D.C. 1840), 546; P.V. Lawson, "The Potawatomi," *Wisconsin Archaeologist* 19, no. 2 (1920): 98

9   Clifton, *A Place of Refuge*, 34; James A. Clifton, "Potawatomi," in *Handbook of North American Indians*, vol. 15: *Northeast*, ed. Bruce G. Trigger (Washington, D.C. 1978), 739

10  Lawson, "The Potawatomi," 98, 102

11  *Report on the Affairs of the Indians in Canada ... 1845*, 34

12  Johanna E. Feest and Christian F. Feest, "Ottawa," in *Handbook of North American Indians*, vol. 15: *Northeast,* ed. Bruce G. Trigger, 772–86

13  *Report on the Affairs of the Indians in Canada ... 1845*, 35

14  A.J. Blackbird, *History of the Ottawa and Chippewa Indians* (Ypsilanti 1887), 98

15  Feest and Feest, "Ottawa," 779

16  E.S. Rogers and Flora Tobobondung, *Parry Island Farmers: A Period of Change in the Way of Life of the Algonkians of Southern Ontario*, Canadian Ethnology Service, paper no. 31 (Ottawa 1975), 278–9

17  Gordon M. Day, "Nipissing," in *Handbook of North American Indians*, vol. 15: *Northeast,* ed. Bruce G. Trigger, 787–91; G.M. Day and Bruce G. Trigger, "Algonquin," in *Northeast*, ed. Trigger, 792–7

18  George Brown and Ron Maguire, *Indian Treaties in Historical Perspective* (Ottawa 1979), 30; J.L. Morris, *Indians of Ontario* (Toronto 1943), 61–2; R.C. Daniel, *A History of Native Claims Processes in Canada 1867–1979* (Ottawa 1980), 63–76

19  See Elizabeth Graham, *Medicine Man to Missionary: Missionaries as Agents of Change among the Indians of Southern Ontario, 1784–1867* (Toronto 1975), 38

20  Benjamin Slight, *Indian Researches; or Facts Concerning the North American Indians; Including Notices of Their Present State of Improvement, in Their Social, Civil and Religious Condition; with Hints for Their Future Advancement* (Montreal 1844), 134–7; Margaret Ray, "An Indian Mission in Upper Canada," *The Bulletin: Records and Proceedings of the Committee on Archives of the United Church of Canada* (Toronto 1954), 10–18; Jameson, *Winter Studies and Summer Rambles*, 3:227–32

21  See Slight, *Indian Researches*, 35ff.; Graham, *Medicine Man to Missionary*, 14–20; G.S. French, *Parsons & Politics: The Role of the Wesleyan Methodists in Upper Canada and the Maritimes from 1780 to 1855* (Toronto 1962), chap. 6; and Donald B. Smith, *Sacred Feathers: The Reverend Peter Jones (Kahkewaquonaby) and the Mississauga Indians* (Toronto 1987).

22  Smith, *Sacred Feathers*, passim

23  Peter (Pahtahsega) Jacobs, "Extract of a Letter from the Same [i.e., Peter Jacobs], dated Lac-la-Pluie, Hudson's Bay Territories, July 10th, 1844," *Methodist Magazine*, 68, 205; Peter Jacobs, *Journal of the Reverend Peter Jacobs, Indian Wesleyan missionary, from Rice Lake to the Hudson's Bay Territory and return* (New York 1858)

24  NA, Salt 1854–55 MS: Salt, Notebook; *Christian Guardian*, 8 February 1911; Rogers and Tobobondung, "Parry Island Farmers," 302

25  Jameson, *Winter Studies and Summer Rambles*, 3:297

26  Ibid., 3:227; H.N. Burden, *Manitoulin, or Five Years of Church Work among the Ojibway Indians and Lumbermen, Resident upon that Island or in its Vicinity* (London 1895), 21

27  Report on the Indians of Upper Canada ("The Sub-committee Appointed to make a Comprehensive Inquiry into the State of the Aborigines of British North America, present thereupon the first part of their general report") (1839; reprint, Toronto 1968), 44–5

28  *Report on the Affairs of the Indians in Canada ...* , *1845*, 34
29  Lorenzo Cadieux, éd., *Lettres des Nouvelles Missions du Canada, 1843–1852* (Montréal 1973), *passim*
30  Florence B. Murray, *Muskoka and Haliburton, 1615–1875* (Toronto 1963), xcv–xcviii; Douglas Baldwin, *The Fur Trade in the Moose-Missinaibi River Valley 1770–1917* (Toronto n.d.), 77–8; John Weiler, *Michipicoten Hudson's Bay Company Post 1821–1904* (Toronto 1973); John W. Pollock, *The Culture History of the Kirkland Lake District, Northeastern Ontario* (Ottawa 1976), 33–5; Elaine Allan Mitchell, *Fort Temiskaming and the Fur Trade* (Toronto 1977); E.G. Higgins and P.A. Peake, *Sudbury Then and Now, A Pictorial History of Sudbury and Area 1883–1973* (Sudbury n.d.), 1–8
31  *Report on the Affairs of the Indians in Canada ...* , *1845*, 35; Morris, *Indians of Ontario*, 27–8; Peter A. Cummings and Neil H. Mickenberg, *Native Rights in Canada* (Toronto 1972), 113–15; Canada, *Indian Treaties and Surrenders from 1680 to 1890*, 2 vols. (Ottawa 1891), 1:112–13 (henceforth *Treaties and Surrenders*)
32  *Report on the Affairs of the Indians in Canada ...* , *1845*, 35; *Treaties and Surrenders*, 1:113; Peter S. Schmalz, *The History of the Saugeen Indians* (Ottawa 1977), 61–72
33  *Report on the Affairs of the Indians in Canada ...* , *1845*, 29; *Treaties and Surrenders*, 1:115
34  Ives Goddard, "Delaware," in *Handbook of North American Indians*, vol. 15: *Northeast*, ed. Bruce G. Trigger, 224; *Report on the Affairs of the Indians of Canada ...* , 1845, 29
35  Robert J. Surtees, *The Robinson Treaties*, Treaty Research Report, Treaties and Historical Research Centre, Indian and Northern Affairs Canada (Ottawa 1986)
36  Morris, *Indians of Ontario*, 34–8
37  Robert J. Surtees, *Manitoulin Island Treaties*, Treaties and Historical Research Centre, Indian and Northern Affairs Canada (Ottawa 1985)
38  Smith, *Sacred Feathers*, 145–6, 159, 206–7
39  G.P. de T. Glazebrook, *Life in Ontario, A Social History* (Toronto 1968), 209
40  Rogers and Tobobondung, *Parry Island Farmers*, 299
41  Paul Radin, "Ethnological Notes on the Ojibwa of Southeastern Ontario," *American Anthropologist* 30, no. 4 (1928): 661–2; Peter Jones, *History of the Ojebway Indians; with Especial Reference to Their Conversion to Christianity* (London 1861), 71
42  See Mark R. Harrington, "Vestiges of Material Culture among the Canadian Delawares," *American Anthropologist* 10 (1908): 408–16.
43  Jones, *History of the Ojebway Indians*, 72
44  Ibid., 71
45  A.F. Chamberlain, "Notes on the History, Customs and Beliefs of the Mississauga Indians," *Journal of American Folklore* 1 (1888): 154–5; George Copway, *The Life and Travels of Kah-gega-gah-bowh (George Copway)* (Philadelphia 1847), 14, 20
46  Murray, *Muskoka and Haliburton, 1615–1875*, 36; Rogers and Tobobondung, "Parry Island Farmers," 273
47  By 1845 guns were common among Indians near settlements. See Kane, *Wanderings of an Artist*, 6 (blacksmith modifies flint lock to cap lock); and Francis Paget Hett, *Georgina: A Type Study of Early Settlement and Church Building in Upper Canada* (Toronto 1939), 44.

48    Rogers and Tobobondung, "Parry Island Farmers," 322
49    Kane, *Wanderings of an Artist*, 2
50    Rogers and Tobobondung, "Parry Island Farmers," 322
51    Henry R. Schoolcraft, *Information Respecting the History, Condition and Prospects of the Indian Tribes of the United States*, 6 vols. (Philadelphia 1851–1857), 1: pt. II, 51, 515, pl. 5 opposite p. 50, pl. 76 opposite p. 516
52    Kane, *Wanderings of an Artist*, 2, 6
53    Rogers and Tobobondung, "Parry Island Farmers," 321
54    Richard King, *Narrative of a Journey to the Shores of the Arctic Ocean* (London 1847), 22
55    Chamberlain, "Notes," 154
56    J.G. Kohl, *Kitchi-gami: Wanderings Round Lake Superior* (Minneapolis 1956), 326
57    Jameson, *Winter Studies and Summer Rambles*, 3:189–90; John J. Bigsby, *The Shoe and the Canoe* (London 1850), 2:125–6; King, *Narrative of a Journey*, 21–2; E.S. Rogers, "Southeastern Ojibwa," in *Handbook of North American Indians*, vol. 15: *Northeast*, ed. Bruce Trigger, 766, fig. 4
58    Kohl, *Kitchi-gami*, 361
59    Ibid., 328–9
60    Ibid., 361
61    George Head, *Forest Scenes and Incidents in the Wilds of North America* (London 1829), 265–9
62    Ibid., 200–2; Rogers and Tobobondung, "Parry Island Farmers," 319–21, pl. 39 (of a lure); Kohl, *Kitchi-gami*, 330; Schoolcraft, *Information*, pt. II, pl. 6 opposite 52, pl. 76 opposite 516
63    Kohl, *Kitchi-gami*, 328
64    Regina Flannery, "The Cultural Position of the Spanish River Indians," *Primitive Man* 13, no. 1 (1940): 1–25; Frederick Johnson, "Notes on the Ojibwa and Potawatomi of the Parry Island Reservation, Ontario," *Indian Notes* 6, no. 3 (1929): 193–216; Diamond Jenness, *The Ojibwa Indians of Parry Island, Their Social and Religious Life* (Ottawa 1935)
65    Chamberlain, "Notes," 155–6; Radin, "Ethnological Notes on the Ojibwa of Southeastern Ontario," 663–4
66    Rogers and Tobobondung, "Parry Island Farmers," 319
67    Ibid.
68    Ibid., 315, 319
69    Paul Kane, *Paul Kane Sketch Pad* (Toronto 1969), sketches 946.15.2 22, 29, 53; Schoolcraft, *Information*, 2:46–8
70    Jenness, *The Ojibwa Indians of Parry Island*, 112; Schoolcraft, *Information*, 2:49–50
71    Edward S. Rogers, "The Dugout Canoe in Ontario," *American Antiquity* 30 (1965): 454–9
72    Slight, *Indian Researches*, 41; Schoolcraft, *Information*, 2:48–9
73    Rogers and Tobobondung, "Parry Island Farmers," 332
74    Ibid.
75    J.M.S. Careless, *The Union of the Canadas, 1841–1857* (Toronto 1967), 106–7, 151
76    "CAR, the great god," as the late Canadian historian A.R.M. Lower termed it. See his *Canadians in the Making: A Social History of Canada* (Toronto 1957), 424–6.

77  For a good overview of the Ojibwa and their snowshoes in the mid-nineteenth century, see Kohl, *Kitchi-gami*, 332–7.
78  P.A. Thompson, "Fish and Game Law Enforcement in Ontario," *Ontario Fish and Wildlife Review* 6, nos. 1–2 (1967): 35–40
79  Jones, *History of the Ojebway Indians*, 104
80  NA, CO 42/388, 265
81  Rogers and Tobobondung, "Parry Island Farmers," 315
82  Ibid., 310
83  Ibid.
84  Ibid., 315
85  Smith, *Sacred Feathers*, 79
86  Murray, *Muskoka and Haliburton, 1615–1875*, 125
87  Kane, *Paul Kane Sketch Pad*, sketches 946.15.21, 22, 24, 27, 32, 34, 37, 39, 47; Jenness, *The Ojibwa Indians of Parry Island*, 112
88  Ibid., 112
89  Kane, *Wanderings of an Artist*, 4–5
90  Rogers and Tobobondung, "Parry Island Farmers," 322
91  Ibid., 305–7; Slight, *Indian Researches, passim;* Burden, *Manitoulin*, 87
92  Chamberlain, "Notes," 153
93  Ibid., 152–3
94  Smith, *Sacred Feathers*, 213
95  Slight, *Indian Researches*, 74; Chamberlain, "Notes," 153
96  Slight, *Indian Researches*, 89; Paul Radin, *Some Myths and Tales of the Ojibwa of Southeastern Ontario* (Ottawa 1914), 1–10; Rogers and Tobobondung, "Parry Island Farmers," 336–7
97  Johnson, "Ojibwa and Potawatomi," 212–15
98  Chamberlain, "Notes," 152; Murray, *Muskoka and Haliburton, 1615–1875*, 102
99  Rogers and Tobobondung, "Parry Island Farmers," 339–40
100  Harrington, "Vestiges," 412–13; Hett, *Georgina*, 114
101  Rogers and Tobobondung, "Parry Island Farmers," 343; Jenness, *The Ojibwa Indians of Parry Island*, 64
102  Rogers and Tobobondung, "Parry Island Farmers," 341
103  Ibid., 289, 303
104  Ibid., 292–302
105  Ibid., 303
106  Slight, *Indian Researches*, 72
107  Kane, *Wanderings of an Artist*, 9–10; Kane, *Paul Kane Sketch Book*, sketches 946.15.33, 946.15.36; Daniel Wilson, *Prehistoric Man, Researches into the Origin of Civilization in the Old and the New World*, 2 vols. (London 1876), 1:393, fig. 84
108  Anon., 1846 Minutes of the General Council; Slight, *Indian Researches*, 72–73; Kane, *Wanderings of an Artist*, 1–2. See Conrad Van Dusen (Enemikeese), *The Indian Chief: An Account of the Labours, Losses, Sufferings, and Oppression of Ke-zig-ko-e-ne-ne (David Sawyer) a Chief of the Ojibbeway Indians in Canada West* (London 1867).
109  Nancy M. Wightman and W. Robert Wightman, "The Mica Bay Affair: Conflict on the Upper-Lakes Mining Frontier, 1840–1850," *Ontario History* 83 (1991): 193–208; Douglas Leighton, "The Manitoulin Incident of 1863: An Indian-White Confrontation in the Province of Canada," *Ontario History* 69 (1977): 113–24;

Surtees, *Manitoulin Island Treaties*; Victor Lytwyn, "Ojibwa and Ottawa Fisheries around Manitoulin Island: Historical and Geographical Perspectives on Aboriginal and Treaty Fishing Rights," *Native Studies Review* 6, no. 1 (1990): 1–30

110    Robert J. Surtees, *The Robinson Treaties*, Treaty Research Report, Treaties and Historical Research Centre, Indian and Northern Affairs Canada (Ottawa 1986)

111    Spirits, for example, inhabited the caves in the escarpment surrounding Burlington Bay. See Jones, *History of the Ojebway Indians*, 255.

112    Slight, *Indian Researches*, 87, 98–100; Jenness, *The Ojibwa Indians of Parry Island*, 29–46, 84; A.F. Chamberlain, "Mississauga Place Names," *Journal of American Folk-Lore* 3 (1890): 74; Chamberlain, "Notes," 157; Johnson, "Ojibwa and Potawatomi," 208–12

113    Jenness, *The Ojibwa Indians of Parry Island*, 65

114    Chamberlain, "Notes," 197

115    Slight, *Indian Researches*, 92–4; Harrington, "Vestiges," 417

116    Slight, *Indian Researches*, 94; Jenness, *The Ojibwa Indians of Parry Island*, 60

117    Slight, *Indian Researches*, 95; Jenness, *The Ojibwa Indians of Parry Island*, 66

118    Slight, *Indian Researches*, 95–6; Jenness, *The Ojibwa Indians of Parry Island*, 65–8; Rogers and Tobobondung, "Parry Island Farmers," 339

119    Slight, *Indian Researches*, 88; Jenness, *The Ojibwa Indians of Parry Island*, 62–3; Rogers and Tobobondung, "Parry Island Farmers," 339

120    Slight, *Indian Researches*, 94; Jenness, *The Ojibwa Indians of Parry Island*, 69–78; Rogers and Tobobondung, "Parry Island Farmers," 337–9

121    Murray, *Muskoka and Haliburton, 1615–1875*, 124

122    Chamberlain, "Notes," 157; Jenness, *The Ojibwa Indians of Parry Island*, 65

123    Jenness, *The Ojibwa Indians of Parry Island*, 89; Rogers and Tobobondung, "Parry Island Farmers," 338; Chamberlain, "Notes," 156; Murray, *Muskoka and Haliburton, 1615–1875*, 126–7

124    Slight, *Indian Researches*, 95; Jenness, *The Ojibwa Indians of Parry Island*, 63–5

125    Ibid., 64–5

126    Glazebrook, *Life in Ontario*; G. Elmore Reaman, *A History of Agriculture in Ontario* (Aylesbury 1970); Joseph Schull, *Ontario Since 1867* (Toronto 1978)

127    See *Toronto Star Weekly*, 2 October 1915, 17

128    Fred Gaffen, *Forgotten Soldiers* (Penticton, B.C. 1985), 28

129    Duncan Campbell Scott, "The Canadian Indians and the Great World War," in *Canada and the Great World War*, vol. 3 (Toronto 1919), 326–7

130    R.A. Hoey, "Economic Problems of the Canadian Indian," in C.T. Loram and T.F. McIlwraith, eds., *The North American Indian Today* (Toronto 1943), 199; Ontario, *Civil Liberties and Rights of Indians in Ontario*, Report of the Select Committee on the Rights of Indians in Ontario, dated Toronto, 19 March 1954, 8, Archives of Ontario, RG 18 D-I-53

131    See Susan DeMille, *Ethnohistory of Farming: Cape Croker 1820–1930* (MPhil, University of Toronto, 1971); Rolf Knight, *Indians at Work* (Vancouver 1978), 156, 158–9; R.M. Dunning, "Some Problems of Reserve Indian Communities: A Case Study," *Anthropologica*, 1964, 6; Schmalz, *The History of the Saugeen Indians*, 182; Rogers and Tobobondung, "Parry Island Farmers," 346–8

132    D.J. Allen, "Indian Land Problems in Canada," in C.T. Loram and T.F. McIlwraith, eds., *The North American Indian Today* (Toronto 1943), 195–6

133    DeMille, *Ethnohistory of Farming*; R.M. Vanderburgh, *I Am Nokomis Too: The Biography of Verna Petronella Johnston* (Don Mills 1977), 73

134   R.A. Hoey, "Economic Problems of the Canadian Indian," in C.T. Loram and T.F. McIlwraith, eds., *The North American Indian Today*, 200–1

135   Ibid., 202

136   Knight, *Indians at Work*, 89, 161; Schmalz, *The History of the Saugeen Indians*, 185–90; Vanderburgh, *I am Nokomis Too*, 92–3

137   For the story of the Dokis Indians and their timber rights, see James T. Angus, "How the Dokis Indians Protected Their Timber," *Ontario History* 81 (1989): 181–99.

138   As late as 1953 nearly 7 000 status Indian children attended Ontario schools; of that figure only 256 were in secondary schools. In 1949 there had been less than 130 in secondary schools. Only 9 students were in the final year of high school (grade 13) in 1953 (Ontario, *Civil Liberties and Rights of Indians in Ontario* [Toronto 1954], 19).

139   Basil H. Johnston, *Indian School Days* (Toronto 1987)

140   R.C. Daniel, *A History of Native Claims Processes in Canada 1867–1979* (Ottawa 1980), 64–76; R.J. Surtees, *The Williams Treaties,* Treaty Research Report (Ottawa 1986)

141   Michael Moore, "Most of Algonquin to be in land claim planned by Indians," *Globe and Mail*, 27 January 1977, 5; "Natives' Claim includes Parliament Hill," *Calgary Herald*, 31 August 1988, A7; Michelle Lalonde, "Land claim controversy shatters cottage-country calm," *Globe and Mail*, 21 May 1990, A4

142   See John Flood, "The Duplicity of D.C. Scott and the James Bay Treaty," *Black Moss*, 2d ser., no. 2 (Fall 1976): 56–63; and Brian E. Titley, *A Narrow Vision: Duncan Campbell Scott and the Administration of Indian Affairs in Canada* (Vancouver 1986).

143   Olive Patricia Dickason, *Canada's First Nations* (Toronto 1992), 328

144   Wayne Dougherty and Dennis Madill, *Indian Government under Indian Act Legislation 1868–1951* (Ottawa 1980), pt. II, 45–55

145   Memorandum prepared by E. St. Louis, "The Record of Canadian Indians in the Two World Wars," 27 April 1950, a document at the Claims and Historical Research Centre, Indian and Northern Affairs, Canada

146   For a sketch of Milton Martin's life, see Enos T. Montour, *The Feathered U.E.L.'s* (Toronto 1973), 130–4.

147   Gaffen, *Forgotten Soldiers*, 53

148   Max King, "With the Indian Boys Overseas," *Pine Tree Chief*, 2 January 1942, quoted in Laurence M. Hauptman, *The Iroquois Struggle for Survival: World War II to Red Power* (Syracuse 1986), 3. The following summer Max King was killed in action in the raid on Dieppe.

149   Anne Rosemary Paudash, "I Married an Indian," *Maclean's*, 1 September 1951, 26–8

150   An interesting interview with Casper Solomon, an Ojibwa elder from Cape Croker, appeared in *Dimensions: Special Editions*, October/November 1980, and was reprinted under the title "Our Elders Speak, Casper Solomon: Elder," in the *Ontario Indian* 4, no. 2 (February 1981): 40. Mr. Solomon and his wife left the Cape Croker Reserve for Port Credit in 1940, where he obtained a position at an oil refinery. The Solomons raised their family of seven children in Mississauga. They moved to Toronto in 1966. He served in 1980 on the Board of Directors of the Native Canadian Centre and taught at the Wandering Spirit Survival School in

Toronto. To the interviewer's question "Was it difficult making the transition, living on the reserve and then moving off, where did you go?," Mr. Solomon replied:

> Actually, it wasn't too difficult because already about that time young people, you know, they had some schooling and they could talk English. They could communicate with white people but we had quite an inferiority complex, you see, because we were brought up to be Indians. The white man was the dominant thing in your life. If you wanted to get anywhere … first you had to be taught by a white person and that's it, and you had to live like he did, that was it. In order to get anywhere you had to conform to that image and if you didn't conform … well, you didn't get anywhere. You weren't told that but that was the way it was.
>
> When I left the reservation, when I first came out; in those days we had no electricity on the reserve, we had no running water, we had no inside toilet. When I left the reservation I saw all these conveniences and also I had quite a inferiority complex. I saw people my own age. They had a job. They were working. They had a skill or some kind of trade, you know, they were, I thought they were, quite smart. Later on I began to work. I went into a refinery. I worked in an oil refinery and there I worked alongside white people and I began to know them a little better, although I didn't socialize with them.
>
> I had a place, I was married and I was bringing up kids but I saw these men at work, you know, I talked to them and as I began to realize they weren't any smarter than I was. In a lot of cases, I thought they were stupid. There was nothing special about them and I was just as smart as they were and I could learn any skill or any kind of work I wanted. I could do whatever they did and maybe sometimes better. It gradually just dawned on me that I wasn't inferior in any way, gradually it dawned on me.

# 8 *The Six Nations in the Grand River Valley, 1784–1847*

CHARLES M. JOHNSTON

## Introduction

The British lost the American Revolutionary War, but their material and strategic standing in the world was, in spite of grim appearances and prophecies of doom, not appreciably altered. The same cannot be said, however, for those Iroquois who fought for Britain and shared her defeats on the battlefield. Unlike the British, their society, economy, and homeland were rudely disrupted, this to a degree that for the most part went unappreciated in the imperial metropole. Preoccupied with its own humiliating circumstances, Britain could find little room for the kind of sensitive response to the Six Nations' plight that might have eased those Indians through the troubles confronting them at war's end.

For one thing, the American Revolution, in which at the outset the Six Nations had sought to remain neutral, placed a heavy burden on their delicate social and political structure in New York. Many Oneida and some Tuscarora, for example, opted for the revolutionary side, whereas the majority of their confederates, notably the Mohawk, declared for the king and rallied to the leadership of Joseph Brant (Thayendanegea), the acculturated and highly reputed Mohawk war chief (see chapter 5). Divided loyalties and the strains of bloody border warfare periodically threatened the fabric of the Six Nations Confederacy and prompted the anxious to wonder about "what [would] happen to the whole [long]house."[1] Their anguish was compounded when, "in the great Hurry of [Bus]iness" that accompanied the peacemaking, the negotiators overlooked earlier British pledges that the Six Nations' rights and property would be restored. Neither in the preliminary discussions nor in the definitive treaty of peace, concluded in September 1783, was provision made for the Confederacy.

This oversight, coupled with the apparent neglect of Native interests generally on the western frontier, aroused strong misgivings in Joseph Brant and John Deserontyon, another Mohawk chief. Since the Americans regarded enemy lands as forfeited, the cornered British sought to persuade the unhappy Iroquois to move north of the Great Lakes to territory still remaining in Britain's hands. Though frustrated by their ally's inability to deliver better terms, Brant and Deserontyon nonetheless accepted the proposal. Some accounts suggest that Brant originally considered settling near Fort Niagara,[2] but if so, he may have given up the idea because of his supposed distaste for living near or amongst the Americans. For the same reason, it would appear, he declined a Seneca invitation to take up residence in New York's Genesee valley.[3]

### The Removal to the Grand River

At any rate, it was left to the beleaguered man on the spot, Sir Frederick Haldimand, governor of Quebec, to make the necessary arrangements to relocate the Iroquois. Fearful of what inaction might bring down on his head, the governor on his own authority despatched a surveying crew to examine a site already fancied by Deserontyon – the Bay of Quinte area. Brant briefly also expressed an interest in this site, but in the end he preferred another, one he had already visited and highly valued – the valley of the Grand River, some 350 kilometres to the west.

Brant's preference for the Grand River reflected his political and strategic calculations. For one thing, the compact consolidation of the loyalist Six Nations in that quarter would furnish a possible jumping-off point to the Western Indians with whom Britain and Brant wished to maintain a liaison for countering American designs on the interior. Moreover, Brant realized that the Seneca who remained behind in New York would take comfort in knowing that many of their friends among the Mohawk, Seneca, Onondaga, and Cayuga who selected the Grand as a haven would be within easy reach.[4]

More mundanely, Brant may have ruled out the Bay of Quinte because it was "too stony" and hence unfit for farming. But clearly this posed no problem for Deserontyon, who reportedly pronounced the region a "country that suits me"[5] and clung to it, in spite of Haldimand's wishes and Brant's entreaties that he join the larger Iroquois settlement on the Grand. Even though this decision appeared to spark considerable ill feeling, the two men's descendants downplayed it. They claimed that the chiefs were never "personally unfriendly" and that their respective followers had done "better [anyway] by securing two good tracts ... and having two settlements ... [instead of] one."[6]

*Thayendanegea (Joseph Brant),* by William Berczy (1744–1813). One of Berczy's most striking portraits is his full-length image of Joseph Brant at the Grand River, completed c. 1807. Brant died on 24 November 1807. Berczy may have based this portrait on sketches he had made of the famous Mohawk chief in the 1790s.

In any case, once Brant made his decision, Haldimand took steps in the spring of 1784 to arrange the necessary purchase of the Grand River lands from the Mississauga, who had occupied them for nearly a century. The following summer the land transfer was approved, and on 25 October 1784 the governor issued a proclamation conferring some 240 000 hectares in the Grand River valley on the Mohawk and "others of the Six Nations in Consideration of [their] early Attachment to His Majesty's Cause." By the terms of the grant the Six Nations who wished to reside there could do so on a tract "Six Miles deep from each Side of the River beginning at Lake Erie, & extending in that Proportion to [its] ... Head."[7]

The arrangement turned out to be deceptively simple, for over the next generation it produced a host of problems. While Brant regarded the proclamation as an acknowledgment that the lands on the Grand were "absolutely our own,"[8] the authorities stuck by the ancient formula that Indians under the "King's protection" could not convey their lands to others independently of the Crown's wishes. Plainly Brant's desire to enjoy full sway over the tract sprang in part from his plan to bring in a limited number of whites, invariably friends and fellow veterans of the late war. These individuals, it was hoped, could, by example and guidance, instruct the Iroquois males, who regarded agriculture as strictly women's work, in the necessary "arts of husbandry." The need for this kind of tutoring was deemed all the more imperative now that wildlife had declined so markedly in the area. That some such assistance was vital was hinted at when a dispirited Iroquois family, after vainly attempting to raise a crop on the Grand, returned to the Tuscarora village on the New York side.[9]

Most of the nearly 2 000 Indians who migrated to the valley in the spring and summer of 1785, however, stayed on and tried to cope with their new environment. According to a census taken at the time, the Mohawk constituted the largest group (448), followed by the Cayuga, both Upper and Lower (381), assorted Onondaga (245), the Delaware (183), the Seneca, including those from "the West" (78), and a smattering of Oneida, Tuscarora, Tutelo, Nanticoke, Creek, and Cherokee.[10] The Mohawk settled in the vicinity of present-day Brantford and organized the Mohawk village known variously as Ohsweken, New Oswego, or "Brant's Town."[11] The other nations located further down the Grand on both its banks. Thus, the Upper Cayuga and a small group of Oneida occupied an area immediately adjacent to the Mohawk, the Tuscarora formed a community of their own on the eastern side of the river not far from the Onondaga and Seneca encampments, while the Lower Cayuga and Delaware took up lands that occupied roughly half of that part of the valley extending from Brant's Town to Lake Erie. In effect, they duplicated in their new surroundings the separate and distinctive communities they had left behind in their New York homeland.

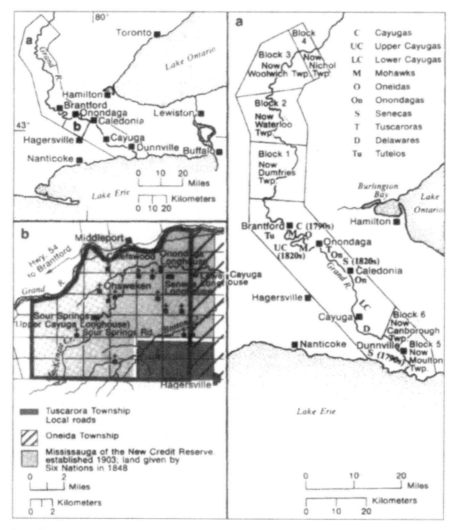

Map 8.1
Area of the Six Nations Reserve
(a) Tribal locations along the Grand River in the 1820s, with blocks 1–6 surrendered to Whites in the 1790s, after Charles M. Johnston, ed. *The Valley of the Six Nations* (Toronto 1964), figs. 2-3; and Augustus Jones, "Map of Grand River Tract," 1791; (b) Six Nations Reserve in 1970.

Meanwhile, several non-Native farmers accepted Brant's invitation to set-tle among the Six Nations, notably John Smith, John Thomas, Alexander West-brook, Hendrick William Nelles, Benjamin Fairchild, and John Dochstadter. The presence of these experienced farmers, while welcomed by Brant and his followers, visibly displeased others. Some officials, for example, feared that the traditional "King's Regulations" governing the disposal of Indian lands would be put in dispute by these dealings. They argued further that the Iroquois, legally regarded as wards of the Crown, could not have whites as their tenants. More to the point, factionalism raised its head when a number of chiefs, led by Isaac and Aaron Hill, expressed fears for the cultural future of the Confederacy should the non-Native influx be tolerated. Their disapproval of Brant's arrangements led in 1789 to a kind of coup against the chief. Brant won out, however, causing both Hills and their entourage to leave the Mohawk settlement and take refuge with Deserontyon at the Bay of Quinte.[12] Other fac-tors of a more personal character may have helped to fuel the quarrel, possibly envy of Brant's power and rivalry for leadership. All the same, Aaron Hill must have agreed in principle with Brant's plan, for his name appears promi-nently on the "deed" or agreement signed early in 1787 actually confirming the white settlers in possession of the "farms" they had already been granted.[13]

The disaffecteds' departure, for whatever reason, strengthened both Brant's grip on the valley and his resolve to have a proper survey undertaken to determine the precise limits of the tract. The survey, completed early in 1791, laid down that the "Bend of the [Grand] River easterly nearly two Miles from its Mouth ... & the Mohawk Village shall be the two fixed Points & that a straight line drawn from one of these points to the other shall form the Center Line of the Indian Lands ... & that two parallel lines to this Six Miles distant on each side of the ... River shall form the bounds between them" and the district earmarked for white settlement to the east.[14]

### The Nature of the Haldimand Grant of 1784

John Graves Simcoe, Upper Canada's first lieutenant-governor, appointed after the British restructured the ill-defined territory of western Quebec in 1791 as the new colony of Upper Canada, took issue with Brant's notions of what constituted the Six Nations' lands. Imbued with ambition and "enthusi-asms" and anxious to make his mark as an imperial administrator,[15] Simcoe made it clear that standing regulations precluded the Six Nations from con-veying their lands to anyone they chose; moreover, such sales might lead to those lands being exploited by unscrupulous "land jobbers." Brant bluntly retorted that the Six Nations were fully capable of protecting their own inter-ests. Second, they could easily sell some of their territory because they did not need it all – the tract being too large to be efficiently farmed by them alone. Finally, the sales were essential, as the Six Nations might have to depend on assured income from such transactions.[16]

These arguments about Joseph Brant's right to sell land appeared lost on Simcoe, however, and in 1793 he issued a patent or deed for the Grand River tract contrary to Brant's perception of it. It stated, in effect, that none of it could be disposed of, except through the good offices of the Crown;[17] the Indian lands, in short, did not form an estate in fee simple – Brant's contention – but a leasehold. Predictably, the angry chief refused to accept this patent, a move that prompted the acerbic Simcoe to threaten the "curtailment of [the tract] to one half of the River."[18] This threat, however, was not carried out. Indeed Simcoe himself revised his stand on prospective sales by urging the Six Nations, if they felt so obliged, to sell their lands to the "highest bidder" only. But just as obviously, the governor fully expected the Crown to have a supervisory role in the proceedings. On the other hand, Lord Dorchester, governor of Quebec and Simcoe's titular superior, whose edicts the lieutenant-governor of Upper Canada often tried to ignore, was prepared to be more liberal in his interpretation of the Six Nations' claims.[19] At any rate, convinced of the justice of his case, Brant, armed with a power of attorney from over thirty chiefs, sold off six large blocks, or roughly half the original grant, an area approximately 140 000 hectares in extent.

When Simcoe left the colony in 1796, the problem of land sales was thrown into the hands of his successor, the much less commanding Peter Russell, the administrator and president of the Executive Council. After Britain urged Russell to set Brant's transactions aside, the chief threatened an armed march on York, the colonial capital, and set out to exploit plausible rumours of a planned French attack on the St. Lawrence. The threats worked – British officials at York wanted no repeat of the Pontiac resistance. The military weakness of Russell in Upper Canada and the intervention on Brant's behalf of such highly placed persons as the British minister to the United States also helped to bring about the resolution of the problem. On 5 February 1798, the Crown formally sanctioned the land conveyances, a move that thoroughly delighted Brant, who remarked to a friend that "as to the title I believe there's no danger now."[20]

The chief was to be proved wrong. The decision taken in 1798, the authorities firmly asserted, did not confirm Brant's claim that the Indians' lands were held in fee simple and "absolutely" theirs. This assertion was brought to the attention of one John Norton (Teyoninhokarawen) when he went to England in 1804 to argue the Six Nations' case. An impressive and highly literate person of mixed Scottish and Cherokee blood, Norton was an adopted Mohawk who, while serving as an interpreter on the Grand River, had become Brant's close friend and confidant. Although politicians, reformers, and leaders of society received him well in Britain, Norton made no headway on the legal front and failed to change the bureaucracy's interpretation of the status of the Grand River lands. Norton's efforts were thwarted principally by the energetic opposition of officials in the Indian Department in Canada, notably his arch-rival, Col. William Claus, the deputy superintendent general. Claus, who plainly envied Norton's ability and popularity while despising his low social station,[21] also earned Brant's displeasure over the years.[22] The feud between Norton and Claus ended only with their deaths a generation later. Long before that, Brant himself died at his home on Burlington Bay, in November 1807, with the disagreement on the nature of the Six Nations' lands left unresolved.

### Joseph Brant's Attempts to Introduce British Culture among the Iroquois

With Norton's assistance, Brant had worked as well to secure the cultural and spiritual well-being of his followers, notably the "Christian Mohawk." Through his own exertions, timely help from Haldimand, and the labour of non-Native friends – the Smith and Thomas families – the Church of St. Paul, or the Mohawk Chapel, was put up in 1785, and plans laid for a school and the appointment of a teacher. The superintendent of Indian affairs, Sir John Johnson, endorsed these moves, for clearly they would help to strengthen the Indians' attachment to Britain. Another means of keeping Brant in "good humour" was the assignment to the Mohawk Chapel of the bulk of the "Queen Anne's Plate" (together with a pulpit cloth and two black tables), the ornate communion service presented to the Mohawk by that monarch three-quarters of a century earlier and displayed in their original church at Fort Hunter in the Mohawk valley.[23]

Brant, a devoted Anglican, did his utmost to promote Christianity on the Grand. In 1787 he helped to complete a new edition of the Mohawk Prayer Book, which included the chief's own translation of the Gospel of St. Mark. His confidant, Norton, in 1804 brought out for the British and Foreign Bible Society a Mohawk translation of the Gospel of St. John.[24] Brant failed, however, in his repeated efforts to secure a resident Church of England missionary for the Grand River. The remoteness of the area, faulty communications, and the demands facing the agency that was expected to provide this service – the Society for the Propagation of the Gospel (SPG) – were offered as excuses for ruling out the appointment. Brant continued to complain about the all-too-infrequent visits of, first, the itinerant John Stuart and then Robert Addison, who was posted at Niagara. Not until 1827 did Brant's sought-after resident missionary materialize.

Joseph Brant's home at the north end of Burlington Bay. A drawing by Eliza Field Jones.
From Peter Jones, *History of the Ojebway Indians* (London 1861), opposite 209

A mid-nineteenth-century sketch of the Mohawk Chapel at the Mohawk village at Grand River, by Eliza Field Jones, the wife of Kahkewaquonaby, or the Reverend Peter Jones.
From Peter Jones, *History of the Ojebway Indians* (London 1861), opposite 213

Furthermore, it had become all too apparent that the chief's varied attempts to have his people accept Christianity and to become acculturated to European ways were running into stiff opposition. Conservatives who feared a dangerous erosion of traditional Iroquoian values if Brant continued to have his way were strengthened by the teachings of Handsome Lake. At the turn of the century this legendary Seneca prophet inspired a well-received campaign to restore the Iroquois' time-honoured rites and in the process fashion what would later be called the religion of the Longhouse.[25]

## The Grand River Iroquois after Brant's Death

In the 1810s much else happened to shape the fortunes (and misfortunes) of the Six Nations Confederacy. Brant's death, the emergence of Norton as the Mohawk's war chief, the running feud between him and Claus, and the War of 1812, which sharpened that feud, were among the major flashpoints. The Confederacy's lacklustre response to the outbreak of war in 1812, which contrasted markedly with its involvement in the British Empire's earlier troubles, stemmed from a variety of factors. The twenty years spent adjusting to new circumstances in Upper Canada (a span in which its population had virtually stood still),[26] the dispute over lands and status, and the concern that the metropolis's interest in the Iroquois' problems was on the wane all contributed. And yet, while the Iroquois took little or no part in the battles at Detroit and Stoney Creek, they did participate, at considerable cost to themselves, in the important engagements at Queenston Heights, Fort Erie, and Beaver Dam. Even so, unflattering and, on the face of it, unfair references were often made to the Six Nations' wartime contributions, criticisms reinforced by the complaints of post-war travellers from overseas. The gist of the complaint, or in some cases lament, was that the Confederacy in the 1820s no longer exhibited those rough but nonetheless "noble" virtues characteristic of the eighteenth-century Iroquois.[27] Instead, they were seen to be degenerating under the impact of the more vicious aspects of European civilization and to be facing total extinction.

Arrayed against these mournful judgments were those missionary reports that abounded in hopeful assurances that the Iroquois could be rescued from oblivion by speedy conversions and proper care. To make the point, they also noted that the Six Nations' population had increased by about 20 percent (to approximately 2 200) since the last census taken before the War of 1812.[28] Among those reporting favourably were the Episcopal Methodists who established missions among the Oneida and built a schoolhouse for the Upper Mohawk at the Salt Springs in 1827.[29] Meanwhile the SPG, active on the frontier since Brant's day, had belatedly sent a resident missionary, William

Hough, to the valley the year before. Failing health abruptly shortened his career there, and within a year another agency, the New England Company, virtually took over from the society and appointed its own missionary to the so-called Mohawk Station. The company, based in London, which had been seeking to Christianize Aboriginal people in the older seaboard colonies since the seventeenth century, had after the American Revolution shifted its attentions first to New Brunswick and then to Upper Canada.

In 1827 it despatched to the Grand the Reverend Robert Lugger, an experienced educational missionary, who was anxious to establish schools in the Iroquois villages along the river. For a time he collaborated actively with Joseph Brant's son, John (Tekarihogen), the

Chief John Brant (1794–1832), son of Chief Joseph Brant.

From Thomas L. McKenney and James Hall, *History of the Indian Tribes of North America, with Biographical Sketches and Anecdotes of the Principal Chiefs*, 3 vols. (Philadelphia 1842–44), vol. 2, opposite 139, Metropolitan Toronto Reference Library, T15499

"head chief of the Mohawks,"[30] who, like his father, played a productive role in advancing the cultural interests of his people. Out of the collaboration came the preparation of a Mohawk grammar. Lugger's efforts among the already-Christianized Mohawk succeeded, but the missionary had great difficulty persuading sceptical Seneca, Onondaga, and Cayuga, particularly those who adhered to the religious code of Handsome Lake, to accept the Gospel. Lugger also had difficulties with the Methodists, who vigorously and imaginatively promoted their own missionary efforts among the Iroquois. In the end the Methodists received considerable backing from a sympathetic John Brant and from the so-called Upper Mohawk, who, it seems, became convinced that Lugger was trying to undermine the chief's authority.[31] The missionary heatedly denied the charge.

Though put off stride by the Methodists, Lugger scored a triumph of his own when he gathered support to found a school of industry for the Mohawk. This innovation would, to use his words, usher in the "civil improvement" deemed so essential to the religious variety. Unlike his Methodist contemporaries, Lugger was convinced that education ought to go hand in hand with conversion and not be a mere second step in the civilization of the Indian.[32] This led to the establishment in 1831 of the Mohawk Institute as a day school for instructing Iroquois youth in agriculture, basic trades, and domestic science. Four years later, as part of a plan to train a cadre of select young adults as teachers for their people, the institution was turned into a boarding school, one that survived for a century and a quarter.[33] Only with a school like the Mohawk Institute, Lugger and his backers argued, could the Grand River Iroquois prepare themselves to meet the challenge of living amidst an expanding settler community.

Indeed, by this time the non-Native presence in and beyond the valley had become highly visible. Brantford, so named by its inhabitants in 1827, had taken shape earlier in the decade. In 1830 the Indian land titles that its white citizens had long held were officially confirmed when the Mohawk handed over 320 hectares as a village plot. Another portion still unconfirmed was auctioned off on the Mohawk's behalf in 1831. The availability of new land and an ambitious canal project contributed to the town's commercial boom in that pre-railway age.

William Hamilton Merritt, the ebullient "projector" of the pioneering Welland Canal, which had begun operations in 1829, ushered in the new era. Merritt and his supporters, who wanted to enhance the natural advantages of the St. Lawrence River, discussed with officials at York the feasibility of doing the same for the Grand. After their undertaking received a charter as the Grand River Navigation Company, it obtained, with government approval, a pledge of funds from the Six Nations, a piece of business arranged without the knowledge of any responsible spokespersons for the Confederacy. It soon became apparent that the investment was ill-advised and produced no return for the Iroquois treasury, only angry recriminations and heavy financial losses.[34]

### The Consolidation of the Six Nations' Territory on the Grand River

Meanwhile, settlements continued to make heavy inroads on lands still occupied by the Six Nations. Apart from the agreement reached on Brantford in 1830, four other major surrenders were made over the next decade to accommodate the influx of non-Indians. In the next four years the townships of North and South Cayuga, together with Dunn Township and the remainder of Canborough and Moulton townships (which had been sold off when Blocks 5 and 6 had been conveyed in 1798), were surrendered to Mennonites and to settlers like John De Cou, a prominent miller from Niagara who went into lumbering and quarrying.

As white immigration increased, there was much unauthorized squatting on Indian lands and more and more unofficial transactions concluded between individual Iroquois and land-hungry non-Native purchasers. Although many of these were formally ratified after a special review in 1835, these agreements isolated the Indian settlements stretched out along the Grand River, making them vulnerable to further white incursions. This alarmed both the authorities and the Six Nations' leadership. In response, the government of Upper Canada passed an order-in-council, 27 November 1840, which recommended that the whole of the remaining Six Nations lands, apart from a compact bloc reserved for their exclusive benefit and free from white encroachment, be surrendered to the Crown. The lands outside the compact bloc would be evaluated and put on the market, with the proceeds earmarked for the Indians' betterment.[35] By this means the authorities hoped that the needs of white settlement would be met and that the Six Nations would benefit financially through the more intensive use of the lands remaining to them.

Samuel Peters Jarvis, who had been appointed Upper Canada's superintendent of Indian affairs in 1837, strongly advocated the scheme.[36] Clearly, some influential chiefs shared his enthusiasm, for on 18 January 1841 they readily agreed to sign the so-called surrender document that the eager superintendent had prepared for the occasion. The Six Nations' deputation comprised the influential John Smoke Johnson, a Mohawk veteran of the War of 1812 and the Rebellion of 1837, and six other chiefs who purportedly represented the other nations of the Confederacy.

But within days other Six Nations spokespersons denounced their action and charged that Jarvis had acted in a domineering manner. The Iroquois signatories were accused of failing to follow traditional procedures and of having spent insufficient time debating the issue. This Johnson strongly denied, and both he and Jarvis set out to discredit the opposition in turn, calling their credentials into question and alleging that the opponents of the scheme were being manipulated by an unscrupulous land speculator.[37] The row strongly echoed the factional struggle that had erupted earlier between the acculturated leadership – in this instance represented by Johnson – and the more conservative element at Grand River. The controversy led to great strife in the 1840s, and the issue, ever since the establishment of the reserve in 1847, has continued to agitate the Six Nations community (see chapters 9 and 10).

In any case, the 8 000 hectares originally contemplated for the reserve were almost tripled out of respect for the chiefs' fears that the smaller tract would not meet the varied requirements of all those Iroquois families who elected to settle on it. In all, the reserve, as confirmed in 1847, consisted of some 22 000 hectares, located primarily in the townships of Tuscarora, Oneida, and Onondaga.

## *NOTES*

1    Archives of Ontario (AO), Kerby Collection/Claus Papers, no. 6, John Deserontyon to Daniel Claus, 3 December 1778

2    Wisconsin State Historical Society, Draper MSS, 13F24; microfilm copies in Burlington (Ont.) Public Library

3    Ke-che-ah-gah-me-qua [Eliza Field Jones Carey], *Sketch of the Life of Captain Joseph Brant, Thayendanegea* (Montreal 1872), 7

4    Barbara Graymont, "Thayendanegea," *Dictionary of Canadian Biography*, vol. 5: *1801–1820* (Toronto 1983), 803–12

5    Draper MSS, 13DF35

6    Ibid., 13F72

7    Charles M. Johnston, ed., *The Valley of the Six Nations: A Collection of Documents on the Indian Lands of the Grand River*, 2d ed. (Toronto 1971), 41–51

8    Draper MSS, 12F29–30

9    Ibid., 13F113

10    Johnston, *Valley of the Six Nations*, 52

11    Isabel T. Kelsay, *Joseph Brant: Man of Two Worlds* (Syracuse 1984), 621

12    Ibid., 427–8

13    Johnston, *Valley of the Six Nations*, 70–1

14    Ibid., 57

15    S.R. Mealing, "The Enthusiasms of John Graves Simcoe," Canadian Historical Association, *Report*, 1958, 50–62

16    William L. Stone, *Life of Joseph Brant-Thayendanegea*, 2 vols. (New York 1838; reprint, New York 1969), 2:397

17    National Archives of Canada (NA), Q329, 91

18    Ernest A. Cruikshank, ed., *Correspondence of Lieutenant-Governor John Graves Simcoe with Allied Documents*, 5 vols. (Toronto 1923–31), 2:114–16

19    Johnston, *Valley of the Six Nations*, 81–2; Draper MSS, 12F39–391

20    New York Historical Society, O'Reilly Collection, vol. 12, Joseph Brant to Israel Chapin, 16 June 1797. For the diplomatic and military background to these events, see S.F. Wise, "The Indian Diplomacy of John Graves Simcoe," Canadian Historical Association, *Report*, 1953, 36–44; and Bradford Perkins, *The First Rapprochement: England and the United States, 1795–1805* (Philadelphia 1955).

21    C.F. Klinck and J.J. Talman, eds., *The Journal of Major John Norton, 1816* (Toronto 1970), cxii

22    Draper MSS, 13F72

23    J.W. Lydekker, *The Faithful Mohawks* (Cambridge 1938)

24    Klinck and Talman, *The Journal of Major John Norton, 1816*, xlvii–xlviii

25    For an admirable discussion of these themes, see Anthony F.C. Wallace, *The Death and Rebirth of the Seneca* (New York 1969). Also helpful are Annemarie A. Shimony, "Conservatism among the Iroquois at the Six Nations Reserve," *Yale University Publications in Anthropology* 65 (1961): 203ff.; and Sally M. Weaver, "Seth Newhouse and the Grand River Confederacy," in M.K. Foster, J. Campisi, and M. Mithun, eds., *Extending the Rafters: Interdisciplinary Approaches to Iroquoian Studies* (Albany 1984), 165–82.

26  NA, Claus Papers, 10:29–30
27  John Howison, *Sketches of Upper Canada, Domestic, Local and Characteristic* (Edinburgh 1821), 161–4
28  Six Nations Agency Office, Statistical Report for 1827
29  Elizabeth Graham, *Medicine Man to Missionary: Missionaries as Agents of Change among the Indians of Southern Ontario, 1784–1867* (Toronto 1975), 20
30  Draper MSS, 13F25; Isabel Kelsay, "Tekarihogen," *Dictionary of Canadian Biography*, vol. 6: *1821–1835* (Toronto 1987), 760–2
31  Charles M. Johnston, "To the Mohawk Station: The Making of a New England Company Missionary – The Rev. Robert Lugger," in Foster, Campisi, and Mithun, eds., *Extending the Rafters*, 77–8
32  J.D. Wilson, "No Blanket to Be Worn in School: The Education of Indians in Early Nineteenth Century Ontario," *Social History/Histoire Sociale* 7 (1974): 293–305
33  New England Company Papers, 1923, 148–9. Today the Woodland Cultural Centre is located at the site, in the renovated Mohawk Institute.
34  See B.E. Hill, "The Grand River Navigation Company and the Six Nations Indians," *Ontario History* 63 (1971): 32–40
35  This section is based on material in NA, RG 10 (Indian Affairs), particularly vol. 505, 185–6; vol. 506, 88. See also NA, CO 42, "Report on the Affairs of the Indians in Canada, part i, 1844," vol. 515. The Samuel Peters Jarvis Papers at the Metropolitan Toronto Reference Library (MTRL) were also useful, B 58, pp. 249–50, 253ff.; B 59, pp. 30–2.
36  Jarvis's chequered career is examined in J. Douglas Leighton and Robert J. Burns, "Samuel Peters Jarvis," *Dictionary of Canadian Biography,* vol. 8: *1851–1860* (Toronto 1985), 430–3. He was suspended from his office in 1845 on the grounds of incompetence and financial irregularities.
37  John Smoke Johnson's statement at a meeting at the Johnson Settlement, 20 February 1841, NA, CO 42, vol. 516, Report on the Affairs of the Indians in Canada, Appendix 16, pp. 222–3. For information on the Indians' protests and criticisms of the surrenders of 1841, see MTRL, Jarvis Papers, B 59, pp. 30–2; NA, RG 10, vol. 506, p. 88. For references to the authorities' repudiation of the opponents of the surrender, consult MTRL, Jarvis Papers, B 58, pp. 249–50, 253ff.; NA, RG 10, vol. 505, pp. 185–6.

# 9 The Iroquois:
# The Consolidation of the Grand River Reserve in the Mid-Nineteenth Century, 1847–1875

SALLY M. WEAVER

## Introduction[1]

The Grand River community has many features that set it apart from other First Nations bands in Canada and other Iroquoian communities on the continent. When the Six Nations left their national villages along the Grand River and settled together in 1847, they established the most populous reserve in Canada and the largest Iroquoian settlement in North America. For the first time in Iroquoian history, all the nations – Mohawk, Oneida, Onondaga, Cayuga, Seneca, and Tuscarora – lived together in one community. Because of this consolidation, the Six Nations Confederacy Council became the natural vehicle to govern the Six Nations, unlike the situation on other Iroquoian reserves in Ontario, where the councils of individual nations persisted, or on the reservations in New York State, where the Confederacy was not rejuvenated following the Revolutionary War.

Despite the government's ill-fated investment of their funds in the Grand River Navigation Company, the Grand River Iroquois were also the wealthiest band in Canada during the nineteenth century. From the sale of their lands along the river between 1830 and 1853, they created a band fund of over $800 000. From this fund they paid salaries to their own superintendent, interpreter, forest warden, doctors, and teachers. As well, because the majority of the band's members adopted Christianity and took to farming in an energetic way, the Indian Department considered the reserve its showpiece, a highly successful example of Indian adjustment to Canadian society. At the same time the community contained a small but strong core of Longhouse followers, those who adhered to the more traditional form of Iroquoian culture in fuller fashion than Iroquois on other reserves on the continent. Thus, the Grand River reserve has always been a populous, multinational, and wealthy First Nations community, containing striking contrasts between the culturally conservative Longhouse people and the more acculturated Christians. The reserve community was consolidated in the mid-nineteenth century under the Confederacy Council's direction.

## Establishing the Reserve Community, 1847–1857

By the 1830s the depletion of their lands threatened to leave the Six Nations people scattered along the river on isolated pockets of land, more vulnerable to land speculators than in the past (see chapter 8, Map 8.1). Following the government's decision to consolidate the Six Nations in one continuous tract, the chiefs, in January 1841, surrendered the remaining lands to the Crown for sale, with the exception of 8 000 hectares to be set aside for a reserve as well as the farms then occupied by Indian families along the river.[2] Shortly after this a number of the chiefs, worried that the reserve would be too small, convinced the government to nearly triple the reserve in size.[3] Thus, in 1847, when the families settled on the tract along the Grand River valley, the reserve contained over 22 000 hectares of land.

### The New Reserve

As most of the over 2 200 Iroquois lived near Brantford, the chiefs asked that the reserve be located there, on the south side of the river, between present-day Brantford and Caledonia. Since then the reserve has occupied all of Tuscarora Township and the southern part of Onondaga Township, both in Brant County, and the western part of Oneida Township in the Haldimand-Norfolk region. (See Map 8.1.) Subsequent land surrenders during the nineteenth century, including the 2 400 hectares in the southeast corner granted the Mississauga (Ojibwa) of the New Credit in 1847, reduced the original 22 000 hectares to its current size of 17 960 hectares. Additional small parcels of land, totalling 111 hectares, still belong to the Six Nations within the city limits of Brantford.

With the decision to consolidate all the nations on one territory, the Six Nations people had to abandon their separate villages, now encircled by settlers, along the Grand River. The Iroquois left behind their cleared fields, their log cabins, and other improvements. In moving to the new reserve (surveyed in 1842 in preparation for their relocation), once again they faced the problem of clearing the land, for the reserve was heavily forested with maple, oak, beech, and some white pine.

In preparation for the resettlement, the chiefs asked the government to appoint a local superintendent to manage their affairs, and as with other band management expenses, they agreed to pay the salary of this individual from their band funds. Subsequently, the Indian Department in 1844 appointed David Thorburn, who served as the Six Nations' visiting superintendent until his retirement in 1862. The designation of "visiting" superintendent was quite appropriate, as Thorburn lived in Queenston, visiting the Six Nations mainly for council meetings. While his immediate job was to manage the resettlement, Thorburn's overall responsibility was to represent the authority of the government to the Six Nations. He enforced government legislation and acted as the major communication link between the community and the Indian Department.

The task of settling the Six Nations with a minimum of hardship fell jointly to the chiefs and Thorburn. Together they had to make policies, for example, on who should be allotted land, what size the lots should be, and whether or not the nations should be settled in separate areas of the reserve. But before they could do all this, they had to remove the squatters.

*Squatters*

White squatters had moved onto the reserve mainly between 1839 and 1844 and had occupied many of the newly surveyed plots.[4] Having worked hard to clear small parcels of land and build shanties and log houses, they resisted relocation.[5] Their opposition made their eviction costly and sometimes dangerous. Some did not want to abandon the land they had improved even after receiving appropriate compensation. Still others, after eviction, returned to the reserve to remove the timber from their improvements for which they had received compensation.[6] Determined to keep their farms, squatters repeatedly petitioned the Legislative Assembly of Canada and appealed to the courts. The courts failed to defend Iroquois interests. The Six Nations, in fact, even had to pay for improvements made by squatters who had settled on the reserve after the government posted notices of eviction in 1844.[7]

Although the eviction process was unpleasant, especially in the few instances of squatters defending their property with firearms, most of the 157 squatter families were evicted by 1853 – but at a considerable cost to the Six Nations.[8] The monies paid the squatters for their improvements came from the Six Nations' band funds. In theory those Iroquois families who took possession of squatters' farms were to repay the cost of the improvements to the band funds, but in practice the chiefs did not enforce the repayments. Consequently, the council recovered very little of the £8 000 ($32 000) in eviction costs.

*Assigning Land*

Once the removal of squatters was under way, the chiefs began assigning reserve land to Six Nations members. Between the spring of 1847 and the end of 1848, they and Thorburn systematically allocated forty-hectare plots to most Six Nations families. The few families of Delaware, Nanticoke, and Tutelo, all allied groups, received land as easily as the Six Nations people. Although the chiefs and Thorburn completed most of the assignments by 1848, as late as 1851 a few families were still moving onto the reserve from their villages down-river.[9]

Despite the visiting superintendent's preference for settling the various nations in separate locations, the chiefs argued against it, since intermarriage was extensive.[10] The final settlement pattern, however, did reveal heavy concentrations of individual groups in certain areas of the reserve.[11] In general, the Cayuga, Seneca, and Onondaga settled in the northeastern part of the reserve known today as "down below," a designation reflecting these groups' original location down-river. The upper tribes – the Mohawk, Tuscarora, and Oneida – were concentrated in the central and western areas referred to today as "up above." Because the upper tribes became predominantly Christian during the nineteenth century, the term "upper end" is often used by the Six Nations to refer to the more acculturated Christian element in the community. In the same fashion, the term "lower end" is applied to the predominantly Longhouse area of the reserve, where the conservative culture is still maintained.[12]

Although a few Six Nations families lived in Onondaga Township, on the north side of the river, this part of the reserve remained unallotted at this time.[13] The Indian Department preferred to concentrate the people on the main body of the reserve, but its effort to discourage Indian occupation of the area on the north side failed, as did its efforts to persuade the chiefs to surrender this part of the reserve in 1848.[14]

The question of who should receive land on the reserve arose at the outset of the allotment process. Thorburn wanted only the Six Nations people to occupy the land, but the chiefs, in fact, assigned some plots to whites and a few black families, stipulating that the blacks must remain on the lands assigned them and not move elsewhere on the reserve.[15] In these instances the families had developed friendship and kinship ties with the Six Nations people, and the chiefs saw no need to deny them a place in the new community. The more difficult cases arose with mixed marriages, mostly of Mohawk women to white men. Here, again, the chiefs overruled Thorburn and assigned land to the families in the name of the Indian wife. Thus, by 1851, 325 nuclear families, including widows with children, had received plots, with nearly half of them having teams of oxen or horses for clearing the land.[16] (See Table 9.1.)

*Farming*

With the reserve lands assigned, families now re-established their farms. This required almost seven years of toil, fraught with the risks of drought and frost.[17] By 1857 the community had cleared less than 10 percent of the land for cultivation and pasture. The hardship of farming was further complicated by the difficulties of obtaining cash for seed if insufficient seed grain had been set aside the previous fall, or if smut damaged the preserved seed during winter storage. For cash the Six Nations depended heavily on their annuities, the spring and fall distribution of their interest monies that came from the capital fund after the costs for administering the reserve were deducted. The community used the interest monies, amounting to $12 a person in the 1850s, to purchase seed for spring planting and to ease distress in the winter if the fall harvest was poor.

During the 1850s the Six Nations' farming practices resembled those of the neighbouring white farmers. In some instances, however, Iroquois farmers took less care with seed grain and tended to run short of fodder for cattle before the spring pasture season.[18] Barns were not yet common and the Iroquois farmers often turned their livestock out of the sheds to browse in unfenced areas earlier in the spring than was the case among local non-Native farmers. In addition, subsistence gardening was more prevalent among the Longhouse families than among the Christians at the upper end of the reserve. While some of the advanced Mohawk farmers began marketing oats, wheat, and barley, cash was not easily obtainable. Those who farmed needed to establish credit with local white merchants, for no stores existed on the reserve. By the mid-1850s the lack of credit off the reserve had created a new set of problems.

*Debts*

The Indian Protection Act of 1850, drafted purposely to protect First Nations land and property, prohibited non-Indians from holding Indians responsible for debts if they lived on reserves.[19] The same legislation also prohibited the seizure of goods purchased by Indians from their annuities as payment for debts. Although merchants around the reserve knew of this legislation, they continued to advance credit to the Six Nations people, especially to the well-to-do families. When the amount of the Indian debt, however, continued to rise and Brant County merchants failed to receive payment, they petitioned

Table 9.1
Population by Nation

| | 1785 | 1810 | 1843 | 1857 | 1875 | 1900 | 1910 | 1920 | 1930 | 1949 | 1970 | 1973 |
|---|---|---|---|---|---|---|---|---|---|---|---|---|
| Mohawk | 464 | 451 | 793 | 933 | 1 020 | 1 615 | 1 827 | 1 893 | 1 866 | 2 400 | 3 783 | 3 974 |
| Cayuga | 381 | 408 | 421 | 470 | 801 | 991 | 1 041 | 1 127 | 1 165 | 1 344 | 2 354 | 2 525 |
| Onondaga | 245 | 196 | 283 | 267 | 339 | 343 | 364 | 371 | 322 | 346 | 542 | 560 |
| Tuscarora | 129 | 289 | 192 | 209 | 266 | 382 | 416 | 444 | 431 | 487 | 780 | 789 |
| Oneida | 162 | 141 | 199 | 172 | 217 | 330 | 367 | 378 | 396 | 551 | 786 | 802 |
| Seneca | 78 | 212 | 107 | 105 | 190 | 214 | 217 | 235 | 237 | 228 | 333 | 345 |
| Delaware | 231 | 41 | 127 | 87 | 113 | 164 | 170 | 167 | 171 | 179 | 255 | 256 |
| Nanticoke | 11 | 82 | 47 | 76 | 25 | — | — | — | — | — | — | — |
| Tutelo | 74 | 9 | 40 | — | — | — | — | — | — | — | — | — |
| Other | 68 | 27 | — | — | 4 | — | — | — | — | — | — | — |
| Total | 1 843 | 1 856 | 2 223* | 2 319 | 2 975 | 4 039 | 4 402 | 4 615** | 4 588 | 5 535 | 8 833 | 9 251 |

\*    There is a discrepancy between the total (2,223) in the original census and the actual total (2,209).
\*\*   The 1920 census contains the phrase "less 4 included twice = 4611" after the total.

*Sources:* The census figures for 1785 come from Charles M. Johnston, ed., *The Valley of the Six Nations* (Toronto 1964), 52; for 1810 from Johnston, *Valley*, 281; for 1843 from Johnston, *Valley*, 307; for 1857 from Six Nations Agency, Council Minutes, February 1857, 141; for 1875, 1900, 1910, 1920, 1930, and 1949 from Six Nations Agency Archives, Extracts from Paylists, on December of each of the cited years; and for 1970 and 1973 from the Six Nations Agency, Official Band Lists, 31 December of each year cited.

the Legislative Assembly to repeal the Indian Protection Act. Although they failed to have the statute repealed, their intimidation was effective. Twice during that decade, in 1854 and again in 1858, the chiefs agreed to pay the personal debts of their band members from the interest monies.[20]

The procedure for settling the debts proved time-consuming. The Indian Department appointed a special commissioner, usually a local business person from Brantford, to screen the debts to ensure that Indians were not being overcharged. If the receipts were in order, the commissioner then issued the amount, at the same time cautioning the merchant not to expect similar treatment in the future. When, in 1859, the total debt of $17 000 had been repaid, the chiefs complained about the inequity of the procedure.[21] The debts paid had been those of the wealthier Indian families whom the traders had trusted, while the poorer families, not advanced credit, suffered even more, as their payments were withheld that year to pay the debts of the wealthy. Thereafter both Thorburn and the chiefs admonished the community to avoid building up debts. As the merchants became more cautious in advancing credit, the Six Nations families took greater care to establish a good credit rating at the local stores. By the end of the century a good reputation with merchants was a source of considerable pride in the families as well as a necessity in carrying on their farming activities.

*Resources*

A few unscrupulous whites and Six Nations men not disposed to farming profited by illegally cutting and selling timber from the reserve for the railroad construction business. The government prohibited the commercial sale of timber from the reserve unless it had been licensed by the superintendent, but the timber on a family's land could be used for building houses, sheds, fences, and barns. Compared to farming, timber sales produced quick cash with little effort, and as the years passed, the timber regulations, which the chiefs initially opposed, proved almost impossible to enforce.[22] At night, with a full moon, timber was easily cut and hauled onto barges to be taken downriver for sale. In the rare instances in which the timber predators were apprehended, the costs of prosecuting proved so high that the money returned to the Six Nations' band fund was minimal. In 1874, for instance, only $33 was deposited in the band fund after the sale of $400 worth of illegally cut timber.[23] By the late 1860s most of the commercially valuable stands of white pine had been cut on the reserve and the superintendent no longer felt that enforcing the regulations was realistic.

With the exception of timber, which the chiefs and Six Nations people clearly saw as each family's private property, other resources on the reserve were treated as communal property. The sulphur springs, called Sour Springs, were reserved for the use of all band members who valued their medicinal qualities. Gravel deposits were rented to non-Indians, the rental fees being returned to the band fund.

## The Council

Despite differences over timber conservation, the chiefs and their determined and forceful superintendent generally worked well together. Thorburn, whom the chiefs referred to as "Old Ironsides," used a range of tactics, from cajoling to coercion, to persuade the chiefs to decide issues as he preferred. But the chiefs firmly defended their prized autonomy. As a result, the chiefs usually disregarded Thorburn's request to use precedents to guide council decisions. The chiefs preferred to handle each individual case on its own merits.

The creation of the multi-national Six Nations Reserve in 1847, together with the government's policy of indirect rule, gave the Confederacy Council legitimacy in both the community and the Indian Department. When the Iroquois resettled along the Grand River over half a century earlier, they reconstituted the Confederacy Council, creating a Canadian counterpart to the old council at Onondaga (New York), which collapsed at the outbreak of the Revolutionary War. During the pre-reservation period at Grand River (1785–1846) the national councils of the individual nations governed their respective villages, allocating land and settling internal disputes.[24] The entire Confederacy Council before 1847 met only for matters affecting the Six Nations as a whole, such as land transactions or dealings with the Grand River Navigation Company. After 1847 the full council condemned separate meetings of the national councils as divisive.

With the partial exception of the smaller Seneca and Oneida nations, hereditary chiefs continued to be appointed to the full council at Grand River. The ideal number of fifty chiefs in the official roll call[25] was greatly augmented by the appointment of assistant chiefs, men in line for hereditary positions but who held, theoretically, second place to the principal chiefs. In addition, there were a few appointments of self-made chiefs, or to use the Six Nations term, "Pine Tree" chiefs; these were men of outstanding abilities, often with oratorical skills and sound judgment. Finally, the council contained a few war chiefs, men such as the Mohawk's John Smoke Johnson, who had fought with the British in the War of 1812. Although the principal chiefs were in theory the most important, in practice at Grand River the assistant chiefs and the self-made chiefs played an equally powerful role. In the final analysis, personal ability, not official status, became the basis for influence and respect in the council. This applied as well to the chiefs from the dependent nations.

In the conventional lore of the Confederacy, the chiefs from the dependent nations – the Tuscarora, Delaware, Tutelo, and Nanticoke – had lesser status and were not included in the elaborate condolence ceremony, which mourned the death of a hereditary chief and installed his successor.[26] In theory, they could speak on issues only through their host nations, the Cayuga and Oneida. In practice, however, these chiefs played a full role. They deliberated openly on particular matters, voted on the allocation of funds, accompanied official delegations, and held council offices such as that of secretary. The dependent nations also appointed assistant chiefs and had war chiefs, but they did not appoint self-made chiefs. Thus, even though the status of the chiefs from the dependent nations was less than that of the chiefs from the original five nations, at times their influence was just as great.

The actual number of chiefs at Grand River invariably exceeded the normal number of fifty. From 1864, when the first official list of chiefs is available,[27] to the turn of the century, the total number of chiefs appointed at any one time ranged between sixty-two and seventy-six (see Tables 9.2 and 9.3). The high number was due to the appointment of assistant chiefs, for there were only nine self-made Pine Tree chiefs during the last half of the nineteenth century and the number of war chiefs gradually diminished as the old veterans died. The dependent nations, not included in the original roster, also appointed chiefs. The Nanticoke normally had two chiefs, the Delaware two, the Tuscarora four, and the Tutelo one. (Only the Tutelo eventually lost their representation in council when extensive intermarriage, primarily with the Cayuga and Tuscarora,[28] led to the loss of their official status on the band lists.)

The more populous nations – the Mohawk, Cayuga, and Tuscarora – had little difficulty in filling vacancies when a chief died, but the less numerous Seneca and Oneida often had fewer chiefs than they were entitled to appoint. In some cases, particularly among the Seneca, the titles were "extinct" because they had never been filled at Grand River after the resettlement in 1784. In other cases, the families lacked male heirs for the matrons to appoint and, for various reasons, these titles were not filled by men "borrowed" from related lineages within a clan as custom allowed. In a very few instances, disagreements over who should be appointed, or over which matrons held the right of appointment, caused vacancies. In general, however, the Confederacy Council was viable. Families were proud of owning chieftain titles, and as the century passed, the vacancies caused by death and occasionally by impeachment for improper conduct were readily filled.

In the historic condolence ceremony, new chiefs were "raised up" by one of the two moieties among the Grand River Iroquois. The ceremony was held in the Lower Cayuga Longhouse if the deceased chiefs belonged to the

Table 9.2
Official List of Chiefs, 1864
*Principal and Assistant Chiefs*

| No. | Name | Nation/Group |
|---|---|---|
| PC* No. 1. | Joseph Lewis, Principal Chief | Mohawks Upper |
| Mud Turtle – PC 2. | James Givens | " |
| – PC 3. | Nicholas Burning | " |
| Bear – PC 4. | Isaac Hill | " |
| 5. | Jacob Carpenter | " |
| 6. | David Carpenter | " |
| Wolf – PC 7. | John Carpenter acting for David's son | " |
| Bear – PC 8. | Isaac Lewis | " |
| Bear – PC 9. | Jacob Hill, Bay of Quinte | " |
| 10. | Joseph Fraser | " |
| 11. | David Hill Farmer | " |
| 12. | Peter Burning & Moses Walker 1 PC Wolf | " |
| 13. | John Smoke Johnson | Mohawk Lower |
| 14. | Nicholas H. Burning | " |
| Wolf – PC 15. | Geo. H.M. Johnson not acting | " |
| 16. | Joseph Johnson | " |
| 17. | Henry Clench | Aughawaga |
| 18. | Jacob General | Peter Green |
| 19. | Joseph Porter | " |
| 20. | Nicodemus Porter | " |
| 21. | John Buck | Onondaga Clear Sky |
| 22. | Geo. Buck | " |
| 23. | Aaron Hill | " |
| 24. | Isaac Hill | " |
| 25. | William Buck | " |
| 26. | David John | " |
| 27. | John Gibson | " |
| 28. | Peter Key | " |
| 29. | Joseph Snow | " |
| 30. | Powless Henry | " |
| 31. | John Williams | " |
| 32. | Jacob Johnson | Oneida Joseph |
| 33. | Peter Odasade | " |
| 34. | Peter John | Barefoot Onondaga |
| 35. | Jacob Jamieson | Upper Cayuga |
| 36. | John General | " |
| 37. | Abram S. Hill | " |
| 38. | Isaac Jacobs | " |
| 39. | Nelson Martin | " |
| 40. | David Hill Jacket | " |
| 41. | Isaac Aughawaga | " |
| PC 42. | Joseph Monture | Lower Cayuga |
| 43. | George Monture | " |
| 44. | John Warner | " |
| 45. | John Hill | " |
| 46. | William Jacobs | " |
| 47. | William Henry | " |
| PC 48. | John Fishcarrier | " |
| PC 49. | Jacob Silversmith | " |
| 50. | James Monture | " |
| 51. | John Skyler | " |
| 52. | John Obediah | Tuscarora |
| 53. | Jacob Williams | " |
| 54. | William Green | " |
| 55. | Thomas Isaac | " |
| 56. | William Johnson | " |
| 57. | Sage Harris | " |
| 58. | David Hill Seneca | Kanadaga Seneca |
| 59. | Jacob Hill Seneca | " |
| 60. | Seneca Johnson | " |
| 61. | Cornelius Anderson | Nanticokes |
| 62. | William Longfish | Young Family |
| 63. | James Latham | Nanticokes Old Family |
| 64. | John Wilson | Delawares |
| 65. | John Cayuga | " |
| 66. | Abm. Maracle | Bay of Quinte Mohawk |

*Source:* Six Nations Agency Minute Book, 1864–67, 1–3

* PC = Principal Chief

Cayuga, Oneida, or dependent nations (known as the younger nations moiety), or in the Onondaga Longhouse if the chiefs were of the older nations – the Onondaga, Mohawk, or Seneca. As tradition prescribed, the bereaved chiefs were offered the condolences of those of the other moiety, who admonished them to wipe away their sorrow and recall the purpose of the League and the great peace, established by Deganawidah. Noted ritualists conducted the elaborate ceremony, which began with the mourning nations welcoming the condoling chiefs at the wood's edge, near the longhouse. It continued through the condoling chant and the recitation of the "laws" of the League, and ended with the charge given the new chiefs to learn the ways of the council and act in the best interests of the entire Confederacy.[29] In the 1870s and 1880s, the Onondaga chief John Buck, the wampum keeper, and the young Seneca chief John A. Gibson were the ritual leaders for the elder nations, both men being prominent Longhouse chiefs and well respected in the council. For

Table 9.3
Number of Chiefs Appointed to Council, 1847–1899

|  | 1847[1] | 1864[2] | 1867[3] | 1875[4] | 1881[5] | 1895[6] | 1897[7] | 1899[8] |
|---|---|---|---|---|---|---|---|---|
| Mohawk | 15 | 18 | 18 | 15 | 21 | 20 | 16 | 13 |
| Oneida | 5 | 6 | 8 | 4 | 4 | 12 | 10 | 9 |
| Onondaga | 9 | 12 | 12 | 18 | 15 | 15 | 15 | 14 |
| Cayuga | 11 | 17 | 25 | 18 | 15 | 14 | 16 | 15 |
| Seneca | 5 | 3 | 3 | 8 | 5 | 8 | 7 | 5 |
| Tuscarora | 8 | 6 | 5 | 7 | 4 | 4 | 3 | 5 |
| Delaware | 2 | 2 | 3 | 0 | 1 | 1 | 1 | 1 |
| Nanticoke | 1 | 3 | 1 | 0 | 2 | 2 | 2 | 0 |
| Tutelo | 1 | 0 | 0 | 0 | 1 | 0 | 0 | 0 |
| Total | 57 | 67 | 75 | 70 | 68 | 76 | 70 | 62 |

1  Council Minutes, 1847–48, compiled from attendance record

2  Council Minute Book, 1864–67, 1–3

3  Council Minute Book, 1867–72, 50–2

4  List of chiefs in petition of chiefs to David Laird, superintendent general of Indian affairs, 18 January 1875, NA, RG 10, Red series, vol. 1949

5  Council Minute Book, 1878–83, 125–6

6  Six Nations Agency Archives, Chiefs Distribution Book, 1890–1907, 44–5

7  E.M. Chadwick, *The People of the Longhouse* (Toronto 1897), 86–96

8  Department of Indian Affairs Annual Report for 1899 (Ottawa), 571

the younger nations, Cayuga chiefs William Wage (Pine Tree), the council's forest bailiff, Jacob Silversmith, and Joseph Montour performed the same duties.[30] As a memory device, the Cayuga used a condolence cane containing fifty pegs, each accompanied by a pictograph representing the fifty chiefs in the proper order of the roll call.[31] In more modern times the Onondaga side tended to use kernels of corn, placed in a certain order, for the same purpose,[32] but most of their ritual leadership in the late 1800s came from the young blind chief John A. Gibson (1849–1912), whose remarkable memory needed no prodding and whose knowledge of the League's lore surpassed that of all others.[33]

Given the nature of hereditary appointments, men were sometimes made chiefs who had little interest in political affairs or the reserve in general. When one considers as well other factors, such as old age, ill health, transportation difficulties, and farming demands, it is not surprising that the actual attendance of chiefs at the council meetings during the 1840s and 1850s averaged between twenty and thirty. When matters of a controversial nature were discussed, the attendance increased to over forty chiefs. Aside from the sustained session in 1847–48, when the chiefs allotted land to families, meetings occurred three to four times a year, usually for several days at one sitting. The chiefs made their way on foot or horseback to the Onondaga council house in Middleport and boarded with local residents for the duration of the session.

Councils were called either by Thorburn when he wished to introduce new business or by the chiefs when they wanted information or wished to bring issues to the visiting superintendent's attention. Although Thorburn technically presided over the session, the chiefs handled business in their traditional way and reported the decision through the interpreter to the clerk, who prepared the official minutes in English. The Onondaga firekeeper, usually Chief Echo, opened the meeting by welcoming the gathering. The speaker of council, the eminent Mohawk chief John Smoke Johnson, then announced the items for discussion. (See Table 9.4, page 194.) The Mohawk and Seneca chiefs first discussed each matter, and upon reaching a decision "passed it across the fire" to the Cayuga and Oneida chiefs on the opposite side of the house, who reviewed it together with the chiefs from the dependent nations. They reported their decision to the Mohawk speaker of council for consideration by the Onondaga chiefs. If the decision was unanimous and considered by the Onondaga chiefs to be beneficial to the council and the Six Nations people, the Onondaga chiefs simply announced the verdict, but if disagreement had surfaced among the chiefs, they referred the matter back for further consideration in the hope of achieving unanimity. Even with unanimous decision, however, if the Onondaga chiefs considered it harmful to the people, they could refuse to sanction it and urge reconsideration.

Table 9.4
Six Nations Council Officers

*Interpreter*

| Chief Peter Smith | Mohawk | ? | 1840s–59 |
|---|---|---|---|
| Chief George H.M. Johnson | Mohawk | PC* | 1859–83 |
| Chief Alexander G. Smith | Mohawk | AC** | 1883–87 |
| (Warrior) William Reep | | | 1887–97 |
| Chief William Smith | Mohawk | AC/PC | 1897–1923 |

*Secretary*

| Chief Josiah Hill | Nanticoke | PC | 1880–1915 |
|---|---|---|---|
| Chief David Jamieson | Cayuga | PC | 1915 pro tem |
| Asa R. Hill | | | 1915–22 |
| Arthur Anderson | Tuscarora | | 1922 pro tem |
| David S. Hill | Seneca | | 1922–24 |

*Speaker of Council*

| Chief John Smoke Johnson | Mohawk | Pine Tree | 1858–70s |
|---|---|---|---|
| Chief Nicholas H. Burning | Mohawk | Pine Tree | 1870s–92 |
| Chief David Hill Seneca | Seneca | PC | 1892–98 |
| Chief Alexander G. Smith | Mohawk | AC | 1898 |
| Chief Elias Lewis | Mohawk | PC | 1898–1903 |
| Chief John Charles Martin | Mohawk | Pine Tree | 1903–16 |
| Chief Alexander G. Smith | Mohawk | PC | 1916–17 |
| Chief William D. Loft | Mohawk | PC | 1917–18 |
| Chief Andrew Staats | Mohawk | PC | 1918–22 |
| Chief Levi General | Cayuga | PC | 1922–24 |

*Deputy Speaker of Council*

| Chief Nicholas H. Burning | Mohawk | Pine Tree | 1870s |
|---|---|---|---|
| Chief David Hill Seneca | Seneca | PC | 1880s–92 |
| Chief John Buck | Onondaga | PC | 1892–93 |
| Chief David Thomas | Mohawk | PC | 1894–98 |
| Chief Nicodemus Porter | Oneida | PC | 1898–1903 |
| Chief Jacob S. Johnson | Oneida | Regent | 1903–16 |
| Chief Jacob General | Cayuga | | 1916–17 |
| Chief Andrew Staats | Mohawk | | 1917 |
| Chief Daniel McNaughton | Cayuga | PC | 1917-18 |
| Chief Levi General | Cayuga | PC | 1918–22 |
| Chief Chancey Garlow | Mohawk | AC | 1922–24 |

\* PC = Principal Councillor
\*\* AC = Assistant Councillor
*Source:* Sally M. Weaver, from Six Nations Council Minutes and other archival sources

Given the large size of the council, the achievement of consensus required extensive periods of deliberation, sometimes even days. Thorburn often left the chiefs on their own for that time, returning when they were ready to announce their decision or when they wished him to clarify a point. The chiefs deliberated mainly in Mohawk, the council's official language. Henry Andrews, the clerk, then recorded the decision in English in the Six Nations' minute book, as did his successor, Nanticoke chief Josiah Hill, the council's first secretary (1880–1915).

During the 1840s and 1850s, Peter Smith, a Mohawk chief, held the crucial office of interpreter. Although some chiefs spoke English, primarily those from the upper tribes, few could read or write it, and the interpreter had to be trusted to deliver an unambiguous translation of the chiefs' decision to the superintendent. He also conveyed the superintendent's directives and information to the chiefs and was generally responsible for giving the superintendent an accurate view of the chiefs' concerns. Because the job of interpreting brought power, prestige, and a good salary, many chiefs coveted the post.

National Archives of Canada, c-85137

Iroquois chiefs from the Six Nations community, Grand River, with wampum belts, 14 September 1871. John Smoke Johnson, Mohawk chief and speaker of council, appears standing to the right of John Buck, Onondaga chief and wampum keeper. To the right of John Buck is John Smoke Johnson's son, George Johnson, Mohawk chief and government interpreter. Geroge Johnson was the poetess Pauline Johnson's father.

Attempts to unseat the interpreter were not uncommon. This occurred with Chief Peter Smith when, in 1859, he was impeached on grounds that had nothing to do with his considerable interpreting skills.[34] He was replaced by the increasingly powerful young Mohawk chief George H.M. Johnson, the son of the highly respected speaker of council, Chief John Smoke Johnson[35] and the father of the Mohawk poetess Pauline Johnson.[36] George Johnson had just built a magnificent home in Onondaga, called Chiefswood, which the band council refurbished a century later and opened to the public as a historic museum.

The speaker of council and the interpreter were powerful officers in the daily management of the council's affairs, and with two exceptions a succession of eminent Mohawk chiefs filled both these positions until the turn of the century. Onondaga chief George Buck held the more traditional position of wampum keeper, but the actual job of safeguarding the historic wampum belts, which commemorated agreements between the Iroquois and their allies, was done by his brother, Onondaga chief John Buck, until his death in 1893.[37] At that point the task fell to David Sky, George Buck's successor, who as a young man was installed in 1883.[38]

In the council the Onondaga chiefs held the ritual offices, while the Mohawk chiefs occupied the administrative positions. This reflected the larger cultural pattern at Grand River in which the Mohawk spoke for the more acculturated nations associated with Christianity and "progress," and the Onondaga for the more traditional Longhouse nations. Collectively, the chiefs fulfilled the difficult but vital role of representing the views of the Six Nations to the Indian Department. But the deep-seated cultural division in the community often made consensus on certain issues difficult, if not impossible.

*Religion*

By 1860 the pattern of religious affiliation was set, with Longhouse adherents comprising about 20 percent of the population and the Christians about 80 percent. This pattern, which would hold for over a century, reflects more than a difference in religious persuasion. It represents two cultural philosophies that influence individual decisions in a wide variety of fields, such as education, social change, the economy, material lifestyle, and local governance. As the nineteenth century passed, these separate philosophies became more firmly entrenched in community life, especially as external pressures for change increased and Victorian society's intolerance for religious and cultural differences intensified.

Despite enhanced pressures from Christian missionaries, Longhouse adherents maintained the full ritual cycle of their faith in their three longhouses on the reserve: the Sour Springs, or Upper Cayuga longhouse, southwest of Ohsweken; and the Onondaga and the Lower Cayuga longhouses located "down below" on the reserve. Their basic objective was to retain the traditional customs of the Iroquois; the languages; the Confederacy form of government; the social structure, which included the matrilineal lineages, clans, and moieties; and the various rituals and herbal remedies for healing. Longhouse chiefs and preachers admonished their people to follow the teachings of Handsome Lake, the Seneca prophet,[39] and to treat the ways of the white people cautiously. As a result, the Longhouse community "down below" became the centre for the preservation of the orthodox Iroquois culture. There, living in close proximity, Longhouse families practised their faith without the close scrutiny – and sometimes critical comment – of the Christian Iroquois. Among the Iroquoian reserves in Canada and the United States, the Grand River Longhouse community has become recognized as the locus where the more traditional form of Iroquois culture is best preserved.[40]

*Education*

Although Christianity had made significant inroads among the Mohawk, Oneida, and Tuscarora even before the migration to the Grand River valley in 1784, it became firmly rooted in the community at mid-century. When in the late 1830s the New England Company assigned the Reverend Abraham Nelles and Adam Elliot to the Mohawk Chapel and the Mohawk Institute, respectively, the Anglican Church became the most powerful Christian denomination on the reserve, with a larger following than the Baptists and the Methodists combined.[41] The Anglican missionaries' judgment carried considerable weight off the reserve[42] as well as among the upper nations on the reserve, and on a few occasions they even successfully influenced the council's decisions. In 1859 their intervention in the council's selection process resulted in Chief George H.M. Johnson, then the official interpreter for the New England Company,[43] becoming the Confederacy Council's new interpreter. Johnson performed his duties as interpreter and forest warden in an outstanding fashion until his early death in 1884, precipitated by a brutal beating he received in enforcing the timber regulations on the reserve.

Largely because of their heavy investment in the Mohawk Institute, the New England Company missionaries came to expect special privileges in their dealings with the Six Nations. The Mohawk Institute, built in 1831, became a residential school in 1834. Students of both sexes were instructed in English from texts recommended by the provincial education department. Girls were given additional training in the domestic arts and boys in the mechanical skills of carpentry, masonry, and wagon-making, in addition to agriculture. Controversy, however, surrounded the question of attendance. After a conflict between Thorburn and the company's missionaries arose in 1847, the government suspected that the missionaries had greatly inflated the attendance figures to 120 pupils.[44] The Earl of Elgin reported that only 30 pupils were taking classes at the time he visited the institute in 1851.[45]

Disagreement over a land grant and the type of education offered at the Mohawk Institute led to a serious confrontation in 1847 between the visiting superintendent and the Anglican missionaries. According to Thorburn, the missionaries neglected both agriculture and formal education.[46] Their refusal to forward reports on the schools only angered him further. The New England Company's request for eighty hectares of Indian land adjacent to the Mohawk Institute for use as a manual training farm initiated the dispute.[47] Although Thorburn supported the teaching of farming skills, he opposed the missionaries' persistent efforts to have the land permanently transferred to the company. Previously, the Indian Department had sanctioned leases of land to other missionary groups but only on the condition that the land revert to the Six Nations when it was no longer used for schools.

The controversy reached new heights in the late 1840s. Displeased with their failure to secure the type of permanent lease they wished, Nelles and Elliot petitioned higher authorities,[48] charging that the Indian Department encouraged the continuation of the Longhouse faith.[49] Incensed at this allegation, Thorburn responded with a blunt statement on the rights of Indians to freedom of religion, objecting as well to the company's request for an exclusive field of operation among the Six Nations. Thorburn had been highly impressed with the success that Peter Jones, the Methodist Mississauga (Ojibwa) missionary, had had in the New Credit community. As he pointed out to his superiors, the New England Company could not demonstrate such dramatic achievement. In the end, although the Indian Department gave the New England Company a lease, the land and buildings reverted to the Six Nations in 1972 when they were no longer used for educational purposes. Today the Woodland Cultural Centre, operated by the Six Nations, the Mississauga of New Credit, and several other First Nations, occupies the site.

The New England Company offered in 1856 to establish schools on the reserve if the people wanted them.[50] While the chiefs supported the company's educational efforts,[51] as they had some ten years earlier with the Baptists and Methodists, they directed the clergy to build schools only where people wanted them, and not among the Longhouse people whose chiefs opposed them. By 1858 enrolment at the five schools on the reserve reached 150 out of an estimated school population of 400; but attendance remained low and sporadic, and the facilities left much to be desired.[52] Even when the parents supported formal education, children were withdrawn early in the summer for the planting season and returned late in the fall after harvest. The greatest support for schooling came from the upper nations, and this pattern held throughout the nineteenth century.

In summary, during the decade after the consolidation of the nations on the reserve (1847–57), the farming economy was slowly but successfully re-established and the Confederacy Council became the Six Nations government. Up to this time, the Confederacy's right to govern had not been challenged.

## Political Challenges, 1857–1876

Pressure for political reform at Grand River put considerable strain on the Confederacy Council and the Six Nations community in general. Some of the proposed reforms threatened to lessen the Confederacy Council's power, while others jeopardized the council's separate system of administering the reserve under the Indian Department. In effect, the council was caught in the crossfire between officials in Brant County who sought to turn the reserve into a normal township and officials in the Indian Department who wanted to protect the council system yet encourage individual Indians to assume greater political responsibility in society.

### Indian Enfranchisement

The transfer of Indian Affairs from British control to Canadian civil authority in 1860 had long-term implications for Indian policy,[53] but not initially at the Grand River reserve. The most forceful intervention in local affairs came with the passage of the 1857 Enfranchisement Act.[54] Its purpose was to encourage "the gradual civilization" of Indians by providing a mechanism for them to relinquish their unique legal status as wards of the state, thereby gaining the same political rights as other citizens. As the process of abandoning Indian status brought with it the right to vote – the franchise – the procedure was called "enfranchisement." Accordingly, the act set up local enfranchisement committees to hear the cases of individual Indian men (not women) who wished enfranchisement, and to decide whether the candidates were suitably qualified for full citizenship rights. After 1869 Indian women were automatically enfranchised if they married a non-Indian. (Like white women, however, these Iroquois women did not have the right to vote even if "enfranchised.")

Within a year of the act's passage, three Six Nations men, all Mohawk, applied for enfranchisement. Thorburn established a committee that included himself, a local Brantford businessman, and a New England Company missionary, and they proceeded to hear the cases. Ironically, they rejected the first two applicants, brothers Walter and James Kerr, both prosperous and successful businessmen who lived off the reserve, on the grounds of their business debts and non-reserve residence.[55] The third candidate was Elias Hill, a young shoemaker trained at the Mohawk Institute. Hill, after successfully passing "the examination" by reciting the catechism and naming the continents of the world, was recommended for enfranchisement.[56] The chiefs swiftly reacted.

The council immediately protested the legislation, since the Enfranchisement Act removed the chiefs' exclusive powers to determine band membership. The council also objected to the provision in the act that allowed successful applicants like Elias Hill to receive twenty hectares of reserve land,[57] as this threatened to destroy the reserve's remaining land base. But, as with subsequent revisions of the Indian Act throughout the nineteenth century, the chiefs could not prevent its implementation. The council, however, continued to oppose enfranchisement for individuals. Although the Indian Act contained enfranchisement provisions, very few Six Nations people were voluntarily enfranchised during the nineteenth century.

No sooner had the chiefs been confronted with the Enfranchisement Act than a more fundamental and immediate threat to their reserve arose from political pressures in Brant County. Responsible local government had come to the province in the late 1840s. Brantford, a village of 6 500, had become the seat of the new Brant County government in 1853, although the bulk of the county's 25 000 population lay in the newly formed townships.[58] But Tuscarora Township, which was the main part of the reserve, lay outside the county's jurisdiction and under the authority of the Indian Department.

The reform movement that brought responsible government to the province in the 1840s had a strong base in Brant County, mainly in the person of David Christie.[59] A founder of the Clear Grit party, Christie was a zealous liberal reformer and a member of the Legislative Assembly for Brant East from 1855 to 1858. Motivated by his liberal ideals and pressures from the Brantford merchants, Christie wanted to turn the reserve into a regular township in Brant County, complete with the local franchise and taxing responsibilities. In 1858 he introduced a bill in the Legislative Assembly designed to repeal the Indian Protection Act of 1850, which exempted Indians from taxes and debts, and to incorporate Tuscarora Township into Brant County.[60]

Once word of the proposed bill reached the reserve, the chiefs quickly acted. Together with Superintendent Thorburn they took immediate measures to avoid its passage. Their announcement of their agreement to pay individual band members' debts from band funds (as described above) succeeded. Christie withdrew his bill.[61] Had it passed, its effects would have been the same as those of the wholesale implementation of the Enfranchisement Act:

reserve land would no longer have been protected, the county government would have replaced the Confederacy Council, and Indians would have been responsible for their debts to whites. In short, it would have abolished the unique Confederacy Council and the reserve system.

While the Indian Department had fought Christie's zealous efforts, subsequent changes within its own administration caused concern on the Six Nations Reserve. As preparation for the transfer of Indian affairs from British control to the Province of Canada began in the 1850s, the government sought ways to reduce the costs of Indian administration against the public purse. The Indian Department now proposed that the number of chiefs, then totalling over sixty, be reduced to eighteen in an effort to lower the cost of board money paid the chiefs while in session.[62] In the total picture of Six Nations expenditures, this would have brought minimal saving and, in any event, the Six Nations were a financially self-sustaining community. They paid the salaries of all the local officials – the superintendent, the interpreter, the clerk, the local doctor, and the forest warden – from the interest on their capital funds.

*The First Reform Movement*

Although the council had gradually assumed some of the duties of local government during the 1850s, the idea of actually transforming the reserve into a normal municipality, as Christie proposed, had not been envisaged by either the chiefs or Superintendent Thorburn. In fact, the existing Indian legislation contained no provisions for elected band councils on reserves at this time. Thus, when local Six Nations reformers launched the first movement to establish an elected council at Grand River in 1861, no legal ground existed for the type of government they proposed.

Local reformers gained support as a result of the bankruptcy of the Grand River Navigation Company in 1861. The Six Nations, who owned over three-quarters of its stock, lost their entire investment, including some land along the river used for building canals and bridges.[63] To the chiefs, the company's bankruptcy demonstrated the ineffectiveness of the laws intended to protect Indian lands and funds. To the reformers, it proved the chiefs' inability to protect their people's interests, and underscored the need for proper local government, namely responsible officials elected by the community.

Isaac Powless, a bright and articulate young Mohawk, led the reform movement. Although well educated for his day and able to speak most Iroquoian dialects, he had failed to get the job of interpreter for the council in 1859. Whatever role his personal disappointment played remains unknown, but concern over the loss of band funds through the collapse of the Navigation Company undoubtedly motivated his backers. Powless's strongest support came from the Upper Mohawk, most of whom were Christian, although predictably not from the Mohawk chiefs.

In December 1861 Powless circulated a petition on the reserve proposing the Confederacy Council's dissolution and its replacement by an elected municipal government under the aegis of the Indian Department.[64] Some 167 persons finally signed it. The petitioners objected to the hereditary principle for selecting chiefs, arguing that the chiefs were at times uneducated, conservative in outlook, uninterested in political affairs, and free from any direct accountability to the community for their actions.

The council reacted immediately to the petition, but in doing so showed the inherent weakness in such federations – the tendency to fragment under stress.[65] The chiefs agreed to oppose the reform efforts, yet were divided over what strategy to adopt to counteract Powless's actions. In the end they sent two independent delegations, rather than one, to visit Thorburn at Queenston.[66]

The Onondaga delegation headed by chiefs John and George Buck, the newly appointed Onondaga chiefs who would soon become forceful spokesmen for the lower tribes in the council, arrived first. The Onondaga had adopted a laissez-faire approach just as they did in matters of education and medical care. They felt that the nations should unite against reform, but if the Mohawk and other upper nations wished to come under a municipal system, they were free to do so. This infuriated the Mohawk, who headed the second delegation. Under the leadership of Chief John Smoke Johnson, the powerful speaker of council, and his son, Chief George H.M. Johnson, interpreter of the council, the Mohawk criticized the Onondaga for playing into the hands of the reformers by splitting the council and suggesting the reserve be divided. Above all, the Mohawk feared that the council's reaction might demonstrate to the Indian Department its inability to manage its own affairs and act cohesively.

Despite the turmoil created by Powless's petition, the reform movement failed to gain widespread support in the community. Thorburn rejected the petition, for although his task was to promote "advancement" of the Six Nations, he felt the community was not sufficiently "prepared" to adopt a municipal government.[67] Second, the senior officials in the Indian Department who were then examining possible amendments to the Indian Act decided that Indian bands were not yet experienced enough to allow for locally elected councils.[68]

For the council, the Powless petition had been an unsettling experience; for the reformers, a disappointing one. Agitation for an elected system subsequently died down, but there remained in the community a small core of council critics who continued to urge the chiefs to take a more progressive stance on many issues. Their desire for changes was met, in part, with the appointment of a new Indian superintendent in 1862.

*A New Superintendent*

Unlike Thorburn, Jasper Tough Gilkison, the new superintendent, resided in Brantford and could thus oversee the management of Six Nations affairs in a more systematic fashion. Born to a wealthy Brant County family, educated in Britain,[69] and with a background as a railroad executive, Gilkison was well equipped for his administrative tasks. His career with the Six Nations lasted until his retirement in 1891, and during those thirty years he played a major role in overseeing the council's evolution into an effective local government through gradual adaptation.[70]

Gilkison came to office determined to make many changes in the council and the community. Within six months he promoted a whole battery of innovations: a more systematic census-taking procedure; the founding of an agricultural society; the improvement of roads; the building of a new council house; the establishment of a village in the centre of the reserve; and the creation of an improved land-registry system.[71] For the first few months he treated the chiefs with deference and respect, but later his insistent pressuring for change and his authoritarian manner created tension within the council.

The new superintendent improved the census-taking procedures, but his efforts to encourage statute labour for building and maintaining a network of roads at first had limited success. Volunteer labour for road building proved no more popular on the reserve than off, and although Gilkison established a more systematic method of appointing pathmasters to oversee the work, the road program advanced very slowly. His suggestions for an agricultural society initially met with considerable support from the chiefs of the upper nations, and the first few ploughing matches that were held were subsidized by the council's donations of prize money. The formal creation of the Agricultural Society, however, took place six years later, and although Gilkison supported its activities, he played no role in its formation.

The notion of building a village in the centre of the reserve had a certain appeal, and the chiefs were actively involved in planning the street layout and determining the location of a new council house more accessible to the people. Despite the Onondaga chiefs' objections to moving from their old log council house in Middleport, the council decided in favour of a new building and hired Seneca chief John Hill to construct it.[72] The impressive wooden structure was begun in 1863 and finished in 1865, complete with bell tower. In the 1890s it was coated with yellow brick veneer, and since then its bell tower has been removed and its interior renovated several times. It was opened in January 1865 with an elaborate public ceremony at which a few of the prominent Onondaga chiefs "read" and explained the wampum belts to the audience. The chiefs then assumed their formal positions in the new chamber.

The Onondaga sat in the centre, the Mohawk and Seneca to the east, and the Oneida, Cayuga, and dependent nations to the west. The superintendent and interpreter sat on the raised platform at the back, and the secretary in front at a table, taking the minutes. The council house was the seat of the Six Nations government beginning in 1865, housing the meetings of the Confederacy Council until 1924 and the elected council from then until 1978, when the new Six Nations Band Administration Building was erected.

Gilkison's attempts to resolve the difficulties in the administration of justice proved less popular among the chiefs. Prior to settlement on the reserve, the chiefs sitting as separate nations settled disputes among individuals. After the consolidation on the reserve in 1847, the number of land disputes increased, in part owing to the absence of an effective land-registry system. Secondly, the full council did not appear willing to assume the function of

| Clerk? | Supt. | Interpreter |

Oneida          Mohawk
Cayuga          Seneca
Tuscarora
Delaware
Nanticoke    Onondaga
Tutelo

Railing                                    Railing

Audience                          Audience

Front Door

N

Seating Plan of Chiefs in the Ohsweken Council House

arbitration.[73] Even though there were no effective mechanisms for handling civil disputes, Thorburn had actively discouraged the Six Nations people from taking their cases to outsiders for settlement, and he bluntly advised legal officials in Brantford that they could not expect to be paid for their services from band funds.[74] As Brant County became more sensitive to demands on its public purse from the reserve, the issue of paying the costs of criminal justice also arose.

Although Six Nations people committed very few crimes, those who did had no choice but to appear before the courts and sometimes occupy the "lockups" in the city. Criminal justice had always been delivered to Indians through the regular judicial system,[75] limited as it was, and Brant County bore the costs for that system. The Indian Department sought to avoid covering the costs, and resentment in Brant County finally surfaced in 1862. A Brant County Grand Jury recommended that the Legislative Assembly grant normal township status to the reserve as a method for ensuring payment of court costs.[76] Senior officials in the Indian Department, attempting to find some compromise without paying the costs, suggested that a few outstanding Six Nations men be appointed as local magistrates.[77] This would ease the demands on the county and bring judicial services more directly to the people on the reserve. Instead of implementing this suggestion, Gilkison obtained his own appointment as a local magistrate, a move that angered some of the educated and vocal chiefs of the upper nations who could have handled the work equally, if not more, effectively.[78] Only when the council established its own disputes committee in the 1870s was the process of adjudicating local civil disputes settled.[79] Brant County continued to pay the costs of criminal justice.

Gilkison's heavy-handed tactics at times rebounded on him, depriving him of support from those chiefs willing to consider new approaches in the council's operations. This became especially evident in the mid-1860s as the chiefs experimented with committees in an attempt to reduce the time taken in council deliberations. Reaching decisions by consensus among twenty to forty chiefs required an extensive amount of council deliberation, and in instances of particularly difficult decisions, debates could continue for days without any final resolution. This lengthy procedure annoyed Gilkison as well as some of the chiefs of the upper nations who preferred to tend their farms. To speed up decision making, both the chiefs and Gilkison proposed the establishment of ad hoc committees for timber licensing, fire insurance, and cattle theft. Other ad hoc committees were established, but on the whole most were short-lived. In some cases it was easier to appoint a forest warden to control timber cutting, but in general the chiefs were uneasy about delegating authority to a select few.

Woodland Cultural Centre

The Six Nations Indian superintendent and several chiefs. *Standing, left to right:* John Hill, Josiah Hill, Wm. Wedge, Nicodemus Porter; *sitting, left to right:* David Thomas, Jasper Gilkison (Indian superintendent), David Hill.

In an attempt to shorten the lengthy council sessions, Gilkison and other Indian Department officials also suggested that the council establish an executive committee of a limited number of chiefs to handle routine matters of administration.[80] Under this scheme the full council would meet only twice a year (at the time of the annuity payments) or when major issues arose.[81] But the experiment failed. On the few occasions the executive committee actually met, Gilkison proved so overpowering in the discussions that the chiefs rebelled. Quite rightly they demanded to learn why he had bothered to create the committee when it was evident he intended to make the decisions himself.[82] Jacob General, an Oneida chief, objected so forcefully to Gilkison's manner that the council discontinued the experiment. As a result, the superintendent adopted a more diplomatic approach, coming to understand that the chiefs would withhold cooperation if he used coercive tactics.

### The 1869 Indian Act

Although the 1860s witnessed many instances of political unrest in the council, none of them equalled the agitation caused by the Indian Act of 1869.[83]

The act contained the first provisions for elected band councils on reserves. Although the legislation was not automatically applied to bands, the chiefs knew that the government could implement its provisions against their wishes and without their approval. They had reason to feel uneasy, for if the government applied the act, it would remove the Confederacy Council from power.

Even before Parliament passed the act, the chiefs held lengthy debates exploring its possible application.[84] They disliked its regulations on land registration and leasing, and took issue with the sections that automatically enfranchised Indian women who married non-Indian men. These amendments were designed to provide greater protection of Indian land and, in the latter case, to prevent the non-Indian husbands of Indian women from gaining access to reserve lands.[85] Different bands from Southern Ontario and Quebec thoroughly discussed the act at a council held at the Six Nations Reserve in June 1870.[86] While the act did not disturb some of the chiefs of the upper nations, the chiefs of the lower nations wished to establish the point that the Six Nations were Britain's allies, not subjects of the Crown, and therefore as a sovereign power, not subject to Canadian laws.[87] The lower nations became so anxious to remind the Canadian government of their sovereignty that in January 1875 their chiefs prepared a petition outside the council notifying David Laird, the superintendent general of Indian affairs, that the Six Nations were governed by their own ancient laws, not by those of Canada.[88] At the same time they informed him they were preparing a statement of the Confederacy's history and procedures for the Canadian Parliament's approval, hoping this would ensure their future autonomy. It is quite possible that Seth Newhouse's remarkable manuscript on the lore of the Confederacy was an attempt to record the League of the Iroquois' traditions for parliamentary approval.[89] Newhouse, then a newly appointed Onondaga self-made chief, participated actively in reserve politics and wanted to justify the Confederacy's rule and preserve its traditions. But in the end these and other protests failed. The government had already informed the chiefs that the Indian Act applied to the Six Nations people regardless of their wishes, and again in 1878 it bluntly reminded them of that fact.[90] When Newhouse finally presented his manuscript, he failed to receive the council's endorsement of it.[91]

Even though the council remained united in its formal opposition to the Indian Act, strained relations developed between the upper and lower chiefs when, in 1873, the government passed more stringent timber regulations designed to control timber cutting on reserves.[92] By and large the upper chiefs supported these new regulations, whereas the lower chiefs opposed them, charging (with some accuracy) that the upper nations had already cut most of the timber and were now seeking to prevent the lower nations from doing the same.[93] By 1878 the Onondaga chiefs felt so frustrated at these and other

The Six Nations community, 1875.

changes that they asked that they, together with the Cayuga, be given their own reserve under their own superintendent.[94]

The tendency for the council to splinter under stress became ever more apparent. The cleavage between the upper and lower chiefs became a permanent feature of the council. In times of accelerated change, strained relations surfaced, but in more relaxed periods, the division remained dormant.

## NOTES

1   Primary research for chapters 9 and 10 was carried out between 1963 and 1977 on the Six Nations Reserve, in the Indian Agency archives in Brantford, and in the National Archives of Canada in Ottawa. I am especially grateful to the Six Nations Band Council for permission to reside on the reserve in those years, and to the many Six Nations people who so generously taught me their history. In particular I wish to thank Tom V. Hill and Sheila Staats of the Woodland Cultural Centre for their very helpful updating of materials on Six Nations history, and Don Smith, University of Calgary, for his very careful editing of the manuscript. All errors of fact or interpretation in these chapters are entirely mine. I also gratefully acknowledge the financial support for this work from the Canadian Museum of Civilization (formerly National Museum of Man) and the Social Sciences and Humanities Research Council (formerly the Canada Council). These chapters are distilled from a fuller unpublished manuscript on Six Nations political history I completed in 1975 entitled "Iroquois Politics, 1847–1940." I have placed this manuscript on deposit for public access in both the Woodland Cultural Centre, Brantford, Ontario, and the Ethnology Division of the Canadian Museum of Civilization in Hull, Quebec.
2   Canada, *Indian Treaties and Surrenders from 1680 to 1890*, 2 vols. (Ottawa 1891), 2:120–1 (henceforth *Indian Treaties and Surrenders*)
3   Province of Canada, *Report on the Affairs of the Indians of Canada*, Journals of the Legislative Assembly of Canada (Montreal 1847), Appendix T, sec. 3
4   Katherine A. Sample, "Changes in Agriculture on the Six Nations Reserve" (MA thesis, McMaster University, 1968), 21
5   Province of Canada, "Return," Journals of the Legislative Assembly of Canada (Montreal 1853), Appendix FFFF
6   *Six Nations Council Minutes (SNCM)* (Brantford 1847), 54, 108
7   Province of Canada, *Report of the Special Commissioners Appointed on the 8th of September, 1856, to Investigate Indian Affairs in Canada*, Journals of the Legislative Assembly of Canada (Ottawa 1858), pt. 2, Appendix 21
8   Province of Canada, "Return"
9   *SNCM*, 1847, 51
10   Ibid., 7
11   *SNCM*, 1855–58, 66–73
12   Annemarie A. Shimony, *Conservatism among the Iroquois at the Six Nations Reserve* (New Haven 1961)
13   *SNCM*, 1848, 341
14   Ibid., 346

15  *SNCM*, 1847, 80
16  *SNCM*, 1855–58, 66–73
17  F. Douglas Reville, *History of the County of Brant* (Brantford 1920; reprint, 1967), 25
18  Province of Canada, *Report of the Special Commissioners Appointed on the 8th of September, 1856*
19  Province of Canada, *Statutes*, "An Act for the Protection of the Indians in Upper Canada from Imposition, and the Property Occupied or Enjoyed by them from Trespass and Injury," 13 Vict., c. 74, 1850, 13–14
20  *SNCM*, 1858, 93–5
21  Ibid., 209
22  *SNCM*, 1857, 99
23  Canada, House of Commons, "Report: The Select Committee Appointed to Inquire into the Condition and Affairs of the Six Nations in the Counties of Brant and Haldimand in the Province of Ontario," *Sessional Papers*, 1894, Appendix 11, 2
24  Province of Canada, *Report on the Affairs of the Indians in Canada,* Journals of the Legislative Assembly of Canada (Montreal 1845), Appendix EEE
25  William N. Fenton, *The Roll Call of the Iroquois Chiefs: A Study of a Mnemonic Cane from the Six Nations Reserve* (Washington, D.C. 1950), Smithsonian Miscellaneous Collections, III, no. 15, 59–67; Elisabeth Tooker, "The League of the Iroquois: Its History, Politics and Ritual," in *Handbook of North American Indians*, vol. 15: *Northeast,* ed. Bruce G. Trigger (Washington, D.C. 1978), 424–5. Of the 50 hereditary chiefs on the official roster, the Mohawk had 9, the Oneida 9, the Onondaga 14, the Cayuga 10, and the Seneca 8.
26  Fenton, *The Roll Call of the Iroquois Chiefs*, 54
27  *SNCM*, 1864, 1–3
28  Frank G. Speck, *The Nanticoke and Conoy Indians with a Review of Linguistic Material from Manuscript and Living Sources: An Historical Study* (Wilmington 1927)
29  Horatio Hale, "Chief George H.M. Johnson, Onwanonsyshon: His Life and Work among the Six Nations," *American History*, 1885, 131–42
30  Ibid.
31  Fenton, *The Roll Call of the Iroquois Chiefs*, 22–6
32  Ibid., 43
33  A.A. Goldenweiser, "The Death of Chief John A. Gibson," *American Anthropologist* 14 (1912): 692–4
34  *SNCM*, 1859, 3–11
35  Hale, "Chief George H.M. Johnson," 131–42
36  Evelyn H.C. Johnson, "Chief John Smoke Johnson," *Papers and Records of the Ontario Historical Society* 12 (1914): 102–13; Evelyn H.C. Johnson, "Grandfather and Father of E. Pauline Johnson," *Annual Archaeological Report, Appendix to the Report of the Minister of Education, Ontario*, 1928, 44–7; Marcus Van Steen, *Pauline Johnson: Her Life and Work* (Toronto 1965)
37  Augusta I. Grant Gilkison, "What Is Wampum? Explained by Chief John Buck, Firekeeper, July 20, 1887," *Annual Archaeological Report, Appendix to the Report to the Minister of Education, Ontario*, 1928, 48–50
38  Horatio Hale, "An Iroquois Condoling Council: A Study of Aboriginal American Society and Government," *Proceedings and Transactions of the Royal Society of Canada*, 2d ser., vol. 1, sec. 2 (1895): 45–65

39   A.F.C. Wallace, *The Death and Rebirth of the Seneca* (New York 1970), chaps. 8–10

40   William N. Fenton, "The Lore of the Longhouse: Myth, Ritual and Red Power," *Anthropological Quarterly* 48 (1975): 131–47; William N. Fenton, "Northern Iroquoian Culture Patterns," in *Handbook of North American Indians*, vol. 15: *Northeast*, ed. Bruce G. Trigger (Washington, D.C. 1978), 296–321

41   Charles M. Johnston, ed., *The Valley of the Six Nations* (Toronto 1964), lxxvii; J.P. Pryse, "Pioneer Baptist Missionaries to Upper Canada Tuscaroras," *Canadian Baptist Home Missions Digest* 6 (1963–64): 273–82

42   Province of Canada, *Report of the Special Commissioners ... 1856*; Canada, House of Commons, *Report: The Select Committee Appointed to Inquire into the Condition and Affairs of the Six Nations ...* (1874), Appendix 11

43   SNCM, 1859, 41

44   SNCM, 1848, 307

45   PRO, Dispatches, Canada 1851, vol. 1, 151–6. A recent study of the school is Jennifer L.J. Pettit's "From Longhouse to Schoolhouse: The Mohawk Institute, 1834–1970" (MA thesis, University of Western Ontario, 1993).

46   SNCM, 1848, 308–13

47   SNCM, 1847, 72

48   SNCM, 1848, 308–10

49   Ibid.

50   SNCM, 1856, 25

51   Ibid., 54

52   Province of Canada, *Report of the Special Commissioners ... 1856*

53   Duncan C. Scott, "Indian Affairs, 1840–1867," in A. Shortt and A.G. Doughty, eds., *Canada and Its Provinces* (Toronto 1913), 5:331–62

54   Province of Canada, *Statutes*, "An Act to Encourage the Gradual Civilization of the Indian Tribes in this Province and to Amend the Laws Respecting Indians," 20 Vict., c. 26, 1857

55   SNCM, 1858, 70, 227

56   SNCM, 1859, 340–1

57   SNCM, 1858, 139

58   Charles M. Johnston, *Brant County: A History, 1784–1945* (Toronto 1967), 45

59   Johnston, *Brant*, 44–7. For a full sketch of Christie's life see, J.M.S. Careless, "David Christie," *Dictionary of Canadian Biography*, vol. 10: *1871–1880* (Toronto 1972), 168–71.

60   SNCM, 1858, 3

61   Ibid., 175

62   SNCM, 1857, 92

63   Reville, *History of the County of Brant*, 182

64   NA, Record Group 10 (RG 10), vol. 402. Unfortunately, the page number cannot be given, as the volume was not paginated at the time the research was completed.

65   Fenton, "The Lore of the Longhouse," 144

66   SNCM, 1861, 198–9

67   SNCM, 1862, 239

68   NA, RG 10, vol. 528

69   Johnston, *Brant*, 106

70   V.J. Cooper, "A Political History of the Grand River Iroquois 1784–1880"

71  *SNCM*, 1862, 354–6
72  Ibid., 369
73  *SNCM*, 1848, 342–3
74  *SNCM*, 1861, 153
75  NA, RG 10, vol. 718, J.B. Macaulay, Report to Sir George Arthur on Indian Affairs
76  NA, RG 10, vol. 528
77  Ibid.
78  *SNCM*, 1862, 354–5
79  John A. Noon, *Law and Government of the Grand River Iroquois* (New York 1949), 115–84
80  *SNCM*, 1862, 304
81  Chief John Smoke Johnson had himself once made this suggestion; see *SNCM*, 1865, 227
82  Ibid., 269–70, 331
83  Canada, *Revised Statutes 1869*, "An Act for the Gradual Enfranchisement of Indians," 32–3 Vict., c. 6
84  *SNCM*, 1869, 262; 1870, 374–5
85  Sally M. Weaver, "Report on Archival Research Regarding Canadian Indian Women's Status, 1868–1869" (Mimeographed 1971)
86  Anon., *The General Council of the Six Nations, and Delegates from Different Bands in Western and Eastern Canada* (Hamilton 1870); Paul Williams, "The Indian Act 1870–1982: A Study in Consistency," *Ontario Indian* 5, no. 91 (September 1982): 16–21, 52, 56–7
87  Wm. J. Simcoe Kerr, *The General Council of the Six Nations, and Delegates from Different Bands in Western and Eastern Canada* (Hamilton 1870)
88  NA, RG 10, vol. 1949
89  Seth Newhouse, "Cosmogony of De-Ka-na-wi-da's Government of the Iroquois Confederacy: The Original Literal Historical Narratives of the Iroquois Confederacy" (MS); William N. Fenton, "Seth Newhouse's Traditional History and Constitution of the Iroquois Confederacy," *Proceedings of the American Philosophical Society* 93 (1949): 141–58; Sally M. Weaver, "Seth Newhouse and the Grand River Confederacy at Mid-Nineteenth Century," in J. Campisi, M. Foster, and M. Methun, eds., *Extending the Rafters: Interdisciplinary Approaches to Iroquoian Studies* (Albany 1984), 165–82
90  NA, RG 10, vol. 529, 24 March 1870; *SNCM*, 1878, 400
91  *SNCM*, 1885, 177
92  *SNCM*, 1873, 7
93  Ibid., 97–8
94  *SNCM*, 1878, 400

# 10

## The Iroquois: The Grand River Reserve in the Late Nineteenth and Early Twentieth Centuries, 1875–1945

SALLY M. WEAVER

## Introduction

The quarter-century following the passage of the Enfranchisement Act of 1857 was exceedingly difficult for the Confederacy Council, with a steady erosion in its powers of self-government. New legislation and the Indian Department's increased interventionism made its management of reserve affairs far more arduous. Although the reform movement led by Isaac Powless had failed, pressures from the community on the Confederacy Council built up and became polarized. The Longhouse people wanted the Six Nations' governing body to retain its traditional form, while the increasingly influential Christians often considered the council too conservative in its policies and procedures. The increasing dissension occurred at a time of general prosperity as the new agricultural economy became firmly established.

### The Community Flourishes, 1875–1900

In the late nineteenth century the churches and schools promoted the work ethic, sobriety, and thrift among the Christian families, while the Longhouse preachers continued to urge their followers to adhere to the sober, simple, and more traditional ways of the Longhouse faith. Little interaction took place between these two subcommunities in any formal sense. Indeed, the Christians knew little about the Longhouse faith and often forbade their children from entering the longhouses. The Longhouse followers, consistently pressed and at times publicly harassed by zealous missionaries, held securely to their beliefs, and orthodox parents discouraged any involvement of their children in church activities. Some intermarriage occurred, but neither group approved of it.

The Confederacy Council became the only institution where the two religious traditions met continuously. In full council the chiefs became especially careful not to show favouritism to either group. Thus, the council gave grants for repairs and construction to both longhouses and churches as it did in 1881 when the Seneca members split off from the Onondaga Longhouse to build their own.[1] As neighbours, however, Longhouse and Christian lived easily together, often sharing in farm work and helping each other in times of personal or family crisis. In these informal relations, personal respect and friendships readily developed.

*The Longhouse Religion*

The Longhouse community, numbering almost 700 people in the 1880s and 1890s, practised its rituals in four longhouses, as it does today. The Upper Cayuga, or Sour Springs, Longhouse near Ohsweken attracted both Cayuga and Mohawk families. (See Map 8.1 on page 171.) The other three longhouses, the Onondaga, Lower Cayuga, and Seneca, were and are "down below," where the majority of Longhouse followers live. The ceremonies, conducted entirely in the various Iroquoian dialects, followed the annual agricultural cycle and provided the highlights of the Longhouse year's activities. The ritual cycle began in late January or early February with the elaborate Midwinter Festival or New Year's Celebration, which ended with the ritual burning of a white dog.[2] This was followed in the spring by the maple sugar and seed-planting rituals, and in the summer by the strawberry, bean, and green corn celebrations. The final event was the Thanksgiving or Harvest Ritual, held in the fall to thank the Creator for the ripening of the crops.[3]

In each longhouse the faith keepers, three men and three women appointed by the clans to oversee the planning of events, organized the ceremonies. Noted ritualists, well versed in the proper chants, addresses, and prayers, led the intricate ceremonies. The women prepared the food, the customary corn bread, and the soup, the latter prepared from dried corn that was pounded, leached by ashes, and cooked with small bits of pork and occasionally beans.[4] Men who sometimes donned a traditional style of Iroquois costume with leggings, shirt tied with a sash, and the unique Iroquois headdress often led dances and songs. The small drums and the horn or turtle-shell rattles used to accompany the singers and dancers were considered prize possessions, as they are today.[5] While the clothing men usually wore to the celebrations was indis-

Pageant, Six Nations, late 1890s.
From David Boyle, "The Pagan Iroquois," *Archaeological Report 1898. Being Part of Appendix to the Report of the Minister of Education Ontario* (Toronto 1898), pl. 3, National Archives of Canada, c-33569

tinguishable from that worn by Brant County farmers, the women often dressed up for the occasion, putting brightly coloured shawls over their shoulders, but wearing their normal full-length gingham or cotton skirts.

The Longhouse faith provided its adherents with an elaborate set of beliefs and practices for healing. Followers used various herbal remedies in the home and consulted well-known herbalists, who had a large repertoire of healing potions derived from traditional Iroquois pharmacopoeia and colonial practices. If the sick person wished, he or she could join one of the many active medicine societies on the reserve – the False Face, Otter, Bear, Buffalo, and Eagle – some of which specialized in curing particular ailments.[6]

The Longhouse people lived from birth to death within their own community, guided by its well-integrated system of values and morals. Shortly after birth the child received an Indian name that belonged to its mother's clan. The name was used mainly for ceremonial purposes, not for addressing the individual.[7] From infancy the parents took the child to the ceremonies and introduced the boy or girl to the Longhouse traditions. Marriage, traditionally an informal ritual, was left to the agreement of the bride and groom's kin groups. Marital fidelity was expected.[8] Although there was no divorce in a legal sense, couples did separate, in which case the children remained with the

Buffalo and Erie County Historical Society, c25,504

A Seneca woman in the late nineteenth century.

mother and her lineage. The choice of marriage partner was largely left to the young people, although a few marriages were arranged by the respective mothers of the couple, as was the traditional practice. On death, the deceased person was buried in the graveyard of the Longhouse he or she had attended, and the death feast was held ten days later, at which time the spirit was believed to leave the body and ascend to the home of the Creator.

The Longhouse philosophy of life, embodied in the elaborate Code of Handsome Lake, was straightforward.[9] The Longhouse people followed the teachings of Handsome Lake and adhered to the "Indian way." They led

Old and new Onondaga longhouses, with a few graves, at the Six Nations Reserve, late 1890s.

From David Boyle, "The Pagan Iroquois," *Archaeological Report 1898. Being Part of Appendix to the Report of the Minister of Education Ontario* (Toronto 1898), pl. 6, National Anthropological Archives, Smithsonian Institution, 961-c-4

proper lives by taking care of their children and parents, by remaining faithful to their spouses, and by refraining from gossiping, gambling, and drinking alcohol. They avoided materialism in favour of a simple style of life free of petty jealousies and harmful acts such as witchcraft. Above all the Longhouse people followed their own traditions, not those of the white man as taught in the schools and churches. Their preachers recited this moral code at both the Midwinter Festival and the "Six Nations' meetings" held annually in the fall at one of the longhouses on the reserve, urging their members to live by these values and beliefs in their daily lives. Men and women held in high esteem in the Longhouse community gained this respect on account of their knowledge of the traditions, and also through the personal example they set in closely following the Code of Handsome Lake in their private lives.

*Christianity*

By the late nineteenth century, missionary activity had become highly successful, resulting in the formation of new congregations and the building of additional churches. The most prominent denomination remained the Anglican Church, which was financially supported by the New England Company. The last of the five Anglican churches that still stand on the reserve was completed in 1908. The Baptists, the second largest church group, had three churches on the reserve. Although the size of the Methodists' congregation was only one-half that of the Baptists, they also operated three churches.[10]

By 1890 the denominational pattern showed the Anglicans with one-half of the Christians' membership, the Baptists with nearly one-third, and the Methodists with nearly one-sixth. (See Table 10.1.) The few remaining Christians belonged to either the Roman Catholic or Presbyterian churches, or were affiliated with other small missions on the reserve, such as the Brethren, the Mormons, or the Salvation Army.

The individual congregations in each of the denominations ranged from ten to over sixty families. They participated actively in both religious services and the administration of the churches. At Sunday School the missionaries as well as Six Nations men and women taught the children. The children's highlight of the social year was the annual Sunday School picnic in the summer; the families brought a huge lunch, and the adults organized baseball and other games. Six Nations men and women regularly filled the various church offices, as wardens, deacons, and elders. Upon their shoulders rested the maintenance and repair of the church buildings. Various fund-raising activities – teas, suppers, strawberry socials, garden parties, and picnics – provided the necessary funds for new furnishings, organs, and books. The women prepared the food and brought it to the church hall or, occasionally, to the council house, where larger crowds could be fed. The menus included every variety of berry pie, cakes, cookies, stews, and, most popular of all, oysters. People dressed up for these occasions, the women wearing brightly coloured long gingham dresses and the men often donning jackets and dress shirts. At many of these events, members of the congregation, missionaries, and chiefs gave speeches. One of the local brass bands provided the music, or in the smaller gatherings, men, women, and children performed solos or offered choral singing.[11]

*Social Activities*

Voluntary associations played an important role in the community. These associations offered individuals educational and leadership opportunities, and for the community they provided entertainment and public service. The Temperance Society was one of the first to establish a firm hold in the community, and although a few Longhouse people belonged during the nineteenth century, most of its supporters were Christians. The members held monthly meetings either in private homes or in the small halls built by the five branches of the Temperance Society. The executives of the branches brought in

Table 10.1
Christian Affiliation among the Six Nations

|  | 1865 | 1890 | 1924 | 1929 | 1934 | 1939 | 1944 | 1949 | 1954 | 1959 |
|---|---|---|---|---|---|---|---|---|---|---|
| Anglican | 1 141 | 1 062 | 1 329 | 1 403 | 1 510 | 1 575 | 1 640 | 1 845 | 1 875 | 2 556 |
| Baptist | 370 | 635 | 849 | 906 | 980 | 990 | 1 050 | 1 022 | 1 285 | 2 179 |
| Methodist | 340 | 337 | 805 | — | — | — | — | — | — | — |
| United Church | — | — | — | 739 | 890 | 900 | 1 010 | 1 184 | 1 228 | 621 |
| Presbyterian | — | 9 | — | — | — | — | — | — | — | 103 |
| Roman Catholic | — | 23 | — | — | — | — | — | — | — | 92 |
| Other Christian | 238 | 101 | 462 | 468 | 518 | 547 | 625 | 697 | 737 | 277 |
| Longhouse | 657 | 684 | 858 | 975 | 1 010 | 1 020 | 1 195 | 1 255 | 1 260 | 1 393 |
| Unknown | — | 554 | — | — | — | — | — | — | — | 83 |

*Source:* Sally M. Weaver, from archival sources

speakers, and after the meeting the women offered a lunch. In the summer, well-attended picnics, often near "69 Corners" (at the junction of today's Sour Springs and Chiefswood roads), carried the temperance cause to larger audiences. Speakers from the reserve and elsewhere often preached in fire-and-brimstone fashion against the evils of intoxicating beverages, and older men gave testimonials on how they had reformed or how they had avoided temptation. After various prayers and hymns, the families ate their picnic lunch, met friends, exchanged the latest news, and discussed how their farming was progressing. The Temperance Society held an annual meeting either at Grand River, at Muncey with the Oneida, or at Lewiston, New York, with the Tuscarora. The council often granted funds to assist in the expenses of these large gatherings.

The reserve's most popular public celebration came on the 24th of May. Beginning in the early 1860s, the council held a celebration of Queen Victoria's birthday, at which large quantities of bread and cheese were given to the sick and needy. As the years passed, however, "Bread and Cheese Day" became more elaborate. Everyone received bread and cheese at noon, before the program of speeches by chiefs, local dignitaries from Brant County, and various distinguished visitors. Always the speakers recalled the prominent role the Six Nations had played in the Revolutionary War and the War of 1812. The program usually ended with reaffirmations of loyalty to the queen and to England. In effect, Bread and Cheese Day became the national holiday of the Six Nations, providing them with an opportunity to reaffirm their own identity and traditions.

There were also unusual public events, such as the visit of the governor general and the Countess of Dufferin in August 1874 and the arrival of Prime Minister Sir John A. Macdonald in September 1886. The chiefs spoke at these celebrations. When the council house became the centre for such occasions, the council might freshen it up with a new coat of paint or decorate it with the large banners carrying the clan symbols that had been donated to the council by the Ontario genealogist Edward Chadwick.[12]

The autumn's most popular event became the annual agricultural show and ploughing match. Wishing to promote agriculture, improve livestock, and "encourage honest industry," Chief William Smith and Joseph Powless, both prominent Mohawk farmers, founded the Six Nations Agricultural Society in the fall of 1868.[13] Membership and competitions were restricted to Six Nations people because they wanted to manage their own organization, although the organizers welcomed non-Indians as spectators and often used them as judges for the competitions. In one year the membership expanded from the original dozen to thirty-three.[14]

Despite increasing community interest and an expanding membership, at

National Archives of Canada, c-6134

Sir John A. Macdonald, on his visit to the Six Nations Reserve, 7 September 1886.

first the society struggled for funds. Continued donations from the New England Company and a small grant from the Ontario Department of Agriculture, beginning in 1873, kept it alive in its early years. Initially, according to the society's secretary, the chiefs were "yet too much prejudiced against such innovations" to support its activities financially. Public interest continued to build, however, and visits to the show by Joseph Howe, the superintendent general of Indian affairs in 1870, and other dignitaries brought it considerable publicity. The prize lists expanded to include prizes for sheep, swine, and poultry as well as for horses and cattle; the number of farmers in the competition for the best grains, particularly wheat and barley, increased. For women the Ladies Department offered competitions in peach and plum preserves, corn and wheat bread, butter, jellies of all kinds, embroidered and knitted work, and quilting. Men also competed in crafts, as the exhibition gave prizes for lacrosse sticks, axe handles, and walking canes. By 1875 the society had almost a hundred members, and keen local interest in brass bands led to the popular band competitions.

By 1880 the annual exhibition had outgrown the available space in the council house. The society built a large, Maltese cross–shaped exhibition hall in a five-hectare park, across from the Ohsweken council house. They soon added more dining halls and additional cattle sheds, as well as a horse-race track in the park. Although the society had originally agreed to pay for the building entirely out of the annuities of its members, band funds were eventually used, as was a portion of the Ontario government grant for $7 000 made to unorganized townships.[15] Under persistent pressure from the upper chiefs, the council in 1879 began to grant the society $200 annually towards the fall fair and to donate $70 towards the ploughing match.

The Agricultural Society, a major force in the community in improving agriculture and livestock, became the showcase for local farmers' work. For the organizers on the executive, the exhibition required months of careful planning and preparation. As the years passed, it expanded to three days and became a major event in the fall, with the schools closing on the Friday to permit the children to participate in the competitions.

Like the first fall fair, the original ploughing match in 1862 attracted few participants. But with the organization of the Agricultural Society in 1868, the ploughing competitions became more popular, and by the 1870s over two dozen men competed. In 1875 Lord Dufferin donated a valuable Scottish-made, high-cut plough as the main prize.[16] The governor general made this donation annually until 1886, when the council and the Agricultural Society paid for the prize plough. Competition was keen. George "Pigtail" Johnson, noted for his effective war cries, started the competitions. When the designated time for ploughing expired, Johnson let forth again with his war cry,

The Six Nations Agricultural Society Fair, Ohsweken, Ontario, early twentieth century.
From Frederick H. Abbott, *The Administration of Indian Affairs in Canada* (Washington, D.C. 1915), opposite 64

signalling to the participants to stop their teams of draft horses. The judges took over and, after measuring the furrows, decided on the winner.[17]

Like the Agricultural Society, the Plowmen's Association became the showcase for Six Nations ploughing expertise. The success of Six Nations men in matches in the surrounding counties soon followed. Three generations of men in William Capton's family won provincial championships as well as coveted prizes of trips to Britain for international ploughing competitions.

*Farming*

Farming reached its peak in the 1890s. In 1891 more land was held in farms than at any other time in reserve history.[18] The farms supported the large number of children in the typical Six Nations family, often six to twelve. Generally, farms ranged in size from twenty to forty hectares, worked chiefly by a father and his sons. Each family had a few cows, which supplied milk for drinking and making butter and cheese, and some chickens, which provided eggs. When the family needed meat, it slaughtered a pig or a cow. Small gardens of corn, potatoes, and various vegetables supplied everyday food needs, and some families had fruit trees and berry patches. Vegetables were stored for the winter in root cellars, and during the summer and early fall, the women worked hard to preserve summer produce for the winter.

Despite the heavier clay soils, the Six Nations farmers produced the same crops as their non-Indian neighbours: wheat, hay, and oats, with oats becoming the major crop by 1891.[19] Because of the difficulties Six Nations farmers faced in getting loans for farming, they used fertilizer less frequently and consequently their crop yields were sometimes less than those outside the reserve. On the whole, however, the Iroquois used similar farming practices. Reapers, mowers, and threshing machines were owned by Six Nations farmers, and teams of horses had by now replaced oxen for ploughing.[20]

As the decades passed, pigs and poultry became more popular on the reserve, although cattle and horses remained the more common livestock. Some of the wealthier farmers began to specialize in certain types of cattle and swine, and a few raised sheep (although this never became popular because sheep became the prey of stray dogs). Farmers interested in improving their livestock through better breeding and caring practices participated in the branch of the Farmers' Institute established on the reserve in 1895. The Six Nations' weekly *Indian Magazine* (1894–98), subsidized by the Farmers' Institute, regularly published suggestions on how to improve crops and livestock.

Although fencing became more common at the turn of the century, cattle occasionally wandered into neighbouring cornfields. Eventually, active farmers pressured the council to establish by-laws regarding fencing, sheep protection, and cattle impounding.[21] The most noticeable change came with the building of larger and more impressive barns. The wealthier farmers made their barn foundations of stone masonry. Almost always barns were erected in barn-raising bees involving anywhere from twenty to a hundred men. While the men cut and shaped the massive timbers with axes and adzes, and then erected the frame, the women cooked the meals and entertained themselves in quilting bees. When barns burned down by lightning, the council provided some fire insurance to cover the loss of the timber and cattle, but neighbours and friends provided the labour to build the new barn. The loan program, which the council initiated in 1895 at the urging of the Farmers' Institute,[22] accelerated the building of barns in the Six Nations community.

Fall harvesting, like barn building, was often done in bees, but by the 1890s farmers employed hired hands from both inside and outside the reserve. As wage labour became more plentiful off the reserve, especially in the Niagara Peninsula during berry-picking season and near Galt (Cambridge) for flax pulling, a serious shortage of local manpower developed. In most families teenage boys helped with the farm chores, while the girls assisted their mothers with the household work and the care of the younger children. School attendance dropped noticeably during the spring planting and fall harvesting seasons, as it did off the reserve, an unavoidable pattern in families that could not afford hired help.

*Education*

Christian families took a more critical look at the school facilities on the reserve in the 1870s. Of the thirteen schools serving the Six Nations in 1874, including the Mohawk Institute, nine were operated by the New England Company, two by the Wesleyan Methodists, and two by the chiefs, financed by band funds.[23] But the standard of education remained uneven and the school system was plagued by many problems. The buildings, of log and frame construction, were in poor repair, and the few windows provided inadequate light and ventilation. While the stoves required constant stoking in the winter, no provision existed to provide wood systematically to the schools, nor for that matter to supply necessary equipment such as slates, books, paper, and desks. This made life in the classroom most uncomfortable. By 1874 only a third (547) of the school-age population (1 504) were even enrolled. Attendance itself was irregular and absenteeism common.[24] Of the thirteen teachers in 1874, eight were Six Nations men and women who had received their own education at the Mohawk Institute. But teacher turnover was very high.

Courtesy of Lloyd King

The No. 8 school in the Six Nations Reserve, mid-twentieth century. About one dozen of these small elementary schools were located throughout the community.

In 1878 a number of the upper chiefs succeeded in convincing the council to vote $1 500 as an annual expenditure on education from their band fund.[25] This grant matched the amount given yearly by the New England Company. To this sum, the Indian Department added $400, its first financial grant to education on the Six Nations Reserve. With the council's grant, the new Six Nations' School Board was formed, composed of three men appointed by the council, three missionaries, and the superintendent, Jasper T. Gilkison. The first Indian school board in the province immediately began its work to improve the educational system on the reserve.

After assessing the state of the school buildings, the school board established a program of repairs and maintenance. The council provided firewood to the existing schools and also gradually built new schools under the direction of the council's inspector of public works.[26] The board dug new wells to ensure a safer water supply. It carried out inventories of teaching equipment and annually reordered whatever was needed. The council soon offered awards for outstanding scholastic achievement and provided grants to assist in board and tuition costs for higher education.

The reserve schools taught the same subjects as elsewhere in the province: grammar, spelling, writing, arithmetic, geography, and history. At the Mohawk Institute these subjects were supplemented by domestic training for the girls and instruction in farming and trades (blacksmithing, shoemaking, carpentry, and stone masonry) for the boys.

By 1884 the Brant County school inspector regularly inspected the reserve schools. Over time the average daily attendance increased. From 1881 to 1901 it rose from 30 percent of those enrolled to 45 percent.[27] Some Six Nations pupils went beyond the primary school level, and by 1888 five students attended the collegiate in Brantford and two more were training to be teachers at the Provincial Normal School in Toronto.

National Archives of Canada, c-85125

Pauline Johnson (1861–1913), the best known of the Six Nations students who attended Brantford Collegiate Institute. At the turn of the century Johnson was one of Canada's most popular poets and entertainers. Today she is best remembered for her poetry celebrating her Amerindian heritage. The photo was taken c. 1890.

After the turn of the century a few of the sons of the more dedicated farmers were sent to the Ontario Agricultural College at Guelph for specialized training. Some parents went to great lengths to ensure that their girls, as well as their boys, received further schooling. Some drove their children daily by horse and buggy to the collegiates in the towns near the reserve, and others boarded their children in town during the week, scrimping and saving money to afford the additional expense.

University training was rare but not absent. Oronhytekha, a Mohawk from the Six Nations Reserve, graduated from the University of Toronto in 1866. Thomas Green, the first engineer from the reserve, took his training at McGill University and was supported by annual grants from the council in the 1870s. At the same time, George Bomberry completed his medical degree in Montreal and the Reverend Isaac Barefoot was ordained as an Anglican clergyman; Reverend Barefoot would teach for many years at the Mohawk Institute.

The success of these young men inspired others to follow, and this in its turn created further pressures to improve the reserve's standard of education. When the New England Company discontinued its annual educational grant in 1897, the council maintained its contribution. The appointees on the school board, sometimes chiefs, but as often individuals without council affiliation, showed great dedication and energy, and helped raise the educational level of the population.

*Health and Social Welfare*

Under Superintendent Gilkison's persistent counselling, the chiefs turned their attention to the field of social welfare and health. Medical services had first been provided to the Six Nations in the 1820s by Robert Kerr, a military surgeon,[28] but the care offered by Kerr and other itinerant physicians was extremely limited. In the early 1840s the chiefs hired Dr. Alfred Digby, a Brantford physician, and paid him from band funds to serve the community, primarily to inoculate against smallpox.[29] The Six Nations suffered from the same diseases as non-Indians in the valley, where the incidence of "fevers and agues," various forms of malaria, was high on account of the damming and flooding caused by the Grand River Navigation Company. In 1853 the council went a step further by hiring Dr. Robert H. Dee on a full-time basis to provide medical services to the reserve. Dr. Dee initially lived in a mission house on the Grand River and visited the homes in his horse and buggy. Throughout his thirty-six years of service, a series of assistant physicians helped him, but he bore the prime responsibility for the community's health care until his retirement in 1889. The Six Nations themselves paid him from their band fund and gave him an annual allowance for purchasing drugs.

Although the Longhouse followers preferred to use their own herbal remedies and curing rituals, the Christian community's demands upon Dr. Dee increased to the point that the council built a large, impressive brick residence for him in Ohsweken in 1885. Office calls now became increasingly common, as Dr. Dee preferred to perform minor surgery at his home rather than in his patients' houses, where the crowded conditions enhanced infection. After 1885 he sent the more serious cases to the newly built hospital in Brantford, and in these instances the council often assisted in the payment of the costs.[30] Tuberculosis, one of the most dreaded diseases because it often proved fatal, required long periods of isolation and convalescence at the Muskoka sanatorium in Gravenhurst (or in later years at sanatoriums in Hamilton and Brantford).

Diseases such as typhoid fever, whooping cough, and scarlet fever continued in the community but with an incidence no greater than among non-Indians in similar rural settings.[31] The overall death rate at Grand River, however, was estimated at twice that of the national average: 20 deaths per 1 000 population compared to the national figure of 10 deaths per 1 000.[32] The high rate can best be attributed to the late seeking of treatment, after the disease had become well advanced. But the high birth rate counteracted the death rate, leading to a gradual overall increase in the band population, from 2 600 in 1868 to 4 000 in 1898.

In an effort to improve public health and sanitation in the community, the council in 1900 adopted a series of health by-laws patterned on those in the surrounding counties.[33] The Six Nations' Public Health Act led to the creation of a board of health, responsible for the enforcement of the by-laws on safe water supplies in the schools and homes, and on quarantining procedures in cases of smallpox or typhoid outbreaks. When a small outbreak of smallpox occurred on the reserve in 1901, the Board of Health supported the doctor's quarantine measures and provided the affected families with food and supplies during their period of isolation.[34]

Superintendent Gilkison recognized the important link between welfare and health in the 1870s and encouraged the chiefs to expand their jurisdiction into the field of social welfare. Gradually the council offered more assistance to the indigent, the elderly, and the chronically ill and disabled. The council provided such assistance if the immediate family was unable to do so, and in several instances it turned back requests on the grounds that immediate kin could provide such assistance. The doctor, who implemented the council's policies, became the local welfare officer. After visiting patients and their families, he filled out orders for relief or hospital care, and later reported the costs to the chiefs in his quarterly sessions with them.[35] In instances of permanent disability the council pensioned band members at $25 a year, and it

Woodland Cultural Centre, Clarence Jamieson Collection

Dr. C.U. Holmes, the doctor to the Six Nations Reserve in the early twentieth century, and several Iroquois chiefs, between 1900 and 1910. *Standing, left to right:* Alex Lottridge, Jacob S. Johnson, Josiah Hill, Peter M. Jamieson, George Gibson; *seated, left to right:* Dr. C.U. Holmes, David John, William Smith.

offered temporary assistance to widows and children without immediate financial support. Generally, however, poor and indigent families were few in number, and the council's help was needed only in extreme circumstances. Immediate kin normally handled family crises of death, sickness, and hardship. Despite the high rate of infant mortality, families had many children, which led to large kinship networks of the matrilineal type among the Longhouse followers and of the bilateral type among the Christians. Beyond these networks, neighbours and longhouse and church members were called upon for support, or volunteered assistance, when needed.

The doctors and chiefs also recognized the relationship between community health and housing but could do little to reduce the overcrowding in the small log houses. By the 1880s housing styles began to diversify and increase in size. Mohawk chief A.G. Smith, the Anglican interpreter, built the first brick residence, a large and imposing structure, in 1880. By 1900 fifteen brick houses reflected the growing differences in wealth and social standing in the community. Although log houses still predominated at the turn of the century, numbering 359 in 1900, the number of larger frame dwellings had increased, totalling almost 200 by 1900.[36]

John Buck with his family, outside his log house, Six Nations Reserve.
Photo by J.N.B. Hewitt, early twentieth century, National Anthropological Archives, Smithsonian Institution, Photo No. JNB Hewitt, Photo Album III, III-10

Chief A.G. Smith's home in the Six Nations Reserve.
From J.B. Mackenzie, *The Six-Nations in Canada* (Toronto 1896), opposite 90

*Community Improvements*

The council's road program produced significant improvement in transportation on the reserve by the 1880s. Barring the common spring washout problems, horse and buggy travel was much easier and farmers could readily get their grain to markets in Hagersville, Hamilton, and Brantford.

Annually the council appointed forty-two pathmasters to oversee the statute labour on the roads. Under this system the concession roads onto which the farm lots abutted were graded and maintained in a systematic way. The council also undertook the more specialized and costly tasks of building bridges and culverts, financing the construction from the annual interest on the band fund. Working with Superintendent Gilkison, the chiefs determined where bridges and culverts were needed and set priorities on the projects. Gilkison and Josiah Hill, the inspector of public works, drew up the specifications, and local Six Nations men, mainly chiefs, tendered bids to the council for the work.[37] The council would have the structure inspected before releasing payment, and the contractors would remedy any subsequent problems having to do with faulty construction.

Increasing centralization in the Indian Department, however, affected the roads program. In 1883, for example, the department required its own engineers to approve the specifications for construction. Although the chiefs resented this infringement on their long-standing local procedures, they were forced to comply with the new policy.[38] Furthermore, as iron construction for bridges became more common, outside contractors tended to be hired for the work.

Ohsweken, the "capital" of the Six Nations territory, had expanded by the 1890s. In addition to the council house and the doctor's residence, the village had as its leading buildings the new Six Nations Agricultural Exhibition Hall and the Tuscarora Baptist Church. James Styres's store, across from the council house, sold all manner of foodstuffs. In a second section Styres stored and sold grain. Seneca chief John Hill, a skilled carpenter, made window sashes, door-frames, and coffins from lumber prepared in the Styres Planing Mill next door in a third section of the store. Upstairs, over the store, was "Styres Hall," used on occasion for public meetings and those of the Orange Lodge (formed in 1886). Oneida chief Jacob Salem Johnson owned and operated a second large store; his descendants would carry on the family enterprise until the early 1970s. No. 2 school, a red-painted wooden structure, was also located in the village. Visitors or chiefs attending council stayed in Alex Lottridge's Western House, a small, well-furnished hotel.

Walking in the village became hazardous in the spring because of the rain and mud, and in the 1890s the residents (with the help of a council grant) built a plank sidewalk. Six Nations people came into the village daily to purchase goods or to visit on their way to the council-operated saw and grist mill just south of the village, at Frog Pond. In the winter, people sat around the wood-burning stoves in the stores to chat in front of the bulletin boards full of notices of local events. But despite Ohsweken's central location, the Indian Department refused to relocate its Indian Office to the village. The office remained in Brantford, requiring residents to travel the sixteen kilometres either on horseback or by horse and buggy, or to take the train from Onondaga station.

*Land Claims*

As pressure for reserve farmland increased in the early 1880s, the Six Nations' land claim to the headwaters of the Grand River became more urgent. In 1882 a small group of active Mohawk farmers, led by Mohawk chief William Smith, founded the Union Association to persuade the council to pursue the land claim.[39]

The Haldimand Deed of 1784 had granted the Six Nations a tract of land from the mouth of the Grand River to its source, to a depth of six miles (ten kilometres) on each side,[40] but the Simcoe Deed of 1793, which was intended to confirm the Haldimand Deed,[41] did not include the land above Nichol Township (see Map 8.1). Nor did land surveys of the tract, approved by Joseph Brant, extend beyond Nichol's north boundary. The Union Association contended that the lands above the Nichol boundary remained the Six Nations'. Under the leadership of Chief William Smith and spurred on by Peter Hill Farmer, a progressive Mohawk farmer,[42] the Union Association repeatedly urged the chiefs to take the claim to the government. The group held regular meetings, kept minutes, and raised funds through tea meetings and oyster suppers so that they might hire a lawyer from Toronto to prepare their case.

After the chiefs agreed to pursue the matter, the Confederacy Council sent a small delegation to Ottawa. Although the meeting with the federal officials was cordial, they denied the validity of the Six Nations' claim.[43] The council then, in 1888, supported William Smith's efforts to carry the case to the colonial secretary in London, England.[44] The council endorsed the brief the Union Association's lawyer had prepared, and with funds raised in the community, Chief Smith visited London in 1889. But the results proved disappointing. As with all such deputations, the British authorities turned the matter back to the Canadian government, whose position remained firm. The government held that Governor Haldimand had not originally purchased land above Nichol Township and therefore was in no position to grant those lands to the Six Nations.[45] Moreover, the federal officials claimed that Joseph Brant and the Six Nations chiefs had accepted the early surveys, which showed the tract's northern boundary to be at Nichol Township. While firmly believing that the land at the headwaters rightfully belonged to the original Haldimand grant, the chiefs took no further action, as the British authorities had confirmed the Canadian government's rejection of the claim.

Disappointed with its limited progress on the land claim, the Union Association turned its attention to controlling pasture lands in the Mohawk area, the southwestern part of the reserve.[46] Active farmers, like Peter Hill Farmer, worked with the Union Association to persuade the council to pass by-laws to assist farming. The council eventually complied with these demands, passing the regulations in the 1890s,[47] although the chiefs were often reluctant to enforce them.

Farming by-laws were an area of importance to many chiefs, as a matter of a larger political principle. By-laws meant that the council was adopting the governing mechanisms of Canadian society. Since the legal basis of the by-laws lay in the Indian Act, many chiefs opposed instituting them, as their existence would acknowledge the act's application to the reserve. But many of the chiefs of the upper nations felt differently and actively encouraged the use of by-laws.

### Political Change

The split between the Christian and the Longhouse chiefs became more pronounced in the Confederacy Council in the 1880s. Led by the powerful Onondaga chiefs, the lower nations became increasingly alarmed at the upper nations' promotion of modifications in the council's procedures. The Onondaga traditionalists believed that the council's old procedures fully met the needs of local government. In principle they opposed the Indian Act and any measures taken by the government to restrict their powers. For them the legitimacy of the Confederacy lay in the rich lore of the League and the success it had brought the Six Nations both in colonial times and in their adjustment to life along the Grand River.

In contrast, the chiefs of the upper nations, led by the Mohawk, wanted to be innovative, to try new procedures, and to adopt new policies, as long as their control over local affairs was not endangered. Wanting to reduce the lengthy and often unproductive council debates, which many of them considered tedious, the "progressives" proposed voting as a means of reaching decisions or breaking deadlocks.[48] During debates on the Indian Act they often took a selective approach, accepting and using certain provisions of the act, such as the by-laws, and opposing others. But whenever federal legislation or

National Archives of Canada, c-33643

A session of the Six Nations Council, council house, Ohsweken, c. 1900. The Six Nations superintendent and other government representatives appear at the desk in front; the Onondaga, the firekeepers of council, in the centre; the Seneca and Mohawk at the right; the Oneida, Cayuga, Tuscarora, Delaware, and Nanticoke at the left.

action by the superintendent threatened to diminish their powers in ways unacceptable to them, they defended their position. Their education and ability to read and speak English enabled them to understand legislation, deal directly with the superintendent, and argue their case in a forceful fashion.

After the government passed the Indian Advancement Act of 1884 (whose sole purpose was to institute elected councils),[49] the chiefs of the upper nations became increasingly aware that they must defend the hereditary council in terms of its contemporary utility as a local government. In short, the upper chiefs became political pragmatists, anxious to ensure the continuity of the council by making it responsive to community demands and the reality of the Indian Department's power. On account of their Christian background and progressive ideas, they took little interest in the rituals of the Confederacy, including the elaborate condolence ceremony for installing new chiefs.[50] Instead their interests lay in streamlining the council's business procedures, establishing the committee structure, and enhancing its success as a local government.

By the 1890s the upper chiefs held the balance of power in the council. They occupied the administrative positions, chaired the committee meetings

and took the minutes, and formulated many, but not all, of the council's posi-
tions on major issues. By 1900 three-quarters of the chiefs were Christian,
reflecting the religious composition of the community. Leadership in the
council rested with the core of influential progressive chiefs, such as Josiah
Hill (Nanticoke), the influential farmer William Smith (Mohawk), the
Anglican interpreter A.G. Smith (Mohawk), the former Department of Indian
Affairs official J.W.M. Elliot (Mohawk), Joab Martin (Mohawk), the
Ohsweken storekeeper Jacob Salem Johnson (Oneida), and the skilled carpenter (who had built the council house) John Hill (Seneca). Active in their
respective churches and the Agricultural Society, they were innovative in their
outlook. Yet, they remained proud of the hereditary council's accomplishments, particularly the adoption of by-laws which, at one point, they
recommended to the St. Regis (Akwesasne) Mohawk.[51] A small core of Longhouse chiefs, including John A. Gibson (Seneca), John Buck (Onondaga),
David Sky (Onondaga), and Abram Charles (Cayuga) – all respected authorities on the lore and ritual of the Confederacy – represented the conservative
position.

Even though Christian and Longhouse chiefs held different views on how
the council should operate, routine business proceeded smoothly. Council
attendance remained exceptionally high, averaging forty to fifty chiefs out of
the official roster of some seventy-six appointments in 1895.[52] (See Table
10.2, pages 236–7.) Vacancies in titles caused by death were readily filled,
and very few disputes arose over succession to titles. Although the council
was still more conservative than the successful farmers wished, and more
innovative than the traditional Longhouse followers desired, the chiefs collectively steered a successful course through these conflicting pressures, including the initial controversy surrounding the federal franchise.

*The Federal Franchise*

Under the Franchise Act of 1885, adult Indian males in eastern Canada who
met the necessary property requirements gained the right to vote in federal
elections without losing their Indian status. The prime minister, John A.
Macdonald, who had personally promoted the Indian franchise as part of his
general assimilation policy, visited the reserve in early September 1886 to
persuade the Six Nations that voting would not jeopardize their special status.
But he failed to convince the chiefs who had already advised the people to
abstain from voting and attending political meetings.[53]

A few of the influential chiefs of the upper nations, however, felt that the
Six Nations' views would be better represented in Parliament if their people
exercised the franchise. These men actively participated in political rallies on

Table 10.2
Six Nations Chiefs, 1897

| Nation | Clan | Chief's Title | Office Holder | Appointed | Assistant Chief | Appointed |
|--------|------|---------------|---------------|-----------|-----------------|-----------|
| Mohawk | Turtle | Tehkarihoken | Elias Lewis | 1878 | Abram Lewis | 1876 |
| Mohawk | Turtle | Ayonwatha | David Thomas | 1870 | Isaac Doxtater, Sr. | 1880 |
| Mohawk | Turtle | Sadekariwadeh | Peter Powless | 1877 | Daniel Doxtater | 1877 |
| Mohawk | Wolf | Sahrehowaneh | Isaac Davis | — | *None at present* | |
| Mohawk | Wolf | Deyonhehgweh | John W.M. Elliott | — | James C. Elliott | — |
| Mohawk | Wolf | Orenrehgowah | Isaac Doxtater, Jr. | 1887 | *None at present* | |
| Mohawk | Bear | Dehhehnagareneh | Joab Martin | 1887 | George W. Hill | 1888 |
| Mohawk | Bear | Rastawehserondah | John Fraser | 1877 | A.G. Smith | 1874 |
| Mohawk | Bear | Sosskoharowahen | William Staats | 1887 | William Smith | 1861 |
| Oneida | Wolf | Odatschedeh | William Green | 1886 | *None at present* | |
| Oneida | Wolf | Kanongweyondoh | Jacob Salem Johnson* | 1893 | — | |
| Oneida | Wolf | Dehyonhhagwedeh | Nicodemus Porter | 1855 | Joseph Porter, Sr. | 1860 |
| Oneida | Turtle | Shononhsese | *Extinct* | | | |
| Oneida | Turtle | Dwenaohkenha | George Peter Hill | 1880 | William Captain Hill | 1888 |
| Oneida | Turtle | Atyadonentha | Abram Hill Jacket | 1888 | Augustus Hill Jacket | 1888 |
| Oneida | Bear | Dewatahonhtenyonk | *Extinct* | | | |
| Oneida | Bear | Kaniyatashayonk | *Extinct* | | | |
| Oneida | Turtle | Owatshadehha | John General | 1851 | Archibald Jamieson | 1888 |
| Onondaga | Deer | Dathodahonh | Nicholas Gibson | 1870 | Philip Hill | — |
| Onondaga | Beaver | Ohnnehsahhen | Peter John Key | 1878 | — | |
| Onondaga | Beaver | Dehhatkatons | Elijah Harris | — | — | |
| Onondaga | Snipe | Honyadagewak | David John | — | — | |
| Onondaga | Ball | Awekenyade | *Extinct* | | | |
| Onondaga | Turtle | Dehhahyatgwaeh | Johnson Williams | 1848 | — | |
| Onondaga | Wolf | Hononweyehde | David Sky | 1885 | — | |
| Onondaga | Deer | Kohwanehsehdonh | John Jamieson | — | — | |
| Onondaga | Deer | Hahehonk | William Echo | 1875 | — | |
| Onondaga | Hawk | Hoyonhnyaneh | Joseph Porter, Jr. | 1887 | — | |
| Onondaga | Eel | Sohdehgwasenh | Levi Jonathan | 1875 | — | |
| Onondaga | Turtle | Sakokehheh | William Peter Buck | 1887 | — | |
| Onondaga | Turtle | Raserhaghrhonh | *Extinct* | | | |
| Onondaga | Turtle | Skanawadeh | Gibson Crawford | — | — | |
| Cayuga | Bear | Dehkaehyonh | Abram Charles | 1863 | James Webster Sky | 1888 |
| Cayuga | Ball | Kajinondawehhon | Robert David | 1897 | Franklin David | — |
| Cayuga | Bear | Katawarasonh | *Extinct* | | | |
| Cayuga | Bear | Shoyonwese | Austin [B]ill | 1897 | Samuel Kick | — |
| Cayuga | Turtle | Atyaseronne | *Extinct* | | | |
| Cayuga | Wolf | Dyonyonhgo | Joseph Jacobs | 1886 | William Hill | 1886 |
| Cayuga | Wolf | Dehyondhowehgo | Joseph Henry | 1888 | Phillip Miller | 1883 |
| Cayuga | Snipe | Dyonwatehon | William Henry | 1883 | John Henry | — |
| Cayuga | Snipe | Atontaraheha | *Extinct* | | | |
| Cayuga | Bear | Deskaheh | Benjamin Carpenter | — | David General | — |

*(Table 10.2 continued)*

| Nation | Clan | Chief's Title | Office Holder | Appointed | Assistant Chief | Appointed |
|--------|------|---------------|---------------|-----------|-----------------|-----------|
| Seneca | Turtle | Skanyadahehyoh | John [Arthur] Gibson | 1872 | George Key | 1887 |
| Seneca | Snipe | Sadehkaonhyeas | Michael Smoke | 1884 | *None at present* | |
| Seneca | Snipe | Satyenawat | *Extinct* | | | |
| Seneca | Hawk | Shakenjowane | *Extinct* | | | |
| Seneca | Turtle | Kanohkye | David Hill Seneca | 1836 | John Hill | 1865 |
| Seneca | Bear or Snipe | Nisharyenen | *Extinct* | | | |
| Seneca | Snipe | Kanonkeedawe | Johnson Sandy | 1890 | — | |
| Seneca | Wolf | Deyonnehohkaweh | George Gibson | 1887 | — | |
| | | | | | | |
| Tuscarora | Turtle | Sagwarithra | Solomon Nash | 1873 | — | |
| Tuscarora | Turtle | Nehawenaha | *Not represented in Canada* | | | |
| Tuscarora | Turtle | Tyogwawaken | Moses Hill (deceased) | — | | |
| Tuscarora | Bear | Nakayendenh | *Not represented in Canada* | | | |
| Tuscarora | Bear | Dehgwadehha | *Not represented in Canada* | | | |
| Tuscarora | Bear | Nehchanenagon | *Not represented in Canada* | | | |
| Tuscarora | Wolf | Nayohkawehha | William Williams | | — | |
| Tuscarora | Wolf | Nayonchakden | *Not represented in Canada* | | | |
| Tuscarora | Snipe | Karihdawagen | Joseph Green | 1886 | | |
| Tuscarora | Snipe | Thanadakgwa | *Not in Canada* | | | |
| Tuscarora | Beaver | Karinyentya | *Not in Canada* | | | |
| Tuscarora | Beaver | Nehnokaweh | *Not in Canada* | | | |
| Tuscarora | Beaver | Nehkahehwathea | *Not in Canada* | | | |
| | | | | | | |
| Nanticoke | Wolf | Sakokaryes | Josiah Hill | 1873 | | |
| Nanticoke | Wolf | Rarihwetyeha | Richard Hill | 1873 | | |
| | | | | | | |
| Delaware | Cold Ashes | Withkumoorhool | Nelles Monture | 1887 | | |

**Pine Tree Chiefs**

| | | | | | | |
|--------|------|---------------|---------------|-----------|-----------------|-----------|
| Onondaga | | Wakanehdodeh | Alexander Hill | 1865 | | |
| Onondaga | | Wakanehdodeh | Isaac Hill | 1865 | | |
| Cayuga | | Wakanehdodeh | William Wage | — | | |
| Seneca | | Wakanehdodeh | David Vanevery | — | | |

* Regent.
*Source:* E.M. Chadwick, *The People of the Longhouse* (Toronto 1897), 86–96

the reserve. During the campaign of 1891 they persuaded the council to cancel a session so that the Liberal candidate could use the council house for electioneering.[54] In 1893 Chief William Smith, a strong Liberal, even addressed the Liberal convention in Ottawa.[55] By 1896 the chiefs had granted both political parties equal treatment in the use of the council house for campaigning.[56]

In the election of 1887, the first after the franchise was granted, ballots were cast by 250 Six Nations men out of a voters' list of approximately 441.[57] The reserve electorate (voting in the South Brant riding) divided their support nearly equally between the Liberal and Conservative candidates in the contests of 1887 and 1891. Both elections returned a Conservative government to Ottawa, but a Liberal member of Parliament from South Brant, William Paterson.[58] In the election of 1896, the last before the withdrawal of the Indian franchise, the high turnout of Six Nations voters was credited with swinging the riding to Robert Henry, a Conservative candidate, although the Liberals won power in Ottawa. In 1898 Sir Wilfrid Laurier and his administration implemented their long-standing pledge to disenfranchise Indians on the grounds that they were wards of the government.[59]

The federal elections had caused such excitement that the council reversed itself and in 1898 requested the government to retain the Indian franchise.[60] However, the implications of the federal franchise for local politics became evident when those individuals who favoured an elected council asked why Indians could vote federally but not locally. Clearly, the federal franchise provided a valuable argument for the Six Nations reformers who wished to replace the hereditary council with an elected one under the Indian Advancement Act. Consequently, in 1903, when the reformers petitioned the government for the return of the federal franchise, the chiefs refused to endorse their request.[61]

*Political Accommodation*

Among the upper nations in the late nineteenth century, education, industry, and achievement became the basis for personal respect and leadership in voluntary associations and church activities. As the council assumed a prominent role in community affairs, a number of families among the upper nations sought to influence its decisions, particularly in the field of education. In 1894 a small group of men known as the Progressive Warriors organized to promote an elected council system under the Indian Advancement Act. They wanted a council progressive in outlook, accountable to the people through elections, and recruited on the principle of personal achievement rather than hereditary privilege.

The Progressive Warriors, most of whom were educated at the Mohawk Institute, where the training they received was superior to that offered in reserve schools, articulately presented their arguments. Active in church affairs and in the Orange Lodge in Ohsweken, they participated fully in the community. In background they reflected the reserve's increasing occupational diversity. Their group included farmers, store owners and storekeepers, mill operators, carpenters, contractors, and, in two instances, a physician and a minister. In their ranks the Mohawk, Delaware, and Cayuga nations dominated. Some participants had relatives who had joined the earlier reform movement (led by Isaac Powless), the group that had promoted municipal government in the 1860s. With one exception they had no claim to hereditary title.

In 1894 the Progressive Warriors petitioned the federal government to establish an elected council on the reserve.[62] Even though the principle of democratic government appealed to the Indian Department, its officials in this instance did not feel that the 212 signatures on the petition (representing only 20 percent of the adult men) showed sufficient support for such a radical change. In fact, the Indian Department saw no need for reform, as the hereditary chiefs were making progressive strides in managing the community. Discouraged by this reception, the Progressive Warriors reduced their activities. Although they renewed their efforts in 1898, they gained no further support from either the community or the Indian Department. In the meantime, the more traditional council members from the lower nations became more assertive.

Uneasy about the changes introduced by the progressive leaders in the council, the Onondaga and Seneca chiefs wanted to renew the traditional practices in the council and reaffirm the Confederacy's sovereign status. As a result, in 1899 they reintroduced the long-ignored practice of opening the council meetings with white wampum, symbolizing the legitimacy of the proceedings.[63]

Since 1890 the lower nations' chiefs had periodically petitioned the government to seek confirmation of Six Nations sovereignty. These memorials

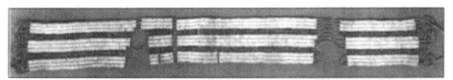

"Gus-wen-tah," or the Two Row Wampum. The belt consists of two parallel rows of purple wampum beads on a white background. The three rows of white beads stand for peace, friendship, and respect. The two rows of purple beads symbolize the British government and the Six Nations Confederacy. Each of the two rows represents a single vessel travelling down the same river, without interfering in the course of the other.

Woodland Cultural Centre

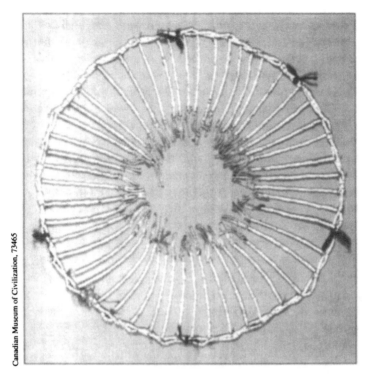

Canadian Museum of Civilization, 73465

This entwined circle with its fifty pendant strings, each one representing one of the chiefs of the original Five Nations, records the
foundation of the Six Nations Confederacy.

invariably referred to the historic wampum belts, particularly the Covenant
Belt[64] and the Two Row Wampum Belt, as evidence of the Six Nations' alliance
with the Crown. Proud of its history, the council gave permission in 1899 to
William Beauchamp, an American ethnologist writing on the Confederacy's rituals, to photograph the remaining wampum belts in the council's possession.[65]
A few months later, the council itself appointed a committee of chiefs to write
down the oral traditions. Thus, from the dictation of the eminent local authority
Seneca chief John A. Gibson, they recorded and approved the official version
of the Confederacy's lore.[66] The chiefs quickly responded to invitations to
surrounding historical societies to give public talks on the Six Nations' history,
and generously assisted anthropologists writing on the Six Nations' customs,
such as J.N.B. Hewitt (1892, 1900-26),[67] Horatio Hale (1895),[68] William
Beauchamp (1901),[69] Edward Chadwick (1897),[70] David Boyle (1898, 1905),[71]
F. Waugh (1916),[72] and A.A. Goldenweiser (1913, 1914).[73]

The council stood at its zenith in the 1890s. It steered a careful, but highly successful, course between the conflicting demands of the Progressive

Warriors and the Longhouse traditionalists by acknowledging some of the demands of both groups. The key to the council's success lay in the influential chiefs of the upper nations, who, holding the balance of power in the council, tried to accommodate the forces of reform and conservatism in the community. As adept political pragmatists, the chiefs acknowledged the presence of the Indian administration, understood its workings, and used its respect for "progress" to justify the continuance of their council. Their ability to act as brokers between the conflicting interests in the community led to the smooth functioning of the council. Although not innovators, these upper chiefs facilitated major advances in education, road construction, farm improvement, and public health, leading many people on the reserve and in the Indian Department to view the council as a strong, progressive force. Understandably, people on the reserve today remember the Confederacy Council of this era primarily for the leadership role it took in accommodating the community's two cultural traditions.

## The End of an Era

In the early twentieth century, agriculture remained the community's primary economic base. Farmers began to market more dairy produce and to specialize in various breeds of cattle and swine. Increasingly the younger generation worked, in season, berry picking off the reserve or sought permanent jobs in nearby towns. The Six Nations Agricultural Society recovered after its exhibition hall was struck by lightning and burned to the ground in 1908. The society built a new hall, and the fall fair attracted even larger crowds.

Although women had always played a major role in church activities and in organizing the fairs, they now formed their own voluntary associations. In 1905 they founded the Ohsweken Women's Institute to promote better education for rural women. Through its activities the Six Nations women became skilled organizers and effective community leaders. During the First World War many of them took up Red Cross work.[74] By sponsoring box socials, masquerade parties, and booths at the fall fair, women on the reserve raised money to buy a piano for one of the schools and food for the sick and needy. They encouraged education by giving prizes at the school fairs, and they successfully campaigned for a systematic immunization program for the schoolchildren.

In keeping with Victorian values, several enthusiastic church women, together with some missionaries and the Indian superintendent, formed a local branch of the Moral Reform League in 1907. Dedicated to improving the moral standards in the community, this organization's zealous leadership quickly became unpopular by preaching a strict puritanical morality at every opportunity. The league's short life was a welcome relief to Longhouse and church people alike.

The annual cycle of ceremonies continued in the four longhouses, and although changes occurred in the matrilineal kinship system, particularly in the use of clan names among the Mohawk, Longhouse followers still traced descent matrilineally.[75] Although the Indian Act prescribed rules of inheritance for transferring property from the deceased to his wife and children, the chiefs respected the matrilineal system among the Longhouse people and supported the wishes of those of their followers who adhered to it. Hereditary chieftain titles continued to pass matrilineally through families with few irregularities.[76]

Community health remained an important part of the council's activities, and the Board of Health (1901–24) actively promoted better sanitation facilities on the reserve.[77] A tent hospital was erected in Ohsweken in 1908, and although originally intended to house tubercular patients (there were then fifty active cases of TB on the reserve), it handled patients with all types of illnesses.[78] However, the drafty bell tents provided little comfort to the dozen patients. After the women's tent blew down in a wind storm in 1911, the chiefs ended the experiment.

The council continued to repair old schools and to build new ones. It also maintained the roads program. Under insistent pressure from families of the upper nations, the chiefs considered the adoption of regulations for compulsory school attendance, despite a petition from the Longhouse community against such a policy.[79] Both the Christian families who wanted more progressive policies and the Longhouse families who now actively petitioned the

National Archives of Canada, c-33568

Superintendent Gordon J. Smith in the office of the Six Nations Indian Agency, Brantford, Ontario, c. 1912.

chiefs to block such changes, pressured the council. In the midst of these demands, the council tried to expand its powers in local management, but it encountered an increasingly rigid Indian Department bureaucracy. The department denied the council any role in selecting physicians paid from band funds. It also rejected the request to institute a loans program for house construction and informed the council that its educational proposals were too costly to implement. The council's work became exceedingly difficult as political unrest increased.

*Unrest*

The Progressive Warriors (commonly called "Dehorners" in keeping with their objective of removing the horns of office from the chiefs and installing an elected council) reorganized in 1906 under the title of the Indians Rights Association. Under a more effective and educated leadership, the Dehorners pressed the council to adopt provincial standards of education on the reserve. When this failed, they petitioned the federal government in 1907 and again in 1910 for an elected band council.[80] Although some of their most active spokespersons were Delaware, leadership and support came largely from the Mohawk, Upper Cayuga, Tuscarora, and a few Seneca families. In principle, the Dehorners opposed hereditary rule, believing that local government should be progressive in its policies and accountable to the people through elections. They actively campaigned for public support by holding annual picnics and supper meetings, and by using the local press in Brantford and Caledonia.[81] In 1910 they sent a delegation to Ottawa to enlist government support. But in spite of their organizational skills and energetic campaign, they could not increase their support beyond 25 percent of the community. While sympathetic to their aims, Indian Department officials (concerned about the possibility of unrest on the reserve) informed the Dehorners that unless they obtained the backing of a clear two-thirds majority in the community, the government could not consider instituting an elective system.[82] This discouraged the Dehorners, and although their leaders (with a few exceptions) remained committed, they no longer actively campaigned as they had in the past.

While the Dehorners pressed for an elected government, the Longhouse community vigorously reaffirmed its customs and traditions. In an effort to improve relations between the two groups, the chiefs passed a resolution that in the future Longhouse followers would be referred to as "Deists," not "pagans," as was often the case on the reserve.[83] Although well intended, the resolution had little impact. When the chiefs of the upper nations sponsored a ceremony to reaffirm loyalty to the Confederacy in 1914, some of the Longhouse chiefs withheld their support. They argued that the council no

National Archives of Canada, PA-120204

Dehorners on a mission to Ottawa to request the institution of an elected Six Nations council, Ottawa, Ontario, 31 March 1910.

longer followed the proper procedures and that the Christian chiefs neither respected nor understood the workings of the Confederacy.[84] By 1917 relations in the council had deteriorated to the point that the chiefs had to urge Onondaga chief David Sky, the wampum keeper, to return to council and read the wampum belts for the gathering.[85] Attendance at the council fell to the lowest in history, averaging twenty to twenty-five chiefs out of the seventy appointments. The appointment of a firekeeper to preside over the meetings sometimes proved difficult on account of the high absenteeism among the Onondaga chiefs.

In the years immediately preceding the First World War, the operations of the council began to break down under the cross-cutting pressures of the Dehorners on one side and conservative Longhouse chiefs on the other. The more immediate factor, however, was the loss of the old leadership in council, brought about by the death of such influential chiefs as John A. Gibson in 1912 and Josiah Hill in 1915.[86] For decades these men had been powerful moderating forces in the council, tempering relations and proposing conciliatory measures. As they and other chiefs died, more militant young men of both Longhouse and Christian affiliation succeeded them. Confronted with a more assertive council, the Indian Department grew increasingly uneasy about the daily management of Six Nations affairs and more determined to contain the unrest.

When news of the outbreak of war with Germany in August 1914 reached the council, the chiefs immediately voted $1 500 towards the patriotic fund and offered to support the enlistment of their young men if this was needed.[87] But relations turned sour when Ottawa refused to acknowledge their status as allies of the Crown.[88] When the Canadian military authorities solicited the chiefs' help in recruiting, the council shifted ground, disclaiming Canada's right to military jurisdiction over Six Nations men. Instead, the council reaffirmed its allegiance to Great Britain, deciding to support recruitment only if asked by the king himself.[89] The council maintained this position throughout the war, and it actively opposed the program established by Ottawa in 1916 to register all able-bodied males in Canada and to control agricultural production for the war effort.[90]

## The First World War

Most of the community did not share the council's opposition to the Canadian military effort. Indeed, young men eagerly volunteered and many past military age tried in vain to enlist. Early Six Nations recruits joined the 4th Battalion, but most went into the 114th Battalion of the Haldimand Rifles, formed in the fall of 1915 under the command of Col. E.S. Baxter. After Baxter's death in

1916, the command fell to Lt.-Col. Andrew T. Thompson, a lawyer and former member of Parliament from Cayuga who formed lasting friendships with the Six Nations men and officers of the battalion. In all, 292 men enlisted from the reserve,[91] forming two complete companies in the 114th Battalion. In their honour, the Women's Patriotic League on the reserve embroidered a magnificent regimental flag with Iroquois clan motifs and tomahawks in recognition of the Indian contingent. It hangs today in the council house.

The Six Nations men were among the first Canadian troops to encounter gas warfare in the trenches in France.[92] Their leadership and bravery brought them high acclaim.[93] In April 1915 Lieut. Cameron D. Brant, a great-great-grandson of Joseph Brant, was the first soldier from Brant County to be killed in action, fighting at Ypres with the 4th Battalion. Of the 292 Six Nations men who enlisted, 29 were killed in action, 55 were wounded, and 5 died from sickness.[94]

During the war years the Women's Patriotic League worked tirelessly for the soldiers. They knitted socks and mitts, collected proper clothing, and raised money to send cigarettes and gifts overseas. They ensured that Six Nations men without relatives received mail, and in some of their work they were supported by funds from the council. When the men returned at the end of the war, they formed the Veterans' Association. The association raised funds to help widows and orphans, and one returned soldier, Lieut. Fred Loft,

Courtesy of Affa Loft Matteson

Lieut. Fred Loft of the Six Nations, with his company of men in the Forestry Corps, Canadian Expeditionary Force, Windsor Park, England, July 1917. The Six Nations council had named Loft a Pine Tree chief shortly before he went overseas.

founded the first national Indian organization in Canada in 1919, the League of Indians of Canada.[95]

## The End of Confederacy Rule

The war left its mark on local politics in a very different manner. Disappointed, if not bitter, over the council's failure to support the Canadian military effort, some of the Six Nations soldiers in France signed a petition in 1917 urging the government to establish an elective council on the reserve. Although the Indian Department still declined to endorse an elected system, the petition carried considerable weight after the war, when Canadian nationalism increased and reformers could make a strong appeal on the reserve to "the loyalist cause."

Following the war, the application of the Soldiers Settlement Act to the reserve only heightened the unrest.[96] The act, designed to assist veterans to improve their farms or establish new farmsteads, required that reserve land be assigned to returned men. The chiefs strongly objected to the act, viewing it as an infringement on their right to allot land. They also disputed the Canadian government's assumption that it had authority over Six Nations territory. Despite the council's resistance, lands were assigned to veterans. By 1920 the difficulties between the council and the Indian Department had become acute.

Displeased with the slow rate of voluntary enfranchisement, the government amended the Indian Act in 1920.[97] Henceforth, an Indian, under the act, could be compulsorily enfranchised without application if a panel of three properly appointed persons judged him to be fit for full citizenship status. The amendment, known locally as the Compulsory Enfranchisement Act, caused a furore on the reserve, increasing to an intolerable level the chiefs' resentment of government interference in their affairs. In an attempt to free themselves from the government's authority, the chiefs reasserted the Confederacy's sovereignty[98] and hired A.G. Chisholm, a lawyer from London, Ontario (and later George Decker, a lawyer from Rochester, New York), to prepare their case for them. They raised funds on the reserve, and in 1921 and again in 1923 they sent Deskaheh, Cayuga chief Levi General, to London, England, and then to Geneva, Switzerland, to carry their case before the League of Nations.[99] Deskaheh, a member of the Upper Cayuga Longhouse, had become a forceful leader in the council and was supported by the Mohawk chiefs. He led the pro-Confederacy faction in its struggle to retain power.[100] In the end his efforts failed to bring the Confederacy recognition as a sovereign power, but his activities attracted considerable public attention[101] and rallied strong support for the chiefs on the reserve.

By early 1923 minimal cooperation between the chiefs and the superintendent made even routine business difficult. In an effort to break the impasse, the government appointed Col. Andrew T. Thompson to investigate the situation. However, Thompson's close association with the First World War veterans who had petitioned for an elected council immediately cast doubt on his impartiality and on the government's motives. Confederacy supporters boycotted the hearings he held in Ohsweken. Few people were surprised when his report recommended the abolition of the Confederacy Council.[102]

In September, a month after the release of Thompson's report, Duncan Campbell Scott, the deputy superintendent general of Indian affairs, secured cabinet approval to establish an elected council. The chiefs and Col. C.E. Morgan, the local superintendent, had been holding council meetings in the agricultural exhibit hall in Ohsweken while the council house underwent repairs. On the morning of 7 October 1924 they convened the proceedings in the normal way. Then, at noon, without prior notice to the chiefs, Colonel Morgan read the order-in-council removing the Confederacy from power. He then announced the date for the first election of the band council. Although they had expected the government to make such a move, the chiefs were unprepared for the announcement. When Morgan finished, the chiefs quietly disbanded and gathered outside in shock. On Morgan's orders, the Royal Canadian Mounted Police (RCMP) seized the wampum used to sanction council proceedings and other council records from the council house, and deposited them in the safe at the Indian Office in Brantford. On the doors of the hall they posted a proclamation announcing the date and procedures for the first election.

In its last years the Confederacy Council bore little resemblance to the highly effective council of the 1890s. Although the council's militant leadership had alienated some of the more moderate chiefs in the early twentieth century, the hereditary council still held strong majority support in the Six Nations community in 1924. Even the Dehorners regretted the fashion in which the federal government had so abruptly ended the council's rule at the Grand River.

National Archives of Canada, c-33642

Proclamation announcing the first election for positions on the Six Nations council, October 1924.

National Archives of Canada, c-33571

First elective council of the Six Nations, 1924. Colonel Morgan, the Six Nations Indian superintendent, appears in the centre of the first row, fourth from the right, among the councillors.

After the elections in mid-October 1924, the newly elected councillors (two from each of the six electoral districts on the reserve) took their seats in the council house. Since then the elected council has governed the reserve, receiving support from 20 to 40 percent of those eligible to vote in the elections.

## Post-war Development

Following its establishment in 1924, the elected council adopted new policies in many fields.[103] With support from the province, it purchased road graders and began a more extensive road improvement program. The elected council enforced compulsory education and applied the provincial standards of education to the school system. It hired qualified teachers, many of them Six Nations women. A small but increasing number of children proceeded to high school and post-secondary training. With a $7 000 contribution from the band funds, the twenty-bed Lady Willingdon Hospital was opened in Ohsweken in 1928. Until his retirement in 1951, Dr. Walter Davis managed the hospital. While not Indian himself, Dr. Davis, the reserve's doctor, had been raised in the community by a Six Nations family. The women at the upper end of the reserve formed a ladies' auxiliary, to raise funds for bed linen, dishes, and other needed items for the hospital. They visited patients, brought them gifts

Lady Willingdon Hospital.
Photo by J.N.B. Hewitt, National Anthropological Archives, Smithsonian Institution, Photo. No. III-15

and reading material, and organized Christmas parties and other kinds of entertainment.

Although many families still farmed, the inability of a number of Six Nations families to secure loans for farm machinery (because of the legal status of reserve lands) led them into new occupations. Families sometimes moved to Hamilton, Buffalo, and Detroit for work in industry. High steel rigging, although dangerous work,[104] was popular and lucrative, and employment opportunities led individuals to travel widely throughout Ontario and New York State, returning home on weekends or upon the job's completion. During the Depression of the 1930s some of these families returned to the reserve where they could grow their own food and share accommodation with relatives. The Temperance Society was gradually transformed into the Benevolent Lodge during these years, and the many branches on the reserve raised funds to cover funeral costs and support families in times of hardship.

Although the reserve gradually became a rural non-farming community in the 1930s, the old agriculturally based voluntary associations remained as the most prestigious organizations on the reserve. The fall fairs of the Agricultural Society and the ploughing matches attracted large crowds, and the Women's Institute still received strong support from the women of the upper nations. Women became even more active in the community.[105] As teachers and nurses they exerted pressure in the home and the community to improve the education and public health standards on the reserve. The Orangemen's Lodge continued to hold meetings in Ohsweken. But the most active group was the Veterans' Association, which, in a flurry of activity in the early 1930s, raised money to erect a monument in the park adjacent to the council house, to honour the Six Nations men who were killed in the First

World War.[106] The Veterans' Association remained active during the Second World War, when it was joined by Six Nations women who again formed a local branch of the Red Cross to support their young men and women overseas. During the war approximately 225 members of the Six Nations community served in either the Canadian or American forces; one of their number, Brigadier Milton Martin, commanded the 14th and 16th Infantry Brigades of the Canadian Army.[107]

Following the 1924 change-over in local government, the Confederacy chiefs continued to hold meetings in the Onondaga Longhouse and to raise up new chiefs in the condolence ceremony.[108] Joined at times by the Mohawk Workers, a faction of Christian hereditary council supporters,[109] they worked for the reinstatement of the hereditary council. As the years passed, however, some of the Lower Cayuga Longhouse members came to support the elected council, maintaining that religion and politics were separate fields of activity.[110] Without governing functions, the hereditary council had gradually become much like a theocracy, reinforcing the values of the Longhouse culture and becoming more tightly integrated with the Longhouse religion.[111]

The cultural duality of the Six Nations community has persisted over generations despite pressures for change. The Longhouse culture has remained viable,[112] and the highly acculturated Christian group has developed a style of life that today is barely distinguishable from that of non-Indians in Southern Ontario, although its members still strongly identify as Iroquois.

As a whole, the Six Nations community has a keen interest in its own history, taking particular pride in the traditions of the Confederacy and in the prominent role of the League in colonial times. Over the years a number of Six Nations people have written on certain aspects of their community and its local history, among them John Brant-Sero,[113] Asa B. Hill,[114] E.H.C. Johnson,[115] Ethel Brant Monture,[116] Elliot Moses,[117] Julia Jamieson,[118] Enos Montour,[119] Alma Greene,[120] Elmer Jamieson,[121] and George Beaver.[122] Research by Six Nations people on their own history is carried out at the Woodland Cultural Centre in Brantford in the renovated Mohawk Institute building. Significant historical documentation on Six Nations history has been collected and catalogued in the centre's research library, while its collection of rare books covers the Eastern Woodlands area.[123] Its museum and gallery, under the direction of Tom V. Hill, have facilitated the patriation of Iroquoian wampum in recent years[124] and supported research on the history of the early Mohawk village.[125] The centre has also prepared materials on Six Nations veterans,[126] and it provides a research guide for the many Six Nations persons who seek assistance in reconstructing their family genealogies.[127]

# NOTES

1 *Six Nations Council Minutes (SNCM)*, 1881, 215
2 Horatio Hale, "The Iroquois Sacrifice of the White Dog," *American Antiquarian and Oriental Journal* 7 (1885): 7–14
3 David Boyle, "The Pagan Iroquois," *Annual Archaeological Report, Appendix to the Report of the Minister of Education, Ontario*, 1898, 81
4 F.W. Waugh, *Iroquois Foods and Food Preparation* (Ottawa 1916), Memoir 86
5 Gertrude P. Kurath, *Dance and Song Rituals of Six Nations Reserve, Ontario*, Bulletin 220, National Museum of Man (Ottawa 1968)
6 A.A. Goldenweiser, "On Iroquois Work, 1912," *Summary Reports of the Geological Survey Branch of the Canadian Department of Mines for the Calendar Year 1912* (Ottawa 1914), 472–3
7 Ibid., 367
8 *SNCM*, 1891, 106–7
9 A.C. Parker, *The Code of Handsome Lake, the Seneca Prophet*, Bulletin 163, N.Y. State Museum (Albany 1913)
10 The Anglican Church formed its first congregation around the Mohawk Chapel built by Joseph Brant in 1786. St. John's, the second Anglican church, was built originally in the Tuscarora village in the 1830s, but it was later moved across the river to the main body of the reserve in 1884. In quick succession, St. Paul's (Kanyengeh) was built in 1865, Christ Church (Cayuga) in 1874, and St. Luke's in 1888. St. Peter's Church, the last of the Anglican churches, was built in Ohsweken in 1908. The Baptists, the next largest church group, had three churches, the largest being the Tuscarora Baptist Church in Ohsweken, its congregation dating from 1840, when missionary activity began. The Medina Baptist Church was erected in 1860, and the last, Johnsfield Baptist, in the 1890s. The Methodists, with half the size of the Baptist congregation, operated in three churches, the earliest being the Delaware Methodist Church, dating to missionary work in the 1840s. Stone Ridge Church, west of Ohsweken, was erected in 1898, and the last one, Grand River Methodist, after the turn of the century.
11 *Indian Magazine* (Brantford), 1894–98
12 Edward M. Chadwick, *The People of the Longhouse* (Toronto 1897). Chadwick (1840–1921), an authority on Ontario genealogies, was very interested in the Six Nations. For an interesting account of the oratorical skills of Chief A.G. Smith, see Hugh Dempsey, *Red Crow, Warrior Chief* (Saskatoon 1980), 166–72. For details on Lord Dufferin's visit, see William Leggo, *The History of the Administration of the Right Honorable Frederick Temple, Earl of Dufferin* (Montreal 1878), 254–65. Good reviews of Sir John's visit appear in the Brantford *Courier*, 8 September 1886, 1–2; the Brantford *Expositor*, 8 September 1886, 2; and the Brantford *Weekly Expositor*, 10 September 1886, 4. Denise Kirk, local history librarian, Brantford Public Library, kindly located these references to John A Macdonald's visit.
13 *Six Nations Agricultural Society Minutes (SNASM)* (Ohsweken 1868). These minutes are in the possession of Mr. Arthur Anderson Sr.
14 *SNASM*, 1869
15 *SNCM*, 1882, 313

16   Elliot Moses, "A Brief Historical Sketch of the Six Nations Plowman's Association" (Address given to the Six Nations Plowman's Association, 26 October 1963)

17   Ibid.

18   Katherine A. Sample, "Changes in Agriculture on the Six Nations Reserve" (MA thesis, McMaster University, 1968). Sample calculates that the average acreage of cropland per farm, for example, tripled between 1861, when it was slightly over 4 hectares, and 1891, when it was almost 12 hectares. Improved lands, which included all lands used for crops, pasture, orchards, and gardens, doubled from 1861 to 1891, to an average of 16 hectares. As farming became more widespread, the average farm size decreased. Thus, the average in 1861 of almost 36 hectares per farm dropped to under 24 hectares by 1891, the lowest in reserve history. By 1891 over one-half of the nearly 700 farms on the reserve were between 4 and 20 hectares in size, while one-quarter of them were between 20 and 40 hectares. The more active and aggressive farmers had expanded their holdings to the extent that forty-three men owned farms between 40 and 80 hectares, and six held farms of over 80 hectares.

19   Sample, "Changes in Agriculture on the Six Nations Reserve," 57

20   Elliot Moses, "Seventy-Five Years of Progress of the Six Nations of the Grand River," *Waterloo Historical Society* 56 (1969): 19–26

21   SNCM, 1895, 425

22   Ibid., 424

23   Canada, Department of Indian Affairs, *Annual Report* (Ottawa 1874), 13. For a historical overview of education at Grand River, see Abate Wari Abate, "Iroquois Control of Iroquois Education: A Case Study of the Iroquois of the Grand River Valley" (PhD dissertation, University of Toronto, 1984); and Woodland Cultural Centre, *School Days: An Exhibition on the History of Indian Education* (Brantford 1984). For primary- and secondary-level teaching purposes, *School Days* has excellent photographs. A highly useful teaching unit for grades 7 and 8, entitled *Reserve Communities: A Six Nations History Unit* (Brantford 1987), has been prepared by the Woodland Cultural Centre. This unit overviews Six Nations history from pre-contact times to the present. For earlier grades, especially grades 5 and 6, see Bruce Hill, *Six Nations* (Toronto 1986).

24   Canada, Department of Indian Affairs, *Annual Report* (Ottawa 1874)

25   SNCM, 1878, 380

26   Julia D. Jamieson, *Echoes of the Past: A History of Education from the Time of the Six Nations Settlement on the Banks of the Grand River in 1784 to 1924* (Ohsweken 1969)

27   Canada, Department of Indian Affairs, *Annual Report* (Ottawa 1881), 305–7; Canada, Department of Indian Affairs, *Annual Report* (Ottawa 1901), 35

28   Johnston, *The Valley of the Six Nations*, 110

29   Sally M. Weaver, *Medicine and Politics among the Grand River Iroquois* (Ottawa 1972), 41–7

30   Ibid., 44

31   Boyle, "The Pagan Iroquois," 189

32   J.A. MacRae, *Report Re Sanitary and Some Other Matters: Six Nations Reserve* (Ottawa 1899), 613

33   Canada, *Six Nations Public Health Act: Regulations of the Six Nations Indians of the Grand River* (Ottawa 1900)
34   Sally M. Weaver, "Smallpox or Chickenpox: An Iroquoian Community's Reaction to Crisis," *Ethnohistory* 18 (1971): 361–78
35   Weaver, *Medicine and Politics*, 46
36   Canada, Department of Indian Affairs, *Annual Report* (Ottawa 1900), 506
37   SNCM, 1882, 370
38   Ibid., 1883, 481
39   Peter Hill Farmer, "Minutes and Notes of the Six Nations Union Association" (Ohsweken, Ont. 1882–87), Archives of the Canadian Museum of Civilization, Hull, Quebec
40   Canada, *Indian Treaties and Surrenders from 1680 to 1890* (2 vols., Ottawa 1891; reprint, 3 vols., Toronto 1971), 1:251–2 (henceforth *Treaties and Surrenders*)
41   Ibid., 9–10
42   Fred W. Voget, "A Six Nations' Diary, 1891–1894," *Ethnohistory* 16 (1969): 345–60
43   Canada, *Sessional Papers,* no. 20B (Ottawa 1887)
44   SNCM, 1888, 34
45   Canada, *Sessional Papers* (Ottawa 1887), 37. For a description of recent Six Nations land claims, see Donald J. Bourgeois, *Research Report on the Six Nations Indian Land Claim to the "Tow Path" along the Grand River,* prepared for the Ministry of Natural Resources (Toronto 1982); and Donald J. Bourgeois, "Six Nations Indian Land Claim to the Bed of the Grand River," *The Historical Research Report Series,* Report No. 1, prepared for the Ministry of Natural Resources (Toronto 1986).
46   Farmer, "Minutes and Notes of the Six Nations Union Association"
47   Six Nations, *Consolidated Regulations of the Six Nation Indians of the Grand River* (Ottawa 1910)
48   SNCM, 1880, 37–8, 128–33
49   Canada, Indian Advancement Act ("An Act for Conferring Certain Privileges on the More Advanced Bands of the Indians of Canada, with the View of Training them for the Exercise of Municipal Powers"), 47 Vict., c. 28, 1884
50   Horatio Hale, "An Iroquois Condoling Council," *Transactions of the Royal Society of Canada,* 2d ser., vol. 1, sec. 1 (1895), 43–65; reprinted in William Guy Spittal, ed., *The Iroquois Bill of Rites and Hale on the Iroquois by Horatio Hale* (Ohsweken, Ont.: Iroqrafts 1989), 339–61
51   SNCM, 1899, 367–8
52   John A. Gibson, "Names of Chiefs of the Six Nations According to the Rules and Order of the Confederation," *Distributors Book, 1890–1907* (Brantford 1895)
53   SNCM, 1885, 386
54   SNCM (Ohsweken), 1891, 68
55   Malcolm Montgomery, "The Six Nations and the Macdonald Franchise," *Ontario History* 57 (1965): 17
56   SNCM, 1896, 299
57   National Archives of Canada (NA), RG 10, vol. 2287
58   Montgomery, "The Six Nations and the Macdonald Franchise," 23
59   Ibid., 25
60   SNCM, 1898, 141–8

61  *SNCM*, 1903, 349
62  NA, RG 10, vol. 2284, Petition to T.M. Daly, Spring 1894
63  *SNCM*, 1899, 376
64  Diamond Jenness, "Three Iroquois Wampum Records," *Annual Report of the National Museum of Canada for 1931* (Ottawa 1932), 25–9
65  *SNCM*, 1899, 228; William N. Beauchamp, "Wampum and Shell Articles Used by the New York Indians," *New York State Museum Bulletin* 41 (1901): pl. 14, figs. 174–9
66  *SNCM*, 1900, 271. Duncan Campbell Scott, the future deputy superintendent general of Indian affairs (1913–32), later published this record. See Duncan C. Scott, "Traditional History of the Confederacy of the Six Nations," *Proceedings and Transactions of the Royal Society of Canada*, 3d ser., vol. 5, sec. 2 (1912), 195–246
67  J.N.B. Hewitt, "Legends of the Founding of the Iroquois League," *American Anthropologist* 5 (1892): 131–48; "Iroquoian Cosmology," *Annual Report of the Bureau of American Ethnology* 21 (1903): 127–339; "Indian Cosmology," *Annual Report of the Bureau of American Ethnology* 43 (1928): 449–819
68  Hale, "An Iroquois Condoling Council," 45–65
69  Beauchamp, "Wampum and Shell Articles," 321–480
70  Chadwick, *The People of the Longhouse*
71  Boyle, "The Pagan Iroquois," 54–211; David Boyle, "The Making of a Cayuga Chief," *Annual Archaeological Report, Appendix to the Report of the Minister of Education, Ontario 1905*, 56–59. For a short review of David Boyle's contact with the Six Nations, see Gerald Killan, *David Boyle: From Artisan to Archaeologist* (Toronto 1983), 180–6.
72  Waugh, *Iroquois Foods and Food Preparation*
73  Goldenweiser, "On Iroquois Work, 1912, " 467–75; A.A. Goldenweiser, "On Iroquois Work, 1913–1914," in *Summary Report of the Geological Survey Branch of the Canadian Department of Mines for the Calendar Year 1913* (Ottawa 1914), 365–72
74  Mabel (Hilton) Hill, *History of the Ohsweken Women's Institute* (Brantford 1965), 6
75  Goldenweiser, "On Iroquois Work, 1912"; Goldenweiser, "On Iroquois Work, 1913–1914"
76  Ibid., 369
77  Weaver, *Medicine and Politics*, 59–66
78  Ibid., 66–70
79  *SNCM*, 1906, 263
80  NA, IA file 32–32, vol. 1, Petitions, 13 March 1907 and 7 April 1910
81  Weaver, *Medicine and Politics*, 24–7
82  NA, IA file 32–32, vol. 1, Pedley to Miller, 20 April 1910
83  *SNCM*, 1908, 73
84  *SNCM*, 1914, 421–4
85  *SNCM*, 1917, 140, 182
86  A.A. Goldenweiser, "The Death of Chief John A. Gibson," *American Anthropologist* 14 (1912): 692–4; Frank G. Speck, *The Nanticoke and Conoy Indians with a Review of Linguistic Material from Manuscript and Living Sources: An Historical Study* (Wilmington 1927), 29
87  *SNCM*, 1914, 46
88  A.I. Hatzan, *The True Story of Hiawatha, and History of the Six Nations Indians* (Toronto 1925), 165–6

89 *SNCM*, 1914, 516–17
90 *SNCM*, 1918, 288, 348
91 Duncan C. Scott, "The Canadian Indians and the Great World War," in *Canada in the Great World War* (Toronto 1919), 3:285–328
92 Enos T. Montour, *The Feathered U.E.L.'s* (Toronto 1973), 110–15
93 Scott, "The Canadian Indians and the Great World War"
94 Canada, *Sessional Papers*, no. 27, Annual Report of the Department of Indian Affairs (Ottawa 1920), 16
95 Frank Montour, *World War I, 1914–1918* (Brantford 1965). For a very thorough overview of Six Nations veterans from the War of 1812 to Viet Nam, see Sheila Staats, *Warriors: A Resource Guide*, Woodland Cultural Centre (Brantford 1986). For good accounts of the work of F.O. Loft, see E. Brian Titley, "League of Indians of Canada: An Early Attempt to Create a National Native Organization," *Saskatchewan Indian Federated College Journal* 1 (1984): 53–63; E. Brian Titley, *A Narrow Vision* (Vancouver 1986), 96–109; and Peter Kulchyski, "A Considerable Unrest: F.O. Loft and the League of Indians," *Native Studies Review* 4 (1988): 95–117.
96 Canada, *Revised Statutes of Canada* (Ottawa 1922)
97 Canada, *Revised Statutes of Canada*, "An Act for the Gradual Enfranchisement of Indians ... "
98 Asa R. Hill, "The Historical Position of the Six Nations," *Papers and Records of the Ontario Historical Society* 19 (1922): 103–9
99 Levi (Deskaheh) General, *General Deskaheh Tells Why He Is Over Here Again* (London 1923)
100 George Decker, *The Redman's Appeal for Justice: The Position of the Six Nations That They Constitute an Independent State* (Brantford 1924)
101 "Appeal of the 'Six Nations' to the League," *League of Nations Official Journal*, June 1924, 829–37; M. Montgomery, "The Legal Status of the Six Nations in Canada," *Ontario History* 55 (1963): 93–105
102 Andrew T. Thompson, *Report by Col. Andrew T. Thompson, Commissioner to Investigate and Enquire into the Affairs of the Six Nations Indians, 1923* (Ottawa 1924)
103 S.M. Weaver, "Six Nations of the Grand River Ontario," in *Handbook of North American Indians*, vol. 15: *Northeast*, ed. Bruce G. Trigger (Washington, D.C. 1978), 534–6
104 J. Mitchell, "The Mohawks in High Steel," in E. Wilson, ed., *Apologies to the Iroquois* (New York 1960), 3–16; Richard Hill, *Skywalkers*, Woodland Cultural Centre (Brantford 1987)
105 Martha C. Randle, "Iroquois Women, Then and Now," *Bureau of American Ethnology*, Bulletin 149 (1951): 167–80
106 Montour, *World War I, 1914–1918*
107 Sheila Staats, *Warriors: A Resource Guide* (Brantford 1986), 26–7
108 William N. Fenton, "An Iroquois Condolence Council for Installing Cayuga Chiefs in 1945," *Journal of the Washington Academy of Sciences* 36 (1946): 110–27; Donald J. Bourgeois, "The Six Nations: A Neglected Aspect of Canadian Legal History," *Canadian Journal of Native Studies* 6 (1986): 253–70
109 Ralph W. Nicholas, "Factions: A Comparative Analysis," in Michael Banton, ed., *Political Systems and the Distribution of Power* (New York 1965), 21–61

110   Marcel Rioux, "Relations between Religion and Government among the Longhouse Iroquois of Grand River, Ontario," Bulletin 126, National Museum of Man (Ottawa 1952), 94–8

111   Denis Foley, "An Ethnohistoric and Ethnographic Analysis of the Iroquois from the Aboriginal Era to the Present Suburban Era" (PhD dissertation, State University of New York at Albany, 1975)

112   Frank G. Speck, *Midwinter Rites of the Cayuga Longhouse* (Philadelphia 1949); Annemarie Anrod Shimony, *Conservatism among the Iroquois at the Six Nations Reserve* (New Haven 1961); Michael Foster, "From the Earth to Beyond the Sky: An Ethnographic Approach to Four Longhorn Speech Events," Canadian Ethnology Service, paper no. 20 (1974)

113   John O. Brant-Sero, "The Six Nations Indians in the Province of Ontario, Canada," *Transactions of the Wentworth Historical Society* 2 (1899): 62–73; John O. Brant-Sero, "Some Descendants of Joseph Brant," *Papers and Records of the Ontario Historical Society* 1 (1899): 113–17; John O. Brant-Sero, "Dekanawideh: The Law-giver of the Caniengahakas," *Man*, n.s., 134 (1901): 166–70

114   Hill, "Historical Position of the Six Nations," 103–9

115   E.M.C. Johnson, "Chief John Smoke Johnson," *Papers and Records of the Ontario Historical Society* 12 (1914): 102–13; E.H.C. Johnson, "Grandfather and Father of E. Pauline Johnson," *Annual Archaeological Report, Appendix to the Report of the Minister of Education, Ontario* (1928), 44–7

116   Harvey Chalmers and Ethel Brant Montour, *Joseph Brant: Mohawk* (East Lansing 1955)

117   Moses, "Seventy-Five Years of Progress of the Six Nations of the Grand River," 19–26

118   Jamieson, *Echoes of the Past*

119   Montour, *The Feathered U.E.L.'s*

120   Alma Greene, *Forbidden Voice* (Toronto 1970)

121   Elmer Jamieson and Peter Sandiford, "The Mental Capacity of Southern Ontario Indians," *Journal of Educational Psychology* 19 (1928): 313–28

122   George Beaver, *A View from an Indian Reserve: Historical Perspective and a Personal View from an Indian Reserve* (Brantford 1993)

123   For a very good popular account of the Eastern Woodland nations, see Tom V. Hill, "The Indians of the St. Lawrence Lowlands," in *The Canada Heirloom Series* (Mississauga 1988), 2:12–25.

124   Tom V. Hill, Paul Williams, and Joanna Bedard, *Council Fire: A Resource Guide*, Woodland Cultural Centre (Brantford 1989); William N. Fenton, "Return of Eleven Wampum Belts to the Six Nations Iroquois Confederacy on Grand River, Canada," *Ethnohistory* 36 (1989): 392–410

125   Ian Kenyon and Neal Ferris, "Investigations at Mohawk Village," *Arch Notes* (Ontario Archaeological Society), January-February 1984, 19–49; Tom V. Hill, "Treasures from Mohawk Village," in *Canadian Collector*, September-October 1984, 15–17

126   Staats, *Warriors*

127   David Faux, "Documenting Six Nations Indian Ancestry," *Families* 20, no. 1 (1981): 31–42

# 11

## The Iroquois of Akwesasne (St. Regis), Mohawks of the Bay of Quinte (Tyendinaga), Onyota'a:ka (the Oneida of the Thames), and Wahta Mohawk (Gibson), 1750–1945

### CHARLES HAMORI-TOROK

In addition to the Six Nations on the Grand River, four other Iroquois communities are located within the province, each with its own distinctive story. The foundation of Akwesasne in the mid-eighteenth century and that of Tyendinaga (Mohawks of the Bay of Quinte) several decades later have already been reviewed (see chapters 5 and 6). The Oneida of the Thames (Onyota'a:ka) arrived from New York State during the 1840s. Forty years later Iroquois from Lake of Two Mountains (Kanesatake or Oka), Quebec, moved to a site near Bala, in Muskoka, in Gibson Township (the Mohawk of Gibson, or the Wahta Mohawk).

### The Akwesasne (St. Regis) Iroquois

The founders of Akwesasne, a Mohawk word meaning "where the partridge drums" (a reference to the rapids nearby),[1] were predominantly Iroquois, although some Algonquian-speaking peoples (mainly Abenaki) from several locations in eastern Canada joined them.[2] At the end of the American Revolution in 1783, their thirty-year-old community straddled both sides of the upper St. Lawrence River, in present-day Ontario, Quebec, and New York State. A decade after the revolution, Akwesasne, originally named St. Regis by the French (before the British Conquest in 1760), still had signs of a strong French influence. After meeting a number of Indians from St. Regis in July 1793, Elizabeth Simcoe, the wife of Upper Canada's lieutenant-governor, wrote in her diary: "They speak French, are much civilized, and have a good deal of the manners of Frenchmen."[3]

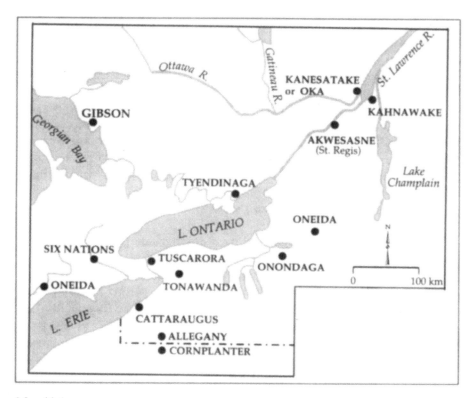

Map 11.1
Six Nations Communities in Ontario, Quebec, and New York State
Drawn by Marta Styk, University of Calgary

Although the Akwesasne Mohawk agreed that many Six Nations Iroquois who had moved to Canada had surrendered title to their lands in New York State, they and their fellow Iroquois at Kahnawake (Caughnawaga) and Kanesatake (Oka) had never done so. In May 1796 the Iroquois signed a treaty with the U.S. government, by which they ceded all their lands except for nearly 100 square kilometres at Akwesasne on the south bank of the St. Lawrence River and two other small parcels of land, for a cash settlement and annuity payments.[4]

Substantial changes came to Akwesasne after 1800. The State of New York appointed three trustees to represent the interests of those Iroquois residing on the south side of the St. Lawrence in 1802. By so doing, the state created an artificial division between the life-chiefs, traditionally appointed by "clan mothers," and the trustees. These two tribal councils, the government-appointed and the hereditary, could not, or would not, cooperate with one another. To add to the Iroquois' dilemma, the British refused to allow those from the American side to live on the Canadian.[5]

The War of 1812 increased the division. Although apparently a sort of gentlemen's agreement initially existed between the British and American authorities not to involve the Akwesasne Mohawk in the hostilities, eventually some joined the British cause, others the American.[6] Following the war, the pro-American Akwesasne Mohawk in the United States recommended that the Americans deny any further annuity payments to those Iroquois who had supported the British. In the end, both governments refused to pay annuities to people living on the "other side of the St. Lawrence River." Beginning in 1841 the Americans paid only registered members of the St. Regis (Akwesasne) Reservation living on the American side, and the British paid only those living in Canada.

In 1836, 381 persons resided on the Canadian side of Akwesasne: 105 men, 109 women, and 167 children under the age of fourteen. This number increased to 450 by the early 1840s. The ethnic composition of the community remained much the same as it had been at the outset: Mohawk from Kahnawake and the Mohawk valley; Onondaga, Oneida, and Cayuga from the Oswegatchie Mission; some Abenaki from the St. Francis River; and some Indians of unknown origin. While Mohawk became the common language, the presence of a clan system indicates that the Mohawk did not predominate. Of the five clans present at Akwesasne, three, the Turtle, Wolf, and Bear, were found among the Mohawk but the Snipe and the Deer were Onondaga

Metropolitan Toronto Reference Library

St. Regis (Akwesasne) as seen by the artist William Henry Bartlett, 1841.

clans.[7] The clan mothers on the Canadian side appointed the twelve life-chiefs who administered the affairs of the Canadian settlement.

During the nineteenth century the Akwesasne Iroquois adopted a way of life that, on the surface at least, resembled that of their non-Native neighbours. They dwelt in log cabins, tilled the soil, and (as a result of their early contact with the Jesuits) regularly attended the Roman Catholic church. Toward mid-century they had on the Canadian side about 200 hectares under cultivation. They continued their practice of slash-and-burn farming. Once they cleared land, they planted it with Indian corn for as many years as possible. They followed with crops such as wheat, peas, beans, oats, potatoes, pumpkins, rye, and buckwheat, until they exhausted the soil, at which point they cleared new land and repeated the cycle. On the average each family cultivated about three hectares. They did not use fertilizer. They cut their hay from the large neighbouring marshes. If their farmland lay at any distance from the settlement, the farmer and his family lived all summer by their fields in a temporary shelter.

Fish constituted an important source of food at Akwesasne in spring and summer. In winter many of the men hunted and trapped. During the summer some young men hired out as raftsmen and boatmen. Some no doubt went farther afield. Unfortunately, the records do not indicate what percentage of the "Iroquois" in the northwest fur trade around 1800 came from Akwesasne, or how many eventually settled permanently in the west, never to return.[8]

Although a degree of political unity initially existed at Akwesasne, external forces worked to split the community. The Americans continued to appoint trustees for the Iroquois, while the British accepted the life-chiefs as the legitimate governing body in Canada. An important unifying factor for the Christian Iroquois, the Roman Catholic Church, was undermined when the Methodist Church in the United States began missionary work at Akwesasne in 1847.

The Canadian government's passage of the Indian Act of 1876 further complicated the lives of the Akwesasne Iroquois. It made patrilineal descent the criterion for registering all status Indians in Canada. On the other hand, New York State continued to determine the descent of the Akwesasne Iroquois matrilineally. This led to ridiculous situations. No longer in Canada could the children of a Canadian Akwesasne woman and an American Akwesasne man be accepted as band members: the father did not reside in Canada. *Vice versa*, on the New York side, the children of a Canadian Akwesasne woman could not be enrolled, as she did not belong to the American Akwesasne community.

To add to the confusion, the Canadian government in 1884 abolished the traditional chiefs' administration of the Canadian Akwesasne community in favour of an elective system. In defiance of the law the Akwesasne clan

mothers appointed twelve life-chiefs as had been their custom and prerogative. The Department of Indian Affairs, however, refused to accept this council and tried to impose democratic elections. The shooting of one Indian and
the jailing of several others marred the vote held in 1899. Aware of the continuing opposition, the department did not initiate new elections once the
terms of the twelve incumbents selected in 1899 expired. Only after tempers
cooled and the opposition weakened did the department reintroduce the elective system. By the early 1930s the traditional chiefs at Akwesasne had died.
Considerable opposition to the elected council remained, but the clan mothers
did not appoint replacements.

The unbearable external pressures on the Akwesasne community caused
great confusion. In 1914 a number readily accepted "Chief Thunderwater" –
an "ersatz" messiah – a black from Cleveland, Ohio, who began political
work at Akwesasne, Kahnawake, and Tyendinaga. By promising to build a
school and a bridge and generally to improve the lot of the Akwesasne people, this charlatan, who used his own mixture of Amerindian ideology and
symbolism, attracted a following. After collecting a sizable amount of money,
Chief Thunderwater disappeared.[9]

During the early 1930s, Alex Chute, an Onondaga Longhouse preacher,
settled at Akwesasne to establish the religion of Handsome Lake. With the
introduction of the Longhouse religion, the Akwesasne Mohawk secured the
ideological foundations necessary to maintain "the old culture" and to justify
the hereditary system of government. This nativistic movement began at a
time when emotions within the community ran high. The ill-fated outcome of
Thunderwater's pronouncements provided fertile ground for the acceptance of
the Longhouse religion. The Longhouse congregation became one of the larger religious groups on the reserve.[10]

### The Tyendinaga Iroquois (Mohawks of the Bay of Quinte)

Akwesasne was the first Iroquois community to become established in what is
now Ontario in the eighteenth century, and the Mohawk community at
Tyendinaga, on the northeastern shore of Lake Ontario, was the second.
Originally, the approximately 120 Mohawk who settled under John
Deserontyon on the shores of the Bay of Quinte were granted about 37 600
hectares. Over the years, however, they lost much of their land.[11] One of the
first surrenders occurred in 1820 when the Tyendinaga Mohawk gave up
some 13 400 hectares in exchange for an annuity of £450. Fifteen years later,
in 1835, the community lost about 6 070 hectares to establish Crown and
Clergy Reserves without, it is claimed, obtaining due compensation from the
government. In that same year, the Mohawk surrendered a further 11 300

hectares. By 1980 their lands along the shores of the Bay of Quinte, the least productive of their original holdings, did not exceed 6 900 hectares.[12]

Before the American Revolution, the Mohawk, influenced by European settlers and the Anglican missionaries, had practised a European style of agriculture in the Mohawk River valley. The ownership of the land by lineages and gardening by females had given way to individual garden plots and cultivation by males. The Mohawk continued this type of tenure on the Bay of Quinte. The men used draught animals and farm equipment common among Euro-Canadian farmers.[13] By the 1830s they lived on farms scattered about the reserve and had cleared some 550 hectares, of which they cultivated over one-third (200 hectares). Mixed farming continued until the First World War, when off-reserve employment and out-migration of band members increased. During the Depression of the 1930s, however, a number of band members returned to take up subsistence farming. Enlistments in both world wars and the increasing mechanization of farming after the Second World War partially explain the decline in farming. Few Mohawk farmers could raise the necessary capital to modernize their operations. Although agriculture no longer constitutes the basis of the reserve's economy, the Mohawk Fair held in September remains as popular as ever.

The government of Tyendinaga has changed greatly as well over the last two centuries. Information about the early period of Mohawk settlement on the Bay of Quinte is limited, but in the early 1960s one elder claimed that the community contained remnants of eleven lineages, comprising three clans: Wolf, Turtle, and Bear. Furthermore, he stated that a lineage matron, whom he referred to as the "family mother," had the responsibility to appoint a male of her lineage to the position of "life-chief." The appointment usually went to the matron's brother or to one of her sons. Eleven chiefs formed the tribal council. If a life-chief did not perform his duties satisfactorily, the matron of his lineage could replace him. The tribal council transacted the business of the Bay of Quinte Mohawk until the late nineteenth century, when the federal government introduced an elective system. As time passed and life-chiefs died, the posts remained unfilled, as it became evident that the Canadian authorities would not recognize their legitimacy. By 1964 only one was said to remain.

For a time, a Grand Council consisting of life-chiefs from all Iroquois communities convened at either the Six Nations Indian Reserve at Brantford or at Syracuse or Tonawanda (near Buffalo) in New York. The council attempted to persuade Ottawa to recognize the Six Nations Confederacy's special status. Many Tyendinaga band members, however, showed little interest in these proceedings. Tyendinaga's elected council, for its part, never recognized the life-chiefs or the part they and others played in the Grand Council.

The Tyendinaga Mohawk's kinship system also became more and more like that of the dominant society. By the mid-nineteenth century they had adopted the same kinship terminology. No longer did they distinguish between a "parallel cousin" (considered as a sibling) and a "cross-cousin" (considered as an in-law). Formerly, one could marry one's cross-cousins, that is, one's mother's brother's or father's sister's offspring; only marriage with parallel cousins, the offspring of a parent's same-sexed siblings, was forbidden. Now they termed both parallel- and cross-cousins as "cousin" and prohibited marriage with either one. Finally, the clans no longer played any role in the Tyendinaga Mohawk's society and administration. By mid-twentieth century they were but vaguely remembered.

Private Huron Eldon Brant, member of the Mohawks of the Bay of Quinte, receives the Military Medal from Gen. Bernard Montgomery for bravery at Grammichele in Sicily.

The Tyendinaga Mohawk have remained allies of the Crown and staunch Anglicans. For their acceptance of Anglicanism, in 1710 the English government presented the Mohawk with a set of silver altar pieces, treasured to this day. When the Mohawk fled the Mohawk River valley, they left behind them the Queen Anne's Silver, as the set is referred to today, safely hidden. In 1793 Captain Deserontyon made his way back to the hiding place and brought the silver back to Tyendinaga. In due course, the Mohawks of the Bay of Quinte and those living on the Grand River divided the altar pieces between them.[14] Strong Anglicans and extremely loyal to the British Crown, the Tyendinaga Mohawk served faithfully in both world wars.

### The Oneida of the Thames (Onyota'a : ka)[15]

Another Iroquois group joined their Grand River, Tyendinaga, and Akwesasne brethren in Ontario sixty years after the American Revolution. Several hundred Oneida arrived during the early 1840s and settled along the banks of the Thames River near London. The Oneida and the Tuscarora had actively supported the Americans during the revolution, but this alliance did not save the Oneida from the ravages of war. They saw their fields destroyed and much of their land confiscated. The Oneida exiles who were scattered between Schenectady and Niagara annually faced long winters of hunger and the hatred of those League members who had remained loyal to the British Crown.

During the decades following the American Revolution conditions deteriorated still further. Some Oneida moved to Kahnawake and Akwesasne. Those who remained in New York State came largely under the influence of Protestant missionaries, whose activities sparked religious factionalism, the "pagan" party versus the Christians. Subsequently, Eleazer Williams, a Mohawk Episcopalian missionary from Kahnawake,[16] devised a plan to move the Oneida to Wisconsin. In the early 1820s several hundred, including some Stockbridge Indians (or Algonquian-speaking Indians originally from what is now New England and eastern New York), emigrated to Green Bay, Wisconsin, leaving about 600 Oneida behind in New York State. Those who remained had further disagreements, which eventually led approximately half the community to purchase about 2 100 hectares of land along the Thames River, next to an Ojibwa and a Munsee (Delaware) community. The Oneida arrived in the 1840s under the leadership of Moses Schuyler and William Taylor Doxtator. As they had purchased the land in common, they held a meeting soon after their arrival to determine how to apportion the land and pass it on to their heirs. The council decided that as much land as an individual could clear would be his "property." Once he had done this, the individual had the right to sell, transfer, or will his property to any band member who had, or whose ancestor had, contributed to the original purchase of the land along the Thames.

As the Oneida established homesteads scattered over their tract, subsistence farming became the community's major activity. The Ontario Oneida grew a number of different crops, some to be consumed immediately, the remainder stored for future use in barns, in root cellars, or in nearby grain elevators owned by non-Natives. Meat, on the other hand, might be dried or salted and packed in barrels. Work bees often undertook farm tasks that required many hands, such as erecting a new barn. The Oneida had only a limited opportunity to acquire cash income. During the summer some individuals worked on the neighbouring flax and tobacco fields of Euro-Canadians. During the winter those who wished to leave the community might find seasonal jobs in the lumber industry. Finally, the sale of any extra farm produce and crafts, such as baskets and cornhusk mats, supplemented their incomes. In the twentieth century, as more and more individuals took jobs in nearby non-Native communities, farming lost its importance and declined.

Once the Oneida had become settled, they instituted a governing council, modelled after the council they had had in New York. As in the past, the matrilineal clans – Wolf, Bear, and Turtle – each appointed a chief and deputy for life to represent them in council meetings. For a time, the hereditary chiefs of the Grand River Iroquois attended the Oneida's councils to validate the appointment of a chief and deputy to council. Through this invitation the Oneida became a part of the Six Nations Confederacy of Canada, and in so doing eased the strain that had emerged at the time of the American Revolution and the War of 1812 when the groups had adopted opposite sides in the conflicts.

The hereditary chiefs settled disputes that might arise from time to time among community residents. Topics of concern were discussed at special council meetings open to all band members so that they might voice their opinions. Debate continued until all agreed. If this proved impossible, the contentious issue was set aside. As advisers the hereditary chiefs had the Pine Tree chiefs, chosen by the clan mothers in consultation with the hereditary chiefs on the basis of their speaking ability and standing in the community. Whenever troubles occurred or any community member had a problem, the Pine Tree chiefs reviewed the case and advised the hereditary chiefs on a course of action. Following Confederation, the Department of Indian Affairs (after it was established in 1880) became more and more involved in Oneida politics. Whenever the chiefs and council could not find a solution to a particular problem, they turned it over to the Indian agent or his superior to adjudicate according to the Indian Act's provisions.

Like all Amerindian groups, strong ties of kinship knit together the Oneida of the Thames. In this matrilineal society the strongest tie existed between a mother and her daughters. Also important were those between grandparents, especially on the mother's side, and their grandchildren. One acquired one's lineage and clan membership from one's mother. One could also acquire membership in the community if one could prove that an ancestor had originally contributed towards the purchase of lands along the Thames River.

As a rule, a father would arrange his son's marriage. Although frowned upon, marriage to a member of the same clan occurred on occasion owing to the small size of the population and a reluctance to marry outside the community. In the late nineteenth century the Oneida underwent further changes in their social and economic way of life. They began to contract more marriages outside the confines of the reserve, and at the same time, clan affiliations lost much of their significance.

The rapidity of change in the twentieth century stimulated unusual factionalism in the Oneida community as well as a move to unseat the Oneida of the Thames's Confederacy Council. In 1915 the dissidents created a second hereditary council; this council had the backing of members of the Longhouse religion who had refused to recognize the legitimacy of the original Oneida of the Thames's council. Within a few years this new body, known as the Six Nations Confederacy Council, became the only one that the Canadian government and the Grand River Iroquois considered legitimate. This action prompted the Oneida of the council to seek help from the Onondaga of New York State. Finally, a third group arose which petitioned the Canadian government in 1934 for an elective governing council, chosen by popular vote.

Although it has been claimed that the majority of the Oneida were not in favour of the idea, the Canadian government accepted the third group's proposal and instituted an elective form of government on the reserve. A chief and twelve councillors elected for two-year terms now governed the community. The Six Nations Confederacy Council refused, however, to accept the elected council. Nevertheless, the federal government authorized the elected council to deal with a variety of community activities, such as education, welfare, housing, and road construction and maintenance.

In the late nineteenth and early twentieth centuries, the majority of the Oneida belonged to one of the Christian denominations: most were Methodists, and a few were Anglicans and Baptists. Some families remained faithful to the Longhouse religion in spite of missionary work among them by Native ministers such as the Reverend Abraham Sickles for the Methodists and the Reverend Henry Chase for the Anglicans. The Longhouse people kept alive the yearly cycle that included the Midwinter, Strawberry, Green Corn, and Harvest ceremonies. Associated with the Longhouse religion were two "curing societies," the False Face and Little Water societies. Belief in the curing societies remained strong, and Christians, as well as Longhouse followers, belonged. Individuals cured by one of the societies could become members of it. Since dreaming was closely associated with curing, another way to gain membership was to have dreamt of doing so. When a person became ill, he or she sometimes consulted individuals recognized for their skills in divining the future from dreams, to gain information as to the appropriate cure. In addition, the Oneida believed deeply in the supernatural and the efficacy of magic potions.

In spite of the challenges they faced, the Oneida made a successful adaptation to their new surroundings in Ontario. They escaped from their impoverished condition in New York to build a new community on the banks of the Thames River. Further north in Muskoka other Iroquois settled four decades later, refugees from Kanesatake, or Oka, at Lake of Two Mountains fifty kilometres west of Montreal.

### Gibson Iroquois (Wahta Mohawk)[17]

The Iroquois who live today at Gibson, adjacent to the town of Bala in Muskoka, arrived over a century ago. They emigrated from the Lake of Two Mountains in the 1880s to their new home in Ontario. They trace their ancestry back to those Iroquois who in the late seventeenth century moved from present-day New York State first to a mission adjacent to the French settlement at Montreal and later to Sault au Récollet on the Island of Montreal. In 1717 the King of France granted the Seminary of St. Sulpice a seigniory at Lake of Two Mountains. Four years later the Sulpician fathers transferred their mission to Lake of Two Mountains and welcomed to it some Algonquian-speaking Indians as well as the Iroquois from Sault au Récollet.

After the British conquest, troubles arose immediately between the Mohawk and the Sulpicians over the issue of the ownership of the seigniory. The Mohawk believed they had been granted the land at Lake of Two Mountains for their use and benefit by the French Crown; the Sulpicians thought otherwise. In the 1870s Methodist missionaries (who supported the Indians' land claim) converted many of the Roman Catholic Iroquois. In 1880 the Department of Indian Affairs asked the Province of Ontario for a block of land within the township of Gibson for the Protestant Lake of Two Mountains Mohawk, where they might establish a settlement and clear the land for farms. As the Protestant Mohawk themselves had selected this location, the government hoped that their migration would resolve the controversy.

A year later, in 1881, the Ontario and Canadian governments reached an agreement by which Ontario sold to the Department of Indian Affairs 10 400 hectares in the township of Gibson where all the Protestant families of "Oka Indians" might settle. Ontario insisted that the Indians must fulfil the "settlement duties" required of all settlers as provided for by the Free Grant and Homestead Act. These duties included the clearing of at least six hectares annually for five years and the construction of a house at least six by seven metres. Finally, after years of discussion regarding the terms of the transfer of land and the Indians' duty to adhere to the terms set forth in the Free Grant and Homestead Act, a reserve was officially created in 1918. The Gibson Indian Reserve, however, contained only some 6 000 hectares, 4 450 hectares less than originally specified.

During the early 1880s, Protestant Mohawk and a few Algonquians had left Lake of Two Mountains and settled on the lands that later became known as the Gibson Indian Reserve. An estimated twenty-five families took up residence near Bala.[18] By 1910, 130 Indians resided in the settlement. In the initial years a few became discouraged and returned to Oka.

In time, the Mohawk cleared land and erected dwellings. They acquired a small house to use as a school and hired a young Indian girl at twenty dollars

Early Iroquois settlers at Gibson. This photo was taken by John Boyd at the Sahanatien Post Office in 1888.

National Archives of Canada, RD 46

a month as the teacher. The community built a proper schoolhouse in 1883. A work bee consisting of the whole community undertook the task of building the first church. In 1909 they built a new Methodist church, this time in a more central location. The decision to move the church, however, proved controversial. The community became split and bitter feelings arose.

For many years after their arrival, these Mohawk depended on hunting and fishing for their livelihood. They caught as many fish as possible during the fall, then smoked or salted the fish for use during the winter. During the late fall they hunted deer and dried the meat for later use. The men tanned the hides from which the women made moccasins worn year-round. They also cut the hides into babiche for use as cordage. With the arrival of spring, the people, young and old alike, tapped the maple trees and prepared syrup and sugar. Spiles of cedar were employed to tap the trees, and log troughs held the sap before it was boiled down in large iron kettles. The people gathered the sap in the morning before the crust on the snow had had time to melt. Maple sugar was used in the cooking of berries and wild apples.

Farming gradually became an important activity. To clear the land, the Indians felled the trees and with hand pikes and/or oxen assembled and burnt the logs. Eventually each farm consisted of from three to eight hectares of cleared land. Whenever a family needed help, neighbours assisted. Each spring the Mohawk ploughed their fields and planted their crops. Each day after supper, which often consisted of corn bread, corn soup, venison, and

Camp Sahanatien, near the Gibson Indian Reserve. The lumber camp was owned by Jim Sahanatien, a member of the Gibson Mohawk community. Fourth from the right, he is seen with the other members of the community, c. 1905.

Ontario Ministry of Natural Resources

meat and apple pies, the Mohawk held a prayer meeting at which they sang Methodist hymns in Mohawk. Corn, harvested in October, was perhaps the most important crop grown, then hay for livestock. Each fall (after the crops had been harvested) the Mohawk held a wood-cutting bee, putting up fire-wood for the winter ahead. By 1900 every farm family had from ten to twenty-five head of cattle, one or more horses, and some pigs and chickens.

Besides working the land, some Gibson Mohawk found seasonal employ-ment in nearby lumber camps. Wages ranged between eight and twelve dol-lars – later as much as sixteen dollars – per month. Board consisted of "yel-low bread," boiled and fried pork, and white beans. With income so earned or by barter, family heads once or twice a month made their way to the stores in Bala, where they purchased food, most often flour, a man often returning home with a 100-pound (45 kilo) sack on his back.

As at other Indian communities in Southern Ontario, farming declined at Gibson after the First World War. By the mid-twentieth century the Gibson Mohawk, like the Iroquois living in the four other Iroquois communities in Ontario, began to experience more changes in their way of life (see chapter 15).

## NOTES

1   James White, ed., *Handbook of Indians of Canada* (New York 1969), 405
2   The Iroquois who founded Akwesasne were soon joined by some Abenaki who had fled their village of St. Francis, near Sorel, following a raid on it by Robert Rogers and his Rangers in 1759. Most of them moved back to their rebuilt mission at Odanak at the mouth of the St. Francis River, immediately east of Montreal. A few Abenaki, however, did remain with the Akwesasne Iroquois. See Gordon M. Day, *The Identity of the Saint Francis Indians*, Canadian Ethnology Service, Mercury ser., paper no. 71 (Ottawa 1981), 74
3   Elizabeth Simcoe, *Diary*, ed. J. Ross Robertson (Toronto 1911), 175
4   Charles J. Kappler, comp., *Indian Affairs: Laws and Treaties*, 5 vols. (Washington, D.C. 1904–41; reprint, New York 1971), 2:45–6; William N. Fenton and Elisabeth Tooker, "Mohawk," in *Handbook of North American Indians*, vol. 15: *Northeast*, ed. Bruce G. Trigger (Washington, D.C. 1978), 477; Jack A. Frisch, "Revitalization, Nativism and Tribalism among the St. Regis Mohawks" (PhD the-sis, Indiana University, 1970), 69–70
5   Fenton and Tooker, "Mohawk," 477
6   Frisch, "Revitalization," 69–70; Fenton and Tooker, "Mohawk," 477
7   Jack A. Frisch, "Tribalism among the St. Regis Mohawks: A Search for Self-identi-ty," *Anthropologica* 12, no. 1 (1970): 209–10
8   A.F. Chamberlain, "Iroquois in Western Canada," *American Anthropologist* 6, no. 4 (1904): 459–63; A.M. Josephy, *The Nez Percé Indians and the Opening of the Northwest* (New Haven 1965); R.E. Lamb, *Thunder in the North* (New York 1957);

Frederick Merk, ed., *Fur Trade and Empire: George Simpson's Journal* (Cambridge 1938); Trudy Nicks, "The Iroquois and the Fur Trade in Western Canada," in Carol M. Judd and Arthur J. Ray, eds., *Old Trails and New Directions* (Toronto 1980), 85–101; Alexander Ross, *The Fur Traders of the Far West*, ed. K.A. Spaulding (Norman 1956)

9   Frisch, "Tribalism among the St. Regis Mohawks," 109–10; Susan (Koessler) Postel, "Hoax Nativism at Caughnawaga: A Control Case for the Theory of Revitalization," *Ethnology* 4, no. 3 (1965): 266–78

10  Frisch, "Tribalism among the St. Regis Mohawks," 115

11  Deborah Jean Doxtator discusses the Tyendinaga land surrenders in "Tyendinaga Land Surrenders: 1820–1840" (MA research essay, Carleton University, 1982). For an overview of Tyendinaga's political history, see Charles Hamori-Torok, "Structures and Politics in Tyendinaga Politics," *Anthropologica*, n.s., 14 (1972): 31–42. K Shelley Price-Jones reviews the early history of the community in "Emerging from the Shadows: The Life of Captain John (Deserontyou), circa 1742–1811, Founder of the Bay of Quinte Mohawk Village" (MA thesis, Queen's University 1993).

12  In the near future the Tyendinaga Mohawk will regain a tiny portion of their lost land. The Mohawk in 1835 leased eighty hectares of their remaining lands, including part of the hamlet of Shannonville, about twenty kilometres east of Belleville, to a Montreal merchant for 999 years, for an annual rent of thirty barrels of flour. The Tyendinaga band council, however, voided the agreement in 1971 when it refused to accept the flour, calling it "unfit for human consumption" (Toronto, *Globe and Mail*, 11 July 1984). A memorandum of understanding was signed on 1 July 1991, between the Mohawks of the Bay of Quinte First Nation and the federal government. Ottawa has agreed to acquire the leased land. As of December 1992, fifty-eight of the non-Mohawk residents indicated their willingness to sell their interests in their property. Once the federal government purchases the land, it will be returned to Mohawk control.

13  J.W. Lydekker, *The Faithful Mohawks* (Cambridge 1938), 176

14  Fenton and Tooker, "Mohawk," 474, 476

15  The following discussion of the Oneida of the Thames is based primarily on Jack Campisi, "Ethnic Identity and Boundary Maintenance in Three Oneida Communities" (PhD thesis, State University of New York, 1974).

16  For more information on Eleazer Williams, consult Geoffrey E. Buerger, "Eleazer Williams: Elitism and Multiple Identity on Two Frontiers," in *Being and Becoming Indian: Biographical Studies of North American Frontiers*, ed. James A. Clifton, 112–36 (Chicago 1989).

17  Based primarily upon Philip LaForce, *History of Gibson Reserve* (Bracebridge, n.d.); Sylvia DuVernet, *An Indian Odyssey* (Islington, Ont. 1986); and Donald J. Bourgeois, personal communication.

18  Charles Angus Cooke provides an excellent account of the background to the departure for Gibson in "Dear Friends of Gibson Reserve," Ottawa *Citizen*, 26 July 1990, A15. Marius Barbeau has written a sketch of Cooke, "Charles A. Cooke, Mohawk Scholar," *Proceedings of the American Philosophical Society* 96, no. 4 (August 1952): 424–6.

*Part Three*

*Northern Ontario, 1550–1945*

# 12 *Northern Algonquians, 1550–1760*

## CHARLES A. BISHOP

The identification of seventeenth- and eighteenth-century Northern Algonquian local groups poses great challenges. For example, was the group name recorded in the historical records the one that the individuals so designated gave themselves? Or was it a name applied to them by their neighbours? Or was it a title dreamt up for them by the Europeans who recorded their encounter with them? Conceivably, different recorders could have applied three or more distinct names to the same group! The problems increase when several Aboriginal groups (each living in a different location) have the same name, but at different dates. Does this mean a single group has shifted from one location to another over a period of time, or is it merely a common group name applied to several distinct peoples?

### The Location of Algonquian-Speaking Groups at Contact

To go some distance in solving the identification problem, one can classify the various groups of Northern Algonquian-speaking peoples in present-day Northern Ontario under broader designations based on possible linguistic and cultural differences. The names Algonquian, Cree, and Ojibwa (Chippewa) came into use after the British conquest of New France. The task of making these identifications using these three broad designations becomes easier for the nineteenth century, since more documentation is available. This in turn can help with the assignment of designations for the extremely problematic seventeenth and eighteenth centuries.

As has been described in an earlier chapter (see chapter 4), local Algonquian-speaking groups termed "Algonquin" by the French (the name "Algonquin" had no meaning in the language of the peoples so designated) lived along the lower Ottawa valley in present-day southeastern Ontario and adjacent southwestern Quebec. To the west in the Lake Nipissing region dwelt the group termed the "Nipissing," who may have been linguistically and culturally intermediate between the Ojibwa farther west and the Algonquin to the east. North of Lake Nipissing resided several Algonquian-speaking groups. In 1640 these latter peoples included "the Timiscimi, the Outimagami, the Ouachegami, the Mitchitamou, the Outurbi."[1] Only the location of the first two peoples can be identified with any certainty. The Timiscimi resided about Lake Timiskaming on the future Ontario-Quebec border, while the Outimagami lived in the vicinity of Lake Temagami between Lakes Nipissing and Timiskaming. About Lake Abitibi to the north dwelt Amerindians of the same name, while to the east of this lake and to the west inland from Lake Superior were the inland Indians known to the French as the "Nation des Bois" or "Gens de Terre."[2] The *coureurs de bois* sometimes called those interior peoples "Têtes de Boule" ("round heads"). The Algonquians termed them "O'pimittish Ininiwac" ("people of the woods").[3] Exact territorial boundaries are impossible to map, as is the boundary between these more southern Algonquian-speaking groups and the northern group termed "Cree" in the nineteenth century who lived south and west of James Bay. We know, however, that Indian trade routes extended from Lake Nipissing to James Bay during early historic times and that at least one Cree group, the Namcasakis, came to trade regularly at Fort Timiskaming.

The names and locations of the various Cree divisions before the nineteenth century are difficult to determine. In the seventeenth and early eighteenth centuries, the term "Kilistinon" or "Christinaux" (or variant spellings)[4] was commonly equated with "Cree." The first mention of the Kilistinon was in 1640 when they were reported to "dwell on the rivers of the sea [James Bay] where Nipissings go to trade with them."[5] The *Jesuit Relations,* or the annual reports of the Jesuits in the years 1656–68, mention four "nations" of "Kilistinons."[6] Nicolas Perrot[7] noted that the Kilistinon of the 1660s "often frequent the region along the shores of Lake Superior, and the great rivers, where moose are commonly found." In 1671 Father Albanel,[8] while at the mouth of the Rupert River on James Bay, identified three groups to the west, "each nation being separated from its neighbours by large rivers." Claude de la Potherie, writing at the end of the seventeenth century from Port Nelson on Hudson Bay, stated that the "Christinaux" lived on the lakes in the interior some 160 leagues (approximately 640 kilometres) from the shores of Lake Superior.[9]

The early historical evidence suggests that Cree occupied Northern Ontario, north of the Algonquian-speaking groups now known as Ojibwa. Whether or not Cree lived in the present-day International Boundary region between Ontario and Minnesota is debatable, since the evidence suggests that the Rainy Lake–Lake of the Woods area might have been inhabited before European contact by a division of the Siouan-speaking Assiniboine. Perhaps

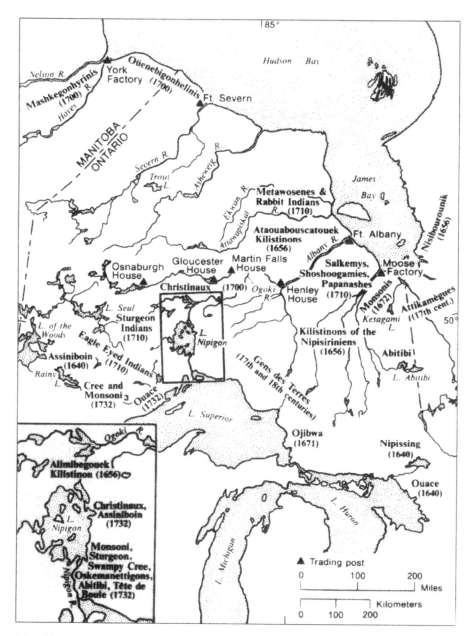

**Map 12.1**

Approximate Locations of Cree and Ojibwa Groups before 1821

Reprinted from *Handbook of North American Indians*, vol. 6: *Subarctic*, ed. June Helm (Washington, D.C.: Smithsonian Institution), 159, by permission of the publisher. Copyright 1981 Smithsonian Institution some Siouan-speakers still occupied settlements in the southwestern portion of Northern Ontario at the time of contact. If so, they had moved west by the mid-eighteenth century.

The boundary between the Cree and the Ojibwa has been the subject of controversy. Some have argued that the Ojibwa blended gradually into the Cree north of the Upper Great Lakes,[10] while others have suggested a somewhat sharper ethnic and territorial boundary.[11] The answer depends largely upon one's interpretation of the available, often imprecise, information. To the southeast, the Ojibwa-Algonquian boundary is equally uncertain, but scholars usually draw an arbitrary line north of the eastern end of Georgian Bay. The term "Ojibwa" appears to derive from the name of a single group, or perhaps cluster of groups, who inhabited the region immediately north of modern Sault Ste. Marie during the seventeenth century. Later, during the eighteenth century, the term was extended to include a number of peoples with a generally similar dialect. In the seventeenth century, however, the various groups were called by distinct names. In the mid-seventeenth century direct knowledge of the Amerindians extended no farther west than the Michipicoten Bay area of Lake Superior. The Indians residing from Georgian Bay to there, for convenience sake, are here called Ojibwa. Some of these peoples, such as the Ouasouarini (Awasse), the Amikouai (Amikwa), and the Oumisagai (Mississauga), retained their separate identities for varying lengths of time after contact with the Europeans. For other groups this was not the case, as they merged with their neighbours and lost their identity. Today, in Canada, all of these peoples are usually referred to as Ojibwa or Ojibway. The French term "Saulteaux," applied to the Ojibwa about Lake Winnipeg, is believed to denote their place of origin near Sault Ste. Marie.[12] The term "Mississauga" is applied to Ojibwa groups living near the north shore of Lake Ontario.[13] Whether they are all descendants of the local group known during the early seventeenth century as Mississauga, who lived along the river of the same name, is questionable.

**Demographic and Cultural Considerations**

All the Northern Algonquians hunted, fished, and gathered berries. Some groups along the southern margin also grew crops (although horticulture was not very important), and some may have occasionally grown corn. Population density and group size depended on the types and abundance of food resources. The widest variety of natural resources existed in the south, and demographic density was naturally highest here. Thus, while the Ojibwa may have occupied a relatively smaller geographic area than the Cree, they had a higher population density. An estimate of some 5 000 Ojibwa between the north shore of Lake Superior and the French River at the time of contact is a reasonable inference from the limited historical data. The total area occupied by the Ojibwa, as defined above, was no less than approximately 40 000 square kilometres, giving a density of one person per eight square kilometres. Any estimate of the Cree population in Ontario is even more speculative. A tentative figure of perhaps 3 000 persons is suggested. If this is indeed accurate, then the Cree, assuming that they occupied the entire region to the Hudson Bay coast, would have had a very low overall population density. The Algonquian-like peoples north of Lake Nipissing and west of the Quebec border may have numbered no more than 600 persons and perhaps had a density comparable with that of the Cree. The overall Northern Algonquian population of Northern Ontario at the time of contact, then, may have numbered slightly more than 8 000 persons. The Assiniboine population, present within northwestern Ontario, cannot be estimated.

The size of groups varied seasonally as well as regionally. Ojibwa summer villages of 100 or more persons were common, and some may have numbered as many as 300 in southern areas. In contrast to their northern cousins, the Great Lakes Ojibwa lived a somewhat sedentary existence, usually ranging from strategically located settlements. The abundance of locally available resources, especially fish (primarily at Sault Ste. Marie) but also small animals, deer, and vegetable products, accounts for their habits and higher population density.

The Ojibwa and perhaps most other Northern Algonquians practised cross-cousin marriage; that is, the preferred mate was a person in the same kin category as one's mother's brother's or father's sister's offspring. In contrast, the offspring of same-sexed siblings of a parent were treated like siblings. The early evidence also suggests that following a marriage, a couple resided briefly with the parents of the bride, during which time the groom performed bride-service chores. Later, the couple might return to live near the groom's parents, though such a decision may have been optional.

Perhaps the Ojibwa are most famous for their totemic clan system. The very word "totem" is derived from the Ojibwa language and has gained widespread usage in anthropology. Among the Ojibwa, every person belonged to a totem group where membership descended through the male line. Each totem group was identified by the name of an animal, bird, fish, or reptile. Individuals possessing the same totem could not marry. Indeed, persons of the same totem considered each other to be close relatives. The North West Company fur trader Duncan Cameron has provided an account of the clan system as it existed among the Ojibwa of the Nipigon country at the beginning of the nineteenth century: "All of those who are of the same mark or totem consider themselves as relations, even if they or their forefathers never had any connexion with each other, or had seen one another before. When two strangers meet and find themselves to be of the same mark, they immediately began to trade their genealogy."[14] At the time of European contact, members of the same totem may have resided near to each other, although in later times individuals possessing the same totem emblem could often be found in several communities.

As was the case with the religion of all Northern Algonquians, the Ojibwa religion made no conceptual distinction between the natural and human world. A variety of spirits, both good and evil, to whom they made frequent offerings filled their world. Human success depended upon a knowledge of the habits of game, on proper respect for the game spirits, and on one's guardian spirit attained through the vision quest. Religious specialists, or shamans, communicated with the spirit world and engaged in curing rituals. The Ojibwa apparently had a number of ceremonies associated with the seasonal cycle. On several occasions Upper Great Lakes' groups held a "Feast for the Dead." The Ojibwa had numerous myths, the most famous of which concerns their creation by the Great Hare Nanobozho.[15]

The Cree, less sedentary than the Ojibwa, moved more frequently and occupied larger hunting ranges. Resources were usually insufficiently concentrated in a given area to permit long-term occupation of a site. They apparently also placed a heavier emphasis on free-ranging game – moose and caribou – except in summer when they could fish. Beaver may have been taken when other resources were scarce or difficult to obtain. Some Cree near the north end of Lake Winnipeg appear to have collected wild rice,[16] while those near the Hudson Bay coast killed seals.[17] In 1695 Father Gabriel Marest, writing from Fort Bourbon (as the French had renamed York Factory, which they then held), remarked: "These Indians have no villages nor fixed dwellings. They are always wandering moving place to place, living upon what they kill. In the summer, they assemble on the lakes where they remain two or three months, and then they go to harvest wild oats [rice] with which they stock their larder." Nearer the Hudson Bay coast, the Cree lived "altogether by hunting. They range the woods continually without stopping anywhere, winter or summer, except when the chase is good, for then they build camps there and remain till they have no more to eat."[18]

From May until October the Cree depended for food on fish, along with various species of waterfowl and, in the west, wild rice. The abundance of wildlife in the late spring and early summer permitted the Cree and their Assiniboine allies to gather together in great numbers.[19] For several weeks they socialized at camping spots on inland lakes and renewed alliances. Prior to the construction of coastal Hudson's Bay Company (HBC) posts, some of the Northern Algonquians, now termed Cree, spent the summer near the north shore of Lake Superior and, while there, visited French traders. After the establishment of HBC posts by James and Hudson bays, they travelled north to trade their furs. During the late fall and early winter, and again in late winter, they hunted moose and caribou. During the harsh midwinter months, the Cree supplemented these foods with grouse, ptarmigan, and varying hare as well as with the meat of fur bearers, especially beaver. Probably the foraging bands deserted areas long before the resources became depleted.

The size of hunting groups is difficult to estimate. The conditions for hunting, the availability of resources in given areas, and seasonal factors affected the size of any given group. No doubt fission and fusion and social factors affected group size at any given moment, depending upon the type and availability of foods being sought.

The Cree religious system closely paralleled that of the Ojibwa. Among the supernatural forces directly affecting their lives was the feared Wittiko, or Windigo, who subsisted on human flesh. The Cree treated game animals with respect and often attributed hunting failure to a breach of a taboo involving proper behaviour towards game spirits, or to sorcery. Few data exist, however, on Cree rituals for the very early post-contact period. One such ritual, the geographically widespread Shaking Tent ceremonial, performed by a shaman to discover information from the spirit world and to inflict harm on others,[20] was probably aboriginal (see chapter 14). Other rituals included the Begging Dance, Scalp Dance[21] and the singing of war songs before making raids on the Inuit living on the east coast of Hudson Bay.[22]

### Initial Contacts with the French and the English

As did the Iroquoians to the south, most Algonquians experienced the effects of European intrusion before face-to-face contacts occurred. The impact of European diseases is unknown, but some believe them to have been a major disruptive force even before the Northern Algonquians had direct contact with the Europeans.[23] When Samuel de Champlain travelled up the Ottawa River in 1613 and later wintered with the Huron in 1615–16, some Northern Algonquians may have made direct contact with his party. Champlain described the peoples north of Lake Nipissing as having lands "stocked with great numbers both of animals, birds and fish."[24] A decade later Gabriel Sagard, the Récollet missionary to the Hurons, stated that the Nipissing made a four- to six-week journey to trade with interior peoples,[25] perhaps the Cree.[26]

The fur trade northwest of Lake Nipissing increased after the 1620s until the intensification of Iroquois raids and European epidemics greatly reduced the Aboriginal population between Huronia and the St. Lawrence valley. In 1662, however, the Ojibwa near Sault Ste. Marie defeated an Iroquois war party.[27] Algonquians who had fled as far west as Lake Nipigon and Green Bay[28] began to return to trade with the French. Military campaigns by the French in the late 1680s further weakened the Iroquois. By the 1690s united attacks by Wyandot, Ojibwa, Ottawa, and other Algonquians made the Iroquois vulnerable (see chapters 4 and 5).

After the 1660s the French fur trade expanded westward as the Iroquois threat decreased. The growing trade had several important effects on the Algonquians of what is now Northern Ontario. First, those nearest to the French settlements along the St. Lawrence could acquire trade items directly, either at Montreal or Quebec, or from the growing number of roving *coureurs de bois*. At this time the Indians considered these items as luxury goods. Certain Algonquians also became middlemen in the trade to more distant groups such as the Cree and Assiniboine. Usually the Ottawa (Odawa) are cited as being the middlemen to more distant peoples, but this term must be used cautiously. During the late seventeenth century the French often extended the term "Ottawa" to as many as thirty different "nations."[29]

**French-English Rivalry and the Fur Trade: 1670–1759**

Until the establishment of the Hudson's Bay Company in 1670, the French had a monopoly on the fur trade north and northwest of the Great Lakes. In the 1670s and 1680s the Hudson's Bay Company erected posts at the mouths of the major rivers flowing into James Bay and Hudson Bay: Fort Charles (Rupert House) at the mouth of the Rupert River in present-day Quebec; Moose Factory at the mouth of the Moose River and Fort Albany at the mouth of the Albany River in present-day Ontario; and York Factory in what is now northern Manitoba. The construction of the HBC posts relieved the Cree and Assiniboine west of Lake Superior of the necessity of obtaining used and poor-quality goods at high prices from Ojibwa and other Algonquian middlemen. The period of intense French-English trade rivalry (which only ended with the fall of New France to the English in 1760) had begun.

As early as 1673 the French complained that the northern English posts diverted many of the Amerindians from bringing their furs to New France.[30] To fight the English traders, the French built a series of posts, several of them temporary ones. They erected a post on Nighthawk Lake near present-day Timmins in 1673, then a post on Lake Timiskaming in 1679.[31] Farther west they founded the important Fort Kaministikwia (Camanistogoyan) near present-day Thunder Bay in 1678, and built Fort La Maune on Lake Nipigon in 1684.[32] The next year they constructed Fort de Français near the forks of the Albany and Kenogami rivers. The French sought to drive the English out of this region. In 1686 Chevalier de Troyes proceeded north from Montreal to

James Bay, where he attacked and captured the three James Bay posts – Fort Charles (Rupert House), Moose Factory, and Fort Albany. Although the English regained their James Bay posts in 1693, they lost York Factory to the French the next year. The English only regained York Factory in 1713 by the Treaty of Utrecht.

All Indians within what is now Northern Ontario had direct access to either French or English trade goods by the 1680s. Most Indians now devoted their time either to travelling in order to trade or to trapping fur-bearing animals. The concentration on the hunting of beaver for the fur trade took a number of Amerindians away from their normal subsistence hunting and fishing. Those closest to the fur-trading posts on James and Hudson bays became increasingly reliant upon the traders for assistance when winter food shortages occurred.

Those Indians who traded directly at the coastal posts, rather than acting as middlemen or trading through middlemen, became known by the Hudson's Bay Company traders as "Home Guards."[33] These Home Guards apparently came from groups who exploited regions nearest to the posts and were willing to assist the traders by hunting geese and caribou for them.[34] The relationship was reciprocal, since the post frequently had to feed "starving" Indians in winter. Occasionally the Home Guard included the offspring of Indian women and company servants.

The regular association of 200 or more Indians with a trading post such as Fort Albany created a "trading post band." (Formerly these Indians had made up autonomous hunting groups.) This relationship and the growing importance of fur-bearing animals to the Native economy may have altered property concepts in some regions. An allotment system of land tenure might have developed among the James Bay Cree and among the Amerindians near Georgian Bay during the late seventeenth century. Although families did not hunt in the same area every year, in the words of John Oldmixon, who wrote in 1741, "hunting grounds were assigned to families or to members by the head of the families every autumn."[35]

Groups further inland from the coast took advantage of the French-English rivalry. Between 1716 and the mid-1750s the French established temporary camps at strategic locations throughout present-day Northern Ontario to intercept and control the flow of trade, which otherwise would have been acquired by the Hudson's Bay Company.[36]

After the French built additional posts along or near Lake Superior during the early 1700s, many Indians further to the southwest made only occasional visits to Fort Albany. French goods became ever nearer at hand after the explorer-trader Pierre Gaultier de Varennes et de La Vérendrye erected posts on Rainy Lake and Lake of the Woods in 1731 and 1732 respectively.[37] Many of the "Clisteens" now ceased making the trip to Fort Albany altogether.

There is evidence that during the period from about the 1720s to the 1770s, the Cree (except for those groups near Hudson Bay who were becoming closely attached to the HBC posts) began to migrate westward from their aboriginal homeland in Northern Ontario to Manitoba and beyond. The accounts of the HBC posts at Berens River for 1815, a slightly later time, describe one aspect of this migration:

> The Indians who inhabit this part of the country belong to the extensive class of Southward or Kristeneaux Indians ... it is probable that these tribes were formerly confined to the East side of Lake Winnipic, but from the diminution of animals, there appears to have been a general migration to the westward, one tribe displacing or rather driving back other tribes 'till at length a great part of the Indians once living on the east side of the Lake are now found to the westwards of it whilst the original inhabitants of the westward are driven still further into the interior.[38]

The anthropologist A.I. Hallowell supplies supporting evidence from oral testimony and genealogical records for the post-contact movements of Ojibwa into the eastern Lake Winnipeg region.[39] Roving bands of Ojibwa from the southeast also began occupying permanently the upper Albany River drainage area by at least the early 1730s. Perhaps they already knew the region, having acted as middlemen traders to the former Cree residents in earlier times. The HBC trader Andrew Graham, writing in the late eighteenth century, documents the spread of the "Nakawawuck." These people, he said, had reached the Nelson River: "They are the most northern tribes of the Chipeways. It is our opinion that they have drawn up to the northward gradually as the Keiskatchewans receded from it."[40]

Graham's remarks alone do not constitute proof of Ojibwa movements, as he remained on the coast of Hudson Bay. Statements, however, by traders at inland trading posts at a slightly later date lend support to the argument. The scholar-trader George Barnston, for instance, writing at Martin Falls in 1839, stated:

> The Greater number of the families belong to that tribe of Sauteux denominated the Suckers – a Band of the Great Chippewa Divisions which appear to have pushed farthest to the northward at least in this quarter ... They are known at York Factory and Severn as Bungees, a name I imagine given to them from their use of the Sauteaux word Pungee – a little. To the northward they keep up an intercourse with the Severn Indians, to the eastward with those of Albany mixing and intermarrying which connections I may say have already produced a Half Cree, Half Sauteux Breed affecting the Language and Character in no slight degree.[41]

The anthropologist Alanson Skinner, who did fieldwork among groups along the Albany River, provides additional support for Barnston's account.[42] Farther south in the Rainy Lake area, Ojibwa had replaced Siouan speakers (probably Assiniboine but perhaps Sioux). According to the North West Company fur trader Peter Grant, the Ojibwa

> assert as an undoubted fact that, formerly the Sciews possessed the greatest part of the country, but, in course of time, as population increased, they emigrated to the westward in search of subsistence ... leaving behind only a few tribes, more attached to their native land. In this state they say their ancestors found the country when, for similar reasons, they emigrated from their ancient possessions to the eastward.[43]

Several other fur traders refer to the post-contact population movements of Ojibwa to the north and northwest of the Upper Great Lakes. By the late eighteenth century, Indian groups, both Cree and Ojibwa, resided in the general regions that they occupy at present. Nevertheless, there continued to be movements of individuals and families thereafter, right to the present day.

To combat the movement of French *coureurs de bois* and their Ojibwa allies, the English reopened Moose Factory in 1730 (abandoned in 1693) and erected their first inland post, Henley House, in 1743 at the forks of the Albany and Kenogami rivers. Henley House was designed as a way station en route to Fort Albany. At the new post the interior Indians could, if need be, obtain food, which was often scarce along the lower Albany River. The company hoped the availability of food at Henley House would encourage the Indians to continue to the bigger post. Unfortunately, the lack of trade goods at Henley House caused much dissatisfaction among the Natives. Only when the French were absent from the Henley House area or when the Indians perceived French trade goods to be of poorer quality or more expensive than English ones, did the interior groups travel to James Bay. Then disaster struck the HBC's first inland post. In 1754, owing to mismanagement, some coastal Cree killed the Henley House traders. Although the post was reopened in late summer 1759, the company again abandoned it after about twenty Indian warriors attacked it a few months later. It was not reopened until 1766.

Following the defeat of the French and before the arrival of independent Scottish and American traders from Quebec, numerous flotillas of canoes from the Indian country north of Lake Superior again made annual trips to HBC posts. Canoe counts from the Fort Albany records indicate that as many as 100 or more vessels would arrive at once, but more often, clusters of two to five canoes appeared. Apparently, each group was headed by a leader and his second in command, designated as a "captain" and a "lieutenant," respectively, by the traders. Robert Temple wrote in May 1762, for example, that

"Captain Mekiss and Lieutenant Nonosecash brot in thirteen Canoes with a good Trade."[44] Upon the flotilla's arrival, both the Indian leaders and the master of the post made speeches. The traders distributed gifts, including alcohol and tobacco, to the senior males. Later the Native leaders received trade goods to be redistributed among their fellows.[45] In most cases, women and children did not visit the post but remained in camp. At Fort Albany the traders usually recorded the names of the chiefs and senior men and, if felt to be important, details about their appearance and behaviour.

Although the way of life of the Algonquians of Northern Ontario can be more fully described in the nineteenth and twentieth centuries (see chapters 13, 14, and 15), some general observations on the mid-eighteenth century can be made. The interior Indians obtained furs, mainly beaver and other valuable species, in snares and deadfalls. In winter they relied for food on moose and caribou supplemented by beaver, grouse, and other small animals. They used the hides of the large animals to make clothing, although some wore beaver robes in winter. They lived in birchbark conical lodges.

The Northern Algonquin hunters ranged from base camps in search of big game and/or fur-bearing animals. Women and children remained near the camp and set snares for small animals, fished, prepared hides, and generally kept things in order. Perhaps the situation was similar to that experienced by the Hudson's Bay Company trader George Sutherland when he wintered with a family of Indians east of Lake Winnipeg in 1777–78. Sutherland recorded that if after several days no game could be found near the camp, the women and children would set up camp at a new location usually no more than twenty-five kilometres from the first. If they made a kill, the group moved to the kill site and as a rule remained there until they had consumed all or most of the meat.[46] The Cree attached to the coastal Hudson's Bay Company posts devoted more time to trapping than the Ojibwa in order to procure cloth and blankets for clothing and bedding. Occasionally, an Indian from the Hudson Bay coast arrived wearing clothing made from polar bear skin.

Despite more than a century of involvement in the fur trade, few Algonquians had, as yet, met a Christian missionary. Their animistic conception of nature and many of their rituals, such as the Shaking Tent rite, bear ceremonialism, and certain mortuary rites, continued relatively unaltered. Nevertheless, some Indians and mixed-bloods did have an opportunity to observe Sunday services held by the traders. They witnessed Christian burial services, and some were so interred. Certainly as early as the 1710s, a few Home Guard Cree about Fort Albany asked to be buried by the traders. When, for example, old Miscamot died in September 1721, he was buried the following day by the traders, "he being desireous when living that he might be buried nigh the English."[47]

Between 1714 and 1760 neither the French nor the English had gained the upper hand in the fur trade in present-day Northern Ontario. This situation ended with the fall of New France in 1760. Although the withdrawal of the French from the fur trade in 1760 resulted in a temporary monopoly for the Hudson's Bay Company, it only lasted one year. In 1761 some Indians visited Moose Factory dressed in clothing acquired from Montreal traders. The rivalry between the Hudson's Bay Company and a new wave of Montreal-based Scottish and American traders exacerbated conflict among the Indians and brought about several irreversible changes in their culture.

# NOTES

1   Reuben G. Thwaites, ed., *The Jesuit Relations and Allied Documents,* 63 vols. (Cleveland 1896–1901; reprint, New York 1959), 18:229

2   G.M. Wrong, ed., *The Long Journey to the Country of the Hurons by Father Gabriel Sagard* (Toronto 1939), 64

3   National Archives of Canada (NA), MG 1 C11E, vol. 13, Canada, *Chaines des postes 1723 et 1725; Sessional Papers,* no. 31 (1879): 84; Alexander Henry, *Travels and Adventures in Canada and the Indian Territories* (Edmonton 1969), 62, 207–8

4   See Frederick W. Hodge, ed., *Handbook of American Indians North of Mexico,* Bureau of American Ethnology, Bulletin 30 (Washington, D.C. 1907; reprint, New York 1971), 1:361–2

5   Thwaites, *The Jesuit Relations,* 18:229

6   Ibid., 44:249

7   E.H. Blair, ed., *The Indian Tribes of the Upper Mississippi Valley and Region of the Great Lakes,* 2 vols. (Cleveland 1911), 2:107–8

8   Thwaites, *The Jesuit Relations,* 56:203

9   J.B. Tyrrell, ed., *Documents Relating to the Early History of Hudson Bay* (Toronto 1931), 263–4

10  Edward S. Rogers, "Changing Settlement Patterns of the Cree-Ojibwa of Northern Ontario," *Southwestern Journal of Anthropology* 19, no. 1 (1963): 64–88; Edward S. Rogers, "Band Organization among the Indians of Eastern Subarctic Canada," in *Contributions to Anthropology: Band Societies,* ed. David Damas, Anthropological series 84, Bulletin 228 (Ottawa 1969), 21–50; Adolph M. Greenberg and James Morrison, "Group Identities in the Boreal Forest: The Origin of the Northern Ojibwa," *Ethnohistory* 29, no. 2 (1982): 75–102

11  Charles A. Bishop, *The Northern Ojibwa and the Fur Trade: An Historical and Ecological Study* (Toronto 1974); Charles A. Bishop, "The Emergence of the Northern Ojibwa: Social and Economic Consequences," *American Ethnologist* 3 (1976): 39–54; Charles A. Bishop and M.E. Smith, "Early Historic Populations in Northwestern Ontario: Archaeological and Ethnohistorical Interpretations," *American Antiquity* 40 (1975): 54–63

12  A. Irving Hallowell, *Culture and Experience* (Philadelphia 1955), 114–15

13  Edward S. Rogers, "Southeastern Ojibwa," in *Handbook of North American Indians,* vol. 15: *Northeast,* ed. Bruce G. Trigger (Washington, D.C. 1978), 760–71

14  Duncan Cameron, "The Nipigon Country," in L.R. Masson, ed., *Les Bourgeois de la Compagnie du Nord-Ouest*, 2 vols. (Quebec 1890), 2:246–7

15  Blair, *The Indian Tribes*, 1:31–40

16  Thwaites, *The Jesuit Relations*, 51:51–7

17  Tyrrell, *Documents*, 262

18  Ibid., 124

19  Thwaites, *The Jesuit Relations*, 54:193; Tyrrell, *Documents*, 18:124–5, 265; Henry, *Travels*, 233

20  Tyrrell, *Documents*, 18:228

21  Hudson's Bay Company Archives (HBCA), B.3/a/57, fo. 1d

22  HBCA, B.3/a/59, fos. 34, 36d

23  Calvin Martin, *Keepers of the Game* (Berkeley 1978), 89–91

24  H.P. Biggar, *The Works of Samuel de Champlain*, 6 vols. (Toronto 1929), 3:41–2

25  Wrong, ed., *The Long Journey*, 86–7

26  Thwaites, *The Jesuit Relations*, 44:249

27  Blair, *The Indian Tribes*, 1:178–81

28  Ibid., 1:173–4

29  Thwaites, *The Jesuit Relations*, 51:21, 54:127; Edmund B. O'Callaghan, ed., *Documents Relative to the Colonial History of the State of New York; Procured in Holland, England and France, by John R. Brodhead*, 15 vols. (Albany 1853–87), 9:160–1

30  E.E. Rich, *The Fur Trade and the Northwest to 1857* (Toronto 1967), 40

31  Elaine Allen Mitchell, *Fort Temiskaming and the Fur Trade* (Toronto 1977), 8

32  Ernest Voorhis, *Historic Forts and Trading Posts of the French Regime and of the English Fur Trading Companies* (Ottawa 1930), 128

33  See, for example, HBCA, B.3/a/13 for 7 August–14 October 1724 and 18 April–27 May 1725

34  HBCA, B.3/a/17, 31 October 1728

35  W. Vernon Kinietz, *The Indians of the Western Great Lakes, 1615–1760*, Occasional Contributions from the Museum of Anthropology of the University of Michigan, no. 10 (Ann Arbor 1940): 237; John Oldmixon, *The British Empire in America, Containing the History of Discovery, Settlement, Progress, and State of the British Colonies on the Continent and Islands of America* (London 1741), 1:548

36  HBCA, B.3/a/10, 16 June 1722

37  L.J. Burpee, ed., *Journals and Letters of Pierre Gaultier de Varennes de la Vérendrye and His Sons* (Toronto 1927), xvi

38  HBCA, B.16/9/1, Berens River report on district. Dale R. Russell's *Eighteenth Century Western Cree and Their Neighbours* (Ottawa 1991) presents several quotations that challenge this description, at least for groups farther west.

39  Hallowell, *Culture and Experience*, 114–18

40  G. Williams, ed., *Andrew Graham's Observations on Hudson's Bay, 1767–1791* (London 1969), 27, 204

41  HBCA, B.123/a/14, Martin Falls's post journal

42  A. Skinner, "Notes on the Eastern Cree and Northern Saulteaux," *Anthropological Papers of the American Museum of Natural History* 9 (1911): pt. 1, 11

43  Peter Grant, cited in Masson, ed., *Les Bourgeois*, 2:241–2

44  Robert Temple, HBCA, B.3/a/54, 24 May 1762

45  Williams, ed., *Andrew Graham's Observations*, 315–24

46  George Sutherland in HBCA, B.3/a/73, 3 May 1778

47  HBCA, B.3/a/10, 13 September 1721. Miscamot had died the previous day.

# 13 *Northern Algonquians, 1760–1821*

## CHARLES A. BISHOP

A Hudson's Bay Company (HBC) account written in 1761 reports traders from Montreal "as thick as Muskettas" inland south of James Bay.[1] Each year saw more and more of these Scottish and American traders entering the north country. Accordingly, in 1767 the company sent its employee William Tomison inland from Fort Severn via the Severn River to Lake Winnipeg to discover the number and the location of opposition traders.[2] He learned that the Montreal traders, or "pedlars" as the Hudson's Bay Company called them, annually despatched large birchbark canoes, well supplied with goods and manned by French Canadian voyageurs, to the interior. In the late 1760s and early 1770s no longer did the Indians north of Lake Superior willingly make lengthy and often exhausting trips to the HBC's coastal posts.

To fight its opponents, the Hudson's Bay Company established four inland posts in 1777: Gloucester House on Washi Lake, about 530 kilometres up the Albany River; Wapiscogamy House (Brunswick House), about 225 kilometres from Moose Factory on the Missinaibi River; and two short-lived posts, one on Missinaibi Lake just inland from Michipicoten and another on Kesagami Lake about 160 kilometres due north of Lake Abitibi.[3] In addition, trader George Sutherland travelled up the Albany River and wintered with a family of Ojibwa in the region east of Lake Winnipeg, perhaps near Lake Pikangikum.[4] Initially, the interior Indians opposed the traders' presence,[5] but this attitude soon changed as the benefits of having two rival posts nearby became apparent.

Both Wapiscogamy (Brunswick) House and Gloucester House succeeded and operated for several years. Gradually the HBC traders adopted some of their opponents' tactics. They learned to vary the location of their camp trades (or small trading outposts) from year to year to elude or cut off the Indians' trade with the opposition. They also continued their exploration of what is now Northern Ontario.

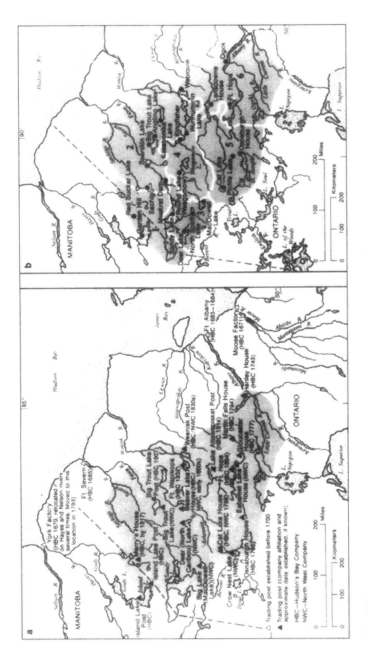

Map 13.1
Northern Ojibwa: Nineteenth-Century Territory
(a) Historic trading posts; and (b) 1970s settlements and bands designated by the government at the time of treaty: (1) Island Lake; (2) Trout Lake; (3) Deer Lake; (4) Caribou Lake; (5) Osnaburgh House; (6) Fort Hope

*Reprinted from Handbook of North American Indians, vol. 6: Subarctic, ed. June Helm (Washington, D.C.: Smithsonian Institution Press), 232, by permission of the publisher. Copyright 1981 Smithsonian Institution*

Despite the Hudson's Bay Company's efforts, the Montreal traders controlled the bulk of the inland trade until the late 1780s. The pedlars had major posts (not including those on Lakes Huron and Superior) at Lake Timiskaming (Fort Timiskaming), Lake Abitibi, Midstinikon Lake (Langue de Terre near Metachewan), Sturgeon Lake, Lake Nipigon, and probably Lake St. Joseph (the remnants of a Canadian post were seen there in 1786). Many other less permanent settlements existed, some of them within 300 kilometres of the Hudson Bay coastline. It is difficult to locate these shifting posts because the independent traders produced few detailed travel accounts and maps. Undoubtedly, however, at one time or another, they occupied most, if not all, of the larger interior lakes and the strategic trade routes during the late eighteenth century.

The Hudson's Bay Company responded by building more posts and more outposts. In 1786 the company established Osnaburgh House at the east end of Lake St. Joseph. For many years this post functioned as a base for outposts at places such as Cat Lake, Red Lake, Lac Seul, Rainy Lake (Lac La Pluie), and Sturgeon Lake. The HBC erected New Brunswick House on Micabanish Lake in 1788, a post on Lake Nipigon in 1792, establishments at Lake Abitibi and Kenogummissee Lake, and then the important freighting depot at Martin Falls in 1794. The Martin Falls post, located at the furthest point up the Albany River that goods could be taken without portaging them, came to replace Gloucester House. From Fort Severn, the HBC established a post at Trout Lake in 1807, and then another inland post in 1813 on Matawagamingue (Mattagami) Lake. The inland posts gave the company traders a firsthand opportunity to observe their rival's tactics (in Montreal in 1783 the pedlars, or independent traders, had merged to form the North West Company,[6] a formidable trading opponent).

To capture the trade, the two rival companies established posts at strategic points designed to block Indians from reaching their competitors. The other tactic of locating next to the competition worked well if one had a superior stock of goods and treated the Native hunters liberally. Competition often bred violence among the traders, as well as among the Amerindians and between traders and Indians.[7]

The most intense rivalry occurred between 1798 and 1804 when a third company, Sir Alexander Mackenzie's short-lived XY Company (a group that split off from the North West Company), competed for furs. Independent traders such as Ezekiel Solomon of Michilimakinac also entered what is now Northern Ontario in search of furs. While rivalry continued in some locations to 1821, the NWC steadily lost ground in the region after about 1805 as fur returns fell.

Few Indians in this territory escaped the effects of the trade rivalry. Despite their time-honoured loyalty to the English, even the Home Guard

Cree took advantage of the competition when the North West Company briefly established a post near the HBC's Moose Factory between 1800 and 1806. Farther inland (where rival posts often were located next to each other), the situation became very tense. Here both companies debauched the Indians with lavish quantities of alcohol and other goods to win their business.[8] If such inducements did not work, the traders might forcefully take the Indians' furs to prevent them from taking them to the opposition. On the other hand, some Ojibwa took debt at two or more competing posts, yet delivered their furs wherever they obtained the best bargain.[9]

The traders relied upon their Native customers for a number of goods and services. The Amerindians supplied the traders with items such as birchbark canoes and various foods, particularly "venison" (caribou meat) and, near Rainy Lake and Lake of the Woods, wild rice. But after 1800 traders at the larger settlements gained some independence from the local Indians by enlarging their summer gardens and fall fisheries.

*East View of Moose Factory,* a watercolour (c. 1804–11) by William Richards. The Hudson's Bay Company warehouse appears on the right, topped by the smaller of the two flags. Immediately in front of the warehouse stands the principal gateway. On the left, topped by the larger flag, are dwelling quarters. The boatyard door, which is shown open, leads to the dock. Outbuildings include the shipwrights' workshop, smith, forge, kitchen, brewhouse, and cattle sheds. Richards, an HBC employee of Welsh and Cree descent, was born in Rupert's Land and worked at Moose Factory as a labourer, canoeman, and cooper.

Glenbow Museum, Calgary, 62.113.1

Despite the construction of palisades about the larger posts, many traders kept a constant vigil against the Indians. At Frederick House in 1813 an Indian murdered the traders and a number of local Indians.[10] The culprit was never captured, nor the post reopened. Farther west, the Crane and the Tinpot, named after their respective leaders, the brothers Ochechak and Tinnewabano, were especially notorious. In September 1803 the Crane threatened Osnaburgh House. On 9 September eight of the Crane's sons declared they would pull the post's stockades down to steal brandy.[11] The following March the factor at Osnaburgh reported that "the Old Crane and 14 of his Sons" had made an effort to take the post, having been living within fifty kilometres of it since January.[12] Two months later "two of the murderous gang belonging to Tinpot" arrived at Martin Falls and killed two Indians.[13] The Martin Falls post expected an attack, particularly after a trader reported that five canoes of Crane had arrived whose "only errand, I plainly perceived is to murder us or some Indians belonging to this place."[14] Finally, after several exhausting and nerve-racking days, during which time the men kept strict watch day and night, the traders pointed two loaded swivel guns at the Crane's tent and ordered them to leave immediately. They did.[15] No incidents were reported thereafter for several years, but the danger remained. The years of intense fur trade competition were indeed a troubled period. According to the traders, other Indians fought amongst themselves, especially when intoxicated, and murders were relatively common.

The more abundant fur trade records in the mid-nineteenth century allow for a full description of the economic activities of the Northern Algonquian (see chapter 14). A short outline of the late eighteenth and early nineteenth centuries can also be provided. Generally speaking, the Indians regarded the summer months as their time of leisure. With food resources more abundant, they assembled in larger groups, socialized, and performed their religious ceremonials. For a few days groups might make short visits to the trading post.

In the summer the inland posts sent out the collected pelts by canoe or batteaux to Montreal or to the coastal HBC posts. Some Ojibwa assisted the Hudson's Bay Company in bringing up supplies at this time, but most interior Indians considered these tasks too arduous and beneath their dignity. The HBC employees were now (for the most part) Orcadians (men from the Orkney Islands north of Scotland); assisted by the Home Guard Cree, they transported the goods part of the way inland from the coast. The North West Company used freight canoes, usually manned by six or eight persons, instead of the larger and heavier batteaux; thus, it relied much less on Native assistance.

After receiving their supplies in late summer, Indians dispersed to their bush camps. From fall to late spring they employed a mixed hunting strategy. Women fished while the men either hunted large game or fur-bearing animals, depending upon their immediate needs for food or for hides for manufacture into garments and snowshoe netting. In the late spring they usually brought in their winter and early-spring pelts. Upon their arrival, the Indians presented their furs to pay their debts incurred before they left for their bush camps.

The HBC's George Sutherland described the hunting pattern of a family of six Ojibwa with whom he had wintered northwest of Red Lake in 1777–78:

> Durring the whole winter – for Ever since we Left our Canoes in the fall – we Generaly Traveled about 8 or 10 miles at a time that is when we repitcht. the men set off soon in the morning with there Sleds and Left the wemen in the tents – and after the men had Traveled about 8 or 10 Miles – then Left the Sleds at a proper place for the wemen to pitch the Tent – then the men set of and hunted all the Day – then they Returned to the place where they Left there Sleds where we always found the wemen and the Tents all Ready made and the Day that we killed anything we had a good Supper.[16]

Sutherland described a feast-to-famine existence: if a moose was killed, the entire camp ate enormous quantities so as not to offend the game spirit. They would consume the animal in about three days. Frequently, another lengthy period would follow when almost nothing was eaten.

The Hudson's Bay Company gave set values to both trade goods and the different species of fur-bearing animals, measured in terms of either the "made beaver" (MB) or, in the area northeast of Georgian Bay, "made marten." Originally, one large prime beaver pelt equalled one made beaver. The value of trade goods varied somewhat depending upon competition. A gun, for instance, might range in value from five to seven made beaver. Often the HBC handed out to leading Indians items of less value, such as brandy and tobacco, to ensure their trust and to encourage them to trap.

The abundance of fur-bearing animals in the late eighteenth century facilitated the Indians' quest for furs. They could obtain trade goods with relatively little effort, especially in regions where rivalry was intense. Nevertheless, the competitive nature of the trade, combined with the competition and conflict among Indian bands themselves to acquire goods, especially alcohol, did lead to excessive over-hunting and, in time, a dip in the fur returns.[17] The decline in beaver forced Indians to trap substitutes like muskrats (musquash). Traders, particularly those of the North West Company, encouraged over-exploitation by relocating trade camps after the Indians had depleted fur-bearing animals in a given area.

In the region north of Lake Superior, beaver remained the predominant fur-bearing animal taken by Indians until 1810. Thereafter, the quantities of other species increased as beaver grew increasingly scarce. This change reflected the Indians' new emphasis on fur trapping.

Apparently the Native trappers took most fur-bearing animals in snares and deadfalls, there being relatively few steel traps in use until well after the middle of the nineteenth century. Later in the nineteenth century, the Lac Seul Indians employed dogs to hunt lynx,[18] but the antiquity of this practice remains unknown. In winter the Indians sometimes simply broke open beaver lodges with hatchets, usually after opening the dam built by the beaver, to lower the water level. This was a very destructive practice, since all the animals in a lodge would die from exposure. Until the two companies' union in 1821, wherever intense competition existed between the Hudson's Bay Company and North West Company, the beaver population declined.

Caribou, referred to in the post records as "deer" or "rein-deer" and their meat as "venison," inhabited all of Northern Ontario prior to 1800. Herds of considerable size were also reported in the lowlands adjacent to Hudson Bay.[19] During the late eighteenth century the traders and Amerindians captured them by constructing hedges and snares along the Severn River.

Elk occurred towards what is now the northern Manitoba border[20] and moose generally throughout Northern Ontario at this time. The moose population appears to have been relatively numerous in the western part of Northern Ontario until after 1800.[21] Peter Grant reported that Indians, in hunting moose, made a circuit to the leeward of the trail until in front of the animal and then quietly moved in on it, a strategy still employed as late as the mid-twentieth century.[22] The northwestern portion of Ontario, above the heavily travelled trade routes to Lake Winnipeg, remained the last refuge of abundant game resources.

Around 1830 the Northern Algonquians fished in a variety of ways. They speared sturgeon in spring and summer[23] and used hooks and lines for other species. Often Indians built traps in which they took whitefish and suckers. The species of fish varied with location. They found lake trout only in the deeper lakes and sturgeon in the major river systems. Other species such as pike, walleye, whitefish, and suckers were present in most regions.

In the spring and the fall, the Amerindians took wild fowl – ducks and geese – and in the summer, loons and grebes. They killed grouse and ptarmigan during the fall and winter. In those years when huge flocks of ptarmigan fed in the marshy grasslands along the coast of Hudson Bay, the Indians shot them.[24] The Indians collected wild rice and blueberries in the areas in which they grew.

The size of winter hunting bands in the late eighteenth and early nineteenth centuries varied depending upon geographical location and seasonal conditions. During the 1770s winter groups in interior Northern Ontario apparently ranged from about eight persons to as many as eighty in some southern areas. In the Rainy Lake–Lake of the Woods area, the Indian population seems to have been somewhat denser. Summer villages of up to 100 persons existed,[25] but winter groups may have been considerably smaller. Between the 1780s and the end of the period, winter groups ranged from about ten to thirty persons. The availability of certain key foods, especially moose and caribou, not fur bearers, dictated the size of winter groups. The fur trader Thomas Vincent, for instance, wrote in his district report for Osnaburgh House in 1814 that Indians "in winter ... endeavour to avoid one another as much as possible on account of spoiling each others hunts and at the same time very probably of starving when a number of them are gathered together."[26]

The location of hunting groups changed within the post-contact period. The distances that Indians migrated, however, varied greatly. Some apparently settled on the Plains, while others moved into what is now Southern Ontario.[27] Still others remained in their pre-contact locations. Many people continued to reside along the north shore of Georgian Bay and near Sault Ste. Marie. The Ojibwa of Weagamow and Trout lakes might not have moved very far, if at all, to the northwest. Likewise, the Cree bands that became attached to the coastal Hudson's Bay Company posts do not seem to have travelled far, although they altered their seasonal pattern of movements once they became closely associated with these posts.

Despite considerable research and much controversy, the question as to whether privatized beaver hunting territories predated European contact remains unresolved. Certainly, however, family hunting territories existed in sections of Northern Ontario by the early nineteenth century. The fur trader Peter Grant wrote of the Ojibwa in the Rainy Lake area in 1804:

> It is customary with them, in the beginning of winter, to separate in single families, a precaution which seems necessary to their very existence, and of which they are so sensible that when one of them has chosen a particular district for his hunting ground, no other person will encroach upon it without a special invitation, and whoever discovers a beaver lodge and marks its situation may consider it his undoubted property, and no other person will attempt to destroy it without his permission. In case of famine, however, any one may abandon his district and seek a better hunt on his neighbour's land without incurring the least ill will or reproach: They say: 'the lands were made for the use of man, therefore every one has an equal right to partake of the produce'.[28]

Other evidence suggests that the system of land tenure described by Grant extended along the North West Company's Great Lakes water route. Trader Daniel Harmon noted in his account of the Indians east of the Rocky Mountains: "Every tribe has its particular tract of country; and this is divided again, among the several families, which compose the tribe. Rivers, lakes and mountains, serve them as boundaries; and the limits of the territory which belongs to each family are as well known by the tribe, as the lines which separate farms are, by the farmers, in the civilized world."[29] An HBC trader, Thomas Fraser of the Abitibi Post, made an almost identical statement in his district report for 1824.[30]

Ecological and economic factors played a role in the adoption of the family hunting territory system. The scarcity of food, especially large game, made it expedient for family groups to claim the right to use specific areas for trapping and obtaining food. Such a strategy made possible the management of vital resources then in short supply. As Harmon noted, "A prudent Indian, whose lands are not well-stocked with animals, kills only what are absolutely necessary to procure such articles as he cannot well dispense with."[31]

Although family hunting territories had already emerged by the early nineteenth century in what is now northeastern Ontario and near the International Border west of Lake Superior, farther north the hunting range system continued until at least the 1820s. Trader Thomas Vincent wrote in 1814 that the Osnaburgh House Indians "have no exclusive right or claim to any particular part to hunt in."[32] The pursuit of large game, still in relative abundance over extensive tracts of land, slowed down the development of the family hunting territory system in Northern Ontario until later in the nineteenth century.

For some time anthropologists have debated the structure of hunting groups in Northern Ontario during the eighteenth century. The available data on this topic remain slight for this time period, but richer for the nineteenth century. (A full discussion of the topic appears in chapter 14.) In the eighteenth century, however, we can say that among the Ojibwa immediately north of Lake Superior, their totem groups, or clans, were important (see chapter 5). The HBC trader George Keith noted in his Michipicoten correspondence book for 1830-31: "They are strongly attached to their clans (for there does exist a Kind of clanship amongst them, distinguished by the Bear Tribe, Cat, Fox, Loon, Crane &c Tribes) or relations and within this degree they are Kind, humane, honest and attentive – In their intercourse with others they are however unjust, arrogant, vendictive, treacherous and comparatively blood thirsty."[33] Moreover, he added, "On the death of the Parents of a family and that none of their offspring consider themselves adequate, the nearest of Kin or clanship seem to possess an undoubted title or claim to take the orphans under their protection."[34]

Less is known of the social organization of the Ojibwa living farther north in the upper Winisk and Severn River drainage systems. The term "Sucker" was sometimes applied to different groups of Indians residing in this region, but it is doubtful whether this label had totemic connotations. One would hardly expect that a series of groups could have prohibited in-marriage or exogamy over such a large geographic region. The best-known group, the previously mentioned Crane, occupied the Sandy-Weagamow-Caribou lakes area north of Lake St. Joseph and south of Big Trout Lake.[35] As previously noted, the group acquired its name from that of its leader, the "Crane," who by the beginning of the nineteenth century was an old man with a large number of sons and daughters.

Further north the Cree social organization had adjusted to the fur-trapping economy in the Hudson and James Bay lowlands by the late eighteenth century. Extended family units lived at various scattered locales inland from the sea coast. Each of the three major coastal posts in Ontario – Moose Factory, Fort Albany, and Fort Severn – possessed trading-post bands composed of the interrelated extended families that wintered in the vicinity. Many of those Cree who traded frequently at the post also performed a variety of post-related chores for the traders, including the semi-annual (spring and fall) goose hunt. As previously indicated, the traders called these Indians "Home Guards" because of their close association with the post and the trader. By the late eighteenth century the Home Guard category included a growing number of mixed-blood descendants of HBC employees and Native women.

As also noted in the previous chapter, cross-cousin marriage apparently characterized all the Algonquians of Northern Ontario.[36] While all Algonquians were polygamous, not all males had more than one wife. Usually leaders had from one to five wives, the number varying with their abilities as hunters, trappers, and politicians. Prominent individuals had more wives and supported their sons-in-law longer than was normally the case.

Some comments can be made about leadership in this time period. Over each group (usually little more than an extended family) there presided a leader, or "captain" (as he was designated by the traders), who possessed limited authority. An individual might obtain his leadership position by primogeniture, that is, by being the eldest son of a previous leader. Nevertheless, personal qualities must also have played an important part in their selection. The traders reinforced the position of leader by according these individuals deferential treatment; in this way they gained the leaders' allegiance and thereby acquired their followers' furs. This was politically expedient, for the loss of a leader's support during the time of fur trade rivalry also usually meant the loss of all his group's furs. From the traders, each leader received a captain's coat and other distinguishing apparel, plus gifts of liquor and tobacco. But as the rivalry between the Hudson's Bay Company and the North West Company intensified, some leaders could not prevent their young men from trading wherever they wished. This undermined a leader's position and may account for the competition among them, as well as for the apparent increase in the number of men who claimed and obtained the title of trading captain. Perhaps the Crane's hostility towards other Indians may in part be explained by their attempt to maintain control over a relatively rich fur and game region – one that possibly remained productive longer than any other area in Northern Ontario.

Little exists in the historical record on the religious and ceremonial activities of the Northern Algonquians in the late eighteenth and early nineteenth centuries. While the traders frequently noted dances and feasts, they rarely described them. The Indians held feasts following a birth, at the naming of a child, and upon a death. The Midewiwin ceremony may have been practised by the Indians near Rainy Lake and Lake of the Woods, but how far to the north it extended is difficult to ascertain. Probably all Algonquians practised the Shaking Tent ceremony, but only the fur trader Andrew Graham (in his eighteenth-century ethnography of the Hudson Bay Cree) described both the tent and the shaman's performance.[37]

## The Home Guard Cree

The establishment of inland trade and competition in the interior of Northern Ontario disrupted the lives of the Ojibwa more than it did those of the Home Guard Cree. The Home Guards actually benefited from the inland competition. After the traders established interior fur trade posts, they hired Cree to man brigades heading inland from the Moose, Albany, and Severn forts. The Cree also continued to trap and hunt geese in both the spring and the fall for the coastal posts. A goose hunt captain, whom the traders treated with deference, presided over the hunt. Possibly this captain coordinated hunting activities in the marsh. Women and children accompanied the men to the marshes to clean and prepare the geese and to keep the hunters' guns loaded. More opportunities for summer jobs about the posts arose as the inland trade made it necessary to enlarge many of the facilities. Competition among the inland traders also resulted in a great quantity and variety of trade items becoming available. Employment opportunities about the post lessened the need to spend time in winter trapping to obtain trade goods.

In the late eighteenth century the Hudson's Bay Company made the goose hunt more efficient when they sent batteaux to the marshes with barrels, salt, and hunting gear. This eliminated the need for the Cree to make regular trips to the post when their supplies ran out or their canoes filled with geese. Prior to the spring and fall hunts the Cree received a ration of oatmeal. In the spring the Cree held a feast before embarking for the marshes.

The spring hunt at Fort Albany usually ran from late April or early May to early June, while that in the fall lasted from early September to early

October. The number of Home Guards participating in the Fort Albany hunt varied from about 100 to 150 persons, of whom perhaps 30 were male hunters. Usually, a few more Indians participated in the spring hunt, since some who had wintered further inland had by now returned to the coast. But in the fall they moved inland for trapping rather than linger on the coast to hunt geese.

During the winter, life for the Home Guards remained much the same as in the mid-eighteenth century. To hunt and trap, they still scattered across the lowlands to bush camps composed of extended families. Although the records are not clear, the Cree possibly possessed incipient trapping territories. Some

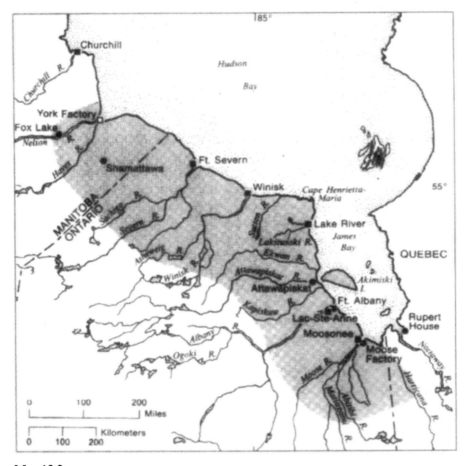

Map 13.2
West Main Cree: Nineteenth-Century Territory

Reprinted from *Handbook of North American Indians*, vol. 6: *Subarctic*, ed. June Helm (Washington, D.C.: Smithsonian Institution Press), 218, by permission of the publisher. Copyright 1981 Smithsonian Institution

Cree apparently managed the beaver found near the coast, perhaps because of company instructions, but not necessarily so. After 1810 the Hudson's Bay Company established a beaver preserve on Akimiska Island that the Cree "guarded."

By 1800 Fort Albany had over 200 Home Guard Cree associated with it, although not all of them participated in the goose hunt. This population constituted a "trading post band" composed of some twenty-five to thirty families, some being the offspring of traders and Cree women. Many of the mixed-bloods blended into the Indian population, but others maintained ties with their fathers and the company. Often the mixed-bloods engaged in post activities such as fishing, cutting and hauling wood, cutting hay for the cattle, and carrying the mail packet to and from other posts. Marriage and kinship linked the Home Guards and many of the Europeans at a particular post in a complex close web of relationships.

National Archives of Canada, c-1917

This watercolour by Peter Rindisbacher shows a Home Guard Indian from York Factory returning with his catch. The man wears a blue, yellow, and red peaked hat, which he has decorated with feathers. He is shown in a blue chief's coat, with an Assomption sash (red, blue, and yellow) around his waist. A red, black, and yellow flat pouch hangs from his neckband. He carries a powder horn. The woman appears wearing a Hudson's Bay Company blanket and carrying a young child in a cradleboard.

## The Decline of the Fur Trade and Resource Depletion:
## Social and Ecological Consequences

The fur trade rivalry affected the Native peoples of Northern Ontario differently, most adversely perhaps in the area north of Georgian Bay that had been ravaged by the fur trade for over a century prior to the 1770s. Here, as a consequence, the numbers of large animals and fur bearers available to the Ojibwa were reduced.

North and west of Sault Ste. Marie the situation differed again. As late as 1770 game of all sorts (including beaver, otter, moose, and caribou) abounded. Although these animals had been hunted in response to the fur trade for over a century (except close to the Great Lakes), the ecological balance was not seriously disturbed until the years of intense competition between the Hudson's Bay and North West companies. Almost immediately the Ojibwa began to overexploit both the fur bearers, especially beaver, and the large animals upon which the Indians' survival greatly depended. Competing traders put heavy demands upon the Ojibwa. Not only did their reliance on country food lead them to encourage the Indians to provide meat for the posts, but their demand for furs led to the overexploitation of fur-bearing animals. In addition, the traders required moose and caribou hides to make windows, to construct snowshoe netting, and to wrap fur bundles for shipment.

The Northern Algonquians usually proved willing partners in the fur trade. Those who attempted to maximize the amount of goods they could receive, made little attempt to preserve the natural resources. Despite the surviving evidence of aboriginal resource-management practices, the Indian belief that game would remain so long as they treated the hunted animals with the proper respect led some Native people to overlook the ecological consequences of their behaviour.

As early as 1800 the area near Rainy Lake and along the North West Company's heavily travelled route leading to the northern plains had experienced a considerable decline in game. Daniel Harmon wrote in 1807 that the country about Sturgeon Lake "has been a Beaver Country, but now those Animals are become scarce, for they have been continually hunted by the Natives for more than a hundred years."[38] Likewise, the fur trader Duncan Cameron, recognizing the effects of nearly thirty years of rivalry, reported in 1804 on the decline of beaver in the Nipigon country.[39]

In any event, the steady demand for furs, combined with the inability of a single group to maintain control over the resources of a specific area, did not allow the fur-bearing animals time to recover. Consequently, the quantities of pelts taken by both companies declined after 1800. As beaver became scarce, Indians focused on "small furs" – muskrat, marten, and mink. Their struggle to obtain enough furs to meet their demands for trade goods intensified.

The returns at Osnaburgh House illustrate the decline in beaver pelts. Between 1788 and 1799 the post annually obtained over 1 100 large or whole beaver skins and sometimes considerably more despite intense rivalry with the North West Company. But in 1821 (the last year before the union of the two companies) a mere 163 pelts were traded.[40] The declining quantities of furs meant that fewer traders and trading posts were needed.

Almost simultaneously, as a result of the growing scarcity of moose and caribou, the Ojibwa's quest for food became more time-consuming and difficult. Out of necessity, some Indians began to rely heavily on fish and hare. The region north of Osnaburgh House and south of Big Trout Lake, the land of the Crane, was one of the last to have caribou in significant numbers. By the 1820s, however, the Crane experienced great difficulty in securing sufficient big game for food and clothing. The Crane now met with disaster. During the winter of 1825–26 no less than seven Crane starved to death.[41] After this catastrophe, they reluctantly, but out of necessity, turned to a subsistence based upon rabbits.

The decline of big game had other effects. Up to this point the Indians had made much of their clothing from the hides of caribou and moose. The absence of "leather" meant that they now had to make much greater use of rabbit-skin parkas and blankets. But the cyclical nature of the hare population tended to make reliance upon this animal, whether for food or clothing, precarious. To compensate, the Indians often sought hides for moccasins and snowshoe lacings from the traders' store. To assist hungry Indians who arrived during the winter, traders began also to stock larders of fish and potatoes. The perilous reliance on hare had still another consequence: it required the Indians to hunt hare at the very time they needed to obtain more furs to trade for badly needed trade goods.[42]

Changes in ecological and trade conditions had a number of social consequences. The switch to small game led to a change in the division of labour. Males as well as females now found themselves fishing and setting hare snares, activities formerly undertaken primarily by women.[43] Furthermore, wrote Thomas Vincent from Lac Seul in 1825, "their former pride and ambition to excel each other is vanished. A young man may now be seen wearing an old tattered Rabbit Skin garment that a few years ago he would have considered a degrading covering for a helpless old Woman."[44] Farther south at Sault Ste. Marie and Michipicoten, by the 1820s Indian apparel was, apart from the rabbit-skin robe, made mainly from European cloth.

The Northern Algonquians' new dependence on small game animals led to the separation of families for much of the year. Except on rare occasions, there was not sufficient food in any given locale to maintain groups of twenty persons or more, unlike during the late eighteenth century. Families had to disperse and focus their efforts on hare and fish in the areas where these could be found.

The new ecological and trading conditions fostered greater individualism. The traders' preference to deal with individuals rather than small groups headed by captains underscored the significance of individual success in trapping. Consequently, some Indians as early as the 1810s – and much earlier in regions to the south – began marking beaver lodges to indicate private ownership. Yet, because others ignored these efforts, neither private rights nor game-management practices basic to the system of family hunting territories emerged for at least a decade or so after 1821.

Between 1770 and 1820 the Indians in what is now Northern Ontario grew increasingly desirous of European trade goods. So long as rivalry remained intense and furs abundant, they could obtain these goods cheaply and with relatively little effort. As resources became depleted, however, Indians had more difficulty doing so. Such items as axes, awls, files, knives, kettles, twine, fish-hooks, guns, powder, and shot had to be obtained from the post. Likewise, when hare became scarce, the Indians sought European cloth, capots, leggings, and blankets, although these were not always available or affordable. The search for fur to buy trade items, one contemporary trader wrote, "keeps the very best Indian in constant employment every day of the year & not to live as Indians were wont to live 20 years ago but merely to exist."[45] Despite this "miserable life" and some changes in social and economic organization, the Northern Algonquians practised an amazing array of adaptive strategies to maximize returns and thereby reduce efforts. As a result, they retained much of their old culture and belief system.

## NOTES

1  Hudson's Bay Company Archives (HBCA), B.135/a/33, 26 July 1761
2  HBCA, B.198/a/10. For a detailed account of the fur trade in the "Little North," the region east of Lake Winnipeg, south of the Hudson Bay lowland, and north of the International Boundary waters, between 1760 and 1821, see Victor P. Lytwyn, *The Fur Trade of the Little North: Indians, Pedlars and Englishmen East of Lake Winnipeg, 1760–1821* (Winnipeg 1986).
3  Elaine Allen Mitchell, *Fort Temiskaming and the Fur Trade* (Toronto 1977), 20–4
4  HBCA, B.3/a/73, 23 November 1777; Charles A. Bishop, *The Northern Ojibwa and the Fur Trade: An Historical and Ecological Study* (Toronto 1974), 329–31
5  HBCA, John Thomas to Edward Jarvis, Moose Factory, 10 June 1780
6  Gordon Charles Davidson, *The North West Company* (1919; New York 1967), 12–13

7   HBCA, B.57/a/2, fos. 2–2d, 6 September 1809. See also Glyndwr Williams, ed., *Hudson's Bay Miscellany 1670–1870* (Winnipeg 1975), 107–10.
8   HBCA, B.155/a/11, fo. 19, 7 January 1796. This often had devastating results. The fur trader James Sutherland, for instance, stated on 7 January 1796:

> Three more Indians being kill'd last fall at Lake Sturgeon when they were Drunk, this is exclusive of the two murdered by Mr. Bests Brandy ... besides two more who I hear is dead from surfits of liquor ... Dreadful is the devastations now which spiritous liquors is making among the Indians, between us at one end, the N.W. Company at the Other and Cameron and Co. in the middle who vieing with each other who shall pour the spirituous poison most down their throats, and not only this but those who survives the deadly draught are become more abandon'd to every vice by corruption and the evils arising from opposition from those who should have taught them better principles so that the poor natives have entirely lost that natural Innocence and simplicity of manner for which they were formerly distinguished.

9    HBCA, B.155/a/9, 28 September 1793
10   Mitchell, *Fort Temiskaming and the Fur Trade*, 30–3
11   HBCA, B.155/a/18, fo. 10, 9 September 1803
12   HBCA, B.155/a/18, fo. 11d, 3 May 1804
13   HBCA, B.123/a/8, fo. 20, 24 May 1804
14   HBCA, B.123/a/8, fo. 20, 27 May 1804
15   HBCA, B.123/a/8, fos. 20d–23, 24 May–2 June 1804
16   HBCA, B.3/a/73, 3 May 1778
17   Mitchell, *Fort Temiskaming and the Fur Trade,* 39
18   HBCA, B.107/a/9, 1 November 1830; B.107/a/16, 23 December 1837, Lac Seul Post Journals
19   John Richardson, *Fauna Boreali-Americana or the Zoology of the Northern Parts of British North America* (London 1829), 250; Samuel Hearne, *A Journey from Prince of Wales's Fort in Hudson's Bay to the Northern Ocean,* ed. J.B. Tyrrell (Toronto 1911), vi, 236
20   HBCA, B.220/a/1, fo. 28d, 30 December 1807; B.220/a/2, fo. 14d, January 23, 1810
21   HBCA, B.123/e/4, fo. 9
22   See Edward S. Rogers, *The Round Lake Ojibwa*, Occasional Paper no. 5, Art and Archaeology Division, Royal Ontario Museum, University of Toronto (Toronto 1962), c42
23   HBCA, B.155/a/5, 25 May 1791, Osnaburgh House post journal
24   HBCA, MG 19, D2, Surin House, vol. 1, Post 1: Journal of William Falconer, 1768–69, 1, 20, 21, 22, 23, and 28 February 1769
25   J. Carver, *Travels through the Interior Parts of North America in the Years 1766, 1767, and 1768* (Minneapolis 1956), 115; Alexander Henry, *Travels and Adventures in Canada and the Indian Territories between the Years 1760 and 1776* (Edmonton 1969), 240–1
26   HBCA, B.155/e/1, fos., 3d–4
27   Edward S. Rogers, "*The Southeastern Ojibwa,*" in *Handbook of North American Indians,* vol. 15: *Northeast,* ed. Bruce G. Trigger (Washington, D.C. 1978), 760–71. Also please see note 38, chapter 12.

28  L.R. Masson, éd., *Les Bourgeois de la Compagnie du Nord-Ouest* (New York 1960), 2:236. See also Harold Hickerson, *Land Tenure of the Rainy Lake Chippewa at the Beginning of the Nineteenth Century*, 41–63.

29  W. Kaye Lamb, ed., *Sixteen Years in the Indian Country*, 237

30  HBCA, B.1/e/3

31  Lamb, *Sixteen Years in the Indian Country*, 237–8

32  HBCA, B.155/e/1, fo.3d

33  HBCA, B.129/b/4

34  Ibid.

35  Edward S. Rogers and Mary Black Rogers, "Who were the Cranes? Group and Group Identity Names in Northern Ontario," in Margaret Hanna and Brian Kooyman, eds., *Approaches to Algonquian Archaeology*, Proceedings of the Thirteenth Annual Conference, the Archaeological Association of the University of Calgary (Calgary 1982), 147–88

36  See Duncan Cameron's remarks about the Ojibwa (1804), quoted in Masson, *Les Bourgeois de la Compagnie du Nord-Ouest*, 2:247.

37  Glyndwr Williams, ed., *Andrew Graham's Observations on Hudson's Bay, 1767–91* (London 1969), 161–2:

> The conjurer is often employed by other Indians to enquire concerning any affair or to retrieve any misfortune that has befallen them; or avert such as threaten them ... On such occasions a round, narrow high tent (named Shebastakekan) is erected by the conjurer, by sticking strong sticks into the earth at a distance from each other, and about eight feet high; the top open but the rest covered with skins, so that no person can see what is going on. At a distance from the ground a stage is erected by tying poles across. Upon this the magician mounts to perform his duty. He makes a great many frightful howling etc. and shakes the whole fabric with violence; and is all over reeking with sweat. The exercise continues several hours before his familiar condescends to dictate an answer; and when the conjurer comes out he appears quite frantic, staring wildly with frightful gestures. During the process all the other natives sit round with the most profound silence. The performer is painted black, and as ugly as the infernal genius he invokes. All the fires are put out, and one of the aged men stands by with the greatest gravity to light a pipe, and introduce it under the skins when called for.

38  Lamb, *Sixteen Years in the Indian Country*, 107

39  Masson, *Les Bourgeois de la Compagnie du Nord-Ouest*, 2:245, 297

40  Bishop, *The Northern Ojibwa*, 246, Table 38 (consolidated fur return records from the Osnaburgh House Account Books)

41  HBCA, B.155/a/37, fo. 17d

42  HBCA, B.124/e/4

43  HBCA, B.107/a/8, January 1830

44  HBCA, B.3/e/10

45  Charles McKenzie in HBCA, B.107/e/4

# 14 Northern Algonquians and the Hudson's Bay Company, 1821–1890

## EDWARD S. ROGERS

## Introduction

When the Hudson's Bay and the North West companies joined forces in 1821, the new partnership (to be known as the Hudson's Bay Company) gained a virtual monopoly over the fur trade in what is now Northern Ontario. Only in the Boundary Waters region (Rainy River–Lake of the Woods) did a competitor, the American Fur Company (established in 1809),[1] threaten their trade. This challenge itself ended in 1833 when the Hudson's Bay Company agreed to pay the American Fur Company £300 annually to remain out of the Rainy River country.[2] Even after the HBC sold its rights to Rupert's Land in 1869–70, a monopoly situation existed for several decades in Northern Ontario, until the late nineteenth century when freetraders once again entered the country.[3]

## The Hudson's Bay Company Gains a Monopoly

After amalgamation, the Hudson's Bay Company introduced new policies and consolidated its operation. It reduced staff[4] and closed some posts and many if not all of the outposts. By 1856 the company had only twenty-five posts in operation throughout Northern Ontario.[5]

Among the new policies implemented was a ban on the trading of liquor at the company's posts.[6] The Hudson's Bay Company also introduced conservation measures. For years the intense competition between the different trading companies had led to the over-trapping of fur-bearing animals, especially beaver. As early as 1824 the Hudson's Bay Company instructed its traders to tell the Native people not to hunt furs during the summer. Two years later the

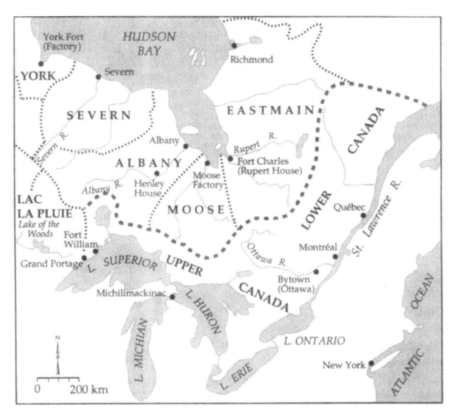

Map 14.1
Fur Trade Districts in the 1830s
Drawn by Marta Styk, University of Calgary; based on maps of the 1830s in Glyndwr Williams, *Highlights of the First 200 Years of the Hudson's Bay Company* (Winnipeg 1976); originally published in *The Beaver* (Autumn 1970), 14–15

traders in the Severn district forbade the Indians to trap any beaver.[7] But all such attempts at conservation failed. The Indians replied that they relied on the beaver for both food and clothing. The traders persisted and tried to discourage them at least from trapping during the summer.[8] In time most fur bearers recovered their numbers. As the trade improved, the company opened old posts and occasionally established new ones, such as the short-lived post at Winisk.[9] Big Trout Lake (closed in 1825) reopened in 1844 and Cat Lake in 1873.[10]

## The Algonquians Respond

By the 1820s the Northern Algonquians had experienced important cultural changes. Further modifications in their material culture and in their subsistence patterns occurred over the next seventy years. Thanks to the greater abundance of written information one can describe in some detail their mid- and late-nineteenth-century culture and social organization.

*Equipment for Survival – Mostly Old*

During the mid-nineteenth century the Northern Algonquians used several traditional lodge types – the conical, ridge-pole, and dome-shaped lodge.[11] To build such structures, they began by selecting light poles for a foundation, which they then covered with birchbark, spruce boughs, hide and/or bits of canvas. They carpeted the earth floors with spruce boughs that the women replaced every few days. At the centre of the lodge they left a cleared space for an open fireplace, or in the case of the communal ridge-pole lodge, they placed several fireplaces in a line down the centre. To start the fire, they used a fire-drill,[12] smouldering punk, or a strike-a-light obtained in trade. Such lodges were snug, with the exception of those covered with spruce boughs (through which the winter winds rattled). In summer hailstones could pierce the birchbark lodges.[13]

Canadian Museum of Civilization, G.S. 594

Two types of Ojibwa lodges (the conical and dome-shaped), with a birchbark canoe in the foreground.

Canadian Museum of Civilization, 48790

A moss-covered conical lodge, with a toboggan leaning against it.

During the last half of the nineteenth century, the Indians introduced a new style of housing: the moss-covered conical lodge.[14] Usually they built these during the fall and occupied them most of the winter. At each campsite, the Amerindians frequently set up fish- and meat-drying racks, smoke lodges, and cache racks, especially if they occupied the site for any length of time. Until recently they put up few other structures. Farther south in the Boundary Waters region, where some Indians began to farm, they built more substantial dwellings and livestock barns based on the settlers' models.

The Northern Algonquians perfected appropriate means of transport for the Subarctic. In winter they wore snowshoes that had frames of birch wood[15] and were laced with moose- and/or caribou-hide thong. The round-toed style was traditional among the Indians of Northern Ontario, but towards the end of the period, the pointed style came into use. As caribou and moose disappeared during the early nineteenth century, the Indians adapted by finding other sources of thong to lace their snowshoes. First, they cut up beaver and other hides for this purpose; but the company disapproved, and its agents soon began importing "leather" to trade with, or give, the Indians.[16] The traders had a difficult time, however, obtaining sufficient hides for the making of babiche.[17] If babiche was unavailable, the Indians made snowshoes totally of wood, without any webbing, somewhat like skis.[18] Such snowshoes had come into use by the late nineteenth century.

Canadian Museum of Civilization, 36782

An Ojibwa in traditional winter dress, with snowshoes.

For the transportation of personal possessions, furs and/or game, the Amerindians constructed toboggans. They made them out of two birch boards cut out with an axe and crooked knife, the front ends steamed and then bent upwards. With crossbars in place, the Indians lashed the parts together with thongs. Both men and women hand-drew the finished toboggans.

For summer transportation, the Northern Algonquians built light birch-bark canoes, ideally adapted for northern travel. These canoes carried heavy loads over rough lake waters and through the many river rapids. The materials for construction – birchbark, cedar wood, spruce roots, and gum – were all readily available except within the Hudson Bay Lowlands. In emergencies, the Amerindians used log rafts to travel downstream or sometimes, in the spring break-up, large blocks of ice.[19]

Photo by George M. Dawson, National Archives of Canada, c-79651

Ojibwa women mending a birchbark canoe, North-West Angle of Lake of the Woods, October 1872.

Although little clothing was needed in the summer,[20] the subarctic winters forced the Northern Algonquians to perfect appropriate warm clothing. Originally, they used beaver, moose, and caribou hides,[21] sewing with sinew from the backs of caribou and moose.[22] As big game declined, however, in the early nineteenth century hare skins became the predominant material[23] for parkas, leggings, hoods, and moccasins for children.

When the supply of hides from big game first became limited, the men rejected clothing made of hare skins, considering it degrading. The lack of caribou hides and the cold weather, however, convinced them to adapt. By 1830 most males were probably clothed in hare skins. Women wore a one-piece hare-skin dress with attached sleeves, secured at the waist with a caribou- or moose-hide belt.[24]

To make rabbit-skin clothing, the women cut the skins spirally into narrow strips. They then "spun" these strips in such a fashion that the cord so formed had hair completely around its circumference. The women then wove the strips on an upright frame into rectangular pieces. Finally they sewed the requisite number of pieces together to produce the appropriate item of clothing. The Northern Algonquians wove hare-skin blankets and wore hare skins turned inside out as socks. When the hides of big game became scarce, the women might make moccasins of fish skins, either walleye or pike.[25]

Until the late nineteenth century the traders at the interior posts had a very limited quantity of cloth.[26] Whenever it was available, the women used cloth to fashion various items of clothing. For the men, they sewed leggings, breech clouts of white stroud, shirts, and capots, or "coats."[27] A hare-skin coat would be an additional covering in periods of intense cold. Women wore dresses of blue stroud with separate sleeves tied across the back of the neck and decorated leggings. Both men and women might wear a pointed cloth cap which hung down the back to the waist. The Indians decorated their caps with feathers and attached the tail-end of the cap to their belt with an owl-bone pin.[28] Sometimes a trader presented an exceptionally good trapper with a coat and occasionally a handkerchief.[29] A "chief" might be given a suit of black cloth, boots, and hat, and his wife a bright tartan wool dress piece and tartan shawl.[30]

Some Amerindians incorporated bird feathers of different colours into their hair as it was braided, and wore brass rings in their ears and on their fingers.[31] Many, if not all, of the Northern Algonquians decorated themselves with designs painted in one or more colours.[32] By the mid-nineteenth century the Indians near the big coastal posts such as Fort Albany and Moose Factory,

Photo by R.S. Cassels, National Archives of Canada, PA-123309

Ojibwa women by the Hudson's Bay Company factor's home, Lake Temagami, 21 August 1894.

and near Lakes Superior and Huron, wore European clothing. At the more isolated posts they had to rely more on furs, especially rabbit-skin robes and blankets.

Hunting and trapping equipment, although not especially complex, varied. From an early date the traders supplied the Northern Algonquians with firearms,[33] which they used to hunt caribou, moose, grouse, ptarmigan, ducks, and fur-bearing animals. Until they acquired percussion weapons in the 1890s, flintlocks were the only guns generally available.[34] Flintlock owners constantly came to the post to have their inefficient weapons repaired. Sometimes they reported the loss of fingers caused by their guns exploding.[35] Even if the guns did not break, it often happened that the hunters expended all their ammunition on partridge hunting in the fall,[36] making the flintlocks no more than extra baggage for the remainder of the winter.

Since ammunition was expensive[37] and sometimes unavailable, and the early guns themselves unreliable, the Indians continued to use their traditional hunting equipment. They did have bows and arrows,[38] some blunt-headed for small game and others presumably tipped with bone or stone. Besides the simple bow, they had a crossbow, a device derived most likely from the

Canadian Museum of Civilization, 23947

Ojibwa boys, Bear Island, Lake Temagami, July 1913.

traders. No doubt the Natives also used spears when hunting big game in late winter, but this practice is not documented.[39] To attract moose within range of the hunter during the rutting season, they used a birchbark caller.[40]

Fishing equipment included traps that the Indians placed in suitable rapids to catch whitefish in the fall.[41] The Fort Severn people also employed them during the spring to take trout.[42] Apparently, some Indians farther south sometimes constructed traps during the spring to take suckers.[43]

The Northern Algonquians also set lines, mostly in late winter when the lakes were still covered with ice, to catch lake trout and ling. A great deal of labour was necessary to cut through a metre or so of ice. At the same time, they might use a hook and line to jig for the same species.[44] A short wooden pole, home-made, stout line, and a hook, either made from a pail handle or secured from the traders, were all the equipment needed. The home-made spears used to take sturgeon during their spring spawning runs had iron points obtained from the traders.[45] Other species of fish might also be taken with spears or, on occasion, with bows and arrows. Around the Great Lakes area the Indians caught whitefish with dipnets.[46]

Gill nets were relatively rare until the late nineteenth century.[47] Initially, the Indians used gill nets primarily in summer, as it was difficult to set them under the ice in winter. Placing a gill net under the ice, even when one possessed an iron chisel for cutting the many holes necessary, required a great deal of work. Moreover, when setting a net, the Indians still had to clear

Indian fish traps, District of Patricia, 1927.

broken ice out of the holes they had cut. For this, they used a wooden scoop or shovel, the same as those they made to clear away the snow from about the camp.[48] In time, however, the Indians came to use the efficient gill nets more and more throughout the year, until they replaced most, if not all, other items of fishing equipment. By 1900 most Indians owned at least one.

The Northern Algonquians in the mid-nineteenth century had a variety of traps and snares.[49] Probably they most commonly employed the samson-post deadfall for taking fisher, marten, mink, weasel, and fox.[50] Towards the end of the nineteenth century the Indians at the southern end of James Bay began to use the kicker deadfall.[51] With it the trappers took the species listed as well as lynx.[52] No doubt the Northern Algonquians also made deadfalls with trigger releases different from the two mentioned, but unfortunately no data exist indicating what these might have been.

The Indians utilized snares primarily to capture such game as hare and lynx.[53] On occasion they erected much larger snares for bear, and some Northern Algonquians used these for moose. The first type of snare, the spring-pole, could not be relied upon to function properly when temperatures went very far below freezing. Under such conditions, the moisture in the green sapling used for the pole froze. It could not spring upward and strangle the prey when an animal tripped the release. For the noose the Indians employed caribou sinew,[54] but when this was unavailable, they purchased "rabbit snare twine" from the traders.[55] They could use the second type of snare, the tossing-pole type, throughout the year.

Photo by F.W. Waugh, Canadian Museum of Civilization, 45678

A deadfall, Lac Seul, northwestern Ontario, 1919.

Occasionally the Indians bought steel traps to capture beaver, fox, and muskrat, although such traps were not always obtainable from the traders.[56] Moreover, nineteenth-century steel traps were also quite heavy and costly, which reduced their popularity.[57]

Additional equipment included birchbark containers and/or metal vessels for collecting berries. The Amerindians built special racks on which to dry blueberries. To collect wild rice, they took sticks to knock the grains from the stalks into a canoe as it passed through the rice field. They had spiles, birch-bark and metal containers, and moulds for the extraction and processing of the sap from maple trees. Both wild rice and sugar maple grew only in the more southerly parts of Northern Ontario.

## The Search for Food and Furs

Although the traders frequently commented that the Native people were "starving hard," little indication exists that death by starvation often occurred.[58] Malnutrition, however, was a likely contributing factor in some deaths. Many more Indians might have died for want of food if they had not received aid from the traders.[59] The Hudson's Bay Company provided the hungry Indians with fish, occasionally potatoes, oatmeal, and flour, and under extreme conditions might kill a company dog to feed a destitute family.[60]

In the nineteenth century the Northern Algonquians had to alter drastically their subsistence strategy. Big game (formerly a principal means of support) had practically disappeared from the country by 1830, and beaver became greatly reduced in numbers.[61] The shift from a reliance upon moose and caribou to a much greater dependence upon fish and hare subjected the Northern Algonquians to great difficulties.[62] Approximately every seven to ten years, hare almost disappeared from the country, and fish randomly varied in numbers. When such reductions in food occurred simultaneously, the Indians were hard-pressed.[63] Fortunately, big game did return slowly at the end of the nineteenth century.[64]

As the Indians shifted to a subsistence strategy based upon small game, they no longer ranged as widely in search of food and furs (see chapter 13). They became restricted to favourable fishing locales or hare-snaring grounds. Similarly, as the numbers of the fur-bearing animals fell, trapping became increasingly critical. Accordingly, the Northern Algonquians claimed private ownership of beaver by marking the animals' lodges. In time, all the fur-bearing animals found within the territory customarily exploited by a particular hunting group came to be considered that group's property. Consequently, other groups recognized vague boundaries to each hunting group's land. By the late nineteenth century most of the Indians of Northern Ontario operated traplines within specified territories.[65]

The Indians' adoption of gardening, primarily the raising of potatoes, also led them to stay in the same area. The Ojibwa in the Boundary Waters area had gardens in the early nineteenth century.[66] Farther north, gardening began in the 1870s, but there the Indians only grew potatoes.

In the mid-nineteenth century the Northern Algonquians normally lived in small family groups throughout most of the year. Sometimes, however, a particular location was rich enough in natural resources to support several groups for the greater part of the year. And at least once annually (usually for a few weeks in the summer), a number of families assembled at their traditional gathering centres. Individuals also briefly visited a trading post (see chapter 13). As the years passed, however, Indians spent more and more time each summer near the trading post. As the volume of trade goods shipped into the interior increased, the Hudson's Bay Company employed many canoe men on the brigades transporting the winter's furs to the coast and hauling inland new consignments of goods for the coming winter's trade. Work on the brigades was difficult, and on occasion the men suffered accidents, sickness, and death.[67]

At first, the brigade workers left their families at a bush camp near the area where they would spend the coming winter. But in time they brought them to the posts, where they remained after the fur brigades departed. The Indians in the vicinity of the post lived principally on fish and small game.[68] When the berries became ripe, they gathered blueberries and gooseberries. Although the traders discouraged the Indians from trapping fur-bearing animals during the summer, they continued to do so, but not as intensively as during the winter.[69]

With the approach of fall, families left their gathering centres and dispersed to their fall camps. If overtaken by freeze-up, they abandoned their canoes and proceeded on foot to their trapping grounds. Upon reaching their fall encampments, they hunted as much country game as possible and preserved it for the winter. The Northern Algonquians took large numbers of whitefish with traps during late October and early November.[70] They filleted the fish and then smoke-dried them over a smouldering fire. With a wooden spoon they broke up some of the smoked fish into a powder, to which they added berries. The Indians stored the fish pemmican in specially designed birchbark boxes.

Other sources of food generally remained available throughout the fall. Waterfowl returned from the north on their way south. In the late fall the Indians also hunted bears. Although moose failed to reappear in sufficient numbers during the nineteenth century, the Indians still hunted them intensively during the fall. At this time of year they also gathered cranberries.[71] In the Boundary Waters region the Indians harvested wild rice. Garden produce

Wild rice harvesting, Lac Seul, 1919.

furnished additional food for a number of people. During the fall the Northern Algonquians near the International Border and Lakes Superior and Huron dug up their potatoes and stored them in root cellars, to be drawn upon during the winter. They put aside a few seed potatoes for planting the following spring.

Fall lasted but a few weeks. As it drew to a close, the Indians made further preparations for winter. They repaired their snowshoes and toboggans, or made new ones. Until the beginning of winter the Indians stayed at their fall campsites. Each group comprised two to three families, a dozen or so individuals, closely related to one another. Occasionally, if the resources in the vicinity permitted, as many as eight to ten families, fifty or so people, might live together. When, as usually occurred, food resources within convenient travel distance of the camp dwindled below a certain point, the group moved. At such times, in order to locate sufficient

Netting snowshoes, Long Lake, northwestern Ontario, 1916.

food and furs, the group might split into two or more units – the larger the group, the more likely division would occur.

Several or more kilometres separated each winter camp to allow each group sufficient territory. The members of each camp usually remained within a circumscribed area. If, however, little or no food could be found, the occupants could move beyond their accustomed range in search of food.

Everyone made the most of the few available daylight hours. The elders, often accompanied by the children, jigged for fish or tended snares set for hare. The able-bodied men went farther afield in search of big game if they had seen signs of any in the area. At the same time, they set and tended their traps and snares. The women tended the camp, cooking, collecting firewood and boughs, and checking their snares for hare.

While the intensive competition between the North West Company and the Hudson's Bay Company had greatly reduced the number of fur-bearing animals, none had been exterminated. Beaver recovered their numbers by the mid-nineteenth century. At times some areas even became overpopulated. Whenever their population became too great, the beaver became susceptible to outbreaks of tularimia, which quickly reduced their numbers.[72] Marten, a fur-bearing animal once in as great demand as beaver, never appears to have recovered its former numbers.[73]

Once open water appeared in the spring, each group evacuated its winter camp and moved to a new location situated on higher ground. Before the spring thaw got fully under way, the Indians gathered a supply of firewood and boughs. They hunted the first migrating ducks and geese, and speared sturgeon. During late April, whitefish "disappeared" but suckers replaced them. The Indians took suckers in abundance from the smaller streams.[74] The Ojibwa in the Boundary Waters region often made their spring camps in maple groves and tapped the trees for the sap.[75]

Either in late spring or early summer, the Indians constructed their birch-bark canoes. In areas where the soil and growing season permitted, they also prepared gardens and planted crops. As summer approached, the scattered hunting groups prepared to leave their spring camps. Once the lakes and rivers had cleared of ice, they joined others – mostly, if not all, close kinsmen – at a gathering centre where they held feasts and dances.[76] At the centres people came and went regularly. If no trading post existed at the traditional gathering centre, individual families (after renewing acquaintances) might singly, or in small groups, proceed to one. At the post they exchanged furs for European goods and might see a Christian missionary. If one was available, the Indians attended services and had baptisms and weddings.

Making a birchbark canoe, Long Lake, 1916. In the first photograph the
Indian women are sewing the birchbark to the frame. In the second,
F.W. Waugh, an anthropologist, appears to be taking notes on the process.
The final photo shows the completed canoe on the water. Waugh took all
but the second photograph.
Canadian Museum of Civilization, 36693, 36687, 36742

*Social Life*

Enough data exist to describe the Northern Algonquians' social organization in the mid-nineteenth century (see also chapter 13). They had several types of social groupings. The smallest was the nuclear family, and the largest, the named group and/or trading post band. In between were the hunting group, the band, and, among some Northern Algonquians, the "clan."

The domestic or household unit, the core usually being the nuclear family, consisted of a man, his wife (or wives), their children, and possibly one or more dependents, such as an elder or an orphan. Polygamy was practised and a man might have as many as seven wives,[77] although two or three appear to have been most common. The number of offspring varied greatly. Some couples had none. Some men, especially those with more than one wife, might sire fifteen to twenty children, perhaps more. The husband or father dominated the household, but the women shared in the responsibilities as partners.

The family, the basic social unit, associated with other households in their winter camp. The members of each camp were usually related to each other in one way or another. The winter hunting group or camp often consisted of families whose heads were brothers and, if he was still living, their father. Although the Northern Algonquians preferred such an arrangement, it was not always possible to achieve owing to the differentials in sex ratios and deaths within a family. Accordingly, there existed hunting groups that included brothers-in-law or more distant kin. Rarely, however, would a hunting group include an individual without a kinship relationship to some group member.

Leadership of such winter groups remained informal. The leader, the individual who could provide food and other necessities, was to be "responsible"[78] for his followers. He advised and counselled his followers in spiritual matters and tried to protect them from harm, whether arising from natural or supernatural forces. Dictatorial behaviour on the leader's part would likely have caused the group to split apart.

The composition of each hunting group changed, on occasion, for various reasons. On the death of the leader, the surviving domestic units might realign themselves with other hunting groups. A leader's unpopularity also might lead to a change. The most likely reason for change, however, was if a group had grown too large to be supported by the resources available in its traditional territory; then it would have to divide into smaller groups.

Those hunting groups that assembled, as a rule, every summer (but sometimes at other times of the year as well) formed a band, the members of which were closely related. In the north, a band consisted of not more than one hundred or so individuals. But farther south, in the Boundary Waters region, much larger gatherings occurred, with as many as one thousand or more people involved. Although little information is available, no doubt each band had a name by which it was known.

From the meagre evidence that survives, it appears that band members recognized a senior male as their leader. But, as with the hunting group leader, he had no real authority, merely moral suasion. A leader held his position because of his charisma and, no doubt, his supernatural powers. He was neither elected to nor inherited the position. Consensual democracy prevailed. On the leader's death the band might break apart and regroup into new bands. In the early part of the nineteenth century, however, the traditional bands either became fragmented or amalgamated as a result of the establishment of trading posts in their country. Then a new social and quasi-political unit arose, the "trading post band."

## The Trading Post Band

Once the fur trade became stabilized in 1821, the trading post band emerged, first at the big coastal posts such as Fort Albany and Moose Factory. The Hudson's Bay Company now dictated where the Indians could trade. It permitted them to transfer from one post to another, but only on the recommendation of a chief factor.[79] Periodically post traders attempted to conform to the new rule by dealing only with their regular customers and sending "strange Indians" away.[80]

The Indians within a circumscribed area about a Hudson's Bay Company post came to form a trading post band. Each such band consisted of the former bands or segments thereof that had resided in the vicinity. The size of a trading post band varied, though usually several hundred people were involved.

Initially, the number of Native visitors at a particular post fluctuated greatly. They might arrive at any time of the year, with the general exception of February, spring break-up, and fall freeze-up. Those coming the greatest distances usually left their families behind, especially during the winter months. Once they arrived, they remained for only brief periods of time, just long enough to trade their furs and obtain a few trade goods. During the summer the visitors sometimes remained longer, particularly when awaiting the return of the brigades with new supplies. As time passed, however, more and more men and their families assembled at the post for longer periods each summer, especially at those times that the company needed men for the brigades. At Christmas, New Year's, and Easter, as many families as possible gathered for a week to ten days at the trading post to barter furs for goods, attend religious services, hold feasts, and participate in dances. Furthermore, during the winter, families experiencing hard times travelled to the post in search of aid. If possible, the traders supplied them with what food they could spare, usually no more than a little fish and potatoes.

At the trading posts the Northern Algonquians encountered an alien culture and witnessed, and sometimes participated in, a foreign lifestyle. The varied activities that the Northern Algonquians viewed at a trading post and the relations they entered into stimulated change in their own societies. Trade goods of European manufacture, "country made articles," and other things of European origin (including genes) brought about changes in the Aboriginal way of life. As already noted, the Indians began to adopt gardening, trapping territories, and dog traction and sleds in response to the traders' presence.

Intermarriage occurred during this period, as traders and their servants often took Native women for wives. From such unions came a class of mixed-bloods, such as the Orkney-Cree. The Hudson's Bay Company did not encourage the practice, though, as it placed an additional strain on the resources available at the post to feed these women and their children.[81] Intermarriage continued, but to what extent remains to be determined.

As the years passed, more and more Native people (especially the mixed-bloods) worked for the traders, particularly in the summer on the fur brigades. The traders also employed some men and women to fish for the posts.[82] Other Indians supplied the traders with hare,[83] ptarmigan, waterfowl, and caribou meat. A number tended the gardens[84] and, where cattle were kept, cut marsh

Archives of Ontario, Acc. 10144

Hudson's Bay Company voyageurs on their way to Flying Post (near Biscotasing, Ontario) with supplies, c. 1900.

grass for fodder. Often the traders hired a Native person to tend the sled dogs during the summer months.[85] Indians also cut firewood, hauled in building logs, and acted as guides.[86] Generally twice during the winter, two Indians from each post acted as "trippers" to carry the packet between the various establishments, especially to headquarters with relevant news regarding the trade. The post supplied its trippers with pemmican, oatmeal, and cornmeal, as they had little or no time to hunt en route.[87]

In the late eighteenth century the traders generally dealt with "captains" and "lieutenants"; these men would be the leaders of one or more families (see chapter 13). The practice of dealing with individual trappers began only in the 1820s, at which time the use of the terms "captain" and "lieutenant" practically disappeared. The company, however, encouraged certain Indians to act on its behalf to ensure that the trappers at the post in their quarter did not take their furs to another HBC post or, when the independent traders again began to operate in Northern Ontario, to a freetrader. Evidence exists that the HBC traders arranged for the "election" of such individuals to the position of chief.[88] Certainly, in the mid-nineteenth century traders began to speak of chiefs.[89] In some instances the trader might give a chief a black cloth suit, boots, and a hat, and his wife a bright tartan wool dress piece and tartan shawl.[90]

Fort Albany, c. 1867–68.
Photo by Bernard Rogan Ross, Provincial Archives of Manitoba, Hudson's Bay Company Archives, HBCA Photograph Collection, 1987/363-A-6/5 (N8283)

*Other Social Units*

Apparently at various times and for varying lengths of time, social units larger than the bands existed – if the traders' comments reflect the Northern Algonquians' reality.[91] The Cranes, first described in the previous chapter, constitute one of these social units or "named groups," which were composed of more than one band. The Sucker, a similar group, occupied lands west of the Crane, between Sandy and Deer lakes. Also in this general area dwelt the Pelican, perhaps a similar social unit. These named groups were not political entities and none had an overall leader. The members, however, traced close kinship relationships among themselves. They also tended to intermarry more frequently than seek a spouse from among other groups. Each group constituted a territorial unit. Their imprecise boundaries shifted only slightly during the known existence of the groups.[92]

One other social unit, referred to in the literature as a "clan," "gens," "dodem," or "totemic group," apparently existed at this time among the Ojibwa who inhabited the southern portion of Northern Ontario. As described in chapter 13, the clan group took its name from a particular species of animal, bird, or fish. During the mid-nineteenth century the clan functioned primarily to regulate marriage. Although not always observed, the rule was that one could marry only an individual from another clan. One inherited one's clan affiliation from one's father.[93]

The Northern Algonquians were a peaceful people, although personal hostilities and warfare did occur. Generally, however, whenever troubles arose, the opposing parties simply separated, each moving to a different location. In this manner, physical violence (but not shamanistic attacks) could be avoided. Yet the traders did report some cases of assault and occasionally murder. While the incentives for these attacks were not always clear, certainly in some cases at least, the desire to steal furs and/or trade goods possessed by the victims played a role. Retaliation and revenge followed, contributing to further murders.[94]

*Conflict among the Northern Algonquians and with the Traders*

There is little concrete evidence that organized warfare took place among the Algonquians of extreme Northern Ontario. The Ojibwa of the Lake of the Woods–Rainy River areas, however, undertook raids against their traditional enemies, the Sioux, who lived in what is now Minnesota. A war party consisted of young males. Raids continued at least until the middle of the nineteenth century.[95]

Generally speaking, the traders and the Northern Algonquians maintained a friendly relationship with one another. Exceptions existed, especially before the middle of the nineteenth century. The Crane certainly gained a reputation in the early nineteenth century for aggressive behaviour towards the traders[96] (see chapter 13). In practice, conflict arose mainly on account of the occasional petty theft, such as stealing fish from the nets or the nets themselves, cutting down the garden fences to steal potatoes, breaking into a store, or stealing furs.[97] More serious incidents occurred when Indians attempted to burn a post by setting fire either to the woods nearby or to the post itself, as in the case of Fort Severn, destroyed by fire in 1827.[98] Only occasionally was the life of a trader threatened.[99]

Troubles between the traders and the Northern Algonquians probably never ceased entirely, but the number of reported cases declined after the mid-nineteenth century. The increasing influence of the Christian missionaries during these decades possibly contributed to the amicable relations that generally existed between the Euro-Canadians and Native peoples in what is now Northern Ontario.

## The Missionary Enters

In 1820 the Hudson's Bay Company invited the Church of England to provide clergy for Rupert's Land. The Reverend John West of the Church Missionary Society was appointed chaplain to the Red River settlement.[100] Later, the society began missionary work among the Indians. In 1849 Bishop David Anderson arrived in the Red River settlement to begin his ministry in the Diocese of Rupert's Land.[101] Two years later the Anglican missionary John Horden landed at Moose Factory, where he remained until his death in 1893.[102] Using the Cree syllabic script devised by the Methodist missionary James Evans, Horden translated and published many religious works for his parishioners.[103] In 1872 the Anglican Church established the Diocese of Moosonee in the eastern part of the Diocese of Rupert's Land, Horden being appointed its first bishop.[104]

The first Anglican missionaries made short excursions to survey the mission field. Bishop Anderson made one of the first such trips in 1852, when he travelled by canoe from the Red River settlement down the Albany River to Moose Factory on James Bay. There he ordained John Horden (who became the first bishop of Moosonee in 1872).[105] Horden made several important trips into the interior, including a journey in 1880 from York Factory to Big Trout Lake, where eight years earlier the Anglicans had established a mission.[106] In 1895 Big Trout Lake obtained an ordained minister on a full-time basis. In that year William Dick, who had been stationed there since the 1880s as a catechist, was ordained.[107] Dick, a Cree, perhaps an Orkney-Cree, from York Factory, converted and served the spiritual needs of most of, if not all, the

Indians of the Severn River basin for many years. In the meantime, the Native minister Thomas Vincent worked as a missionary at Fort Albany. In 1863 he visited Osnaburgh on his way to Lac Seul, and in 1870 he went on another tour of the Albany River basin.[108] Many Indians residing between the shores of Hudson and James bays and the upper reaches of the Albany, Attawapiskat, Winisk, and Severn rivers became converted to the Anglican faith in the last half of the nineteenth century. John Sanders, a mixed-blood from Fort Mattagami, became the first ordained Anglican minister of Ojibwa background. Bishop Horden ordained him as a priest in 1879.[109]

Methodist missionaries had entered what is now northwestern Ontario before the Anglicans. In 1838 James Evans, accompanied by the Ojibwa Peter Jacobs and Thomas Hurlburt, left for a two-year tour of the Lake Superior region.[110] Hurlburt worked with the Native people of Fort William.[111] Another Methodist, William Mason, established a mission at Rainy River in 1839.[112] With the company's approval, Evans departed in 1840 to establish a mission at Norway House, well beyond the country examined during his previous trip. He took with him as far as Rainy River the Ojibwa Henry Steinhauer, whom

Ontario Ministry of Natural Resources, Vince Crichton Collection

John Sanders, a Native Anglican minister, Missanabie, late 1890s.

he left there to assist in the conversion of the Indians of that region.[113] Ultimately, however, the early Methodist work in northwestern Ontario failed, and even Native workers like Peter Jacobs, Henry Steinhauer, and Allen Salt,[114] who worked in the area in the mid-1850s, made few converts. For seven years (1840–47) the Methodists had also maintained a missionary, George Barnley, at Moose Factory.[115]

The Methodists' success came at Norway House, in present-day northern Manitoba, where James Evans made a lasting contribution. It was here that he devised the syllabic script for writing Cree that soon spread throughout the Subarctic and was used by Methodist and Anglican clergy.[116] From Norway House, missionaries made excursions as far as Island and God's lakes, where they met Indians from northwestern Ontario who had come to trade. The mission-

Peter Jacobs, an Ojibwa Methodist minister, in the costume he wore in the Northwest.

From Peter Jacobs, *Journal of the Reverend Peter Jacobs. Indian Wesleyan Missionary, from Rice Lake to the Hudson's Bay Territory* (New York 1858)

aries pushed on further east, eventually coming into contact with Indians under the Anglicans' influence.

Roman Catholic missionaries, the third group to seek converts in Northern Ontario, had difficulty in gaining access to the Indians of the area because of the initial opposition of the Hudson's Bay Company.[117] In the 1840s, however, the Oblates established a mission at Abitibi Post, from which Catholic priests made forays into the James Bay region. In 1892 they founded a mission on the western shore of James Bay at the mouth of the Albany River.[118] Farther west, Roman Catholic missionaries travelled to the Fort William area in the 1830s and later to the Boundary Waters region.[119]

*The Algonquians' Religion – A New Mix*

With the arrival of missionaries in what is now Northern Ontario, a new ingredient was added to the religion of the Northern Algonquians, who had already some exposure to Christian practices and ideas through the traders.

Photo by John Macfie, 1955

Marker on the grave of Moses Bluecoat, Fort Severn, Ontario, inscribed in both English and Cree syllabics.

The Crane contacted missionaries on their own initiative in 1855.[120] Only the traders could have influenced them to do so. Burial customs began to change, as more and more Indians requested to be buried the way the Europeans were.[121] The traders held divine services on Sundays and also at Easter and other Christian festivals. They said grace at meals, sometimes refused to work on Sunday, and no doubt on occasion openly lectured the Indians about their "superstitious" ways.[122] Intermarriage with the traders also increased the Indians' awareness of Christian concepts and behaviour. As a result of their exposure to Christianity, a number of Indians added some of its concepts to their own faith, without rejecting their own beliefs and rituals.

Fundamental to the Algonquians' religious outlook was the concept of "power" (see chapter 7). According to their system of beliefs, power resided in most, if not all, living and non-living objects and phenomena. A human being acquired power through dreams in which the spirits might bless him or her. But, in addition and more important, one could obtain power by means of a vision quest. About the time of puberty, boys and girls went into the bush to fast for ten days and nights. The top of a hill was selected or a platform was built high in a tree where the youth would spend the necessary time. One or more spirits would, if the individual was so favoured, take pity upon him or her and become the individual's guardian for life. One might increase one's power during one's lifetime through further fasting. The spirits often took pity upon orphans who were mistreated (as many were), giving them power to overcome their adversities.

Although most, if not all, individuals had power, some had more than others. Those who possessed the most became the religious leaders. Those who strove to become shamans or people of power (medicine men) sought spirit helpers such as *missipisiw* ("great lynx") and/or a number of other spirit helpers who, when needed, could be combined into one superior power known as *missape* ("great man"). The ability to control and manipulate power dominated the lives of the Ojibwa. The Cree of the Hudson Bay Lowlands, on the other hand, appear to have been less concerned with manipulating power, although they too were capable of doing so.

Power could be employed for several purposes but basically for good or evil, depending upon one's perspective. Those with "medicine" used their power to protect the group to which they belonged from supernatural (or natural) harm. From the point of view of members of the group, such use of power was good. But the object of such use thought otherwise. At Cat Lake in 1883, for example, the "Chief" neared death. He had given up eating because he thought someone had "conjured" him and therefore he had lost hope.[123] Power could also be employed to protect and punish, to prophesy future events, and to divine the whereabouts of missing people and lost objects.

Several types of "medicine" people existed in the nineteenth century; the roles they assumed depended, at least in part, on the form of blessing they had received. The two most notable were the Shaking Tent practitioner and the "herbalist." The herbalist, or doctor, prescribed a variety of medicines to cure illnesses and injuries.

As among the Algonquians of Southern Ontario (see chapter 7), the Shaking Tent practitioner performed a special ceremony to divine or punish a transgressor. When requested, he had assistants erect a special structure that consisted of four to eight poles set vertically and quite deep in the ground in a circle a metre or so in diameter. The poles extended upward

Ojibwa herbalist preparing medicine and treating a patient.

From the Bureau of Ethnology, *Seventh Annual Report, 1885–86* (Washington, D.C. 1891), 159, National Anthropological Archives, Smithsonian Institution, Photo No. 481

The structure for a Shaking Tent at Kapisko, an out-post of Albany, c. 1930.
Photo by Walter Watt, Provincial Archives of Manitoba, Hudson's Bay Company Archives, HBCA Photograph Collection, 1987/363-A-6/14 (N8284)

two to three metres and were held in place with one or two hoops that encircled them. One hoop was always placed at the top and sometimes a second one about halfway up. The structure was covered completely with birchbark or hide (perhaps occasionally canvas) except that the top was left uncovered to allow the spirits to enter. The structure was erected during the day, but the performance could not be held until darkness fell. Then the person of power lifted a corner of the covering at the bottom and crawled inside. From within the Shaking Tent, the medicine person called upon his or her spirit helpers to come and assist. Soon they arrived and the individual commenced to converse with them. Those in the audience with questions they wanted answered addressed them to the person in the tent who in turn asked the spirit helpers to find the answers. The Shaking Tent performer prophesied events and on occasion called the souls of offenders into the Shaking Tent, where punishment was inflicted upon them, including death.

The Northern Algonquians in the nineteenth century performed rituals to appease the spirits of slain game. The bear was of extreme importance in this respect, but other species were not neglected. Smoking was often of ritual significance and might, for example, be used in an attempt to control the wind. The Indians commonly used tobacco to propitiate the spirits.

The Midewiwin, a religious society among the Ojibwa, put on special performances to cure the sick. If a person became ill, he or she might request the society to help. If it did so, the patient became a member of the society and paid fees for the privilege. The society was composed of eight grades in ranked order, starting with the lowest of the four earth grades. After moving through these earth grades, one might enter the first of the four sky grades. The higher one went, the more expensive the initiation fees became. Few gained the higher grades, and the Ojibwa considered those who did to have immense spiritual powers. Accordingly, they were greatly feared.[124]

By the end of the nineteenth century, the Northern Algonquians had been under the influence of Christian missionaries, directly and indirectly, for some twenty-five to sixty years and of the traders for much longer. They were affected in quite different ways. Some rejected outright the teachings of the missionaries. Others grasped the new religion wholeheartedly but without a full understanding of its contents. Most allowed themselves to be passively converted. Nowhere, however, did the traditional beliefs and practices completely disappear. The Indians generally appear to have made an accommodation to the missionaries' teachings, mixing some of the new with some of the old. From this fusion arose minor and short-lived nativistic movements.

One such movement began at Fort Severn in the early 1840s. Hymns used among the Native people of York Factory found their way to Fort Severn, where the Indians became intrigued with them. Two Indians, presumably medicine persons, used a vision quest to interpret these hymns and then "presented themselves before their countrymen as extraordinary messengers from heaven." They reported: "A splendid mansion, extensive enough to contain all the Indians, but designed for them alone, and abundantly supplied with every source of enjoyment, was stated to be in course of preparation, and to be let down from heaven in a few years." As part of the new belief, all dogs were to be killed, a prescription carried out in large measure everywhere the movement spread, with the exception of Moose Factory. At Fort Severn an old woman and a youth became fervent converts to the movement and carried the message to Fort Albany, where most of the people became involved. From there it spread to Moose Factory. The efforts of Methodist missionary George Barnley of Moose Factory and of the Hudson's Bay Company factor at Fort Albany[125] finally stopped the movement. No doubt throughout the rest of the century, similar movements arose but went unnoticed.

*The Algonquians Begin to Lose Ground*

Until the nineteenth century, the Northern Algonquians had been free to follow their own way of life with a minimum of direct interference by the traders. But now all of this slowly changed. Although the fur trade economy was stable in these years, Algonquians in the southern part of the area confronted for the first time prospectors, miners, lumbermen, government agents, and independent traders.

Following in the footsteps of the traders and missionaries, government representatives became a major force in the lives of Ojibwa and Cree in the last half of the nineteenth century.[126] By 1850 the land and resources along the north shore of Lake Superior had gained importance as Euro-Canadians had expanded their activities westward. The Robinson-Superior Treaty (1850) became the first of several signed treaties between the government and the Northern Algonquians (see chapter 7). In 1873 the Ojibwa west of the Robinson-Superior Treaty surrendered their lands in what is now northwestern Ontario and southeastern Manitoba in Treaty No. 3, and later the Ojibwa ceded in Treaty No. 5 (1875) the Berens River basin.[127] As a result of the treaty each Indian received annually an annuity payment of five dollars and a medical examination. At the treaty signing, reserves were specified, but for the time being the Indians remained free to hunt and fish on their traditional territories (if on Crown lands). No further surrenders of land occurred until Treaty No. 9 in 1905. Accordingly, the Indians throughout the remainder of Northern Ontario remained free of government supervision.

As Southern Ontario became completely settled in the mid-nineteenth century, more development occurred in Northern Ontario. This had begun before the Indians actually signed the treaties. Non-Natives conducted commercial fisheries during the 1840s at Fort William before the signing of the Robinson-Superior Treaty in 1850. The entrepreneurs netted, salted, and shipped large quantities of whitefish to Canadian markets.[128] Such commercial enterprises increased rapidly after the government secured title to the land.[129] At the same time, the improved transportation system gave greater access to the area. In 1855 the Sault Ste. Marie canal opened, and for the first time sea-going vessels could reach the western extremity of Lake Superior.[130] During the early 1880s the Canadian Pacific Railway slowly made its way across the southern section of Northern Ontario, to be completed in 1885. In the Boundary Waters region, logging and related activities began during the late 1870s and intensive commercial fishing, especially for sturgeon, during the mid-1880s.[131]

Each new development brought further changes that, in time, affected the Indians. The commercial fisheries necessitated the erection of shipyards and construction of fishing boats. To alleviate conditions of low water in the Boundary Waters region, which restricted boats of deep draft in their movements, dams had to be built. The first one was constructed near Kenora in 1887–88, raising the level of the Lake of the Woods by an estimated one metre.[132] The dams flooded neighbouring lands to varying degrees. The flooding resulted in a reduction in the crop of wild rice, the quantity of marsh grass

Map 14.2
Treaties
From "First Nations Ontario," prepared by Indian and Northern Affairs Canada and the Ontario Native Affairs
Secretariat, 1991. Revised 1993

that could be cut for fodder, and the numbers of fish and muskrats that Indians could obtain. Sometimes the flooding also submerged the Ojibwa's improved farmlands, barns, and houses.[133]

Farther north, the Native peoples remained isolated from the federal government. As late as 1892 federal authorities believed themselves unable to interfere in the affairs of the Indians north of the height of land above Lake Superior. In that year Indian Agent Donnelly of Port Arthur wrote to the deputy superintendent general of Indian affairs: "I wish to Report to your Department, that about the first of June last, a Band of Crane or Swampe Crees attacked a camp of Ojibwa Indians at night time and killed fourteen

A COLLAGE OF SIX PHOTOGRAPHS, ALL TAKEN BY THE
TREATY NINE COMMISSION, 1905–1906

Mrs. Black, Missanabie, 1906.
National Archives of Canada, PA-59571

Indian girls, Brunswick House, 1906.
National Archives of Canada, PA-59561

Group of Ojibwa women and girls at Fort Mattagami, 1906.
National Archives of Canada, PA-59589

(Left) Two older Amerindians, Flying Post, 1906.
National Archives of Canada, PA-59575

(Below) Miss Doherty (on the extreme left) and her pupils at the Bear Island School on Lake Temagami, 1906.
National Archives of Canada, PA-59576

(Bottom) Ojibwa men at Fort Hope, 1905.
National Archives of Canada, PA-59539

men, women and children and the Cranes had four killed, this occurred at Crow Lake near the Albany River."[134]

On receipt of this letter, the deputy wrote the superintendent: "Neither of the Bands of Indians mentioned therein are Treaty Indians, and the Crow Lake, near the Albany River, must be outside Treaty limits ... it is difficult to see what can be done to bring the offenders to immediate justice, owing to their distance from civilization."[135]

The superintendent then contacted the North-West Mounted Police, who were of the same opinion: "The sending of men to Crow Lake would be a costly expedition, a season's work, and if the Government once shows any sign of supervision appeal will be made, as elsewhere, for continued protection, etc."[136] Yet, in the decades to follow, even the remote Northern Algonquians would be forcibly subjected to Euro-Canadian laws and customs.

## NOTES

1   Washington Irving, *Astoria or Anecdotes of an Enterprise beyond the Rocky Mountains* (Philadelphia 1961), 1, 16

2   The agreement lasted until 1844 (Harold A. Innis, *The Fur Trade in Canada* [Toronto 1956], 330; E.E. Rich, *Hudson's Bay Company 1670–1870*, 3 vols. [Toronto 1960], 3:525–6).

3   Provincial Archives of Manitoba (PAM), Hudson's Bay Company Archives (HBCA), B.030/a/008, fo. 4

4   W.J. Noxon, ed., *The Diary of Nicholas Garry, Deputy Governor of the Hudson's Bay Company* (Toronto 1973), 112

5   H.Y. Hind, *Report on the Exploration of the Country between Lake Superior and the Red River Settlement* (Toronto 1858), 415–16

6   HBCA, B.155/a/036, fo. 8; B.155/a/039, fo. 23; B.155/a/051, fo. 6

7   See Arthur J. Ray, "Some Conservation Schemes of the Hudson's Bay Company 1821–1850, an Examination of the Problems of Resource Management in the Fur Trade," *Journal of Historical Geography* 1, no. 1 (1975): 49–68; HBCA, B.155/e/11, fo. 3; B.198/e/007, fo. 2; B.220/a/004, fo. 2d; B.198/a/073, fo. 25

8   HBCA, B.220/a/012, fo. 9d

9   HBCA, B.234/a/001; B.234/e/001

10   HBCA, B.220/a/006; B.220/a/004, fo. 22d, 26, 27; B.198/3/007, fo. 1d; Charles A. Bishop, *The Northern Ojibwa and the Fur Trade: An Historical and Ecological Study* (Toronto 1974), 137

11   F.W. Waugh, "Field Notes," 1916, no. 2, Canadian Museum of Civilization; John J. Honigmann, "The Attawapiskat Swampy Cree, an Ethnographic Reconstruction," *Anthropological Papers of the University of Alaska* 5, no. 1 (1956): 41–4

12   Waugh, "Field Notes," no. 1

13   HBCA, B.155/a/072, fo. 4

14  Edward S. Rogers, "Changing Settlement Patterns of the Cree-Ojibwa of Northern Ontario," *Southwestern Journal of Anthropology* 19, no. 1 (1963): 64–88

15  HBCA, B.220/a/004, fo. 108

16  HBCA, B.155/a/038, fo. 13; B.220/b/001, fos. 5–5d

17  HBCA, B.220/a/004, fo. 8d; B.220/a/005, fo. 9d

18  HBCA, B.155/a/039, fo. 16Ad; B.198/a/073, fo. 15; B.220/a/005, fos. 9d, 19d, 22, 25d

19  HBCA, B.198/a/073, fo. 31d; E.S. Rogers, personal knowledge

20  Richard King, *Narrative of a Journey to the Shores of the Arctic Ocean* (London 1847), 32; Robert M. Ballantyne, *Hudson's Bay; or Every-Day Life in the Wilds of North America, During Six Years' Residence in the Territories of the Honourable Hudson's Bay Company* (London 1857), 239

21  HBCA, B.198/a/073, fo. 31d

22  Waugh, "Field Notes," no. 1

23  HBCA, B.155/a/038, fo. 26d; B.155/a/038, fo. 9

24  Waugh, "Field Notes," no. 1; Ballantyne, *Hudson's Bay*, 240; Paul Kane, *Wanderings of an Artist among the Indians of North America* (Toronto 1925), 39

25  E.S. Rogers, personal knowledge

26  HBCA, B.220/a/005, fo. 6

27  HBCA, B.15/a/039, fo. 29d

28  Waugh, "Field Notes," no. 3; Ballantyne, *Hudson's Bay*, 240–1

29  HBCA, B.155/a/038, fos. 20d, 24

30  Martin Hunter, *Canadian Wilds* (Columbus 1935), 260

31  King, *Narrative*, 32

32  HBCA, B.155/011, fo. 2d

33  B.J. Given, "The Iroquois Wars and Native Firearms," in M.-F. Guedon and D.J. Hatt, eds., *Papers from the Sixth Annual Congress 1979*, Canadian Ethnology Service, paper no. 78 (1981), 84–94

34  HBCA, B.030/a/007, fo. 9. Once the new guns were introduced, the Indians rejected flintlocks. HBCA, B.239/e/015, fos. 14–15

35  HBCA, B.198/a/065, fo. 61; B.198/a/073, fos. 6, 15, 15d, 18, 20d, 28, 28d; B.220/a/004, fos. 9, 10 Ad, 12, 18; B.220/a/008, fo. 43; B.220/a/012, fo. 13; B.220/a/013, fo. 17; B.220/a/036, fo. 14; B.220/a/023, fo. 22d

36  HBCA, B.220/a/005, fo.13; B.198/a/073, fos. 15d, 17, 18

37  Hunter, *Canadian Wilds*, 29

38  Ballantyne, *Hudson's Bay*, 240

39  Probably they did employ bone harpoon heads for taking beaver.

40  Waugh, "Field Notes," no. 4

41  HBCA, B.155/a/039, fo. 22d; B.155/a/077, fo. 5; Waugh, "Field Notes," no. 3; Honigmann, "The Attawapiskat Swampy Cree," 37; E.S. Rogers and Mary B. Black, "Subsistence Strategy in the Fish and Hare Period, Northern Ontario: The Weagamow Ojibwa, 1880–1920," *Journal of Anthropological Research* 32, no. 1 (1976): 6–9

42  W.B. Scott, personal communication

43  HBCA, B.123/018, fo. 19d; B.220/a/033, fo. 1

44  HBCA, B.220/a/006, fos. 32, 34

45  HBCA, B.155/z/001, fos. 160, 217

46  Ballantyne, *Hudson's Bay*, 238

47  HBCA, B.220/a/004, fo. 5d

48 HBCA, B.220/a/006, fo. 10d; B.155/a/068, fo. 4d; B.155/a/076, fo. 15d; Waugh, "Field Notes," no. 1
49 HBCA, B.030/a/007, fo. 18d; B.030/a/11a, fo. 15; B.155/a/038, fo. 11d
50 J.M. Cooper, *Snares, Deadfalls, and other Traps of the Northern Algonquians and Northern Athapaskans* (Washington, D.C. 1938), 63
51 Ibid., 63–4
52 Ibid., 63
53 HBCA, B.030/a/007, fo. 18d; B.030/a/011a, fo. 15
54 HBCA, B.155/a/039, fo. 21d
55 HBCA, B.155/a/038, fo. 11d
56 HBCA, B.155/z/001, fos. 160, 166d, 175d, 217; B.198/a/073, fo. 10
57 Hunter, *Canadian Wilds*, 259; Richard Gerstill, *The Steel Trap in North America* (Harrisburg 1985)
58 Mary Black Rogers, "Varieties of 'Starving': Semantics and Survival in the Sub-Arctic Fur Trade, 1750–1850," *Ethnohistory* 33, no. 4 (1986): 353–83. Several recorded cases of starvation can be found in HBCA, B.155/a/037, fos. 17d, 20, 23, 24; and HBCA, B.198/005, fo. 2.
59 HBCA, B.220/a/012, fos. 25–6; B.220/a/013, fos. 33, 33d; B.220/a/015, fos. 26d, 27; B.220/a/018, fo. 25d
60 HBCA, B.030/a/007, fo. 2d; B.220/a/014, fos. 19, 20, 35; B.220/a/016, fos. 26d, 27d; B.200/a/028, fos. 25d, 30; B.220/a/016, fo. 29; B.220/a/012, fos. 25, 25d; B.220/a/013, fo. 33d
61 HBCA, B.155/a/036, fo. 21; B.155/a/037, fo. 24; B.155/a/039, fo. 39d; B.198/a/073, fo. 22d
62 HBCA, B.155/a/037, fo. 24; B.155/a/038, fos. 14,18, 19d; B.220/a/015, fo. 17; B.220/a/016, fo. 43; B.220/a/010, fo. 35d; Bishop, *The Northern Ojibwa*, 186; Rogers and Black, "Subsistence Strategy"; Hind, *Report*, 248–9; HBCA, B.155/a/038, fo. 19d; B.155/a/039, fo. 21d
63 HBCA, B.155/a/036, fo. 17
64 HBCA, B.155/a/078, fos. 11d, 17, 23d; B.220/a/042, fos. 24d, 25, 28, 31d, 33, 59d, 61d, 64, 64d, 66d, 67d; B.220/b/001, fo. 13d; B.220/z/002
65 Harold Hickerson, *Land Tenure of the Rainy Lake Chippewa at the Beginning of the 19th Century* (Washington, D.C. 1967), 41–63; C.A. Bishop, "The Emergence of Hunting Territories among the Northern Ojibwa," *Ethnology* 9, no. 1 (1970): 1–15; Edward S. Rogers, *The Round Lake Ojibwa* (Toronto 1962), Occasional Paper no. 5, Art and Archaeology Division, Royal Ontario Museum, c22
66 Hind, *Report*, 139, 241, 244
67 HBCA, B.220/a/009, fo. 5d; B.220/a/019, fo. 4; B.220/a/023, fo. 4d; B.220/a/026, fo. 9; B.220/a/027, fos. 5d–6; B.220/a/030, fos. 7, 10; B.220/a/033, fo. 4
68 HBCA, B.198/a/073, fo. 4d
69 HBCA, B.220/a/012, fo. 9d; B.220/a/025, fos. 6, 6d, 7
70 HBCA, B.220/a/004, fo. 5d; Rogers and Black, "Subsistence Strategy"; HBCA, B.220/a/008, fo. 12d
71 HBCA, B.200/a/004, fo. 6d
72 HBCA, B.220/a/024, fos. 25, 26
73 HBCA, B.220/a/019, fo. 21; B.220/a/020, fo. 32; B.239/e/001, fo. 2d
74 HBCA, B.220/a/019, fo. 21d; B.155/a/039, fo. 23d
75 Ruth Landes, "The Ojibwa of Canada," in *Co-operation and Competition among*

*Primitive Peoples*, ed. Margaret Mead (Boston 1961), 92

76   HBCA, B.030/a/011a, fo. 17d; B.030/a/011b, 3 August; B.155/a/079, fo. 7d

77   HBCA, B.003/z/001, fo. 4d

78   Jerry McKay, Big Trout Lake, personal communication

79   HBCA, B.155/a/004, fos. 7d, 8; B.198/a/065, fo. 51

80   HBCA, B.155/a/075, fos. 7–7d; B.220/a/040, fo. 2d; B.220/a/041, fos. 2, 12d

81   In 1824 the Hudson's Bay Company passed an order-in-council that no more Indian or half-breed women were to be taken by servants as wives without the permission of the chief factor of the department (HBCA, B.155/a/036, fo. 18d). This injunction was repeated in 1825 (HBCA, B.123/a/022, fo. 10).

82   HBCA, B.155/a/062, fo. 5; B.155/a/068, fo. 8; B.155/a/075, fo. 25; B.220/a/042, fo. 48d

83   HBCA, B.155/a/068, fos. 11, 12, 14d, 15d, 16

84   HBCA, B.155/a/068, fos. 1, 7; B.220/a/032, fo. 8; B.220/a/040, fo. 25

85   HBCA, B.220/a/023, fo. 2; B.220/a/027, fos. 4, 36, 42; B.220/a/0422, fos. 10d, 15, 38d; B.220/a/043, fo. 15d; B.220/a/044, fo. 18

86   HBCA, B.155/a/075, fo. 6; B.155/a/075, fo. 25d

87   HBCA, B.220/a/020, fo. 38

88   HBCA, B.030/a/007, fo. 9; B.030/a/009, fo. 1

89   HBCA, B.155/a/036, fo. 7d; B.220/a/006, fos. 29d, 34, 37d; B.220/a/007, fos. 27, 29d; B.155/a/075, fos. 8d, 9d, 17; B.220/a/038, fos. 7d, 19d; B.220/a/043, fo. 43d; B.030/a/007, fo. 1d; B.220/a/044, fo. 60d; Hunter, *Canadian Wilds*, 259–60

90   Hunter, *Canadian Wilds*, 240

91   It is difficult to sort out such social units, since the traders often used such terms as "band" or "tribe" to refer to no more than a nuclear, or at most, an extended family; see, for example, the Cranes' Band, HBCA, B.155/a/036, fos. 19, 20d; B.155/a/037, fos. 4d, 17d, 24; B.155/a/041, fo. 3; "Crane Tribe," HBCA, B.220/a/025, fos. 23, 31, 32; HBCA, B.220/a/026, fos. 3d, 19d, 30, 31; "Goose Tribe," HBCA, B.220/a/029, fo. 15d; "Sucker Tribe," HBCA, B.220/a/005, fos. 2d, 6; "Moose Tribe," HBCA, B.155/a/063, fo. 6; "Bear Band," HBCA, B.155/a/036, fo. 10; "Bear Breast Band," HBCA, B.155/a/036, fo. 23d.

92   Edward S. Rogers and Mary Black Rogers, "The Puzzle of the Crane Indians," *Rotunda* 12, no. 4 (1980): 11–19; Edward S. Rogers and Mary Black Rogers, "Who were the Cranes? Groups and Group Identity Names in Northern Ontario," in *Approaches to Algonquian Archaeology*, ed. Margaret G. Hanna and Brian Kooyman (Calgary 1982), 147–88

93   It has been suggested that the "clan" was a concept that came late to the Ojibwa (Fred Eggan, "Social Anthropology, Methods and Results," in *Social Anthropology of North American Tribes*, ed. Fred Eggan [Chicago 1955], 527. On the other hand, Harold Hickerson, *The Chippewa and their Neighbors, a Study in Ethnohistory* (New York 1970), 49–50, argued against this position. Bishop agreed with Hickerson's argument that clans were pre-contact. Bishop went on to argue that as Ojibwa moved into Northern Ontario from a region about Sault Ste. Marie, the new environmental conditions were not favourable to the maintenance of a clan organization and therefore the limited corporate functions reported by ethnologists working in the area represent only the remnants of a once-flourishing clan organization. Yet he does concede that "the question of clans is still open for further debate" (Bishop, *The Northern Ojibwa*, 274).

94   HBCA, B.155/a/035, fo. 25; B.155/a/036, fo. 6d; B.155/a/037, fo. 20; B.155/a/038; fo.

24; B.155/a/039, fo. 5d–7; B.155/a/062, fo. 18d; B.155/a/074, fo. 1d; B.155/a/075, fos. 34–34d; B.155/a/078, fos. 19d–20; B.155/a/079, fo. 26; B.220/a/005, fos. 3–3d; B.220/a/008, fos. 29d–30, 31d, 33; B.220/a/016, fo. 34; B.220/a/016b, fos. 72–73, 76, 77, 77d–78, 82d–83, 117d–118; B.220/a/033, fo. 6b, 37d

95   Hind, *Report*, 27, 46

96   HBCA, B.155/a/039, fo. 29d; B. 155/a/037, fos. 13, 13d; B.155/e/022, fo. 2d

97   HBCA, B.155/a/078, fo. 18; B.155/a/079, fos. 7, 7d; B.155/a/041, fos. 14d–15; B.030/a/007, fos. 7d, 18d; B.155/a/038, fo. 27d

98   HBCA, B.155/a/079, fo. 10; B.220/a/005, fo. 11d

99   HBCA, B.155/a/036, fos. 6d, 7d; B.220/a/043, fo. 61d

100  Richard A. Willie, "John West," *Dictionary of Canadian Biography*, vol. 7: *1836–1850* (Toronto 1988), 900–1

101  Thomas C.B. Boon, *The Anglican Church from the Bay to the Rockies* (Toronto 1962), 66–7

102  John S. Long, "'Shaganash': Early Protestant Missionaries and the Adoption of Christianity by the Western James Bay Cree, 1840–1892" (EdD thesis, University of Toronto [Ontario Institute for Studies in Education], 1986); John S. Long, "John Horden," *Dictionary of Canadian Biography*, vol. 12: *1891–1900* (Toronto 1990), 445–7

103  James Scanlon, ed., *Letters from James Bay 1883–1885, Bishop John Horden* (Cobalt 1976)

104  Boon, *The Anglican Church*, 120

105  David Anderson, *The Net in the Bay, or, Journal of a Visit to Moose and Albany* (London 1854); Boon, *The Anglican Church*, 67–8

106  Thomas C.B. Boon, "William West Kirkby, First Anglican Missionary to the Loucheux," *The Beaver*, outfit 295 (Spring 1965): 36–43; HBCA, B.220/b/001, fo. 6

107  J. Lofthouse, *A Thousand Miles from a Post Office* (Toronto 1922), 144

108  T.C.B. Boon, *These Men Went Out* (Toronto n.d.), 32–4; HBCA, B.155/a/076, fos. 18d, 19; B.155/a/079, fo. 5d

109  Donald B. Smith, "John Sanders," *Dictionary of Canadian Biography*, vol. 13: *1901–1910* (Toronto 1994), 920–1

110  Gerald M. Hutchinson, "James Evans," *Dictionary of Canadian Biography*, vol. 7: *1836–1850* (Toronto 1988), 276

111  Arthur G. Reynolds, "Thomas Hurlburt," *Dictionary of Canadian Biography*, vol. 10: *1871–1880* (Toronto 1972), 373

112  Hutchinson, "Evans," 276

113  Isaac Kholisile Makiordisa, "The Praying Man: The Life and Times of Henry Bird Steinhauer" (PhD thesis, University of Alberta, 1984)

114  Jennifer S.H. Brown, "'I wish to be as I see you': An Ojibwa-Methodist Encounter in Fur Trade Country. Rainy Lake, 1854–1855," *Arctic Anthropology* 24, no. 1 (1987): 19–31

115  John S. Long, "The Reverend George Barnley, Wesleyan Methodist, and James Bay's Fur Trade Company Families," *Ontario History* 72 (1985): 43–64

116  Bruce Peel, *Rossville Mission Press: The Invention of the Cree syllabic characters, and the first printing in Rupert's Land* (Montreal 1974); Jo Anne Bennett and John W. Berry, "The Meaning and Value of the Syllabic Script for Native People," *Actes du Vingtième Congrès des Algonquinistes, 1989*, 31–42

117  Soeur Paul-Emile, *Amiskwaski, la Terre du Castor* (Ottawa 1952), 183–4

118  Ibid.
119  Elizabeth Arthur, ed., *The Thunder Bay District, 1821–1891* (Toronto 1973), xxix; Grace Lee Nute, *Rainy River Country* (St. Paul 1950), 34–7
120  HBCA, B.155/a/068, fo. 3
121  HBCA, B.155/a/079, fo. 36; B.198/a/073, fo. 15; B.220/a/008, fo. 15; B.220/a/018, fos. 10d, 16d–17; B.220/a/020, fos. 6, 19d, 27d; B.220/a/040, fo. 6; B.220/a/041, fo. 33; B.220/a/042, fos. 14d, 17d, 18d, 35; B.220/a/043, fo. 7; B.135/a/017, fo. 16d
122  HBCA, B.220/a/044, fo. 9; B.220/a/014, fo. 24d; B.220/a/018, fos. 10d–17; B.220/a/020, fo. 6; B.220/a/021, fo. 19d; B.220/a/037, fo. 4d; B.220/a/038, fo. 31d; B.220/a/039, fos. 3, 24, 26; B.220/a/040, fo. 6; B.220/a/042, fo. 14d
123  HBCA, B.030/z/007, fos. 32d–33
124  On the Midewiwin, see Ruth Landes, *Ojibwa Religion and the Midewiwin* (Madison 1968). The classic account is that by Walter James Hoffman, "The Midéwiwin; or, 'Grand Medicine Society' of the Ojibwa," Bureau of American Ethnology, *Seventh Annual Report, 1885–1886* (Washington, D.C. 1891), 145–300.
125  George Barnley, "Extract of a Letter from the Rev. George Barnley, dated Moose Factory, September 23d, 1843," *Methodist Magazine* 68 (1845): 202–3; Jennifer S.H. Brown, "The Track to Heaven, The Hudson Bay Cree Religious Movement of 1842–1843," in *Papers of the Thirteenth Algonquian Conference,* ed. William Cowan (Ottawa 1982), 53–63; John M. Cooper, *The Northern Algonquian Supreme Being,* Catholic University of America, Anthropological series, no. 2 (1934): 46–7; John S. Long, "The Cree Prophets: Oral and Documentary Accounts," *Journal of the Canadian Church Historical Society* 31 (April 1989): 3–13
126  HBCA, B.030/a/008, fos. 4d–5; B.220/a/044, fo. 42d. 273; B.220/a/044, fo. 42d; J. Alcock, *A Century in the History of the Geological Survey of Canada* (Ottawa 1947), 48–54
127  W.E. Daugherty, *Treaty Research Report: Treaty Three* (Ottawa 1986); Kenneth S. Coates and William R. Morrison, *Treaty Five (1875–1908)* (Ottawa 1986)
128  Ballantyne, *Hudson's Bay,* 249
129  See Arthur, *Thunder Bay District 1821–1892,* 96, 103–4
130  Hind, *Report,* 189
131  Leo G. Waisberg, *Development, Resources, and Native Societies: The Lake of the Woods Ojibway Case, 1800–1940* (Hamilton 1978), 27, 78
132  Ibid., 39
133  Ibid., 38–9
134  National Archives of Canada (NA), RG 10, vol. 2643, file 129823
135  Ibid.
136  Ibid.

# 15 Northern Algonquians on the Frontiers of "New Ontario," 1890–1945

## J. GARTH TAYLOR

As the boundary of the province advanced northward and westward to its present location, the relative isolation of earlier times ended. The building of railways and the subsequent advent of "bush" flying connected Northern Ontario with the outside world. In the wake of the train and aircraft came a whole host of newcomers whose arrival had a profound impact on the land and the Native people. (See Map 13.1b, page 290.)

Prior to 1890 the major representative of the outside world had been the Hudson's Bay Company (HBC). After 1890, however, the arrival of a new wave of fur traders, either independent or representing rival companies, introduced an era of competition. At about the same time, Christian missionaries came more frequently and stayed longer. North of the Albany River government officials, surveyors, prospectors, commercial fisherman, loggers, and miners soon joined them.

### Inroads from the South

The canoe and toboggan were well adapted for their traditional functions, but neither they nor the fur traders' York boats could carry the large quantities of goods required by the settlers and developers who became increasingly interested in exploiting the potential of a new frontier. With the building of railroads, however, old transportation routes and trade networks were quickly abandoned and contact with the outside world dramatically intensified.

Major changes followed the completion of the Canadian Pacific Railway (CPR) in the mid-1880s. Though the line ran mostly south of the height of land, it did cross the northern watershed at several locations, which led to the decline of some traditional supply routes. In the west the CPR station at

Interior of the Fort Albany post, around 1905.
Provincial Archives of Manitoba, Hudson's Bay Company Archives, HBCA Photograph Collection, 1987/363-A-6.1/1
(N8287)

Wabigoon (Dinorwic) became a major jumping-off point into the territory of the upper Albany for surveyors, scientists, and government officials. From 1890 onwards, supplies for the Hudson's Bay Company post at Osnaburgh House were brought in from Wabigoon rather than by the traditional route up the Albany River from James Bay.[1]

Further inroads occurred just prior to the First World War, when the eastern division of the National Transcontinental (later merged with the Grand Trunk Pacific – the western division of the National Transcontinental – and the Canadian Northern into the Canadian National Railways [CNR]) completed a line further to the north, running through Cochrane and Sioux Lookout. Except for a short stretch above Lake Nipigon, this line ran north of the height of land. Because it crossed the headwaters of several major rivers running north and east to James Bay, it had an even greater impact on established trade and supply routes in the Patricia District and the Hudson Bay Lowland than did the CPR.

By 1910 Moose Factory already had a communication link along the Abitibi River to the town of Cochrane. During the summer, the Hudson's Bay Company shipped goods down-river by boat, and in winter, mail from the south was carried along the same route by toboggan.[2] Another railway depot was located on the Moose River system at Mattice, where the company opened an establishment in 1920. This resulted in the closure of English River,

Interior of the Sales Shop, Hudson's Bay Company store, Moose Factory, 1934.
Paddy Houston is shown at the counter.
Provincial Archives of Manitoba, Hudson's Bay Company Archives, HBCA Photograph Collection, 1987/363-M-
140/2 (N79-142)

one of the last of the traditional inland posts in the Moose-Missinaibi river
valley.[3]

During the First World War a water route opened from the railway at
Pagwa, down the Pagwachuan to the Albany River. The Révillon Frères
Trading Company (a subsidiary of Révillon Frères of Paris, which began operations in James Bay in 1904) began to use this route after they had trouble
chartering a ship to take their supplies from Montreal to James Bay. It was
found convenient and later adopted by the Hudson's Bay Company as well.[4]

Another new north-south supply route commenced at Ombabika (Auden
since 1948), farther to the west. This canoe route led, through a series of lakes
and portages, to Eabamet Lake (Fort Hope) on the Albany River. From there,
supplies were carried by a similar water route to the upper Attawapiscat and
Winisk rivers. Supply brigades on this route used canoes that were about six
metres long rather than the customary York boats, formerly employed on the
Albany River. In another departure from tradition, the canoeists rowed rather
than paddled, in commercially produced canvas-covered Peterborough, Lac
Seul, and Rupert's House canoes.[5]

The railways had less impact in the extreme north. There, traditional supply routes remained in operation during the early twentieth century. Fort

Severn continued to operate as a major supply depot, shipping goods inland to Big Trout Lake and other locations in the upper Severn region. Further to the south, outposts in the Lake Winnipeg drainage area continued to obtain supplies via the Berens and Poplar rivers.

In 1930 the Ontario Northland Railway established a terminus at Moosonee,[6] which brought the James Bay Cree into closer contact with the south. It now became possible to ship goods to James Bay by land throughout the entire year. From Moosonee, supplies could be forwarded farther north by sled in winter and boat in summer, and eventually by aircraft in all seasons. Tractor trains came to be another means of supplying northern settlements.

The advent of bush flying gave the aircraft an important role in northern transportation. In the 1920s a number of airlines began operation in Northern Ontario: Laurentide Air Service Limited, Northern Air Service Limited, Jack V. Elliott Air Service, Elliott's Fairchild Air Service, Patricia Airways and Exploration Company Limited,[7] and Western Canadian Airways.[8] By the mid-1930s Canadian Airways made winter flights from Collins to such distant posts as Big Trout Lake and Bearskin Lake, previously considered among the most isolated posts of the fur trade.[9] In these early years of aviation the Ontario government's Provincial Air Service also came into being, primarily to operate in the north.[10]

## The New Traders

The beginning of the twentieth century saw the final destruction of the fur trade monopoly that the Hudson's Bay Company had enjoyed since 1821. Competition arrived, first from the south, from the many access points on the new railways. Individual freetraders needed little outlay to get started in the fur business. According to one observer, the first traders to come in with the railways brought with them "a keg of the strong alcohol, a few cheap gilt watches, some fancy ribbons, coloured shawls and imitation meerschaum pipes, and if they found their bundles would bear a little more weight, they generally put in a little more whisky."[11]

In addition to the individual "whisky peddlers," more respectable opponents emerged to oppose the Hudson's Bay Company "in a straight way," by trading to the Indians "good strong clothing and good provisions."[12] While a number of these small companies (often composed of no more than two to four people) went bankrupt after one or two years, some survived. Organized competition to the HBC became very strong in the early twentieth century.

The Révillon Frères Trading Company became the leading opponent. By 1910 this powerful organization had expanded to the point where it had posts at most of the places where the Hudson's Bay Company traded. During the

Depression of the 1930s, however, Révillon's business declined rapidly. The HBC bought its opponent's assets in Canada in 1936.[13] Smaller organized competitors to the HBC in Northern Ontario included H.C. Hyer of Winnipeg, who moved into the upper Severn area from Island and God's lakes around 1907; the G.A. MacLaren Trading Company, which operated in the Osnaburgh House area from 1901 until bought by the HBC in 1910;[14] and, at a later period, Patricia Stores Limited which traded as far north as Windigo Lake,[15] and the Savant Lake Trading Company.[16]

Competition became keenest towards the end of the First World War, when raw fur prices reached record highs on the world market. A comparison of sample fur prices for 1916 and 1918 indicates that beaver jumped from $5.96 to $14.84, ermine (per forty) from $20.68 to $41.37, marten from $7.06 to $17.76, and otter from $9.61 to $14.84.[17] According to J.W. Anderson, a veteran fur trader, as a result "every Tom, Dick and Harry rushed into the fur trade."[18] The new traders, based at points on the railway, needed only a toboggan, a few dogs, camp equipment, and a roll of dollar bills. (As this observation suggests, cash had become more common in exchange transactions between fur traders and Indians.)

The competition led to an increase in the number of available trade outlets as the larger fur trade companies also operated, in addition to their regular trading posts, smaller outposts. These "camp trades" (small trading outposts such as Big Beaver House, Wunnummin, and Sandy Lake) stocked only basic essentials, such as flour, sugar, tea, and ammunition, and simply exchanged furs for goods without using either cash or credit. Indian or mixed-blood company employees ran many of the camp trades in Northern Ontario.

The rise of competition led to the reintroduction of alcohol, formerly forbidden by the Hudson's Bay Company after its amalgamation with the North West Company. In areas exploited by the whisky pedlars, alcohol had a demoralizing effect on local Indian populations.

*Expansion of Missionary Activity*

Before 1890 Christian missionaries had restricted their outreach to southern regions, such as the Boundary Waters and Abitibi areas, and to the coast of James Bay. A new approach began in the 1890s with a rapid expansion into the northern interior and up the coast of Hudson Bay. Of the three denominations competing for converts – Anglicans, Methodists, and Roman Catholics – the Anglicans had the greatest impact in the northern interior.

Native clergy led the Anglicans' missionary campaign. Bishop Horden at Moosonee instructed and ordained Edward Richards, a James Bay Cree, and William Dick, a Cree catechist from York Factory. Others were trained in the

Long Lake, Ontario, 1906. Note the Hudson's Bay Company post and the neighbouring church with the Indian lodges in front of it.

south, such as Richard Faries, a Cree mixed-blood who was born and brought up at Moose Factory and who spent two years at Montreal Theological College before his ordination in 1898. These men staffed the new mission stations located at strategic inland locations. As mentioned in the previous chapter, William Dick managed the mission at Big Trout from the 1880s until his retirement in 1918. During his ministry he established a mission station at Fort Severn and travelled widely throughout the upper Severn and upper Winisk regions, making converts, baptizing, and marrying.[19] He also trained Native catechists.[20] The Anglicans established another important inland mission at Fort Hope on the upper Albany, where the Hudson's Bay Company had built a post in 1890. Richard Faries directed the mission station until 1899, when it was taken over by Edward Richards. Native catechists ran outposts from the Fort Hope Mission at two other locations on the Albany River: Osnaburgh House and Marten Falls. In addition, Anglican workers made seasonal trips north to the upper Attawapiskat River and as far as the boundaries of William Dick's missionary field on the upper Winisk.

Roman Catholic missionaries also ventured northward during the 1890s, concentrating particularly on the Cree of James and Hudson bays. In 1892 the Oblates, who had formerly made visits to James Bay from Abitibi, established a permanent mission at Fort Albany. From this vantage point, northwest of the old Anglican headquarters at Moosonee, they made summer visits up the coast as far as Winisk, and up the Albany River as far as Fort Hope.[21] Later, the Oblates built permanent missions at Attawapiskat (1912) and Winisk (1934).

The Methodists worked in northwestern Ontario, operating from their older mission posts in Manitoba. One of the early Methodists in Northern Ontario was Reverend F.G. Stevens, who made annual visits to Sandy Lake from 1899 to 1907.[22] After church union in 1925, the United Church of Canada continued many of the former Methodist missions.

The missionaries soon became involved in education and health. In 1902, for example, the Grey Sisters of Ottawa established both a boarding school and a hospital at Fort Albany. The children were brought to the boarding school from coastal Cree communities and from Ojibwa families as far inland as Fort Hope. The Anglican missionary established a day school at Fort Hope in 1910. In 1945 Oblate missionaries started sending Ojibwa children from the upper Albany region to a boarding school at McIntosh, Ontario, on the Canadian National Railway line west of Sioux Lookout.[23]

"Roman Catholic, Anglican, and Methodist missionaries began to impact upon the spiritual life of northern Algonquians about the middle of the nineteenth century, and ultimately Christianity became the dominant religion. Even on the trail, most of the people I travelled with observed morning and evening devotions. Still, elements of older beliefs survived in places, including Sandy Lake, the site of this Roman Catholic mission" – John Macfie (who took this photo in 1955)

From John Macfie and Basil Johnston, *Hudson Bay Watershed* (Toronto: Dundurn Press 1991), 71

Archives Deschâtelets, Ottawa

Father Joseph-Arthur Bilodeau (1886–1963), an Oblate missionary and director of the Roman Catholic Indian school at Fort Albany (1925–38), photographed with Cree in the James Bay area, 1933. Father Bilodeau served for nearly half a century in the Roman Catholic missions on the west coast of James Bay (1919–63).

## Government Involvement

Government surveyors and map makers became more active in Northern Ontario at the turn of the century.[24] The extension of Ontario's northern boundary from the Albany River to Hudson Bay, completed in 1912, placed these lands under provincial jurisdiction (the area south of the Albany River and north of the Great Lakes drainage basin had been transferred to Ontario by 1889).[25]

In the early twentieth century the federal government made treaties with the Amerindians in the area of what is now Northern Ontario. The first treaty with the Indians of the Hudson-James Bay drainage area was Treaty No. 9, signed in 1905 and 1906.[26] It covered all unceded territory from the height of land to the Albany River, which remained the northern boundary of Ontario until 1912. Treaty No. 9 was followed by an extension of Treaty No. 5 by which the Indians ceded the territory around Sandy Lake (1909) and Deer Lake (1910). Finally, the Treaty No. 9 adhesion (1929 and 1930) included all the remaining territory north of the Albany River (see the Map 14.2).

Once the Native people had signed treaties, the federal government set aside land for reserves, each reserve to contain 2.6 square kilometres (one square mile) for every family of five people. Often years passed before the government surveyed the boundaries. Annually, officials of the Indian Affairs Branch, who were usually accompanied by a doctor and an officer of the North-West Mounted Police (later Royal Canadian Mounted Police) visited the various bands. During the summer of 1924, the annual treaty party for the Treaty No. 9 area made its usual trip down the Albany River, departing from Dinorwic and stopping at Osnaburgh House, Fort Hope, Marten Falls, and Fort Albany, but it then used a sea-plane to reach the remaining bands. After this date, the treaty party increasingly travelled by plane.[27]

The annual arrival of the treaty party became an event of major significance to the Indians. The occasion began with a volley of gunfire to greet the canoes bearing the government officials. The status Indians received their annuity payments, which usually amounted to four or five dollars per person, depending on the terms of the treaty. The officials distributed gifts of clothing, blankets, and fish nets, as well as rations for the sick and disabled. The treaty party also contributed to a feast that usually accompanied the celebrations. Occasionally the party met with hostility, as in 1907 at Lake of the Woods when Indians threatened the agent.[28]

Although a police officer accompanied the annual treaty party, law enforcement did not pose a serious problem. One of the few exceptions occurred in 1907, when two North-West Mounted Police officers arrested the conjurer Pesequan (alias Joseph Fiddler) and Jack Fiddler at Sandy Lake and brought them out to trial at Norway House.[29] Pesequan had been involved in the ritual murder of a woman who had been delirious for several days and

National Archives of Canada, C-68920

Signing of Treaty No. 9 at Windigo, Ontario, 18 July 1930. *Standing:* Samuel Sa-wa-nis, John Wesley, Dr. O'Gorman, Chief Ka-ke-pe-ness, and Senia Sak-che-ka-pow.

who had thus, according to traditional belief, constituted a threat to the community. Fiddler's death sentence was later changed to life imprisonment, but he soon died in confinement. Infrequently, the police also had to transport Indians who had gone insane to the outside for treatment.[30]

Although a doctor sometimes travelled with the treaty party, the Indians remained isolated from professional medical attention and facilities. Each trading post normally kept first-aid equipment and a limited supply of medicines. The traders and missionaries might dispense these. Rations for the sick and destitute were also distributed in this manner, and in a few instances aircraft were used to fly emergency cases to hospitals in the south. In spite of occasional epidemics and the obvious limitations of the medical system, there might have been some districts where population increased during the early twentieth century.[31] In other areas, population fluctuated but did not begin to rise until after the Second World War. This was the case for those Indians residing in the upper Severn River drainage basin. Fluctuating numbers of country game may have accounted for this. A severe shortage of country food existed, for example, in 1900[32] and during the winter of 1908–1909.[33]

**Impact on Native Culture: Material Change**

Changes in the material culture of the Indians were easily observable and frequently noted by outsiders. After 1890, for example, traditional shelters gave way to new types of dwellings, one being the moss-covered conical lodge, similar in basic structure to its bark- or hide-covered predecessor, but covered with a thick layer of moss for greater winter warmth (see chapter 13).[34] This semi-permanent structure had to be built in the fall, before the earth froze solid, and was therefore better suited for the more sedentary lifestyle that emerged during this period.

More-permanent structures, styled after those of the settlers, had become common by 1900 in the Boundary Waters area. By the First World War the Indians adopted log cabins in the north as well, at widespread locations such as Pikangikum,[35] Windigo Lake,[36] and the upper Winisk River.[37] Although originally built only by "prominent" individuals, log cabins became the normal winter dwelling by the 1930s. The Indians used both round and squared logs, and commonly made roofs of either the ridge or hip variety. The earliest cabins were heated with open fireplaces of mud,[38] but wood stoves soon became a standard feature.

Some people continued to use conical and dome-shaped lodges as summer dwellings, with canvas supplementing or replacing bark and hides for the covering. Canvas wall tents gradually became more common during the early decades of the twentieth century. Though the wall tent eventually replaced the

An Ojibwa camp near the Ogoki River, north of Lake Nipigon, 1923.
Photo by Joseph Green, Archives of Ontario, Acc. 9348 s15105

Native family by their log cabin, located near Hardrock, which is near Geraldton, north-western Ontario.
Photo by E.C. Everett, Thunder Bay Historical Society, 974.2.72

A Cree settlement near Moose Factory, January 1946. The Cree lived in tents with walls roughly one metre in height. The walls were made of logs chinked with moss and mud.
Photo by Bud Glunz, National Archives of Canada, PA-189737

traditional lodges, it was sometimes attached to such dwellings as an additional room or rooms. The customary open fire heated the lodge, while the occupants used any adjoining tent or tents as sleeping quarters.[39] Such a composite dwelling could house several families and thus probably replaced the traditional multi-family ridge-pole lodge. On the trapline the Indians put up wall tents as winter shelters, which they heated with a light wood stove made from sheet metal.

Winter transportation became more efficient around 1900 with the adoption of dogs for pulling sleds.[40] A good dog team could average about fifty kilometres per day in winter, a distance that could be increased to about eighty kilometres during the lengthened daylight hours of spring.[41] At about the same time as the Northern Algonquians adopted dog teams they began to use two new types of sled. One of these was modelled after the Inuit dogsled and was probably introduced by missionaries and traders familiar with the Arctic. The other, sometimes referred to as a "prospector's sled," was built up on a pair of runners shaped like skis. It travelled more effectively on soft snow than the Inuit sled and kept a load higher and dryer than the traditional toboggan.

Noticeable changes also occurred in summer transportation. Canvas-covered canoes began to replace those made of birchbark shortly after the turn

A dog team returning to Moose Factory, 1934.
Photo by H. Bassett, Provincial Archives of Manitoba, Hudson's Bay Company Archives, HBCA Photograph Collection, 1987/363-M-110/55 (N79-135)

of the century. Unlike the locally made bark canoes, most of the canvas canoes sold by the fur traders came from factories in Peterborough or from Lac Seul and Rupert's House. Native people hired by traders to deliver them to posts as far north as Big Trout Lake usually picked up the empty canoes at the nearest railhead. Each canoe was delivered by a solitary man, who used oars and home-made oarlocks rather than the more traditional paddle. By the 1930s, outboard motors had become a common sight on freighter canoes and were popular with those who could afford them.

By the early twentieth century the Northern Algonquians had discarded most of their former clothing, except for occasional rabbit-skin costumes.[42] Nevertheless, many Native people continued to wear hide moccasins and mittens, frequently decorated with silk embroidery or, more often, glass beads. The more traditional use of coloured porcupine quills had become rare by the turn of the century, although it apparently persisted in the Red Lake area as late as 1915.[43] Those living nearest southern non-Native settlements occasionally donned ceremonial costumes (usually reflecting heavy Plains Indian influence) to celebrate powwows or to entertain tourists.

A useful innovation from Northern Quebec was the sealskin boot, which provided waterproof footwear during the warmer seasons. The Hudson's Bay Company distributed the Inuit-made product to Northern Ontario locations, such as Fort Albany and Attawapiskat.[44] Eventually, the Cree living on the coast of Hudson and James bays started making their own sealskin boots, including one type that had a regular moccasin foot with a sealskin upper.

**Economic Change**

In the Boundary Waters area, many Ojibwa at the turn of the century started to supplement fishing, hunting, and trapping with farming and seasonal wage labour. Indians in the vicinity of Lake of the Woods planted potatoes, pumpkins, carrots, and turnips, all of which they stored underground for the winter.[45] They dried corn and stored it in birchbark storage houses, along with large quantities of maple sugar, berries, fish powder, and dried moose and muskrat meat. Hay was cut, dried, and stored for cows, kept for both meat and milk, as well as for horses.

In the Kenora region, dam construction, which began in the late 1880s, caused widespread flooding. This reduced wild rice yields and also fish and muskrat harvests. Similar results occurred in Lake St. Joseph when an Ontario Hydro dam raised the water level three metres.[46]

North of the Albany River small gardens became common by the turn of the century in such remote localities as Lake St. Joseph, Lake Attawapiskat,

National Archives of Canada, PA-59558

Treaty No. 9 Commissioner Samuel Stewart describes Chief Louis Espagnol (Espaniel), an Ojibwa chief from the Spanish River, as he appeared at the treaty discussions at Biscotasing, 12 July 1906: "Louis was attired in great splendour and his appearance was greatly admired. He had on a Caribou skin uniform with any amount of fringe, as well as pendants of goose bones with tips of deer skin. The Jacket had pockets of red and blue cloth, decorated with beads of various colors. He also wore garters similarly decorated. On his feet were a pair of Caribou moccasins with porcupine designs. He wore a wampum bandolier, and on his breast were two large George 3rd silver medals ... Taking him all in all, Louis was quite a heavy swell, and he was very well aware of the fact."

and the area of Weagamow Lake.[47] The Native people stored potatoes, the main crop in these northern areas, in pits dug in hillsides or under the floors of log cabins. At first only a few individuals grew potatoes, but by the 1930s many did. Imported food became more readily available in the 1940s, and after this, gardening declined rapidly.

In some areas large game animals increased in numbers towards the end of the last century. This provided a welcome addition to the fish-hare diet that had become so common earlier in the century. Caribou, for instance, became more numerous in the Trout Lake area in the 1870s[48] and in the upper Albany area in the 1880s.[49] After having been almost exterminated in the early nineteenth century, moose re-entered Northern Ontario around 1900. The return of these important large game animals made famine less of a threat, and it also provided hides for moccasins, mittens, and snowshoe webbing, all of which had had to be purchased from the traders when locally unavailable.

Fish continued to be a major foodstuff, and fishing provided some Native people with a chance to earn wages from the traders. The development of large-scale commercial fishing for export, however, awaited air transportation in the north. One of the first fish products to be exported by aircraft was fresh caviar, obtained from Indians who fished sturgeon along the Albany River and as far north as Muskrat Dam Lake on the Severn River. To keep the caviar fresh, the Indians first netted the sturgeon and then tethered them to stakes in the water to keep them alive until the sound of an approaching aircraft could be heard. The fishermen quickly hauled out the fish and removed the caviar for immediate shipment to southern markets.[50] This practice, however, soon depleted sturgeon throughout Northern Ontario.

The Beaucage family with a moose taken near Biscotasing in the 1920s.
Archives of Ontario, Acc. 10144

Drying moose meat, Lac Seul, 1919.
Photo by F.W. Waugh, Canadian Museum of Civilization, 45686

A woman scraping a moose hide for tanning, Lac Seul, 1919.
Photo by F.W. Waugh, Canadian Museum of Civilization, 45773

Opportunities for wage labour became more varied. Seasonal employment as tourist guides continued, but now some Indians found jobs with the railways, lumber camps, and mills. After the decline of fur prices in the 1930s, some Native trappers also worked in mines, moving with their families to such places as Red Lake, Pickle Lake, and Favourable Lake. Many, however, found the adjustment from their old lifestyle and the prejudice of non-Native co-workers too great, and returned to the bush after a relatively short time.

As employment opportunities increased in the south, they gradually diminished for the Cree at Moose Factory and Fort Albany. With the arrival of the railways, these posts lost much of their former importance as supply depots. Farther north, however, the fur traders still required individuals to staff the boats from Fort Severn to Big Trout Lake into the 1940s. At times they hired as many as sixty or more men each summer.[51] After the adhesion to Treaty No. 9 was signed in 1929, many were reluctant to go on the brigades until after government officials had arrived. The Hudson's Bay Company voiced its concern, claiming the timing of treaty payments interfered with its employment of the Indians.[52]

Most of the Northern Algonquians in Ontario remained dependent on

Two photos of the Cree village of Fort Severn on Hudson Bay, where the HBC first traded for furs over 300 years ago. The upper photo was taken in the summer of 1955; the lower in August 1964.

Photos by John Macfie, from John Macfie and Basil Johnston, *Hudson Bay Watershed* (Toronto: Dundurn Press 1991), 27 trapping. By 1890 the trade goods regarded as "indispensable" included powder, shot, guns, axes, and nets, and many Indians had also become reliant on flour, pork, tallow, and wool clothing and blankets.[53] During the early twentieth century the inventory of desired trade goods increased to include manufactured canoes, canvas tents, and even, for some, violins and gramophones.

As the desire for trade goods grew, so did the pressure on fur resources, particularly in areas near the railroad, where freetraders encouraged the Indians to violate conservation methods. In these "frontier" locations, Native trappers found a ready market for out-of-season skins and sometimes they continued to trap for ten months of the year.[54] At interior posts the HBC enforced conservation by restricting fur trapping to the period from 25 October to 25 May, although freetraders sometimes encouraged the Indians to do otherwise.[55] The intense pressure on fur resources came from Native and also from non-Native trappers, who spread across Northern Ontario in ever-increasing numbers in the early twentieth century. By 1890 non-Native trappers already encroached on Indian lands near Lake Nipigon and Sturgeon Lake, and by the turn of the century they had reached the vicinity of Osnaburgh House.[56] The high prices for furs after the First World War brought an influx of non-Native trappers to areas as remote as Sandy Lake.[57]

As the veteran fur trader J.W. Anderson pointed out, the non-Native trappers had a higher standard of living and were much harder on fur resources than the Indians.[58] An Indian in the 1920s, living largely off the land, could

National Archives of Canada, PA-59520

These treaty Indians in Abitibi owned a sewing machine (shown on the right), June 1906.

Joe Espaniel, a great-nephew of Chief Louis Espaniel (see page 357), c. 1915. Joe Espaniel came from Pogamising near Benny, on the CPR line between Sudbury and Chapleau. He enlisted in the Canadian Expeditionary Force and was killed overseas. A number of other Northern Algonquians also served in the Canadian Army in the First World War.

Ontario Ministry of Natural Resources, Jim Espaniel Collection get by on an annual trapping income of approximately $300 to $400. As Anderson mentions, however, his non-Native counterpart required a winter outfit of food and equipment amounting to at least $1 000. The search for a greater number of furs contributed to the sharp decline in the number of fur-bearing animals by 1929. Once this happened, non-Native trappers began leaving the region.

Especially hard hit by overtrapping was the beaver. By 1890 the Hudson's Bay Company trader at Osnaburgh House had already expressed fears that beaver had declined and might be exterminated. He attributed this to the fact that the Native people, constantly driven back by the encroachment of hunters from elsewhere, no longer spared a few animals for breeding, "as has hitherto been their custom."[59] The intensive trapping that resulted from boom prices in the 1920s also contributed to the depletion. By 1935 J.W. Anderson reported that the younger Attawapiskat Indians had actually never seen a beaver.[60]

## Social Organization

Traditional forms of social organization changed considerably during the early twentieth century. Probably the "line" Indians (those who moved their primary place of residence from the bush to scattered settlements along the railways) experienced the most profound change. Life in the railway communities, in close proximity to a predominantly male population of non-Native transients, generally had a disruptive effect on old patterns of family and community life. A study completed at Collins, Ontario, indicates that the families relocated to such an environment often experienced a general feeling of apathy and aimlessness. Marriage breakdowns also increased.[61]

Among the bush Indians the effects of contact may have been less disruptive, but even away from the railways their social organization was altered in a number of ways. At the family level, polygyny declined around the turn of the century, after Christian missionaries and government officials explained federal laws against plural marriage.[62] Another change that resulted from external pressure was the adoption of family surnames.[63]

As a rule, missionaries now formalized marriages but parents continued to play an important role in the choice of marriage partner for their children. Marrying outside of one's clan (clan exogamy), once important in the regulation of marriage in the Boundary Waters region, had already started to lose its former importance along the upper Albany river by 1910.[64]

In the area of the upper Winisk and Attawapiskat rivers, the semi-sedentary "all-Native settlement," where people lived in log cabins for ten or more months of the year,[65] gradually replaced the nomadic hunting group. Women and children usually remained in these settlements when the men went

"The Family Circle," Kagianagami Lake, Ontario, c. 1941. Kagianagami Lake is on a tributary of the Albany River just south of Fort Hope, located between the Albany and Ogoki rivers.

Provincial Archives of Manitoba, Hudson's Bay Company Archives, HBCA Photograph Collection, 1987/363-I-82/18 (N9314) to their traplines during the winter months. During the summer those families who visited the trading post at treaty time lived near the posts in cloth tents.

These semi-sedentary all-Native settlements became larger than the earlier hunting groups. The six all-Native settlements existing in the Lansdowne House area during the 1940s, for instance, ranged in size from 42 to 100, with an average population of 62.[66] At such settlements, kinship affiliations continued to be an important factor in determining the composition of the residential group. Primary kin ties connected the vast majority of married couples with other community members.

As the settlements increased in size, a tendency grew to choose marriage partners from within the same community (endogamy). In 65 percent of all marriages in six all-Native settlements, both spouses had resided in the same community prior to marriage.[67] This remarkable incidence of community endogamy is another way in which the all-Native settlements differed from the older hunting groups, which had been largely exogamous units.

Little detailed information on the social organization of the Indians prior to the 1950s exists, making it difficult to plot the distribution of the semi-sedentary all-Native settlements. They appear to have been slow to develop in isolated areas such as Weagamow Lake.[68] At another isolated location, Pikangikum, Ojibwa co-residential groups (all-Native settlements) remained small, with an average of only twenty-three persons as late as 1939.[69] Furthermore, at Pikangikum log cabins remained uncommon, with only an average of 1.5 houses per settlement. Many people must still have spent the winter in tents or traditional lodges.

Interior of Charlie Moore's trapping cabin, Bear Island, Lake Temagami.
Archives of Ontario, Acc. 9164 s15164

Leadership within the all-Native settlements was probably based on several criteria, some traditional and some modern. Although the male head of the largest extended family no doubt remained an important figure, two new roles of great importance emerged: that of camp trader (usually a Native person) and, in the case of Anglican settlements, that of Native catechist. These functionaries sometimes exerted considerable influence over the lives of other people in their settlements. In some cases, people who were already leaders in the more traditional sense filled these roles, thereby giving themselves an even greater authority.

Several factors made the development of semi-sedentary all-Native settlements possible. One was undoubtedly the availability of new and/or increased food supplies, both from store purchases and from local gardening. The use of dogs for sledding also made it easier to transport country food to the settlement, eliminating the necessity of constantly relocating to a new hunting ground.

After the treaties, many of the former trading post bands simply became treaty bands, adopted as convenient administrative units by the agents of

Group of Lake Temagami Ojibwa on Treaty Payment Day, summer of 1913. Chief François White Bear appears in the centre, and the assistant chief Aleck Paul is shown standing to the right, next to Chief White Bear.
Canadian Museum of Civilization, 23991

Treaty No. 9 Indians shown gathering for treaty payments in front of the HBC post, Lansdowne House, Ontario, 1942.
Glenbow Archives, Calgary, NA-3235-68

Voting for the chief at Big Trout Lake, northwestern Ontario, 1947.
Photo by Jake Sieger, Provincial Archives of Manitoba, Hudson's Bay Company Archives, HBCA Photograph Collection, 1987/363-1-83/79 (N9313)

Indian Affairs. Under the supervision of government officials, the treaty band elected a chief, who was expected to make a speech to the entire band at each annual feast. Elected councillors, the number of which was determined by band size, assisted the chief. Both chiefs and councillors received an honorarium ($25 per annum for a chief and $15 for councillors), suits, and medals. Appearances aside, the band had a loosely knit structure, and neither the chief nor his councillors had effective control over band members or revenues; nor did they have real authority over most of those widespread settlements they officially represented. The position of chief created by the government was, however, not a new development. In earlier times, the Hudson's Bay Company had appointed chiefs for various groups of Indians[70] (see chapters 12, 13, and 14).

## Religion

After 1890 Christian beliefs and practices spread, as both Native and non-Native missionaries proselytized throughout Northern Ontario. In northeastern Ontario (where Anglicans and Roman Catholics competed for followers), the majority of the Northern Ojibwa appeared in official records as Christian converts by the 1910s. In northwestern Ontario, Pikangikum, one of the last areas to come under missionary influence, remained non-Christian into the 1930s.[71]

Particularly in those areas under the influence of Native missionaries and catechists, Christianity had a powerful impact. Some Indians around the Bearskin community, for example, experienced a great religious fervour during the winter of 1913–14. Two Indians had a vision in which they travelled to limbo, or the border of Hell, where they saw a lake of fire in which a swarm of souls struggled.[72] After 1920 other Native leaders in the upper Attawapiskat and Winisk areas, inspired by biblical references to walled villages,[73] had palisades built around their all-Native settlements.

In Ojibwa all-Native settlements, located far from mission stations, people gathered in the log homes of the resident Native catechist for daily prayer services. On the trapline they usually took prayer and hymn books in their own language, written in the special syllabics devised by earlier missionaries.[74] In the 1930s Native catechists built churches in many Northern Ojibwa communities, such as Lansdowne House, Webique, and Nikip.

Most Indians in Northern Ontario, including those who formally accepted Christianity, retained some aspects of their traditional belief system. The concept of "power" remained a dominant theme in Native religious thought, even though new sources of power could be found in baptism and other Christian practices. Shamans continued in the twentieth century to perform traditional ceremonies, such as the Shaking Tent rite, and Native herbalists were called upon to cure illness and prescribe love medicines.[75] In many Ojibwa settlements witchcraft continued as a cause of great anxiety, and most cases of illness, accident, and death were attributed to the sorcery of others.[76]

The Midewiwin society still functioned despite government and missionary attempts at suppression.[77] The Midewiwin appears, however, to have declined in the early part of the century in areas distant from its greatest strength in the Boundary Waters area. It had already disappeared along the Albany River by 1909,[78] while at Pikangikum it persisted until the last of the Midewiwin leaders moved to Lac Seul about 1920.[79] Long after the Midewiwin was abandoned at Pikangikum, the dog feast, which once formed part of the Midewiwin ceremonies, was retained as an independent ritual.[80]

Another religious ceremony held in the Boundary Waters area was the Drum Dance. Apparently it originated on the Plains as a nativistic reaction to European contact and spread to the Ojibwa of northwestern Ontario during the late nineteenth century.[81] The Indians made the sacred drums used during the ceremony from wooden washtubs; the tubs were covered with hide and suspended off the ground on four stakes. During the ceremony several men sat around the drum, beating and singing, while others danced. In time the social aspects of the drum ceremony became increasingly important, and it was enacted at powwows along the Winnipeg and Rainy rivers.

## Conclusion

As Northern Ontario came into ever-increasing contact with the outside world after 1890, the Northern Algonquians experienced more and more alterations in their way of life. Among the most noticeable changes were new housing styles, with canvas tents, moss-covered lodges, and log cabins replacing the more traditional dwellings. Winter transportation became more efficient with the widespread acceptance of dogs and the adoption of two foreign types of sled. Another manifestation of change was the rapid decline of the traditional bark canoe, replaced by factory-made canvas canoes that were often propelled by outboard motors.

The subsistence economy of the Indians benefited by the return of moose and caribou to parts of Northern Ontario from which they had earlier disappeared. In the south, Native people supplemented wild food with small-scale farming, which included the raising of horses and cows. Even in the north, with its limited agricultural potential, gardening became fairly widespread, and people raised potatoes, storing them for winter consumption. These improvements in the food situation were partially offset by a decline in the yield of some traditional foods, particularly fish and wild rice, owing to resource development and commercial exploitation.

Trapping remained an important source of cash income but was adversely affected by a decline in the availability of fur, largely the result of overtrapping, abandonment of older conservation practices, and the encroachment of non-Native trappers during periods of high prices. Wage labour partially compensated the consequent loss of trapping income, necessary to purchase an expanding inventory of trade goods and store food. In the south, some took advantage of opportunities for work as tourist guides, commercial fishermen, miners, railway workers, and lumbermen. In the north, freighting remained a source of income into the 1930s.

The emergence of semi-sedentary all-Native settlements in some areas can be related to some of the technological and economic factors already noted. Especially noteworthy were the adoption of log cabins and the use of sled dogs, and the availability of new food supplies. In the Native communities, Christian missionaries and government officials worked to reduce the incidence of polygyny, while at the same time they introduced formalized marriages and the use of family surnames.

Finally, the rapid spread of Christianity characterized this period. Missionaries of various denominations, aided in many cases by Native catechists, succeeded in establishing missions and churches throughout most of Northern Ontario. As a result, almost all of the Cree and Ojibwa were nominal Christians by the 1930s. Nevertheless, many of the traditional religious beliefs and practices persisted side by side with the new teachings and survived into the period after the Second World War.

## NOTES

1   Charles A. Bishop, *The Northern Ojibwa and the Fur Trade, An Historical and Ecological Study* (Toronto 1974), 79

2   J.W. Anderson, *Fur Trader's Story* (Toronto 1961), 18

3   Douglas Baldwin, *The Fur Trade in the Moose-Missinaibi River Valley, 1770–1917* (Ontario Ministry of Culture and Recreation, Historical Planning and Research Branch, Research Report 8, n.d.), 88

4   Anderson, *Fur Trader's Story*, 150

5   See Hudson's Bay Company Archives (HBCA), B.220/a/047, fo. 77; B.220/a/049, fos. 11, 13; B.220/a/050, fo. 8

6   S.A. Pain, *The Way North, Men, Mines and Minerals* (Toronto 1964); Albert Tucker, *Steam into Wilderness* (Toronto 1978)

7   L. Seale Holmes, *Holmes' Specialized Philatelic Catalogue of Canada and British North America* (Toronto 1968), 211–26; C.A. Longwort-Dames, *The Semi-Official Air Stamps of Canada 1924–1934* (Devon 1982), 11–52

8   National Archives of Canada (NA), RG 10, vol. 6889, file 486/28–3, pt. 8
9   *The Beaver*, outfit 265 (March 1935), 63
10   Bruce West, *The Firebirds* (Toronto 1974)
11   Martin Hunter, *Canadian Wilds* (Columbus 1935), 18–19
12   Ibid., 22
13   Anderson, *Fur Trader's Story*, 195
14   Bishop, *The Northern Ojibwa*; HBCA, B.155/a/097, letter 22 May 1910
15   NA, RG 10, vol. 6819, file 490/2–17, Edwards to Scott, 7 September 1928
16   NA, RG 10, vol. 6889, file 486/28–3, vol. 8, Edwards to Awrey, 9 May 1929
17   Bishop, *The Northern Ojibwa*, 83
18   Anderson, *Fur Trader's Story*, 138
19   Anglican Church Records (ACR), *Register of Baptisms and Marriages, Trout Lake Mission 1855–1953*, 2 vols. (Kenora)
20   E.S. Rogers, personal communication
21   Henri Belleau, "Les Missions de la Baie James," *L'Apostolat* 11 (1940): 51
22   F.G. Stevens, "The Crane and Sucker Indians in Far North-Western Ontario," *Missionary Bulletin* 15, no. 1 (1919): 121–6; A.D. (Mrs. F.C.) Stephenson, *One Hundred Years of Canadian Methodist Missions* (Toronto 1925), 123–7; George Lerchs, "The Sandy Lake Cree/Ojibwa," Canadian Ethnology Service MS (Ottawa 1976), 24
23   Soeur Paul-Emile, *Amiskwaski, la Terre du Castor* (Ottawa 1952), 165
24   Morris Zaslow, *Reading the Rocks, the Story of the Geological Survey of Canada 1842–1972* (Toronto 1975), 228
25   The question of Ontario's boundaries is best reviewed in Norman L. Nicholson, *The Boundaries of the Canadian Confederation* (Toronto 1979).
26   J.L. Morris, *Indians of Ontario* (Toronto 1943), 46
27   NA, RG 10, vol. 6888, file 486/28–3, pt. 6
28   NA, RG 10, vol. 6892, file 487/28–3, pt. 1 (Belleville *Daily Intelligencer*, 4 August 1907)
29   David Boyle, "The Killing of *Wa-sak-apee-quay* by Pe-se-quan and Others," *Annual Archaeological Report; being part of an appendix to the report of the minister of education, Ontario* (Toronto 1907), 91–121; Morton I. Teicher, *Windigo Psychosis, A Study of a Relationship between Belief and Behaviour among the Indians of Northeastern Canada* (Seattle 1960), 74; Chief Thomas Fidler and James R. Stevens, *Killing the Shamen* (Moonbeam, Ont. 1985); James R. Stevens, "Zhauwuno-Geezhigo-Gaubow," *Dictionary of Canadian Biography*, vol. 13: *1901–1910* (Toronto 1994), 1128–30
30   Harwood Steele, *Policing the Arctic* (Toronto n.d.), 215, 355
31   W.W. Baldwin, "Social Problems of the Ojibwa Indians in the Collins Area in Northwestern Ontario," *Anthropologica* 5 (1957): 77; R.W. Dunning, *Social and Economic Change among the Northern Ojibwa* (Toronto 1959), 52
32   HBCA, B.220/a/046, fos. 2d, 21, 35d, 36d, 37d, 38d, 40d, 41, 46, 55d, 56d, 60d, 61d, 62, 62d; B.155/b/002, fos. 3d, 15d, 16d, 25d; B.093/a/011, fo. 63d, 66, 66d, 67, 67d, 68, 89d
33   HBCA, B.220/a/047, fos. 95, 111, 124–8
34   William McInnes, "Report on a Part of the North-West Territories of Canada Drained by the Winisk and Attawapiskat Rivers," in *Reports on the District of Patricia*, ed. Willet G. Miller (Toronto 1912), vol. 21, pt. 2, 134; Edward S.

Rogers, "Notes on Lodge Plans in the Lake Indicator (Lac Indicateur) Area of South-Central Quebec," *Arctic* 16, no. 4 (1963): 219–27

35 D.B. Dowling, "Report on the Country in the Vicinity of Red Lake and part of the Basin of Berens River, Keewatin," Canada, Geological Survey, *Annual Report* 7, pt. F (1894): 31

36 J.B. Tyrrell, "Hudson Bay Exploring Expedition, 1912," Ontario Department of Mines, *Annual Report* 22, pt. 1 (1913): 167

37 Willet G. Miller, "Reports on the District of Patricia," Ontario Bureau of Mines, *Report* 21, pt. 2 (1912): 131

38 A. Irving Hallowell, "Notes on the Material Culture of the Island Lake Saulteaux," *Journal de la Société des Américanistes* 30 (1938): 134

39 Ibid., 132

40 F.W. Waugh, Ethnographic fieldnotes on Northern Ojibwa for 1919, MS, Canadian Ethnology Service, Ottawa

41 Anderson, *Fur Trader's Story*, 178

42 Alanson Skinner, *Notes on the Eastern Cree and Northern Saulteaux* (New York 1911), 123

43 Waugh, Ethnographic fieldnotes

44 John J. Honigmann, "The Attawapiskat Swampy Cree, An Ethnographic Reconstruction," *Anthropological Papers of the University of Alaska* 5, no. 1 (1956): 47

45 James Redsky, *Great Leader of the Ojibway, Mis-guona-gueb* (Toronto 1972), 118

46 Bishop, *The Northern Ojibwa*, 71

47 Edward S. Rogers and Mary B. Black, "Subsistence Strategy in the Fish and Hare Period, Northern Ontario: The Weagamow Ojibwa, 1880–1920," *Journal of Anthropological Research* 32, no. 1 (1976): 11–13

48 HBCA, B.022/b/001, fos. 12–14d

49 Bishop, *The Northern Ojibwa*, 90

50 J. Hambleton, "Caviar for Celebrities," *The Beaver*, outfit 275 (June 1944), 46

51 HBCA, B.220/a/048, fo. 91

52 NA, RG 10, vol. 6819, file 490/2–17

53 Bishop, *The Northern Ojibwa*, 94

54 Hunter, *Canadian Wilds*, 29

55 HBCA, B.220/a/051, fos. 55–7

56 Bishop, *The Northern Ojibwa*, 95

57 Lerchs, "The Sandy Lake Cree/Ojibwa," 57

58 Anderson, *Fur Trader's Story*, 163

59 Bishop, *The Northern Ojibwa*, 95

60 Anderson, *Fur Trader's Story*, 188

61 Baldwin, "Social Problems of the Ojibwa Indians," 86

62 R.W. Dunning, *Social and Economic Change among the Northern Ojibwa* (Toronto 1959), 11

63 Mary Black Rogers and Edward S. Rogers, "Adoption of Patrilineal Surname System by Bilateral Northern Ojibwa, Mapping the Learning of an Alien System," in William Cowan, ed., *Papers of the Eleventh Algonquian Conference* (Ottawa 1979), 198–230

64  Skinner, *Notes on the Eastern Cree and Northern Saulteaux*, 150
65  J. Garth Taylor, "Northern Ojibwa Communities of the Contact-Traditional Period," *Anthropologica* 14, no. 1 (1972): 22
66  Ibid., 21
67  Ibid., 25
68  Rogers and Black, "Subsistence Strategy in the Fish and Hare Period," 39
69  Dunning, *Social and Economic Change*, 57
70  HBCA, B.220/a/048, fo. 39
71  A. Irving Hallowell, "Some Empirical Aspects of Northern Saulteaux Religion," *American Anthropologist* 36 (1934): 390
72  HBCA, B.220/a/048, fo. 73
73  J. Garth Taylor, Ethnographic fieldnotes from Webiquie, 8 July–22 August 1970; 14 July–8 August 1972, MSS
74  Baldwin, "Social Problems of the Ojibwa Indians," 65
75  Edward S. Rogers, *The Round Lake Ojibwa* (Toronto 1962), B44
76  Ibid., D17; E.S. Rogers, "Natural Environment – Social Organization – Witchcraft, Cree versus Ojibwa – a Test Case," in *Contributions to Anthropology, Ecological Essays*, ed. David Damas (Ottawa 1969), 24–39
77  J.M. Cooper, "Notes on the Ethnology of the Otchipwe of the Lake of the Woods and of Rainy Lake," Anthropological series, Catholic University of America, no. 3 (1936): 1–29
78  Skinner, *Notes on the Eastern Cree and the Northern Saulteaux*, 154
79  A. Irving Hallowell, "The Passing of the Midewiwin in the Lake Winnipeg Region," *American Anthropologist* 38 (1936): 51
80  Dunning, *Social and Economic Change*, 16
81  Robert E. Ritzenthaler, "Southeastern Chippewa," in *Handbook of North American Indians*, vol. 15: *Northeast*, ed. Bruce Trigger (Washington, D.C. 1978), 756

*Part Four*

*Post–Second World War Years*

Lobstick spruce (on the left, with its middle branches lopped off) marks the winter trail between Weenusk and Hawley Lake, 1955.

Photo by John Macfie, from John Macfie and Basil Johnston, *Hudson Bay Watershed* (Toronto: Dundurn Press 1991), 27

# 16 *The Modern Age, 1945–1980*

## HARVEY McCUE

Army life provided hitherto unattainable freedoms for Indian soldiers. Momentarily it freed them from all the bureaucratic controls and restrictions imposed upon registered and/or treaty Indians by the federal government. But with the Allies' victory in 1945, the demobilized Indian veterans again assumed their former status as "wards of the Crown." In subsequent years the bureaucracy that subjected them grew in size and complexity, especially during the 1960s and 1970s. It continued to act on its ethnocentric and often misinformed view of the Indian. Yet, thanks to an improved educational system their spokespersons gained a confidence in English and a knowledge of the dominant society that allowed them to fight back to preserve their cultural heritage, not to become simply another group of Canadians.

### The Indian on and off the Reserve

*Life on the Reserve*

As the quality of life in Ontario steadily improved after the war, the federal and provincial governments increased their efforts to improve the economic and social conditions in Indian communities. Circumstances beyond their control pulled even the residents of relatively isolated reserves into the modern age. In some cases the introduction of roads, airfields, and the reception of radio and television challenged the cultural and political autonomy of many reserves, frequently with unfortunate results. The limited educational and economic resources of the reserves, especially in the north, left the people illprepared to cope with the industrial world growing up around them.

Modern technology arrived quickly. Spectacular developments occurred in Northern Ontario during the 1960s and 1970s. As late as 1930 the Toronto *Mail and Empire* had written of the "lost tribe of Indians" that inhabited

Weagamow Lake and its environs, located only 350 kilometres north of Sioux Lookout. Within a generation, however, aircraft, radio, "ski doos," telephone, and television transformed the lives of these and many other Indians throughout the province.

Shortly after 1945, hydro-electric power was extended first to the southern, and then to the northern, reserves. In the beginning, large gasoline generators were installed that provided power for the schools and nursing stations, and later for the Indian residents of these communities. Telephone service became available through the use of radio-telephones, although, as was the case with electricity, only Euro-Canadians, such as teachers, principals, nurses, and Hudson's Bay Company (HBC) managers, initially had access to it. At the same time, the federal government greatly increased funding for construction of Indian housing. Throughout Southern Ontario, the square timbered or clapboard house, and in Northern Ontario, the canvas-covered conical lodge or log cabin, began to be replaced by newer but often inadequate "plywood bungalows." These seldom conformed to the requests of the extended families who resided in them. Nor did they always provide even the same protection from cold weather as the buildings they replaced.

The construction during the 1970s of airstrips also greatly changed Northern Ontario Indian communities. Formerly float or ski-equipped single-engine "bush" planes could not land during the spring break-up and fall freeze-up, but wheel-equipped planes, weather permitting, could. The building of airfields that allowed year-round access improved the delivery of food, mail, and merchandise, as well as travel between reserves. Yet transportation costs did not decrease as proponents of the program had predicted. Although subsidization by both the provincial and federal governments took place, an ever-increasing financial burden fell on the Indians who purchased the goods flown north. It also was costly to fly their products, such as fish, furs, and handicrafts, south.

The federal government made a renewed effort to improve medical services, especially in the north, after receiving the report of the James Bay Survey. This study, undertaken during the mid-1940s, had assessed the health conditions of the Indians of James Bay. The Department of National Health and Welfare built nursing stations in northern Indian communities and two hospitals, one in Sioux Lookout (1949) and the other at Moose Factory (1950). Yet the delivery of medical services to supplement those provided by the Christian missionaries remained inadequate. The absence of doctors much of the year in the Indian communities meant that the nurse(s), if any were in residence, assumed the burden of diagnosis and treatment. By default, eye care was left to attentive schoolteachers, the ones most likely to recognize failing eyesight among their students. While dentists hired by Indian Affairs made occasional circuits of the communities, their visits were too infrequent to provide proper dental care. Although Indians received ever-increasing medical aid from Euro-Canadians, they continued to rely on their traditional cures and remedies, especially if the nurses and doctors failed in their treatments.

As living conditions began to change, chronic unemployment, particularly in Northern Ontario, emerged as a major concern. The lack of vocational training and low levels of educational achievement owing to inadequate schooling (in contrast to that of urban areas) were partly responsible. But perhaps more importantly, most reserve communities possessed few economic opportunities – or none at all. Another inhibiting factor was the lack of capital for economic development, as banks would not, as a rule, make loans to Indians residing on a reserve to start a business. Chartered banks defended this position by arguing that, because of the Indian Act, any property on the reserve that belonged to the borrower could not be seized in case of non-repayment of the loan. Other problems encountered by reserve residents, whether in the north or the south, have often been the result of government bureaucracy.

Photo by John Macfie

Boys from Moose Factory, photographed playing hockey at a winter trapping camp at the headwaters of the Mattagami River, February-March 1959. The boys had whittled their sticks from saplings. In the background are beaver pelts curing in the wind and frost. One of the greatest Ontario Indian hockey players was George Armstrong, a former captain of the Toronto Maple Leafs. The son of an Ojibwa mother and a Scots-Canadian father, Armstrong was born at Skead, Ontario, near Sudbury. He played right wing with the Leafs from 1952 to 1971.

For some, the trapping of fur-bearing animals during the winter provided a livelihood. In 1966, for example, there were between 4 000 and 5 000 Indian trappers whose earnings annually amounted to nearly one million dollars. Yet the average yearly income of a trapper was only about $1 000. Although the federal government encouraged Indians to trap, the establishment in most northern communities of day schools that operated from fall until spring meant that a trapper with school-age children lived alone at his winter camp without his family. As a result, trapping and hunting became concentrated around the village. Subsequently, the quantity and quality of furs predictably dropped.

Beginning in the late 1950s, commercial fishing provided another limited source of income for the Indians of Northern Ontario. In less than a decade the returns annually amounted to nearly $500 000. In 1971, however, it was discovered that fish in the rivers and lakes of northwestern Ontario, especially those caught in the English-Wabigoon River system, contained a level of methyl mercury above that deemed safe for human consumption by the World Health Organization. Fishing for such species as walleye and whitefish in areas afflicted with mercury pollution ended. Jobs were lost in the commercial fishing industry, as well as related positions connected with sport fishing. Concern arose regarding the health of Indians, such as those living at the Whitedog and Grassy Narrows Indian reserves, who consumed large amounts of fish out of preference or necessity.

Other sources of income for Indians living in Northern Ontario included firefighting, tree planting, mine work, and – the most profitable work of all – guiding. Indians rented canoes, motors, and accommodation to southern anglers and hunters and acted as their guides. Goose-hunting camps were initiated in cooperation with Indian communities at Fort Severn, Winisk, Kapiskau, Attawapiskat, and Moose Factory. A number of Indians from both Northern and Southern Ontario served in the Canadian navy during the Korean War in the early 1950s.

For Indians living in northwestern Ontario, especially those in the Rainy Lake–Lake of the Woods area, the harvesting of wild rice proved profitable, as a ready market existed in the United States and eastern Canada. To aid this industry, the federal and provincial governments became deeply involved with the bands of the area in an advisory capacity and by providing financial assistance.

Indians living on southern reserves close to urban centres had a greater variety of job opportunities. But under-education and little or no training led to continuing under-employment or chronic unemployment. For many living on southern reserves, seasonal employment – lumbering, guiding, and harvesting fruits, vegetables, and tobacco – offered some relief.

A number of Canadian Indians served overseas in the Korean War. The photo shows (*left to right*) Cree Bill McCauley, Ojibwa Rene Espaniel, and non-Native Sid Sawyer, in late July 1952, in Kure, Japan. All three men came from Biscotasing, Northern Ontario.

Russel Isaacs, an experienced Mohawk high-steel worker. He is shown here as he worked on the construction of the Burlington Skyway Bridge, near Hamilton, in the mid-1950s.
Department of Indian and Northern Affairs, NFB 85403/08-37-00-36

To help reserve Indians, the federal and provincial governments increased funding to create jobs for Indians. Some projects, however, especially in the north, proved nothing more than make-work programs, such as widening paths through the villages and erecting "path signs." Elsewhere, assistance was given for such operations as a charcoal kiln and pheasant farm on the Christian Island Indian Reserve, a furniture factory begun in 1964 on the

Cape Croker Indian Reserve, and a snowshoe factory at Pays Plat Indian Reserve. The improvement of the cranberry marshes on the Gibson Reserve in Muskoka led to the rise of a profitable cranberry business. In 1978, under an agreement with Bata Shoes, an Indian-"owned" and -"operated" shoe factory was built on the Tyendinaga Reserve. Other enterprises promoted through government funding included the establishment of parks and marinas, and the leasing of cottage lots. Many such projects, however, provided only short-term employment during the construction phase, creating few full-time positions.

For some, craft work (such as making baskets, pottery, moccasins, and quill boxes) brought in a little money. After the Second World War several Indian craftspeople, encouraged by the continued interest by consumers in Indian handicrafts, went beyond being merely passive producers and established their own retail businesses. One of the best known is the Whetung Craft Shop on the Mississauga Reserve at Curve Lake north of Peterborough. The Recreation Committee at the Tyendinaga Reserve explored ways and means of training its members in Indian arts and crafts. In 1957 the Six Nations Iroquois formed the Ohsweken Art Group. For a time it held an annual exhibition of Indian artisans' works. In 1970, through the efforts of Art Solomon (and with funding from both the federal and provincial governments), a number of Ontario Indian craftspeople formed the Indian Craft Board of Ontario. With headquarters in Toronto, the organization acted for several years as a wholesaler for crafts produced by Ontario Indians. During this time it attempted to introduce new techniques to the production of traditional Ojibwa and Cree crafts.

None of the projects devised in the 1960s and 1970s could possibly provide permanent employment for all, especially since most reserves in Ontario lacked an adequate economic base. The continuing job specialization in the larger economy beyond the reserve placed those Indians with inadequate education at an even greater disadvantage. In the 1960s and 1970s Indian Affairs created a few permanent local governmental positions such as band administrator, band secretary, and the like, supported by government subsidies. Rarely, though, did the numbers so employed rise above ten to fifteen on many Indian reserves. Most Indians relied on seasonal employment and government assistance for an income.

The economic dependence of individuals and band councils on the federal government strengthened the Department of Indian Affairs' political and financial control over Indian communities and their initiatives. Events on the Golden Lake Reserve provide but one example, although no doubt an extreme one, of the federal government's control. During the summer of 1963 this Algonquin band raised money from tourists through a display of Indian handicrafts and the performance of dances and songs. But the Golden Lake community had to remit the money collected to the Indian Affairs Branch in Ottawa (after 1966 the Department of Indian and Northern Affairs). A year later, band members petitioned their band council to apply for the right to administer all funds raised through their own efforts.

During the 1960s the federal government allowed certain reserve communities a degree of self-government. In 1960, for example, the Walpole Island band council began administering the approximately $80 000 earned each year from fees imposed upon non-Indian farmers, anglers, and hunters who used reserve lands. The council also assumed responsibility for road improvements and other public facilities existing on the reserve. Then, in 1964, Indian Affairs offered the band the right to administer its affairs entirely, the responsibility to be transferred gradually. At the end of the one-year trial period in 1965, the council voted in favour of assuming all the responsibilities of self-government.

As the years passed, more and more reserve communities gained greater administrative and fiscal autonomy. By 1966, approximately one-third of all bands in the province had become responsible for administering their own welfare services. In that same year, the Association of Ontario Mayors and Reeves invited the elected band chiefs to join their organization. The Department of Indian Affairs also encouraged bands to create their own police forces. Walpole Island Indian Reserve did this in 1967. The following year the Cape Croker band council undertook the management of its housing projects. That same year, the department granted the Georgina Island Indian Reserve the right to administer its own welfare, recreation, housing, and road maintenance programs. Following several years of Indian protest, the Ontario government also amended the Education Act to enable band members to sit on local school boards that operated schools attended by Indian children from nearby reserves. The means of selection varied. The Orillia Public School Board selected the representative from the Rama Indian Reserve; the Department of Indian Affairs chose the representative from the Moraviantown Reserve; and the Nipissing Indian Reserve band council appointed two representatives to the local board.

As the number of bands that administered local programs increased, the federal government proposed in 1965 the appointment of a "band manager" on each reserve. Often selected from among reserve residents, band managers provided band councils with an ongoing, day-to-day base for much of the administration of the band. To prepare the new managers, the department instituted an eight-month training program at St. Francis Xavier University in Nova Scotia. By 1980 almost all reserve communities in Ontario had a band administrator who looked after the daily business of the community in consultation with the chief and councillors.

In the 1960s and 1970s recreation programs expanded on the reserves. Softball, snowsnake, and hockey tournaments were organized throughout Southern Ontario, which brought together Indians from many communities. At Ohsweken the winter weekend snowsnake contests attracted players and spectators from across Ontario and the state of New York. Agricultural fall fairs, such as those held at Tyendinaga, Ohsweken, and Parry Island, and the summer powwows staged by the residents of Wikwemikong, Fort William, Saugeen, Six Nations, Curve Lake, and Moosonee provided another release from the tedium of reserve life. Today's dances and costumes, which with few exceptions have been copied from the dances and traditions of the Plains Indians, have become a source of pride and enjoyment for many Indians and non-Indians alike. Throughout Northern Ontario, Treaty Day celebrations marking the anniversary of local treaties provided a focal point for festivities in many communities. With assistance from Indian political organizations, many reserves in Northern Ontario sponsor their own winter carnivals.

By the 1960s, Indians in Ontario began to examine their Indian identity and history. In 1965 the Sarnia Chippewa (Ojibwa) band sponsored a weekend conference to discuss ways and means of preserving Indian culture; Indians from Michigan, Wisconsin, and Minnesota, as well as Ontario, participated. In the previous year Web White had erected a museum on Walpole Island Reserve. Since then other Indian museums have come into existence, the most ambitious being the Woodland Cultural Centre in Brantford, near the Six Nations Reserve.

Archives Deschâtelets, Ottawa

The Bantam Hockey team, 1951/52, of the Fort Frances Indian Residential School – cup champions for the third year.

Indian communities began courses to educate their young people about their ancestors' past. The teaching of their language became an important component, especially in those communities where few or no Native speakers remained. In 1970, for example, the Tyendinaga band council offered a course in Mohawk for adults. At the same time, Ojibwa language instruction began in the schools on the Walpole Island Reserve and at a summer camp established at the Cape Croker Reserve. Ernest Benedict of Akwesasne established the North American Travelling College in 1965. This consisted of a van filled with books, films, and Native crafts that toured Indian reserves for several months each summer. Later, it amalgamated with the White Roots of Peace, another Iroquois cultural organization. For a time (1972–75) the Royal Ontario Museum had a similar project, the Ethnology Museumobile, under the supervision of Basil Johnston of the Cape Croker Indian Reserve, which visited Indian communities throughout Southern Ontario.

Whatever the conditions on the reserve, it remains the spiritual and historical home to most Indians, including those who have moved elsewhere. Likely an individual's ancestors hunted, gathered wild plants, and fished – or in the south raised crops such as corn, beans, and squash – in the area around the reserve. Friends and relatives resided there. On leaving the reserve, Indians often experienced difficult conflicts within themselves owing to the differences between their own values and those of the dominant Canadian society.

*Life in the City*

To escape the depressed economic conditions of many reserve communities, Indians turned more and more to the city. Although Ontario Indians had for many years looked to the urban areas for employment, initially only the most adventurous, or the best educated, actually moved. Those who arrived in the city found ready employment, and being few in number, had little trouble integrating. Beginning in the 1960s, however, an increasing number of Indians without the skills demanded by an industrial society moved to centres like Toronto, Hamilton, Thunder Bay, Timmins, North Bay, Sudbury, and Sault Ste. Marie. Despite the city's employment opportunities, they soon discovered that few jobs existed for those with only an elementary school education and little or no vocational skills or training.

The federal Indian Affairs Branch put in place programs to train Indians for employment in the city. At the Quetico Centre in northwestern Ontario, courses were given in 1960 to train Indians as waitresses, domestics, chambermaids, and kitchen helpers. Funds provided by the Ontario Department of Education, the Department of Indian and Northern Affairs, the National

Endowment Service, and the Quetico Foundation covered in large measure the cost of providing this training. Indian bands whose members enrolled at the Quetico Centre also contributed to the cost of the operation. Five years later twenty Indian families from northern communities arrived at the newly formed Centre for Continuing Education at Elliott Lake, to participate in an urban relocation training program under the auspices of the Canadian Vocational Training Program. Within three years, however, all but one family had returned home. The Moosonee Vocational Training School initiated a similar project. Yet these attempts proved insufficient to assist all those who had left the reserve or who wished to do so. For those who did enroll, the courses offered often proved too limited in the range of job skills provided.

Racial discrimination constituted another obstacle for many Indians attempting to adjust to urban life. The generally white, British-based urban population continued to view the Native person either romantically as a "feathered warrior" or critically as a "drunken transient." Although the Ontario government enacted legislation in the 1950s to prevent discrimination, Indians who came to the city (especially those with little work experience, little formal education, or few, or no, useful skills) found that Euro-Canadian city dwellers could discriminate exactly like their rural kin. Discrimination took various forms: refusal of accommodation and restaurant services; eviction from rental housing without due process; reluctance to hire Indians; and most frustrating of all, bureaucratic delays and lack of interest on the part of both provincial and federal governments.

For many migrants to the city, the only escape from their urban frustrations and their inability to adjust was to return to their home reserves. Others confronted urban challenges by joining together to form "fraternities." The first of these began in Toronto in the late 1960s and became the prototype for the Indian friendship centres throughout Canada. Originally known as the Thunderbird Club, a creation of the Métis Duke Redbird, the organization sponsored social events for Indians residing temporarily or permanently in Toronto, and encouraged a revival of Indian culture.

The original Thunderbird Club lasted only a few years, but the concept survived. The need for such a centre in Toronto certainly existed at that time, since, in 1972, an estimated 12 000 to 14 000 Indians lived in the city. The Native Canadian Centre of Toronto soon came into existence. By 1980 eighteen friendship centres existed in different towns and cities throughout Ontario. During the formative years, the friendship centre in Toronto served as a gathering place for many urban Indians who had succeeded in establishing themselves economically in the challenging environment of the city. In time, the Native Canadian Centre initiated programs to aid the vast number of unemployed and transient Indians scattered throughout the different areas of the city. Social and court workers and counsellors were added to the staff to assist those who came to the centre seeking assistance. Unfortunately, the centre itself could do little to improve the urban Indians' employment situation in Toronto.

Accommodation proved a serious problem for many Indians moving to the city. On the reserve, residents were eligible for housing grants provided by the federal government. However, as soon as they moved off-reserve, federal assistance for housing disappeared. Landlords often overcharged Indians (as well as all others, of course, who rented from them) for run-down premises. By 1967 the Department of Indian and Northern Affairs recognized the rights of Indians who had left the reserve to affordable and suitable housing, and provided grants based on income to enable them to purchase a home. The department allocated an additional $1 000 for buying furnishings. By 1973 this assistance for housing ceased and a program to provide mortgage rates at reduced levels for off-reserve housing applicants replaced it. In the early 1970s, in response to the increasing demand for affordable housing for urban Indians, a number of Indians in Toronto formed the Wigwaman Corporation under the direction of Clare Brant. The corporation secured federal funds to enable it to purchase houses for Indian families to rent and, whenever possible, purchase. The corporation then went further, sponsoring a second project to build an apartment complex for senior citizens of Indian ancestry. Working closely with the Native Canadian Centre of Toronto, the corporation obtained sufficient funding to construct such a complex, which officially opened in 1978.

To meet some of the needs of single women, another Indian group in Toronto founded Anduhyaun Incorporated, a Native women's residence. Verna Petronella Johnston, Josephine Beaucage, and Mildred Redmond were among the women of Indian ancestry responsible for its implementation and success. During this time, Vern Harper persuaded the Toronto Board of Education to recognize the Wandering Spirit Survival School (which he founded) to teach Indian youth in the city the ways of their ancestors and to have pride in their culture. Another survival school, similar in philosophy and programming, began at St. Charles, a village east of Sudbury. Indian parents and professionals connected to the Native Studies programs at Laurentian University in Sudbury initiated the experiment. At both schools, students learned Indian traditions and values in addition to the regular classroom curriculum. Social clubs sprang up such as the Nickle Belt Indian Club of Sudbury, and in Toronto, the North American Indian Club. In addition, Toronto was said to be the home of five Drum societies, each practising its own version of Indian religion.

Interest in Indians and their "traditional lifestyle" grew at an accelerated pace among North Americans during the 1960s and 1970s, particularly among young people who associated a positive stereotype of Indians with an increasing interest in the environment. Many Canadians continued to show interest in buying Indian craftwork for themselves, or as gifts to send overseas to relatives and friends. Some Indians took advantage of the renewed interest in their people and began businesses devoted to the sale of Indian arts and crafts. The Algonquians, a craft shop begun by Margaret Cozry, an Ojibwa from Parry Island, became a successful retail outlet in Toronto and replaced the dissolved Indian Crafts of Ontario. Craft shops also opened in North Bay, Parry Sound, Thunder Bay, and Timmins, usually in close association with friendship centres.

In the 1960s and 1970s Indians in Ontario developed a greater sense of "Indianness." Artists such as Daphne Odjig, Norval Morriseau, Samuel Ash, Blake Debassige, Francis Kagigi, Joyce and Joshim Kakegamic, Roy Thomas, Saul Williams, John Laford, Del Askewie, Fred Green, and the now-deceased artists Carl Ray, Benjamin Chee Chee, and Lloyd Caibaiosai succeeded in producing several distinctive Indian art styles. Other Ontario Indian

Non-Natives join in as the Saskatchewan Inter-Tribal Prairie Dancers beat a drum at the Mariposa Folk Festival on Toronto's Centre Island, Sunday, 8 July 1973.

artists working in the 1970s included Tom Hill, the late Arthur Shilling, and Robert Maracle. The stone carvings of Joseph Jacobs and the pottery of Olive Smith and her daughters are other examples of Indian artistic skills. In Red Lake the Kakegamic brothers of Sandy Lake, Ontario, with the assistance of Indian Crafts of Ontario, established Triple K, a silk-screen shop and gallery. A similar enterprise, Weneebaykok Limited, opened in Moosonee. In 1970, prior to the creation of these two organizations, Tom Peltier founded the Manitou Art Corporation. For several summers, young Indians interested in obtaining instruction in painting, music, and drama attended the school run by the corporation at Little Current on Manitoulin Island. Native writers in the 1960s and 1970s included the poet Duke Redbird, poet and playwright George Kennedy of Lac Seul, author and storyteller Basil Johnston of Cape Croker, Verna Petronella Johnston, Alma Greene, the late Wilfred Pelletier, and Tom Peltier. To encourage and further the creative talents of Indians, Jim Buller established the Association for Native Development in the Performing and Visual Arts in 1974. A creative outlet for aspiring Indian actors, dancers, and writers, it proved an immediate success.

In an attempt to revitalize Native religion, Wilfred Pelletier of Wikwemikong founded the Nishnabe Institute of Toronto. With the initial help of

Ojibwa artist Norval Morriseau, c. 1963.
Department of Indian and Northern Affairs, 04-02-05-10

the Anglican Church, it organized ecumenical conferences. The first assembly was held on the Crow Reservation in Montana in 1970. Thereafter, the participants gathered at the Stoney Indian Reserve, Morley, Alberta. These meetings brought together Indian religious leaders from many parts of North America to discuss their views of religion with Protestant clergy.

In 1970 the Department of Indian and Northern Affairs sponsored the first Cultural Conference for Indians of Canada. Many Indians attended, including some from Ontario. At this and subsequent meetings, the Indian delegates considered ways and means to develop, promote, and preserve their heritage. The second conference was convened at Kamloops, British Columbia. One of the many issues debated at this time was the "repatriation" of Indian cultural remains held in such institutions as the National Museum of Man (now the Canadian Museum of Civilization) and the Royal Ontario Museum.

### Projects for Aiding Indians

During this period, both levels of government and the private sector initiated various projects to "assist" Native people. A great deal of attention was paid to education. As late as the mid-twentieth century, delivery of education remained limited, and in the north practically non-existent. Yet as industrialization weakened the traditional economic base of Indian society and culture, a Western-style education became essential if one wished to participate in some way in the contemporary world.

From Confederation onward, the federal government encouraged Indian education, originally through funding church-run residential schools and mission day schools and later by building and staffing federally owned and maintained schools. The results, however, continued to be disappointing until the 1970s. The low level of academic achievement held back every community. In Ontario, as late as 1968, fewer than twenty Indians attended university. Largely as a consequence of Canada's post-war prosperity and the creation of a modern Canadian social welfare state, the federal Department of Indian Affairs negotiated with the provincial ministries of education in the early 1950s to improve Indian education. Too often teachers in Indian schools were poorly trained, autocratic, and unsympathetic in dealing with their pupils. The curriculum used in reserve schools paid little attention to the residents' culture or their history. The educators also continued to suppress the students' use of their Indian language.

Throughout the 1950s and 1960s both federal and provincial officials in Southern Ontario worked to increase the number of Indian reserve students in nearby provincial elementary schools. This necessitated negotiations between

A scene from the Fort Albany residential school, 6 December 1972.
Department of Indian and Northern Affairs, 06-12-06

the federal and provincial governments, as reserve residents were (and still are) exempt from provincial and municipal education taxes. Thus, the two levels of government had to devise an arrangement that would financially compensate local boards of education for the increase in student enrolment. Once federal money was forthcoming in the early 1960s, Indian children began to be bussed from their reserve homes to schools in nearby towns and villages. In most cases, the decision as to what age the children would be bussed depended largely on how far they had to travel. If the distances were too great, the authorities exempted students in the lower grades and allowed them to attend a reserve school. For older children, however, if no provincial school was located within bussing distance of the reserve, the federal government paid to board the students near one. The integration of Indian children into the provincial school system, however, had limited success. By the late 1960s and early 1970s, certain reserves again began to send their children to the elementary day school on the reserve.

Negotiations began also between Ottawa and Queen's Park for the transfer of additional federal monies to construct off-reserve Indian secondary schools. By the late 1950s two secondary schools, one at West Bay, Manitoulin Island, and the other in Brantford, were under construction. From the outset the explicit and implicit goal of educating the Indians at all levels was to wean them from their Native ways, remove them from the reserves, and change "brown children" into "white people." As literacy in English was the first priority of the Indian school system, English remained the language of instruction. No attempt was made to integrate Native values or languages in the philosophy, pedagogy, and curriculum in Indian classrooms.

In an attempt to find solutions to the many problems besetting Indian education, the Ontario Ministry of Education appointed Walter Currie, an Indian elementary school principal in Toronto, to its staff in 1967. Two more Indian staff were added following his departure, Al Bigwin, another elementary school principal in Toronto, and subsequently Keith Lickers, an elementary teacher from Six Nations. At the same time, the ministry scrutinized school texts to identify and excise racial slurs directed at Indians and other groups. During the 1970s the provincial government also sponsored inquiries into the state of education, including the education of Indians. The provincial government's task force on Indian education, established in 1974, held meetings throughout Ontario. The task force debated submissions from Indian communities (reserve or otherwise). These deliberations resulted in the creation in 1978 of the Ontario Council for Native Education. Federal support for Indian students in post-secondary education emerged as an important social policy in the late 1960s and expanded significantly throughout the 1970s and 1980s.

Bussing Indian students from Walpole Island, c. 1970.
Department of Indian and Northern Affairs, 06-18-06-10

The provincial government also worked to improve the training of teachers of Indian students. It sponsored in 1970, and for two subsequent summers, a five-week course for elementary schoolteachers entitled "Teachers of Indian Children," at Trent University. In the mid-1970s the ministry also produced two resource guides called *People of Native Ancestry*, the first for primary-junior classes and the second for intermediate. The third guide that was designed for senior classes appeared in the early 1980s. During the summers of 1974 and 1975, the Ministry of Education also sponsored a course for Indian teachers at Hamilton Teachers College in Hamilton, Ontario. Out of a total initial registration of 125 applicants, 88 students completed the program and received the ministry's permission to teach.

Another innovation in Indian education occurred in 1969 when Trent University initiated the first Indian studies program in Canada. Two years later, Trent formally established a Department of Native Studies in the Faculty of Arts and Science. With the blessing of the university senate and financial assistance from the Donner Canadian Foundation, Trent attracted an increasing number of Indian students from Ontario and elsewhere in Canada. At the same time, the university appointed Indians and Métis to academic positions in the newly created Department of Native Studies – Harvey McCue, Walter Currie, Ernest Benedict, Fred Wheatley, Marlene Castellano, Raoul McKay, and Joe Couture. Later Lakehead, Western Ontario, York, and Laurentian universities initiated special programs aimed at increasing the number of Indian students in their respective universities. Although the University of Toronto resisted instituting courses in Native studies, it provided scholarships for individuals of Amerindian ancestry.

Educational opportunities for the Indians of Northern Ontario lagged far behind those available in the south (see chapter 15). The limited instruction offered (to grade 8 and in some schools to grade 10) failed to prepare young people adequately for a meaningful place either in their own communities or in Canadian society off the reserve. Education beyond the reserve school could only be obtained by leaving one's family and community to attend secondary school, usually in the south. This could be a frightening experience. In an attempt to ease their transition, the Northern Lights Secondary School was established at Moosonee to allow Indian high school students to study in a familiar milieu. Also at Moosonee, the James Bay Education Centre was built to provide northern Indians with vocational skills to help them gain jobs in the south. Yet in spite of all these endeavours, much remained to be done. In the mid-1960s a concept known as community development gained widespread support.

*Community Development*

In 1964 the federal government brought together a number of Indians and non-Indians to discuss ways to improve life on Indian reserves. Out of this consultation came the concept of community development. Following intensive training sessions in Ottawa, the federal government appointed community development officers, or CDOs as they became known, to work with one or more Indian communities. In northwestern Ontario, for example, CDOs assisted in such projects as the Widjitiwin Corporation, a pulpwood operation that had begun in 1960, and the Amik Association, which (among other enterprises) assisted in the gathering and marketing of wild rice. Within two years, however, issues arose that led Ottawa to abandon the program and to dismiss its field staff. Dissension between the CDOs and the local Indian agents caused the federal government to become disillusioned with the idea of community development. Native leaders had already criticized the fact that most CDOs were non-Indians. Faced with this accusation, Ottawa began to assign Indians to these positions. The Native appointees, however, conducted affairs in their own style, not necessarily in accordance with Department of Indian Affairs directives. This led the federal government to cancel the program.

Two years after the federal government's community development program began in 1964, Ontario created, within the Department of Welfare and Social Services, the Indian Development Branch, later reorganized and renamed the Indian Community Secretariat, and then the Native Community Branch, within the Ministry of Citizenship and Culture. The Ontario government made funds available for a variety of economic and social programs. Free of the sometimes restrictive federal funding regulations, Ontario provided funds to Indian communities for a wide range of projects, usually ones deemed appropriate by the non-Indian rather than the Indian, such as recreational facilities for tourists. The provincial funding paid for parks, trailer camps, and marinas built on a number of reserves – at Dokis, Garden River, Kettle Point, Moose Deer Point, Nipissing, Parry Island, Rama, and Manitoulin Island.

In Northern Ontario the provincial government's game-management practices had a considerable impact. Previously, Ontario government officials relied solely on the enforcement of regulations pertaining to hunting, trapping, and fishing, but in the late 1940s they began to consult and cooperate with Indians to conserve wildlife and make the best use of the natural resources. The provincial government instituted registered traplines, which, it believed, would keep non-Indian trappers out of Northern Ontario, as well as encourage Indians to participate directly in the management of the game resources in their allotted territories. Shortly thereafter, provincial officials began commercial fisheries in many Indian communities throughout north-western Ontario to provide residents with an additional source of income.

While both levels of government attempted to improve Indian education and assist communities economically, the federal government did not lose sight of its long-term goal, the eventual termination of the Indian Act, and of the special status provided those under the act. In 1969 the federal government decided that the time had come to introduce what in the United States was called "termination." It announced its proposals in what became known as the 1969 White Paper.

## The White Paper

Following the Second World War many individuals, both in and out of government, had called for an examination of Canadian Indian policy. In 1946 a joint committee of the House of Commons and the Senate reviewed the Indian Act, first enacted in 1876. The committee's recommendations led to a complete revision of the act. The new act of 1951 enabled Indians to regain their rights to participate in their religious ceremonies (such as the potlatch and Sun Dance) and to drink in public establishments, such as bars and hotels. It ended compulsory enfranchisement, a sorry chapter in the history of government-Indian relations, which enabled the federal government to determine arbitrarily who would cease to be a legal Indian. Once enfranchised, individuals forfeited any rights available to status (legal) Indians from the federal government, including reserve land rights and any settlements arising from negotiations between the band and the government. The revised act allowed individual band councils more authority. While the assimilation of the Indian into the dominant society remained the federal government's stated goal, it would not be forced upon the Indians. Instead assimilation would be a gradual process brought about through the transfer of the responsibility for status Indians from the federal to the provincial level.

In 1964 the Indian Affairs Branch commissioned a social and economic study of seventy Indian reserves within Canada. Harry B. Hawthorn, an anthropologist at the University of British Columbia, headed the research team that produced the two-volume *Survey of the Contemporary Indians of Canada* (the Hawthorn Report). The Hawthorn Commission recommended that the special status of the Indian be maintained, that provincial governments extend more services to Indians, and that those Indians living in remote and isolated areas be prepared for life in urban settings.

In 1965 the Indian Affairs Branch created a number of advisory councils throughout Canada composed of representatives of bands within specified areas. It hoped that these councils would assist in finding solutions to the many problems facing the Indians. The department divided Ontario into nine districts. The Indian bands within each district then elected one representative to the Provincial Indian Advisory Council. The Union of Ontario Indians, a provincial Indian organization, appointed the additional member. The ten members of the Ontario advisory council then selected four from their council to sit on the National Indian Advisory Board.

Three years later the federal government launched a series of national meetings, eighteen in all. As part of the consultation process, Ottawa distributed a booklet entitled *Choosing a Path* to every Indian band in Canada and to as many status Indian homes as possible. The booklet included fourteen questions on a variety of issues but chiefly on the revision of the Indian Act. It posed questions in such a way as to elicit a simple "yes" or "no" answer. The federal government released its White Paper on Indian policy five months after the meetings ended in January 1969.

The White Paper included five major proposals. Parliament would repeal the Indian Act. Second, the federal government would transfer to the provinces federal services to Indians such as health, education, and welfare. Third, the Crown would relinquish title to Indian reserve lands, transferring it to the Indians. Fourth, the federal government would eliminate the Department of Indian and Northern Affairs by the year 1974. Finally, the federal government would continue to honour the lawful obligations contained in the treaties, such as annuity payments. Additional proposals announced the delivery of special programs to aid those bands furthest behind economically.

The White Paper came as a shocking surprise to Indian people. Although the federal government had listened to them, it clearly had already decided upon a specific course of action. Many Native leaders regarded the proposals as assimilationist, the stated goal of the federal government during the previous one hundred years. They saw the assignment of title to reserve lands to individual Indians, or to the band, as an effort to eliminate Indian reserves, an attempt to duplicate the American government policy of termination a decade earlier. Some Indians believed that the proposed transfer of services from Ottawa to the provinces would lead to the abrogation of a historic and legal relationship with the federal government assured through treaties and surrenders of Indian lands and by the terms of the British North America Act (Constitution Act, 1867).

Provincial and national Indian leaders and segments of the non-Indian population challenged the government's plan. Within a year, the Indian Association of Alberta presented to the federal government a paper called *Citizens Plus* that contained a comprehensive and critical condemnation of the White Paper. This critique, the so-called "Red Paper," succeeded in attracting public attention to the Indians' discontent. The Manitoba Indian Brotherhood also responded, in a brief entitled *Wahbung, Our Tomorrows*. The Union of Ontario Indians issued a short statement that reflected the concerns of the authors of the previous two documents. In September 1969, 200 delegates representing the Union of Ontario Indians gathered in Port Arthur, now part of Thunder Bay, to discuss the federal government's new policy towards Indians. At the same time the Association of Iroquois and Allied Indians sent a brief to Ottawa presenting their objections to the White Paper. Strong Indian opposition led the federal government to withdraw its proposals.

## The Private Sector

In the 1950s and early 1960s a growing number of individuals expressed concern for the status and welfare of Indians. In Toronto in 1960 non-Indians and a few Indians founded the Indian-Eskimo Association, which had a board of directors that included Indians and non-Indians from across Canada. As a national body, the IEA, as it came to be known, promoted the political development of Indians and Inuit, and brought to public attention their rich cultural heritage as well as their contemporary concerns. On occasion the IEA acted as a lobby for various Indian issues that arose in the House of Commons. It published a monthly newsletter and convened numerous workshops, conferences, and meetings that directly involved Indians. The IEA served as a training ground for many Indian politicians and community leaders. In 1968 it elected Omer Peters as its president. He was the first IEA president of Indian ancestry.

During this period the Rural Learning Association, an association that emerged in the 1950s in Ontario through the merger of the Ontario Folk Schools and the Farmers Forum, promoted interest in Indian issues by non-Indians. Borrowing heavily on the concept of "folk-schools" that originated in Denmark, the association encouraged its members, as a means of creating change, to exchange and discuss common rural issues.

The qualified success of the concept encouraged some members to wonder if the concept had any application among Indian communities. Certainly the reserves' geographic location qualified them as rural, even though the agricultural base was absent. Marshall Noganosh from the Rama Reserve served as an Indian member of the association and with his assistance and guidance, the first Indian folk-school, organized by the Rural Learning Association, took place in 1963 in Wiarton, Ontario. Encouraged by its success, the association recruited Beatrice McCue from the Georgina Island Reserve and Frank Shawbadees from the Saugeen Reserve as members, and asked them to serve as the organizers of Ontario Indian folk-schools.

Numerous folk-schools took place throughout the remainder of the 1960s and during the 1970s. The organizers selected locations in the province that maximized participation by reserve residents. In the north this usually meant reserves central to several others. Buoyed by the success and interest of participants, the association organized Indian youth folk-schools to enable young Indians on reserves to gather and discuss their shared problems and concerns.

Other organizations held study sessions and conferences in an attempt to learn more about Indians and how the non-Indian might help solve the "Indian problem." Among the many other forums for citizen involvement was the Canadian Association for Indian and Eskimo Education, which before its demise in 1972 held several meetings in Toronto and Ottawa to explore the Indian problem. The Ontario Women Teacher's Association in 1965 provided funds to investigate the images of Canadian Indians portrayed in Ontario school texts.

Throughout the 1960s and 1970s the media made the public increasingly aware of contemporary Indian issues. Newspapers paid more and more attention to Indians, although at times in an overly melodramatic fashion. Books and articles by ethnologists, archaeologists, and other scholars helped to educate those in the academic community and beyond to a more realistic understanding of the Indians' history, culture, and present problems.

## Indian Responses

By the mid-twentieth century divisions arose within many Indian communities on the question of to what degree people must adjust to the dominant Euro-Canadian society. The deterioration, or in some communities the virtual disappearance, of Indian institutions and values brought about by the impact of Western culture, coupled with the continued attempt to assimilate Indian societies, exacerbated the conflict. By mid-century, many of those who wished to adopt Euro-Canadian ways had come to devalue their ancestors' values and beliefs, and to accept the ethnocentric views and "wisdom" of the Euro-Canadian. Some, moreover, sought to minimize the loss of their cultural integrity by attempting to blend the "new" with the "old," as when they fused Christian religious concepts with Native ones, or when they maintained Christian ideas side by side with Indian spiritual beliefs.

With their traditional institutions in disarray and with the increase of the pressures associated with modernization, many Indians became bewildered and confused. The use of traditional values and beliefs diminished among many. By 1960 the usage of Mohawk, Cree, and Ojibwa, the three main languages in use in Ontario, had seriously declined.

But in the 1960s and 1970s an awakening began on many reserves and among the urban Indian population. Civil-rights protests in the United States and an incipient back-to-the-earth movement in North America (which used the positive stereotype of the Indian as a conservationist as a model for the movement) propelled many young Indians into political activities and stimulated them and others to re-examine their histories and cultures more positively than ever before.

## Political Activity

Throughout the 1960s, Aboriginal people in Canada gained in political strength. In 1960 they secured the federal franchise without having to give up their Indian status. The following year the federal government tacitly recognized the reality of Canadian Indian aspirations and distinctiveness when it began to support financially the National Indian Council, formed in 1961. The delegates, consisting of treaty/registered Indians, Métis, and non-status Indians, elected a governing body at the council's first meeting. The council provided an arena for the Indians and Métis of Canada to meet at the national level to discuss common problems. Within a few years, however, it faced a variety of problems. Some felt that the council was too remote from the majority of Indians to speak for them. The legal constraints on federal financial support constituted a more serious problem. By law the Indian Affairs Branch could support only those individuals designated as "Indian" under the Indian Act. In 1964 two new national organizations were born, the National Indian Brotherhood (now the Assembly of First Nations), representing the status and treaty Indians, and the Native Council of Canada, representing the Métis and non-status Indians.

Encouraged by the presence of national organizations, Ontario Indians created their own local political structures, a development that was not really new, since such organizations had emerged from time to time in the past. The Union of Ontario Indians, which at least theoretically represented all the treaty/registered Indians residing within the province, re-emerged in the early 1960s. Both the federal and provincial governments saw the value of a single provincial Indian organization with which they could deal regarding the many issues raised by Indian people. The two levels of government provided funds to maintain the administrative structure of the Union and to assist it in conducting surveys and studies of the Indians' condition. But they gave little money for programs and projects at the grass-roots level. The chiefs of those bands that joined the Union elected the executive, which consisted of a president, vice-president, secretary, and treasurer. Over the years, a number of able individuals, such as Omer Peters, Wilmer Nadjiwon, Fred Plain, Andrew Rickard, and Del Riley, served as president.

With few exceptions, the Union executive worked with both the federal

In the Hiawatha Council Hall, Rice Lake, Ontario, on the occasion of a federal by-election, 31 October 1960. *From left to right:* Lawrence Salleby; Chief Ralph Loucks, deputy returning officer; Lucy Musgrove, poll clerk; Eldon Muskrat, poll constable. On the table is a bust of Chief Tecumseh. These were the first votes cast by a status Indian community since the right to vote in federal elections was extended to all adult Indians on 31 July 1960.
National Archives of Canada, PA-123915

and provincial governments to develop and promote a constructive approach to the ills and needs of its members. Armed with government funds, whose use was often designated by government planners and consultants, the Union of Ontario Indians initiated a variety of economic and social studies of reserve communities. These programs gave ample evidence that the Union responded more to the advice and ideas of non-Indians than to its own membership. The studies sponsored by the Union and the types of consultants appointed often reflected Western theories about social and economic planning and development, concepts foreign to the cultural and historical background of the Native people for whom they were intended. The philosophy and operation of the union reflected little that could be remotely identified as Indian in a traditional sense, either Algonquian or Iroquoian.

The Union of Ontario Indians fell on hard times within a decade. The position of the Union was weakened by its restrained reply to the White

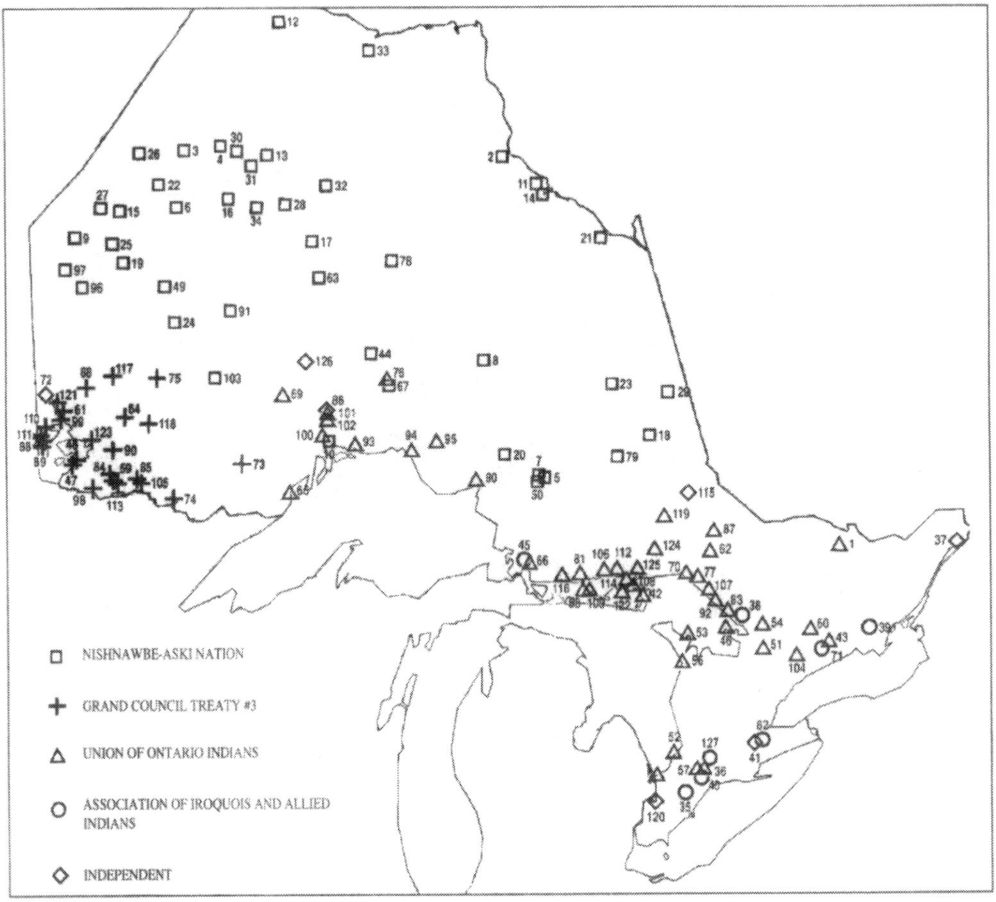

Map 16.1
Indian Association Membership
The associations, located by number on Maps 16.1 and 16.2, are identified by name
on page 403.

From "First Nations, Ontario," prepared by Indian and Northern Affairs Canada and Ontario Native Affairs
Secretariat, 1991. Revised 1993

Paper. The Union soon found itself coming under increasing criticism from its
own membership throughout the province. Furthermore, insufficient field
staff to cope with the increasing workload, together with the "isolation" of the
executive in its Toronto headquarters, added to its problems. In these circumstances, the Union began to fall apart, but it did not disappear. It has continued to maintain a limited presence, owing in part to various claims, such as

**Algonquin**
1  Algonquins of Golden
   Lake

**Cree**
2  Attawapiskat
3  Bearskin Lake
4  Big Trout Lake
5  Brunswick House
6  North Caribou Lake
7  Chapleau Cree
8  Constance Lake
9  Deer Lake
10  Flying Post
11  Kashechewan
12  Fort Severn
13  Kasabonika Lake
14  Albany
15  Kee-Way-Win
16  Kingfisher Lake
17  Lansdowne House
18  Matachewan
19  McDowell Lake
20  Missanabie Cree
21  Moose Factory
22  Muskrat Dam
23  New Post
24  New Slate Falls
25  North Spirit Lake
26  Sachigo Lake
27  Sandy Lake
28  Summer Beaver
29  Wahgohsing
30  Wapekeka
31  Wawakapewin
32  Webequie
33  Weenusk
34  Wunnumin

**Delaware**
35  Moravian
   of the Thames
36  Munsee-Delaware
   Nation

**Iroquois**
37  Mohawks of
   Akwesasne
38  Wahta Mohawk
39  Mohawks of the
   Bay of Quinte
40  Onyota'a:ka
41  Six Nations of the
   Grand River:
   Bay of Quinte Mohawk
   Bearfoot Onondaga
   Delaware
   Konadaha Seneca

Lower Cayuga
Lower Mohawk
Niharondasa Seneca
Oneida
Onondaga Clear Sky
Tuscarora
Upper Cayuga
Upper Mohawk
Walker Mohawk

**Odawa**
42  Wikwemikong

**Ojibway (Chippewa)**
43  Alderville
44  Aroland
45  Batchewana
46  Beausoleil
47  Big Grassy
48  Big Island
49  Cat Lake
50  Chapleau Ojibway
51  Georgina Island
52  Chippewas of Kettle
   and Stony Point
53  Chippewas of Nawash
54  Chippewas of Rama
55  Chippewas of Sarnia
56  Chippewas of Saugeen
57  Chippewas of
   the Thames
58  Cockburn Island
59  Couchiching
60  Curve Lake
61  Dalles
62  Dokis
63  Eabamatoong
64  Eagle Lake
65  Fort William
66  Garden River
67  Ginoogaming
68  Grassy Narrows
69  Gull Bay
70  Henvey Inlet
71  Hiawatha
72  Wabaseemoong
73  Lac des Mille Lacs
74  Lac La Croix
75  Lac Seul
76  Long Lake #58
77  Magnetawan
78  Marten Falls
79  Mattagami
80  Michipicoten
81  Mississauga
82  Mississaugas of the
   Credit
83  Moose Deer Point

84  Naicatchewenin
85  Nicickousemenecaning
86  Lake Nipigon Ojibway
87  Nipissing
88  Northwest Angle #33
89  Northwest Angle #37
90  Ojibways of
   Onegaming
91  Osnaburgh
92  Wasauksing
93  Pays Plat
94  Ojibways of the Pic
   River
95  Pic Mobert
96  Pikangikum
97  Poplar Hill
98  Rainy River
99  Anishinabe of
   Wauzhushk Onigum
100  Red Rock
101  Rocky Bay
102  Sand Point
103  Saugeen Nation
104  Mississaugas of
   Scugog Island
105  Seine River
106  Serpent River
107  Shawanaga
108  Sheguiandah
109  Sheshegwaning
110  Iskutewisakaygun #39
   Independent First
   Nation
111  Shoal Lake #40
112  Sagamok Anishinawbek
113  Stanjikoming
114  Sucker Creek
115  Temagami
116  Thessalon
117  Wabauskang
118  Wabigoon Lake
   Ojibway Nation
119  Wahnapitae
120  Walpole Island
121  Washagamis Bay
122  West Bay
123  Whitefish Bay
124  Whitefish Lake
125  Whitefish River
126  Whitesand
42  Wikwemikong

**Potawatomi**
127  Caldwell
83  Moose Deer Point
120  Walpole Island

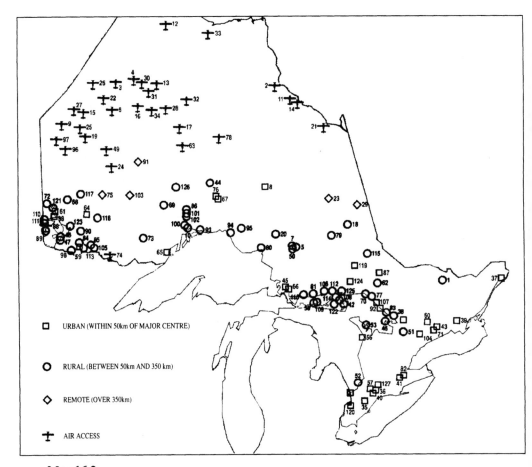

Map 16.2
Access to Amerindian Communities
(refer to list on page 403)
From "First Nations, Ontario," prepared by Indian and Northern Affairs Canada and the Ontario Native Affairs
Secretariat, 1991. Revised 1993

those relating to land, hunting, and fishing rights and Indian burials, which its members have lodged against the federal and provincial governments.

As the Indians became disillusioned with the Union of Ontario Indians, member bands withdrew and established regional organizations throughout the province. In the north, Grand Council Treaty No. 3 came into existence, based on antecedents that had lain dormant for many years. Although it ostensibly spoke for all of the Indians of northwestern Ontario, it really represented only those in the Kenora area, where the headquarters were located. Then in 1973, Grand Council Treaty No. 9 was created by Andrew Rickard, a former grand chief of the Union of Ontario Indians, to represent the Native people of Northern Ontario, with headquarters in Timmins.

The work of Grand Council Treaty No. 9 (now the Nishnawbe Aske Nation) provides an example, similar to that of Grand Council Treaty No. 3, of what Indians are attempting to do to assist their members. The vast distances separating the member bands (scattered as they are from the shores of James Bay west to the Manitoba border, and from the height of land just north of Lake Superior to the tidal flats of Hudson Bay) have hampered its work. The costs in both time and money to serve its widely dispersed member communities are considerably greater than those incurred by Southern Ontario organizations. Despite these difficulties, Grand Council Treaty No. 9 made considerable headway in the 1970s in representing the interests of the Northern Algonquians. As a lobby group, Treaty No. 9 participated in the Porter Commission on hydro-electric power; it led Indian opposition to plans by Queen's Park to divert several rivers in Northern Ontario; and it was instrumental in persuading the Ontario government to create the Royal Commission on the Northern Environment. First chaired by Mr. Justice Patrick Hartt, the commission, which included representatives from the federal and provincial governments and various northern Indian communities, conducted a full-scale enquiry into the needs and special problems facing the environment and citizens of Northern Ontario. Subsequently, Justice Hartt headed the Indian Commission of Ontario, created in 1978 to look into a variety of issues of concern to Indians: the numerous land claims, the gathering of wild rice, and Indian fishing rights in northwestern Ontario.

Grand Council Treaty No. 9, in time, developed a number of social and economic programs for the Native inhabitants of Northern Ontario, including the establishment of the newspaper *Wa Wa Tay News* in Sioux Lookout, an Indian Policing Program, and an alcohol and drug abuse program under the direction of Beatrice Shawanda. Although Grand Council Treaty No. 9, like its sister organizations in Ontario, was often hampered by insufficient funds, it became for a time a political force on behalf of the Native peoples of Northern Ontario, one to be reckoned with by Queen's Park.

A number of Indian groups living in Southern Ontario abandoned the Union of Ontario Indians and established independent organizations. In 1969 one group of dissidents created the Association of Iroquois and Allied Indians, which represented primarily the Indians living in southwestern Ontario. Another splinter group included a number of former officers of the Union of Ontario Indians and Indian reserves, composed of either Algonquians or Iroquoians in the area of Georgian Bay and farther east. In 1971 they formed the Regional Association for Indian Development. Alarmed by the ominous acronym of the new organization, RAID, bureaucrats in Toronto persuaded the leadership, mostly moderate chiefs and councillors, to change its name to Central Ontario Regional Association for Indian Development, or as it came to be known, CORAID. Not politically oriented, the organization concerned itself with the economic and social development of its member communities.

The federal Department of Indian and Northern Affairs and other government agencies, both federal and provincial, funded treaty or registered Indians to organize and operate political organizations such as the Union of Ontario Indians or Grand Council Treaty No. 9. Those of Indian ancestry, whether full-bloods or Métis, who were not registered or enrolled in a band received no support or special consideration. But this changed in the early 1970s when the Department of the Secretary of State recognized these forgotten peoples and provided funds for the Métis and non-status Indians of Ontario and elsewhere within Canada to create political organizations. Thus, the Ontario Métis and Non-status Indian Association was founded officially in 1972 with headquarters in Toronto (later located in Sault Ste. Marie). By 1975 almost all Indian and Métis communities in Ontario belonged to one or more provincial organization. In 1973 the Ontario Native League for Youth was created. The friendship centres sponsored additional organized activities for young Native people. Each summer they brought together a number of young people from different reserves across Ontario for one or two weeks of cultural activities.

The rapid growth of provincial political organizations led a number of potential local Indian politicians to leave their reserves to join the provincial and national organizations. At the same time, other qualified individuals moved away because of the chronic shortage of full-time employment on the reserves. This changed, however, during the late 1970s, as tribal councils emerged and bands acquired more administrative responsibilities, which created new job opportunities in managing band affairs. But those young people who had gone away to school for several years or more and had gained the necessary qualifications to fill the newly created positions often faced a handicap in reserve politics. They might well be considered "outsiders" having no rapport with the local people or understanding of their unique problems.

Sharp divisions existed with each community. Rival factions often prevented potential candidates from running for the position of either chief or councillor. These factions, similar to those found in any other small Ontario community, were based on church affiliation, family relationships, progressive or conservative attitudes, and, occasionally, geographic location in the community.

One other factor has worked against the smooth functioning of the political process: the reliance on federal funding for the planning and development of political structures on the reserves. During the 1970s, however, the federal government attempted to change this situation by granting the bands greater economic freedom. The Department of Indian and Northern Affairs introduced a program of core funding in an effort to improve the operation of reserve councils and the programs they "initiated." Core funding provided monies for the salaries of permanent office employees such as secretaries and band administrators, and this enabled many reserves to secure a stable group of administrative personnel to attend on a daily basis to the affairs of the band and its members. On the other hand, nepotism sometimes has been the guiding principle in the selection of those who hold these positions, a practice that often has intensified the factionalism already present in the community.

*Communication*

The publication of the White Paper and the flurry of responses to it brought the Indians to recognize the need to improve communications between their different organizations, reserves, and settlements throughout Ontario. In 1969 there were some 180 reserves in Ontario inhabited by treaty or registered Indians, perhaps thirty Métis (and/or non-status Indian) settlements, and urban Indians numbering in the thousands. In addition, some thirty Indian organizations and friendship centres were in operation at this time.

During the 1970s several Indian newspapers and newsletters began publication. The Union of Ontario Indians distributed information about Indian concerns, first through its newspaper *Calumet*, an enterprise that waxed and waned over several years, due mainly to a miniscule budget and a small, although dedicated, staff. *Ontario Native Experience* eventually replaced *Calumet* (which had ceased publication by 1970), but in time it shared the same fate. *Ontario Indian* then came into being, a glossy, smartly designed monthly newsmagazine. But it too fell on hard times and ceased publication in 1982. *Sweetgrass* took its place, but not for long. Also from Toronto came *Toronto Native Times*, a publication of the Canadian Indian Centre begun in 1970. The most successful newspaper in the 1970s was the *Wa Wa Tay News*, published since 1974 in Sioux Lookout by Grand Council Treaty No. 9.

Perhaps the most ambitious Native communication project began in 1971. In that year the Ontario Educational Communications Authority (OECA) submitted a plan to a joint U.S.-Canada team working on a project known as the Communications Technology Satellite. The OECA plan called for the establishment of satellite communication between northern Indian reserve communities. Rich in possibilities and exciting in concept, the plan, had it been successful, would have put several Indian communities of Northern Ontario in the vanguard of space-age communication. Unfortunately, underfunding by the Ontario government so curtailed the completion of a final plan that OECA officials felt compelled to terminate the experiment. Nevertheless, considerable improvement in local communication in the north has been achieved through the introduction of FM radio. One of the first stations to be established was at Big Trout Lake in 1974. Since then several other northern Indian communities have followed suit. With an emphasis on local programming, these radio broadcasts provide northern reserve residents with news and entertainment.

*Resistance*

During several centuries of contact between the original inhabitants of America and the Western Europeans, Indians have responded to the presence of Europeans in many ways. Their responses to the pressures brought to bear by the Europeans have taken many forms.

For many, perhaps too many, the use and abuse of alcohol has been one of the most lingering and dangerous forms of response yet adopted. Despite its probable presence among Indians in North America well before the arrival of the European, alcohol in the form of strong, powerful grain alcohol, which served for several centuries as the lubricant that greased the fur trade, gradually acquired a stranglehold on Indian behaviour. Obtained by gift or trade, liquor's intoxicating effects among Indians quickly became evident to all, especially traders who realized the special attraction liquor held for so many of the Indians with whom they traded. Alcohol rapidly established itself as an important commodity in the fur trade and just as rapidly became a factor in the social and cultural lives of Indians throughout the Americas.

For many Indian cultures, alcohol became the medium that enabled individuals to forsake the normal social sanctions that governed daily behaviour. In Ontario the vagaries of a harsh, often unrelenting environment, where survival was at the best of times fraught with the unknown and determined by the forces of nature, helped to create values governing collective social behaviour that maximized cooperation and social harmony and minimized interpersonal aggression. Interpersonal tensions and conflicts were sublimated or redirected by most tribes in Ontario in subtle and non-direct forms of aggression to ensure that the tribes' existence continued in the face of a relentless and hostile environment.

Occasional releases from this necessary restraint took at least two forms: several specific ceremonies, which may have emerged for the sole purpose of providing relief, and certain forms of behaviour when individuals no longer controlled their actions (as in the case of *wiitiko* – when individuals who became "possessed" by an evil spirit threatened individuals and entire groups with physical violence and, occasionally, death). Over time, however, alcohol became the principal means by which individuals could override the sanctions governing interpersonal behaviour and aggression or aggressive acts. Alcohol also over time became a unique method by which individuals could express, verbally or non-verbally, their anger at, and hostility towards, the dominant white forces surrounding them.

Despite its effectiveness as a means of subverting internal values regarding interpersonal relations, alcohol quickly became a serious liability, one threatening the stability of family and reserve life. It forced many young and older adults to live their lives in poverty and despair or to become recidivists guilty of misdemeanours and crimes committed while intoxicated.

The image of the "drunken Indian" became well known in North America in the 1960s and 1970s. For political purposes Canadian and American politicians used the stereotype to play on the disgust that such a portrayal fosters among the electorate. Churchpeople, too, used the image to justify and condone the paternalism and lack of consultation frequently evident in their policies and programs dealing with Indians. Journalists tended to publish stories about Indian misdemeanours involving alcohol but neglected to report on the many accomplishments of Indians who became lawyers, doctors, nurses, artists, teachers, authors, and engineers. The advent of movies and later television did little to change the image of the Indian. The movie or television screen Indian (and few were true Indians, Jay Silverheels – Tonto – from the Six Nations being an exception) was generally cast either as the "noble" or, even worse, as the "drunken blood-thirsty" savage, two stereotypes that still linger. Although not all Indians drank excessively, it took only a few to perpetuate the stereotype. Still, many Indians escaped the harsh realities of the world in which they lived through the use of alcohol.

A major contributing factor to Indians' substance abuse in the 1960s and 1970s lay in the increasing economic disparity between the reserve community and the more affluent dominant society. Lack of vocational skills, lack of job experience, and little formal education created serious problems for Indians who wished to enter the mainstream society. What little regular income many Native families received came from government programs, such as welfare and family assistance, and seasonal employment. The fact that Indians had the highest birth rate of any group in Canada (about three times the national average) increased the stress. Providing physical and social benefits to reserve residents under these conditions proved all but impossible. In response to these conditions, many Indians continued to drink, some to excess, and by the late 1960s, perhaps more than before, Indians were killing themselves through alcohol abuse. The protest was in danger of becoming a death wish. Drownings, fatal injuries resulting from car accidents and physical violence, deaths from freezing or trains, suicides, and infant mortality were often alcohol related. For the youth, the lack of recreational programs and useful employment, on and off the reserve, encouraged an increase in the use of alcohol and other drugs. On reserves, especially those in the north, the incidence among the young people aged ten to twenty-five of drug abuse and hallucinogenic "highs" brought about by sniffing gasoline, nail polish remover, glue, and aerosols reached epidemic proportions during the 1970s. It resulted in suffering and even death, imprisonment in provincial institutions, and a dramatic increase in community tensions.

The Indians' desire for acceptance as equals within Canadian society, coupled with the pressures for them to become "white," has over the years resulted in unbearable strains. The prevailing values in Native society in such sensitive areas as child rearing, interpersonal communication, aggression, materialism, and status tend to be quite different and often opposed to those held by the dominant society. As acceptable or worthwhile as the goal of assimilation might have been (and certainly not all Indians felt that it was), it remained simply unattainable. Regardless of how many institutions and traditions Indians were encouraged or forced for a time to abandon, they continued to remain true to their own heritage.

Surprisingly, much more of the old Indian heritage has been retained than one might expect. Dependence by many Indians on country food or food from the land, whether it be fish, fowl, animals, berries, or medicinal plants, has helped to maintain this attitude. Institutions such as the Longhouse religion among the Iroquois and, to a lesser extent, the Midewiwin among the Ojibwa continued to be a part of the lives of many Indians. A rich body of myths, stories, and legends flourished in the 1960s and 1970s throughout both Algonquian and Iroquoian communities across Ontario. Indian languages continued to be spoken on (and off) many reserves, whether Cree, Ojibwa, Mohawk, or Odawa (Ottawa). The geographical isolation of many reserves contributed to the retention of an Indian ideology and outlook, and a perpetuation of values associated with the family, community, and other aspects of Indian life.

In the 1960s Native political militancy surfaced again as it had in the past. Representatives of the British Columbia–based Native Alliance for Red Power specifically targeted the Royal Ontario Museum, which had mounted an exhibition of paintings of Plains Indians by the early nineteenth-century German artist Karl Bodmer. The titles had been translated into English (but not by any member of the museum staff, since it was an imported show). Unfortunately, the translator used in his texts the term "savage" for Indian, a demeaning term, one repulsive to Native people. The Red Power protesters demanded that the exhibition be dismantled. The confrontation ended amicably, however, after a lengthy discussion. The majority of Ontario Indians, especially the elders, rejected the Red Power advocates' violent rhetoric.

In the mid-1960s another protest surfaced in northwestern Ontario, approximately 1 600 kilometres from Toronto. Indians from Kenora and the surrounding reserves, assisted by a number of non-Native supporters, organized a protest march in 1965 to dramatize the racial discrimination and lack of economic opportunity that existed in northwestern Ontario. The demonstration gained national publicity. In an attempt to defuse the situation, the federal Department of Citizenship and Immigration, through the University of Manitoba, instituted a series of lectures and workshops in Kenora in the hope that each side might acquire a better understanding of the other.

The Kenora protest march of 1965 did not bring about unity among the Indians of Ontario. The Kenora situation was (and still is) a local issue and nothing more. This has been true throughout Ontario, where each Native group has had its own local problems to solve as best it could. Another example was the attempted removal from a school on the Six Nations Reserve in 1968 of several Iroquois pupils by their parents in protest against the provincial educational curriculum that neglected Native people and their way of life. Other isolated incidents occurred. In 1971 CTV aired *The Taming of the Canadian West*, a television documentary that Indians considered derogatory. They succeeded in having it withdrawn from further presentation. During the same year, the Akwesasne Mohawk on the Canadian side blockaded the bridge to the United States in an attempt to force government recognition of the terms of Jay's Treaty that gave the Indians the right to bring goods duty-free across the border. A few years later the Akwesasne Mohawk worked to obtain pollution controls to safeguard the quality of the waters adjacent to the reserve.

A more serious confrontation occurred in Ottawa in 1974, one involving Indians from across Canada. A violent struggle with the RCMP broke out at the conclusion of a national protest that was called the Native People's Caravan. Indian activists, assisted by white radical elements rumoured to have been funded by outside revolutionary bodies, made an unsuccessful attempt to storm the House of Commons. Tempers flared and reason vanished as the attackers clashed with the Mounties.

Native activists again surfaced in the fall of 1974, this time in Kenora. In the nine years since the Kenora protest march of 1965, the Indians of the region had become dismayed and angry over the failure of both levels of government to respond adequately to the potential problem of mercury pollution for the residents of Grassy Narrows and Whitedog reserves. Another point of contention arose over Anicinabe Park in Kenora, which they felt had been taken unfairly from them. Indians wanted it returned to allow them to create a place of refuge for the Indians within, and about, Kenora. Negotiations with the municipal government failed to satisfy their demands. Those who

The occupation of Anicinabe Park, Kenora, 30 July 1974.

occupied Anicinabe Park came from a group called the Ojibway Warriors Society and also included several members of the American Indian Movement (AIM). According to the press, the occupation of the park threatened from time to time to erupt into armed conflict between the Indian radicals and the Ontario Provincial Police. The dispute ended when a leader of AIM was given permission to enter Canada and act as chief negotiator.

Two years later a Toronto chapter of the urban-based American Indian Movement came into existence with financial aid from the Quakers. Like its parent organization in the United States, the Toronto chapter of AIM was composed mainly of a small number of young urban Indians who embraced the politics of rhetoric and confrontation. They identified the causes of tension, even though widespread support among the Indians of Ontario might be lacking. The Toronto AIM chapter became identified with a highly emotional issue, the excavation of a Neutral Indian burial ground at Grimsby, Ontario, by the Royal Ontario Museum during the winter and summer of 1976–77. Del Riley, the president of the Union of Ontario Indians, made a citizen's arrest of Walter Kenyon, who was in charge of the excavation, for desecration of a burial ground. For some time the Union had requested that non-Christian burials be treated with the same respect and dignity as those of Christians. Bureaucratic delay in arriving at a resolution prompted AIM members to take over the office of the museum's chief archaeologist. They demanded that the bones be immediately reburied. A settlement was reached in due course but not until well after AIM had decamped.

The politics of confrontation did not accomplish all that the radical element had set out to do. Without any doubt, however, they did make the white establishment, at least momentarily, stop and think about what it has been doing. Through the media these tactics helped to make the public aware of the fact that the Indians might well have problems in coping with the Great White Father. In general, though, the radical Indian element received little support from the majority of Ontario's Indians in the 1970s.

Another result of the newcomers' presence has been conflict among the Iroquoians, between the "short hairs" ("progressives," that is, of the Christian faith) and the "long hairs" ("traditionalists," that is, of the Longhouse religion), both on the reserve and in urban centres. In 1959 and again in 1968 the traditionalists of the Six Nations reserve near Brantford occupied the band council hall in Ohsweken. By these means they sought to reverse what they conceived to be a gradual deterioration of the long-standing relationship between the Iroquois "nation" and the British Crown. They did not concede that the Canadian government had any jurisdiction over them. The long hairs also felt the hereditary chiefs should be reinstated and the elected council, imposed on the reserve residents in 1924, dissolved.

Chief Joseph Logan is seen (on the left with his hat in his hand) telling his followers to yield to the RCMP and leave the Six Nations Council House, from which the hereditary council had evicted the elected council one week earlier, March 1959.

Another contentious issue arose in the late 1960s: the right of Indian women to remain status Indians under the Indian Act once they married men who were neither treaty nor registered. According to the Indian Act, these women automatically became non-status and lost their treaty rights. Several Indian women of Ontario who lost their status in this manner claimed that this provision of the act violated the Canadian Bill of Rights of 1960. Jeannette Lavell and Yvonne Bedard, both victims of the system, took the matter to the Supreme Court of Canada, which decided against them in 1973.

In the 1970s many Indian women who retained their status rights opposed reinstatement of those who had lost theirs. They pointed out that those Indian women who married non-treaty men were well aware that when they did so they would forfeit their treaty rights. In addition, Indian bands were concerned about the financial impact this change would have on their communities. Extra monies would be needed for housing, schooling, and medical services, and there would no doubt be many other unforeseen costs. By the early

Teacher Jeannette Corbiere gives Jennifer Peltier instruction in Ojibwa at the opening of a ten-week language course for fifteen children aged eight to fourteen at Toronto's Canadian Indian Centre, March 1968. In December 1970 Jeannette Corbiere would lose her Indian status when she married a non-Native. Her unsuccessful case to regain her treaty rights reached the Supreme Court of Canada three years later.

*Globe and Mail* (Toronto), 12 March 1968, neg. no. March 11, 1968, 9-A, L9984

1980s, however, pressure on this matter had increased to such an extent that a parliamentary subcommittee recommended that those parts of the Indian Act that discriminated against Indian women be amended. Parliament did exactly this in 1985, with the passage of Bill C-31. Upon application nearly 100 000 Indian women and children throughout Canada have been reinstated and have gained the benefits of treaty or registered Indians. Reinstatement as a status Indian entitles the individual to receive free medical care, subsidies for housing and higher education, as well as exemption from all federal and provincial taxation on any monies earned on any reserve.

## Land Claims

In the 1970s Indian land claims and the fulfilment of treaty obligations became ever more prominent as Indians went to court over these issues. When this happened, Canadians' image of the Indian as a passive, poor, unemployed, and uneducated welfare recipient began to change. In Ontario the Kenora march of 1965, the Lavell-Bedard case in 1973 before the Supreme Court of Canada, the caution registered in 1973 by the Teme-augama Anishnabai on about 4 000 square miles (10 360 square kilometres) in the Lake Temagami area, the Anicinabe Park occupation in 1974, and the Cornwall Bridge blockade that same year are but several examples of escalating Indian litigation and activism. All of this contributed to a change in the perception held by non-Native Canadians of the Indian as a passive recipient of Western culture. In fact, Indian land claims in the 1970s prompted the Ontario Ministry of Natural Resources to establish the Office of Indian Resource Policy to examine and research the validity of Indian land claims and to deal with other natural resources issues of concern to the Indian people of Ontario.

## Conclusion

The 1970s saw a most positive dimension for the image of the Indian developing in the creative arts – painting, writing, and drama – and in such other fields as law, education, and medicine. The achievements of these Native men and women helped to bring about a shift, albeit gradual, in the public's perception of the Indian in the 1970s, one that was decidedly less negative and less damaging than that held by the non-Indian in the past.

The same cannot always be said for the Indian's self-perception. The years of enforced dependence on the Department of Indian Affairs for direction in most aspects of reserve life, together with the paternalistic approach taken by those officials of the department who considered Indians nothing more than children, produced a numbing effect in the 1960s and 1970s, robbing many Indians of their self-respect and dignity. The success of those who have made it in the mainstream of Canadian society did not, as a rule, filter back to the reserve, and if it did, many Indians did not identify with these professionals as positive models. Furthermore, chronic unemployment, inadequate housing, meagre recreational facilities, and a substandard education – all legacies of the paternalistic policies of Indian Affairs – still persisted in the 1970s, especially on the reserves. The harsh and unrelenting social and economic conditions that scarred most, if not all, Ontario reserves worsened. This inhibited the re-establishment of a positive self-image for many Indian people.

Although Native politicians made headlines in the 1970s with such contentious issues as land claims and Indian rights, at the reserve level the issues of immediate concern to the local residents took a back seat. The failure of the provincial organizations to bolster the self-image of their constituents and to attract widespread provincial grass-roots support is the result of several factors. First, the organizations' leaders have maintained a strong commitment to their own constituents, not to the association's entire membership. This has tended to perpetuate the factionalism so characteristic of small communities and to prevent the serious consideration of issues common to all reserves, such as economic development, appropriate educational standards, and political autonomy. Second, the distance that separated the Indian politicians from the reserve residents in the 1970s reduced the latter's faith in, and support for, those they "theoretically" put in office. The majority of band members believed that their organizations lacked the power to improve local conditions. Since most, if not all, funding for the operation of the reserves came from federal and/or provincial sources, many doubted the ability of their Indian organizations to change local conditions. Furthermore, a substantial segment of the Indian population in Ontario in the 1970s no longer lived on reserves but rather in urban centres, a population that the Indian organizations have in the past ignored. Thus, a large part of the Indian population in the 1960s and 1970s had little, if any, reason to support or take an interest in those bodies that are primarily concerned with reserve Indians.

International events and an increased concern by Canadians of all political persuasions for greater social and political justice would stimulate profound changes among Ontario Indians and their leaders over the next two decades. This period would see enormous changes in Indian politics, leading to the First Nations' inclusion in the constitutional talks of 1992 and the recognition of their inherent right to self-government.

# 17 *Aboriginal Ontario: An Overview of 10 000 Years of History*

DONALD B. SMITH

## Introduction

All authorities agree that the original inhabitants of what is now Ontario lived on this continent for at least 10 000 years before the Europeans' arrival. Archaeologists and Native elders, however, disagree about the place of origin of these first peoples. Most archaeologists believe that human beings migrated to the Americas from Siberia, although the scientists disagree among themselves as to when this might have taken place. On the other hand, many Canadian Indian elders accept as a spiritual truth, revealed in their sacred stories, dreams, and visions, that their distant ancestors originated here. Awareness of this spiritual view is essential if one is to gain an understanding of Canada's First Nations, for it reveals their attachment to the land and to their cultures. It explains Aboriginal Canada's refusal to disappear.

Five hundred years ago the First Nations alone inhabited what is now Canada. In addition to cultural differences, great linguistic diversity existed. The Native peoples belonged to eleven linguistic families (one Inuit and ten Indian), split into over fifty languages. The area now known as Ontario contained members of three Amerindian linguistic families (the Algonquian, Iroquoian, and Siouan) at the moment of European contact. There was no idea of a pan-Indian unity; individuals belonged to their own family, their band, their nation, but did not look upon themselves and all the other Aboriginal groups as one. A sense of a pan-Indian identity across the continent would only truly arise in the last half of the twentieth century.

Canada's Amerindian population at the moment of European contact can best be classified according to cultural areas, as this approach recognizes how climate and regional resources influence the development of societies and technologies. The land mass known today as Canada included six such areas, areas that parallel almost exactly the country's geographical regions: the Arctic, Subarctic, Northwest Coast, Plateau, Plains, and Northeast (or Eastern Woodlands). Ontario included a large section of the Northeast cultural area, the most densely populated, as well as a portion of the Subarctic cultural area with its much smaller population density.

European contact came first in northeastern North America with Europeans who came to dry cod at staging points along the Atlantic coast, and later in the interior with the early fur traders. The establishment of Quebec as a fur-trading post in 1608 and the expansion of the colony of New France in the St. Lawrence valley extended the relationship. Like the English in their colonies to the south, the French believed in the superiority of European civilization and were determined to Christianize and to assimilate the Amerindians. In the St. Lawrence valley the French entrusted this task to Roman Catholic religious orders who established missions for them.

Throughout the entire French regime, only about a hundred marriages between French and Christianized Amerindians occurred in the St. Lawrence River valley, and only a small number of these unions had issue. In contrast, many French *coureurs de bois* married Amerindian women in the interior, away from the European settlements. Several hundred mixed-bloods lived at the junction of the Red and Assiniboine rivers (present-day Winnipeg) by 1815, where they became known as the Métis. A small mixed-blood community existed at Sault Ste. Marie by the early nineteenth century. The mixed-blood descendants of the Hudson's Bay Company's British employees and their Amerindian wives are referred to in several Canadian history texts as "the Country-Born." Today both groups are together termed "Métis."

Inadvertently the Europeans had brought with them diseases that the Native peoples in the Americas had never before experienced – contagious diseases like smallpox, measles, and tuberculosis. These diseases reduced American Indian and Inuit populations drastically. In some areas of the Americas the resulting death rates among Amerindians after European contact are estimated to have reached 90 to 95 percent. While few figures are available for present-day Ontario, the mortality was extremely high, as the statistics provided by the Jesuits among the Huron in the 1630s prove (see chapter 4).

After the conquest of New France in 1760, the English altered some aspects of French colonial policy. The Royal Proclamation of 1763 recognized that Indian lands must be purchased by the Crown before settlement could proceed. This had to be done with the consent of the band concerned – in other words, treaties had to be negotiated. The British upheld the Royal Proclamation in Ontario before Confederation, and in the 1870s the Canadian government extended the policy to the lands it controlled in the area known today as the Prairie provinces. Reserves were set aside by treaty or by various forms of Crown grant in the Maritime colonies. After Confederation in 1867 the Canadian government also formed reserves by special arrangement with individual bands.

For approximately a century after Confederation, non-Aboriginal Canadians believed, as did the early French and English before them, in the necessity of eradicating Amerindian identity and cultures. Systematically the new Canadian state set in motion a policy to eliminate all aspects of Indian traditional life – economic, religious, and social – at variance with the customs of the dominant society. Under the Indian Act of 1876, federally appointed Indian agents gained control over Indian band councils and Christian missionaries were formally entrusted to run the day schools on the reserves and the residential or boarding schools. With only minor modifications this policy lasted into the 1950s.

The federal officials hoped that this system would encourage the "successful" Indians to enfranchise, or to give up their legal Indian status and become part of the general community, becoming full citizens like the Métis. Adult male Indians judged by a special board of examiners to be educated, free from debt, and of good moral character could, upon application, gain their share of their group's lands. Once they obtained the same rights and privileges as every other Canadian citizen, these individuals, their wives, and their descendants became "enfranchised." They ceased to be status Indians, that is, persons classified as Indian under the Indian Act. They gained clear title to their land, which ceased to be part of the reserve. Indian women also lost their status when they married non-status men. Their children, too, were classified as non-status.

Federal administrators hoped that enfranchisement would proceed at a rapid rate and that in the space of several generations the reserve communities in Ontario and throughout Canada would disappear. In actual fact few status Indian men applied, and the vast majority enfranchising in the mid-twentieth century were Indian women who did so involuntarily. In Canada in the 1962–63 fiscal year, for instance, over 650 Indians enfranchised, most of them women who married non-Indians.

Two beliefs predominated at the turn of the century, the first being the assumption of the superiority of European culture and morality. The so-called higher races had a responsibility to aid the "less advanced" to rise to the Europeans' standard. The Amerindian, Inuit, and Métis communities must blend into the larger, "superior" population of European descent. Secondly, it was generally believed that the Amerindians must assimilate for their own good, as they were a vanishing people, a race declining in numbers due to their exposure to a "higher" civilization. Indeed, up to the 1920s, the population of many groups fell because of the continued onslaught of communicable diseases introduced by European contact, such as tuberculosis and smallpox. As late as 1932 Diamond Jenness, the distinguished Canadian anthropologist, wrote in his *Indians of Canada*: "Doubtless all the tribes will disappear. Some will endure only a few years longer, others, like the Eskimo, may last several centuries."[1]

Many Aboriginal people in lightly populated northern areas, distant from large non-Native settlements, escaped the full weight of the Indian Act, the principal federal statute regulating all aspects of status Indian life. Enacted in 1876 and subsequently amended over the years, the act suppressed many Indian traditions and extended the federal government's authority over all aspects of reserve residents' lives. Until the mid-1940s little attention, however, was paid to isolated Amerindian groups like the Cree Indians around James Bay. The military intervention in northern Canada during the Second World War and the search for the north's natural resources in the late 1940s and 1950s brought more Native people into contact with non-Native outsiders.

A new attitude towards Canada's Aboriginal population emerged after the Second World War. Social scientists discredited completely the pseudo-scientific race theory of the late nineteenth and early twentieth centuries. This removed any basis for regarding Amerindians, Inuit, and Métis as inferior peoples. In 1951 Parliament revised the Indian Act greatly, reducing the amount of bureaucratic control over status Indians. By the 1950s it also became very clear that the number of Aboriginal people in Canada was increasing, rather than decreasing. Once said to be a dying race, the Amerindians and Inuit had become the fastest-growing group in Canada, doubling in number every thirty years. Faced with an expanding status Indian population, the federal government in 1969 moved to speed up the assimilation of the Indians, its goal for over a century. It put forward a policy known as the "White Paper," which aimed at repealing the Indian Act of 1876 and terminating the legal distinctions between status Indians and Canadians. It proposed that the Indians lose their special status within the Canadian constitution and become full citizens like everyone else. Secondly, it recommended that the federal government transfer all its administrative responsibilities to the provinces.

The reaction of the status Indians to the White Paper proved so great that the federal government withdrew it in 1971. Amerindian groups refused both to give up their special status and to forget the debt owed them for providing land to the newcomers. Contrary to the government's intent, the White Paper contributed to the formation of the first truly pan-Indian coalition across Canada. Modern Aboriginal politics in Canada, then, dates back to 1969. The new provincial and national Aboriginal organizations effectively fought the White Paper and subsequently the federal government withdrew it. After great pressure from Native groups, the federal government and the provinces also recognized the Aboriginal peoples' "existing" Aboriginal rights in the new Canadian constitution of 1982. The Métis, for the first time, joined the Indians and the Inuit in securing identification in 1982 as Aboriginal peoples.

The assimilationist policy lasted right into the early 1970s, but what once seemed impossible has now been achieved: Aboriginal rights have gained legal acceptance. The determination of the Aboriginal peoples not to disappear and the emergence of a new, officially multicultural Canada have led to a different model. Our new constitution and several recent Supreme Court decisions have repudiated the old policies of working to absorb the Indians, Inuit, and Métis into the dominant society.

In 1990 the Indians, Inuit, and Métis constituted an estimated 4 to 5 percent of Canada's total population. Roughly 500 000 people in Canada have Indian status and are under the Indian Act. Ontario has the largest number of individuals who have status under the federal Indian Act, over 100 000 persons. A marked increase came in 1985 when the federal government allowed those who had enfranchised to regain their Indian status. The greatest number of beneficiaries were Indian women (and their immediate descendants) who had involuntarily lost their status through marriage to non-Indians. Approximately 100 000 individuals across Canada have gained status under the new regulation. A common estimate in 1990 of the number of Métis, individuals who have both European and Aboriginal ancestry but no Indian status, is about 500 000. The Inuit numbered about 32 500 in 1990. In the sparsely populated northern areas of the western provinces, in large sections of Northern Ontario and Quebec, and in the Northwest Territories and much of the Yukon, the Aboriginal people are the majority.

The Indian, Inuit, and Métis peoples of Canada have gained the attention of Canadians and a prominent place on the public policy agenda. Elijah Harper, an Aboriginal member of the Manitoba legislature, played a key role in June 1990 in killing the proposed Meech Lake constitutional accord. He and many other Native people believed the accord ignored Native issues. In the summer of 1990 the troubles at Oka, near Montreal, led to an even greater awareness of Aboriginal grievances. The police assault on a Mohawk road blockade, set up to prevent the town of Oka from expanding a golf course onto land claimed by the Indians, led to a two-and-a-half-month armed standoff. It ended only through Canadian army intervention.

Since the summer of 1990, action on Native grievances has moved at the fastest rate in Canadian history. The federal government has announced that it seeks to settle land claims by the year 2000. It established in the summer of

1991 a "Royal Commission on Aboriginal Peoples" to examine Native issues. Four of the seven commissioners are Aboriginal people. Ontario has recognized the Aboriginal peoples' inherent right to self-government. At last Aboriginal concerns have earned a place on the provincial and national agenda, alongside those of other Canadians.

So much research remains to be done on the history of Ontario's First Nations. *Aboriginal Ontario*, it is hoped, will be but the first of many syntheses and studies of this vitally important subject.[2]

## NOTES

1  Diamond Jenness, *The Indians of Canada* (Ottawa 1932), 264
2  Two recent new studies are Bruce W. Hodgins, Shawn Heard, and John S. Milloy, eds., *Co-Existence? Studies in Ontario-First Nations Relations* (Peterborough, Ont. 1992); and David T. McNab, "Aboriginal Land Claims in Ontario," in *Aboriginal Land Claims in Canada: A Regional Perspective*, ed. Ken Coates (Toronto 1992), 73–99.

# Bibliography
## A List of Titles on the History of Aboriginal Ontario

**Bibliographical and Manuscript Guides**

Abler, Thomas S., Douglas E. Sanders, and Sally M. Weaver. *A Canadian Indian Bibliography 1960–1970*. Toronto: University of Toronto Press 1974

Canada Geographical Board. *Handbook of Indians of Canada* (Appendix of the 10th Report of the Geographic Board of Canada). Ottawa: King's Printer 1913

Helm, June. *The Indians of the Subarctic: A Critical Bibliography*. Bloomington: Indiana University Press 1979

Kidd, Kenneth E., Edward S. Rogers, and Walter A. Kenyon. *Brief Bibliography of Ontario Anthropology*. Art and Archaeology Occasional Paper no. 7. Toronto: Royal Ontario Museum 1964

Krech, Shepard, III. *Native Canadian Anthropology and History: A Selected Bibliography*. Rev. ed. Winnipeg: Rupert's Land Research Centre 1994

McCardle, Bennett. *Archival Records Relating to Native People in the Public Archives of Canada and National Library of Canada and the National Museum of Man: A Thematic Guide*: Ottawa: Treaties and Historical Research Centre, Indian and Northern Affairs Canada 1985

Morrison, James. *First Nations at the Archives: A Guide to Sources in the Archives of Ontario/Les Peuples autochtones dans les archives. Un guide des sources aux Archives de l'Ontario*. Toronto: Ministry of Culture and Communications 1992

Murdoch, George Peter. *Ethnographic Bibliography of North America*. 4th rev. ed. 5 vols. New Haven: Human Relations Area File Press 1975

Ontario. *Akwesasne to Wannumin Lake: Profiles of Aboriginal Communities in Ontario*. Toronto: Ontario Native Affairs Secretariat and Ministry of Citizenship 1992

Snow, Dean R. *Native American Prehistory: A Critical Bibliography*. Bloomington: Indiana University Press 1979

Surtees, Robert J. *Canadian Indian Policy: A Critical Bibliography*. Bloomington: Indiana University Press 1987

Tanner, Helen Hornbeck. *The Ojibwas: A Critical Bibliography*. Bloomington: Indiana University Press 1976

Tooker, Elisabeth. *The Indians of the Northeast: A Critical Bibliography*. Bloomington: Indiana University Press 1978

Weinman, Paul L. *A Bibliography of the Iroquoian Literature*. Partially annotated. Albany: State University of New York 1969

**General Works**

Abel, Kerry, and Jean Friesen, eds. *Aboriginal Resource Use in Canada: Historical and Legal Aspects*. Winnipeg: University of Manitoba Press 1991

Barman, Jean, Yvonne Hébert, and Don McCaskill, eds. *Indian Education in Canada*. Vol. 1: *The Legacy;* vol. 2: *The Challenge*. Vancouver: University of British Columbia Press 1988

Bartlett, Richard H. *Indian Reserves and Aboriginal Lands in Canada: A Homeland*. Saskatoon: University of Saskatchewan Native Law Centre 1990

Brown, Jennifer S., and Jacqueline Peterson, eds. *The New Peoples: Being and Becoming Métis in North America*. Winnipeg: University of Manitoba Press 1985

Buckley, Helen. *From Wooden Ploughs to Welfare: Why Indian Policy Failed in the Prairie Provinces*. Montreal and Kingston: McGill-Queen's University Press 1992

Canada. *Indian Treaties and Surrenders from 1680 to 1890*. 2 vols. Ottawa: Queen's Printer 1891

Canada. *Indian Treaties and Surrenders from 1680 to 1902*. Ottawa: King's Printer 1912

Coates, Ken, ed. *Aboriginal Land Claims in Canada: A Regional Perspective*. Toronto: Copp Clark Pitman 1992

Comeau, Pauline, and Aldo Santin. *The First Canadians: A Profile of Canada's Native People Today*. Toronto: James Lorimer and Co. 1990

Cox, Bruce Alden, ed. *Native People, Native Lands: Canadian Indians, Inuit and Métis*. Ottawa: Carleton University Press 1988

Cumming, Peter A., and Neil H. Michenberg. *Native Rights in Canada*. 2d ed. Toronto: Indian-Eskimo Association in Canada/General Publishing Co. 1972

Dickason, Olive Patricia. *Canada's First Nations: A History of Founding Peoples from Earliest Times*. Toronto: McClelland & Stewart 1992

Dupuis, Renée. *La question indienne au Canada*. Louiseville, Qué.: Les Éditions du Boréal 1991

Dyck, Noel. *What Is the Indian 'Problem': Tutelage and Resistance in Canadian Indian Administration*. St. John's, Nfld.: Institute of Social and Economic Research 1991

Fisher, Robin, and Kenneth Coates, eds. *Out of the Background: Readings on Canadian Native History*. Toronto: Copp Clark Pitman 1988

Francis, Daniel. *The Imaginary Indian: The Image of the Indian in Canadian Culture*. Vancouver: Arsenal Pulp Press 1992

Frideres, James S. *Native Peoples in Canada: Contemporary Conflicts*. 3d ed. Scarborough Ont.: Prentice-Hall Canada 1988

Getty, Ian, A.L. and Antoine S. Lussier, eds. *As Long as the Sun Shines and Water Flows: A Reader in Canadian Native History*. Vancouver: University of British Columbia Press 1983

Grant, John W. *Moon of Wintertime: Missionaries and the Indians of Canada in Encounter Since 1534*. Toronto: University of Toronto Press 1984

Hall, Tony. *1784–1984, Celebrating Together? Native People and Ontario's Bicentennial*. Manitoulin Island, Ont.: Plowshare Press 1984

Harris, R. Cole, ed. *Historical Atlas of Canada*, vol. 1: *From the Beginning to 1800*. Toronto: University of Toronto Press 1987. Published in French under the title *Atlas historique du Canada*, vol. 1: *Des origines à 1800*

Helm, June, ed. *Handbook of the North American Indians*, vol. 6: *Subarctic*. Washington, D.C.: Smithsonian Institution 1981

Jenness, Diamond. *The Indians of Canada*. Ottawa: King's Printer 1932

Kehoe, Alice B. *North American Indians: A Comprehensive Account*. 2d ed. Englewood Cliffs, N.J.: Prentice-Hall 1992

Krotz, Larry. *Indian Country: Inside Another Canada*. Toronto: McClelland & Stewart 1990

Leighton, Douglas, and Patricia Sawchuk. *A Profile of Native People in Ontario*. Toronto: Ministry of Citizenship and Culture 1983

Leslie, John, and Ron Maguire, eds. *The Historical Development of the Indian Act*. Ottawa: Treaties and Historical Research Centre, P.R.E. Group, Indian and Northern Affairs, 1978. Published in French under the title *Histoire de la loi sur les Indiens*

Maracle, Brian. *Crazy Water: Native Voices on Addiction and Recovery*. Toronto: Viking 1993

McMillan, Alan D. *Native Peoples and Cultures of Canada: An Anthropological Overview*. Vancouver: Douglas & McIntyre 1988

Miller, J.R. *Skyscrapers Hide the Heavens: A History of Indian-White Relations in Canada*. Toronto: University of Toronto Press 1989; rev. ed. 1991

———, ed. *Sweet Promises: A Reader on Indian-White Relations in Canada*. Toronto: University of Toronto Press 1991

Morris, J.L. *Indians of Ontario*. 1943; Toronto: Department of Lands and Forests 1964

Morrison, R. Bruce, and C. Roderick Wilson, eds. *Native Peoples: The Canadian Experience*. Toronto: McClelland & Stewart 1986

Morse, Bradford W., ed. *Aboriginal Peoples and the Law: Indian, Métis and Inuit Rights in Canada*. Ottawa: Carleton University Press 1985

Nin.da.waab.jig. *Minishenhying Anishnaabe-aki. Walpole Island: The Soul of Indian Territory*. Windsor, Ont.: Commercial Associates/Ross Roy 1987

Patterson, E. Palmer, II. *The Canadian Indian: A History Since 1500*. Toronto: Collier Macmillan Canada 1972

Peterson, Jacqueline, and Jennifer S.H. Brown, eds. *The New Peoples: Being and Becoming Métis in North America*. Winnipeg: University of Manitoba Press 1985

Petrone, Penny, ed. *First People: First Voices*. Toronto: University of Toronto Press 1983

Richardson, Boyce. *People of Terra Nullius: Betrayal and Rebirth in Aboriginal Canada*. Vancouver: Douglas & McIntyre 1993

Satzewich, Vic, and Terry Wotherspoon. *First Nations: Race, Class, and Gender Relations*. Toronto: Nelson Canada 1993

Slattery, Brian. *Ancestral Lands, Alien Laws: Judicial Perspectives on Aboriginal Title*. Studies in Aboriginal Rights, no. 2. Saskatoon: University of Saskatchewan Native Law Centre 1983

Smith, Dan. *The Seventh Fire: The Struggle for Aboriginal Government*. Toronto: Key Porter Books 1993

Smith, Derek, ed. *Canadian Indians and the Law: Selected Documents 1663–1972*. Toronto: McClelland & Stewart 1975

Steegmann, A. Theodore, Jr., ed. *Boreal Forest Adaptations: The Northern Algonkians*. New York: Picnum Press 1983

Tanner, Helen Hornbeck, ed. *Atlas of Great Lakes Indian History*. Norman: University of Oklahoma Press 1987

Trigger, Bruce G., ed. *Handbook of North American Indians*, vol. 15: *Northeast*.
    Washington, D.C.: Smithsonian Institution 1978
———. "Indians and Ontario's History," *Ontario History* 74, no. 4 (December 1982):
    246–57
Washburn, Wilcomb E., ed. *Handbook of North American Indians*, vol. 4: *History of
    Indian-White Relations*. Washington, D.C.: Smithsonian Institution 1988
Woodland Cultural Centre. *Council Fire: A Resource Guide*. Brantford, Ont.: Woodland
    Cultural Centre 1989
Woodland Indian Cultural Educational Centre. *Warriors: A Resource Guide*. Brantford,
    Ont.: Woodland Cultural Centre 1986
York, Geoffrey. *The Dispossessed: Life and Death in Native Canada*. Toronto: Lester &
    Orpen Dennys 1989

## The Amerindians before European Contact

Dawson, K.C.A. *Prehistory of Northern Ontario*. Thunder Bay: Thunder Bay Historical
    Museum 1983
Ellis, Chris J., and Neal Ferris, eds. *The Archaeology of Southern Ontario to A.D. 1650*.
    Occasional Publication of the London Chapter, Archaeological Society, no. 5 (1990)
McGhee, Robert. *Ancient Canada*. Ottawa: Canadian Museum of Civilization 1989.
    Published in French under the title *Le Canada au temps des envahisseurs*
Wright, J.V. *Ontario Prehistory: An Eleven-Thousand-Year Archaeological Outline*.
    Ottawa: National Museum of Man 1972. Published in French under the title *La
    préhistoire de l'Ontario*
———. "Ontario Prehistory." Canada's Visual History series, vol. 45. National Museum
    of Civilization and the National Film Board of Canada. Published in French under the
    title *La préhistoire de l'Ontario*

## First Contact between the Amerindians and the Europeans

Dickason, Olive Patricia. *The Myth of the Savage: And the Beginnings of French
    Colonization in the Americas*. Edmonton: University of Alberta Press 1984.
    Translated from English by Jude Des Chênes, *Le Mythe du Sauvage*. Sillery, Qué.:
    Les Éditions du Septentrion 1993
———. "Concepts of Sovereignty at the Time of First Contacts." In L.C. Green and Olive
    P. Dickason, *The Law of Nations and the New World*, 141–295. Edmonton:
    University of Alberta Press 1989
Dickinson, John, and Brian Young. "Chapter One: Native Peoples and the Beginnings of
    New France to 1650." In John Dickinson and Brian Young, *A Short History of
    Quebec*. 2d ed. Toronto: Copp Clark Pitman 1993. Published in French under the title
    *Brève histoire socio-économique du Québec*
Dobyns, Henry F. *Their Numbers Became Thinned: Native American Population
    Dynamics in Eastern North America*. Knoxville: University of Tennessee Press 1983
Krech, Shepard, III, ed. *Indians, Animals, and the Fur Trade: A Critique of "Keepers of
    the Game."* Athens: University of Georgia Press 1981
Martin, Calvin. *Keepers of the Game: Indian-Animal Relationships and the Fur Trade*.

Berkeley: University of California Press 1978

McGhee, Robert. *Canada Rediscovered*. Ottawa: Canadian Museum of Civilization 1991. Published in French under the title *Le Canada au temps des aventuriers*

Thornton, William. *American Holocaust and Survival: A Population History Since 1492*. Norman: University of Oklahoma Press 1987

Trigger, Bruce G. *Natives and Newcomers: Canada's "Heroic Age" Reconsidered*. Kingston and Montreal: McGill-Queen's University Press 1985. Published in French under the title *Les Indiens, la fourrure et les Blancs. Français et Amérindiens en Amérique du Nord*

————. *The Indians and the Heroic Age of New France*. Canadian Historical Association Historical Booklet, no. 30. Rev. ed. Ottawa: Canadian Historical Association 1989. The original edition (1977) is available in French.

**The First Nations and the French and English, 1608–1760**

Axtell, James. *The Invasion Within: The Contest of Cultures in Colonial North America*. New York: Oxford University Press 1985

Bailey, Alfred G. *The Conflict of European and Eastern Algonkian Cultures 1504–1700*. 2d ed. Toronto: University of Toronto Press 1969

Champlain, Samuel de. *The Works of Samuel de Champlain*, ed. H.P. Biggar. 6 vols. Toronto: Champlain Society 1922–36

Delâge, Denys. *Le Pays Renversé. Amérindiens et Européens en Amérique du Nord-Est 1600–1664*. Ville Saint-Laurent, Qué.: Les Éditions du Boréal 1985. Translated from the French by Jane Brierley, *Bitter Feast: Amerindians and Europeans in Northeastern North America, 1600–64*. Vancouver: University of British Columbia Press 1993

Havard, Gilles. *La Grande Paix de Montréal de 1701. Les voies de la diplomatie franco-amérindienne*. Montréal: Recherches amérindiennes au Québec 1992

Jacobs, Wilbur R. *Wilderness Politics and Indian Gifts: The Northern Colonial Frontier, 1748–1763*. Lincoln: University of Nebraska Press 1966

Jaenen, Cornelius J. *Friend and Foe: Aspects of French-Amerindian Cultural Contact in the Sixteenth and Seventeenth Centuries*. Toronto: McClelland & Stewart 1976

————. *The French Relationship with the Native Peoples of New France and Acadia*. Ottawa: Research Branch, Indian and Northern Affairs Canada 1984. Published in French under the title *Les relations franco-amérindiennes en Nouvelle-France et en Acadie*

Jennings, Francis. *The Ambiguous Iroquois Empire: The Covenant Chain Confederation of Indian Tribes with English Colonies from Its Beginnings to the Lancaster Treaty of 1744*. New York: W.W. Norton and Co. 1984

————. *Empire of Fortune, Crowns, Colonies, and Tribes in the Seven Years War in America*. New York: W.W. Norton and Co. 1988

————, ed. *The History and Culture of Iroquois Diplomacy: An Interdisciplinary Guide to the Treaties of the Six Nations and Their League*. Syracuse: Syracuse University Press 1985

Kinietz, W. Vernon. *The Indians of the Western Great Lakes, 1615–1760*. Ann Arbor: University of Michigan Press 1940

Richter, Daniel K. *The Ordeal of the Longhouse: The Peoples of the Iroquois League in the Era of European Colonization*. Chapel Hill, N.C.: University of North Carolina Press 1992

Richter, Daniel K., and James H. Merrell, eds. *Beyond the Covenant Chain: The Iroquois and Their Neighbors in Indian North America, 1600–1800*. Syracuse: Syracuse University Press 1987

Thwaites, Reuben G., ed. *The Jesuit Relations and Allied Documents*. 73 vols. Cleveland: Burrows Brothers Co. 1896–1901

White, Richard. *The Middle Ground: Indians, Empires and Republics in the Great Lakes Region, 1650–1815*. Cambridge: Cambridge University Press 1991

**The First Nations and the British, 1760–1867**

Allen, Robert S. *The British Indian Department and the Frontier in North America, 1755–1830*. Department of Indian Affairs and Northern Development, Parks Canada, National Historic Parks and Sites Branch, Canadian Historic Sites: Occasional Papers in Archaeology and History, no. 14. Ottawa: Information Canada 1975

——. *His Majesty's Indian Allies: British Indian Policy in the Defence of Canada, 1774–1815*. Toronto: Dundurn Press 1993

Brown, Jennifer S.H. *Strangers in Blood: Fur Trade Families in Indian Country*. Vancouver: University of British Columbia Press 1980

Cadieux, Lorenzo, éd. *Lettres des Nouvelles Missions du Canada, 1843–1852*. Montréal: Les Éditions Bellarmin 1973

Calloway, Colin G. *Crown and Calumet: British-Indian Relations, 1783–1815*. Norman: University of Oklahoma Press 1987

Devens, Carol. *Countering Colonization: Native American Women and Great Lakes Missions, 1630–1900*. Berkeley: University of California Press 1992

Edmunds, R. David. *Tecumseh and the Quest for Indian Leadership*. Boston: Little Brown and Co. 1984

Graham, Elizabeth. *Medicine Man to Missionary: Missionaries as Agents of Change among the Indians of Southern Ontario, 1784–1867*. Toronto: Peter Martin Associates 1975

Hall, Tony. "Native Limited Identities and Newcomer Metropolitanism in Upper Canada, 1814–1867." In *Old Ontario: Essays in Honour of J.M.S. Careless*, ed. David Keane and Colin Read, 148–73. Toronto: Dundurn Press 1990

Hodgetts, J.E. "Indian Affairs: The White Man's Albatross." In *Pioneer Public Service: An Administrative History of the United Canadas, 1841–1867*, 205–25. Toronto: University of Toronto Press 1955

Kelsay, Isabel Thompson. *Joseph Brant 1743–1807: Man of Two Worlds*. Syracuse: Syracuse University Press 1984

Leslie, John F. *Commissions of Inquiry into Indian Affairs in the Canadas, 1828–1858*. Treaties and Historical Research Centre, Research Branch, Corporate Policy, Indian Affairs and Northern Development Canada. Ottawa 1985

Peckham, Howard H. *Pontiac and the Indian Uprising*. 1947; Chicago: University of Chicago Press 1961

Slight, Benjamin. *Indian Researches; or, Facts Concerning the North American Indians, including Notices of their Present State of Improvement in their Social, Civil and*

*Religious Condition: with Hints for their Future Advancement.* Montreal: J.E.L. Miller 1844

Smith, Donald B. *Sacred Feathers: The Reverend Peter Jones (Kahkewaquonaby) and the Mississauga Indians.* Toronto: University of Toronto Press 1987

Stanley, George F.G. *The War of 1812: Land Operations.* Canadian War Museum Historical Publication, no. 18. Toronto: Macmillan 1983

Sugden, John. *Tecumseh's Last Stand.* Norman: University of Oklahoma Press 1985

Surtees, Robert J. *Indian Land Surrenders in Ontario, 1763–1867.* Research Branch Corporate Policy, Indian and Northern Affairs Canada. Ottawa 1984

———. *Manitoulin Island Treaties.* Treaties and Historical Research Centre, Indian and Northern Affairs Canada. Ottawa 1986. Published in French under the title *Les Traités Manitoulin*

———. *The Robinson Treaties.* Treaties and Historical Research Centre, Indian and Northern Affairs Canada. Ottawa 1986. Published in French under the title *Les Traités Robinson*

Taylor, John Leonard. *Indian Band Self-Government in the 1960s: A Case Study of Walpole Island.* Ottawa: Indian and Northern Affairs Canada 1984

Van Kirk, Sylvia. *Many Tender Ties: Women in Fur Trade Society, 1670–1870.* Winnipeg: Watson and Dwyer 1986

White, Richard. *The Middle Ground: Indians, Empires and Republics in the Great Lakes Region, 1650–1815.* Cambridge: Cambridge University Press 1991

## The First Nations within Canada, 1867–1969

Coates, Kenneth S., and William R. Morrison. *Treaty Research Report: Treaty Five (1875–1908).* Treaties and Historical Research Centre, Indian and Northern Affairs Canada. Ottawa 1986. Published in French under the title *Rapport de recherche sur les traités: Traité Cinq*

Daniel, Richard C. *A History of Native Claims Processes in Canada, 1867–1979.* Research Branch, Department of Indian and Northern Affairs. Ottawa 1980. Published in French under the title *Les réglements des revendications des autochtones du Canada, 1867–1979*

Daugherty, W.E. *Treaty No. 3.* Treaty Research Report, Treaties and Historical Research Centre, Indian and Northern Affairs Canada. Ottawa 1986. Published in French under the title *Rapport de recherche sur les traités: Traité trois*

Daugherty, Wayne, and Dennis Madill. *Indian Government under Indian Act Legislation, 1868–1951.* Research Branch, Department of Indian and Northern Affairs. Ottawa 1980. Published in French under the title *L'administration indienne en vertu de la législation relative aux Indiens, 1868–1951*

Gaffen, Fred. *Forgotten Soldiers.* Penticton, B.C.: Theytus Books 1985

Harring, Sidney L. "'The Liberal Treatment of Indians': Native People in Nineteenth Century Ontario Law." *Saskatchewan Law Review* 56, no. 2 (1992): 297–371

Hodgins, Bruce W., Shawn Heard, and John S. Milloy, eds. *Co-existence? Studies in Ontario-First Nations Relations.* Peterborough, Ont.: Frost Centre for Canadian Heritage and Development Studies 1992

Jamieson, Kathleen. *Indian Women and the Law in Canada: Citizens Minus.* Ottawa:

Ministry of Supply and Services 1978. Published in French under the title *La femme indienne devant la loi: une citoyenne mineure*

Leslie, John, and Ron Maguire, eds. *The Historical Development of the Indian Act.* Treaties and Historical Research Centre, PRE Group, Indian and Northern Affairs. Ottawa 1978. Published in French under the title *Histoire de la loi sur les Indiens*

Montour, Enos T. "Brown Tom's Schooldays." Waterloo, Ont.: Mimeographed 1985

Morrison, James. *Treaty Nine (1905–06): The James Bay Treaty.* Treaties and Historical Research Centre, Indian and Northern Affairs Canada. Ottawa 1986. Published in French under the title *Rapport de recherche sur les traités: Traité neuf*

Surtees, Robert J. *The Williams Treaties.* Treaty Research Report, Treaties and Historical Research Centre, Indian and Northern Affairs Canada. Ottawa 1986. Published in French under the title *Rapport de recherche sur les traités: Traités Williams, 1923*

Taylor, John Leonard. *Canadian Indian Policy during the Inter-War Years, 1918-1939.* Ottawa: Indian and Northern Affairs 1984. Published in French under the title *Politique canadienne relative aux Indiens pendant entre-deux-guerres, 1918–1939*

Titley, Brian E. *A Narrow Vision: Duncan Campbell Scott and the Administration of Indian Affairs in Canada.* Vancouver: University of British Columbia Press 1986

**The First Nations within Canada, 1969–1993**

Cassidy, Frank, ed. *Aboriginal Self-Determination: Proceedings of a Conference Held September 30–October 3, 1990.* Lantzville, B.C.: Oolichan Books 1991

Engelstad, Diane, and John Bird, eds., *Nation to Nation: Aboriginal Sovereignty and the Future of Canada.* Toronto: Anansi Press 1992

Hodgins, Bruce W., Shawn Heard, and John S. Milloy, eds., *Co-existence? Studies in Ontario–First Nations Relations.* Peterborough, Ont.: Frost Centre for Canadian Heritage and Development Studies 1992

McNab, David T. "Aboriginal Land Claims in Ontario." In *Aboriginal Land Claims in Canada*, ed. Ken Coates, 73–100. Toronto: Copp Clark Pitman 1992

Mawhiney, Anne-Marie, ed. *Rebirth: Political, Economic and Social Development in First Nations.* Toronto: Dundurn Press 1993

Ponting, Rick J., ed. *Arduous Journey: Canadian Indians and Decolonization.* Toronto: McClelland & Stewart 1986

Richardson, Boyce, ed. *Drum Beat: Anger and Renewal in Indian Country.* Toronto: Summerhill Press 1989. Published in French under the title *Minuit moins cinq sur les réserves.* Montreal: Libre Expression 1992

Weaver, Sally M. *Making Canadian Indian Policy: The Hidden Agenda, 1968–1970.* Toronto: University of Toronto Press 1981

**The First Nations**

*Algonquin (and Nipissing)*

"Les Algonquins." A collection of articles in *Recherches amérindiennes au Québec* 23, nos. 2–3 (autumn 1993)

Couture, Yvon H. *Les Algonquins. Racines amérindiennes.* Val d'Or, Qué.: Éditions Hyperborée 1983

Day, Gordon M. "Nipissing." In *Handbook of North American Indians*, vol. 15: *Northeast*, ed. Bruce G. Trigger, 787–91. Washington, D.C.: Smithsonian Institution 1978

Day, Gordon M., and Bruce G. Trigger, "Algonquin." In *Handbook of North American Indians*, vol. 15: *Northeast*, ed. Bruce G. Trigger, 792–7. Washington: Smithsonian Institution 1978

Hessel, Peter. *The Algonkin Tribe: The Algonkins of the Ottawa Valley: An Historical Outline*. Arnprior, Ont.: Kichesippi Books 1987

Moore, Kermot A. *Kipewa: Portrait of a People*. Cobalt, Ont.: Highway Book Shop 1982

See also the biographical sketches of the Algonquin in the *Dictionary of Canadian Biography*, vols. 1–12 (Toronto: University of Toronto Press 1966– ): vol. 1 (1000–1700), Batiscan, Iroquet, Oumasasikweie (La Grenouille), Pieskaret, Pigarouich, Tessouat (fl. 1603–13), Tessouat (d. 1636), Tessouat (d. 1654); also the sketch of the Nipissing, Kisensik, in vol. 3 (1741–1770).

*Cree*

Brown, Jennifer S.H., and Robert Brightman. *'The Orders of the Dreamed': George Nelson on Cree and Northern Ojibwa Religion and Myth, 1823*. Winnipeg: University of Manitoba Press 1988

Francis, Daniel, and Toby Morantz. *Partners in Furs: A History of the Fur Trade in Eastern James Bay, 1600–1870*. Kingston and Montreal: McGill-Queen's University Press 1983. Published in French under the title *La traite des fourrures dans l'est de la baie James, 1600–1870*. Sillery: Presses de l'Université Québec 1984

Helm, June, and Eleanor B. Leacock. "The Hunting Tribes of Subarctic Canada." In *North American Indians in Historical Perspective*, ed. E.B. Leacock and N.O. Lurie, 343–74. New York: Random House 1971

Honigmann, John J. "West Main Cree." In *Handbook of North American Indians*, vol. 6: *Subarctic*, ed. J. Helm, 217–30. Washington, D.C.: Smithsonian Institution 1981

Long, John S. "'Shaganash': Early Protestant Missionaries and the Adoption of Christianity by the Western James Bay Cree, 1840–1892." EdD dissertation, University of Toronto (Ontario Institute for Studies in Education) 1986

Macfie, John, and Basil Johnston. *Hudson Bay Watershed: A Photographic Memoir of the Ojibway, Cree, and Oji-Cree*. Toronto: Dundurn Press 1991

Ross, Rupert. *Dancing with a Ghost: Exploring Indian Reality*. Markham, Ont.: Octopus Publishing Group 1992

Soeur, Paul-Émile. *La Baie James. Trois cents ans d'histoire*. Ottawa: Éditions de l'Université d'Ottawa 1952

Trudeau, Jean. "The Cree Indians." In *Science, History and Hudson Bay*, ed. C.S. Beals, 2 vols., 1:127–41. Ottawa: Department of Energy, Mines and Resources 1968

Willis, Jane. *Geniesh: An Indian Childhood*. Toronto: New Press 1973

See also the sketches of Cree Indians in the *Dictionary of Canadian Biography*: vol. 2 (1701–1740), Auchagah, Miscomote, Scatchamisse; vol. 3 (1741–1770), La Colle, Wappisis; vol. 4 (1771–1800), Winninnewaycappo (Captain Jecob); and vol. 7 (1836–1850), Abishabis.

*Delaware (Munceys)*

Gray, Elma E., and L.R. Gray. *Wilderness Christians: The Moravian Mission to the Delaware Indian*. Toronto: Macmillan 1956

Goddard, Ives. "Delaware." In *Handbook of North American Indians*, vol. 15: *Northeast*, ed. Bruce G. Trigger, 583–7. Washington, D.C.: Smithsonian Institution 1978

Heckewelder, John. *History, Manners and Customs of the Indian Nations Who Once Inhabited Pennsylvania and the Neighbouring States*. Philadelphia: Historical Society of Pennsylvania 1876

Weslager, C.A. *The Delaware Indians: A History*. New Brunswick, N.J.: Rutgers University Press 1972

See also the sketches of Delaware in the *Dictionary of Canadian Biography*: vol. 4 (1771–1800), Anandamoakin (Long Coat) and Glikhikan (Isaac).

*Huron (Petun, Wyandot)*

Anderson, Karen. *Chain Her by One Foot: The Subjugation of Women in Seventeenth-century New France*. London: Routledge 1991

Campeau, Lucien. *La Mission des Jésuites chez les Hurons 1634–1650*. Montreal: Éditions Bellarmin 1987

Clarke, Peter Dooyentate. *Origin and Traditional History of the Wyandotts*. Toronto: Hunter, Rose & Co. 1870

Garrad, Charles, and Conrad E. Heidenriech. "Khionontateron (Petun)." In *Handbook of North American Indians*, vol. 15: *Northeast*, ed. Bruce G. Trigger, 394–7. Washington, D.C.: Smithsonian Institution 1978

Heidenreich, Conrad. *Huronia: A History and Geography of the Huron Indians 1600–1650*. Toronto: McClelland & Stewart 1971

———. "Huron." In *Handbook of North American Indians*, vol. 15: *Northeast*, ed. Bruce G. Trigger, 368–88. Washington, D.C.: Smithsonian Institution 1978

Sagard, Gabriel. *The Long Journey to the Country of the Hurons*, ed. G.M. Wrong. Toronto: Champlain Society 1939

Sioui, Georges E. *Pour une Autohistoire amérindienne. Essai sur les fondements d'une morale social*. Québec: Les Presses de l'Université Laval 1989. Translated from the French by Sheila Fischman, *For an Amerindian Autohistory: An Essay on the Foundations of a Social Ethic*. Montreal: McGill-Queen's University Press 1992

Tooker, Elisabeth. "Wyandot." In *Handbook of North American Indians*, vol. 15, *Northeast*, ed. Bruce G. Trigger, 398–406. Washington, D.C.: Smithsonian Institution 1978

———. *An Ethnography of the Huron Indians, 1615–1649*. Syracuse: Syracuse University Press 1991

Trigger, Bruce G. *The Children of Aataentsic: A History of the Huron People to 1660*. 2 vols. Montreal and Kingston: McGill-Queen's University Press 1976

———. *The Huron: Farmers of the North*. 2d ed. Fort Worth, Tex.: Holt, Rinehart and Winston 1990

See also the sketches (*a*) of the Huron in the *Dictionary of Canadian Biography*: vol. 1 (1000–1700), Ahatsistari, Amantacha, Annaotaha, Atironta (fl. 1615), Atironta (d. 1650),

Atironta (d. 1672), Auoindaon, Chihouatenha, Oionhaton (Thérèse), Ondaaiondiont, Savignon, Skanudharoua named Geneviève-Agnès de Tous-les-Saints, Taondechoren (Louis) Taratouan, Tehorenhaegnon, Teouatiron, Tonsahoten, Totiri; vol. 2 (1701–1740), Kondiaronk (Le Rat); vol. 3 (1741–1770), Michipichy, Orontony; and (*b*) of the Wyandots: vol. 5 (1801–1820), Myeerah, Stayeghtha (Roundhead); vol. 7 (1836–1850), Sou-neh-hoo-way (Splitlog).

*Iroquois*

Abler, Thomas S. "The Iroquois." Canada's Visual History series, vol. 28. Ottawa: National Museum of Civilization and National Film Board of Canada, n.d. Published in French under the title *Les Iroquois*

Beaver, George. *A View from an Indian Reserve: Historical Perspective and a Personal View from an Indian Reserve*. Brantford, Ont.: Brant Historical Society 1993

Blanchard, David. *Seven Generations: A History of Kanienkehaka*. Kahnawake: Kahnawake Survival School 1980

Boyle, David. "The Pagan Iroquois." In *Archaeological Report, 1898. Being part of the Appendix to the Report of the Minister of Education, Ontario*, 54–211. Toronto: Warwick Bros. & Rutter 1898

Druke, Mary A. "Iroquois and Iroquoian in Canada." In *Native Peoples: The Canadian Experience*, ed. R. Bruce Morrison and C. Roderick Wilson, 302–24. Toronto: McClelland & Stewart 1986

Du Vernet, Sylvia. *An Indian Odyssey: Tribulations, Trials and Triumphs of Gibson Band of the Mohawk Tribe of the Iroquois Confederacy*. Islington, Ont.: Muskoka Publications 1986

Fenton, William. "The Iroquois in History." In *North American Indians in Historical Perspective*, ed. Eleanor Burke Leacock and Nancy O. Lurie, 129–68. New York: Random House 1971

Graymont, Barbara. *The Iroquois in the American Revolution*. Syracuse: Syracuse University Press 1972

———. *The Iroquois*. New York: Chelsea House Publishers 1988

Hertzberg, Hazel W. *The Great Tree and the Longhouse: The Culture of the Iroquois*. New York: Macmillan Company 1966

Johnston, Charles M., ed. *The Valley of the Six Nations: A Collection of Documents on the Indian Lands of the Grand River*. Toronto: University of Toronto Press 1964

Kelsay, Isabel Thompson. *Joseph Brant, 1743–1807: Man of Two Worlds*. Syracuse: Syracuse University Press 1984

Lafitau, Joseph François. *Customs of the American Indians Compared with the Customs of Primitive Times*, ed. and trans. W.N. Fenton and Elizabeth L. Moore. 2 vols. Toronto: Champlain Society 1974–77

Shimony, Annemarie A. *Conservatism among the Iroquois at the Six Nations Reserve*. New Haven: Yale University Publications in Anthropology 1961

Snyderman, George S. "Concepts of Land Ownership among the Iroquois and Their Neighbors." In *Symposium on Local Diversity in Iroquois Culture*, ed. William N. Fenton, 15–34. Smithsonian Institution Bureau of American Ethnology Bulletin 149. Washington, D.C.: United States Government Printing Office 1951

Spittal, Wm. Guy, ed. *Iroquois Women: An Anthology*. Ohsweken, Ont.: Iroqrafts 1990
Tooker, Elisabeth, ed. *An Iroquois Source Book*. 3 vols. New York: Garland Publishing 1985
Trigger, Bruce G., ed. *Handbook of North American Indians*, vol. 15: *Northeast*. Washington, D.C.: Smithsonian Institution 1978. See the sketches by Thomas S. Abler and Elisabeth Tooker, "Seneca" (505–17); Harold Blau, Jack Campisi, and Elisabeth Tooker, "Onondaga" (491–9); Jack Campisi, "Oneida" (481–90); Marian E. White, William E. Engelbrecht, and Elisabeth Tooker, "Cayuga" (500–4); William N. Fenton and Elisabeth Tooker, "Mohawk" (466–80); David Landy, "Tuscarora among the Iroquois" (518–24); Sally M. Weaver, "Six Nations of the Grand River, Ontario" (526–36)
Wallace, Anthony F.C. *The Death and Rebirth of the Seneca*. New York: A.A. Knopf 1969
Wallace, Paul A.W. *The White Roots of Peace*. Philadelphia: University of Pennsylvania Press 1946

See also the sketches of Iroquois in the *Dictionary of Canadian Biography*: vol. 1 (1000–1700), Dekanahwideh, Donnacona, Ourehouare; vol. 7 (1836–1850), Williams (Thomas); vol. 11 (1881–1890), Onasakenrat (Joseph); and on the individual nations: CAYUGA: vol. 4 (1771–1800), Ottrowana; MOHAWK: vol. 1 (1000–1700), Agariata, Flemish Bastard, Honatteniate, Kiotseaeton, Tekakwitha, Kateri, Togouiroui; vol. 2 (1701–1740), Tekarihoken; vol. 3 (1741–1770), Karaghtadie, Theyanoguin (Hendrick); vol. 4 (1771–1800), Konwatsi'tsiaiénni (Mary Brant), Sahonwagy, Teiorhénhsere' (Little Abraham), Tekawironte (William Johnson); vol. 5 (1801–1820), Atiatoharongwen, Deserontyon (John), Thayendanegea (Joseph Brant); vol. 6 (1821–1835), Kenwendeshon (Henry Aaron Hill), Tehowagherengaraghkwen (Thomas Davis), Tekarihogen (Henry), Tekarihogen (John Brant); vol. 7 (1836–1850), Ohtowa'kéhson (Catharine Brant); vol. 8 (1851–1860), Martin (George), Powlis (George), Williams (Eleazer); vol. 9 (1881–1890), Johnson (George Henry Martin), Johnson (John "Smoke"); vol. 13 (1901–1910), Oronhyatekha; ONEIDA: vol. 1 (1000–1700), Annenraes, Chaudière Noire, Garakontié, Otreouti, Ogenheratarihiens, Tareha; vol. 2 (1701–1740), Gouentagrandi; vol. 3 (1741–1770), Gawèhe, Swatana; vol. 6 (1821–1835), Ainse (Sarah) (Montour, Maxwell, Willson); ONONDAGA: vol. 1 (1000–1700), vol. 2 (1701–1740), Aradgi, Ohonsiowanne, Teganissorens; vol. 3 (1741–1770), Kakouenthiony (Red Head), Ononwarogo; vol. 4 (1771–1800), Hotsinonhyahta' (The Bunt), Ohquandageghte, Teyohaqueande; SENECA: vol. 2 (1701–1740), Aouenano, Cagenquarichten, Tekanoet, Tonatakout; vol. 3 (1741–1770), Kaghswaghtaniunt, Tanaghrisson; vol. 4 (1771–1800), Kaien'kwaahton (Old Smoke); Kayasota'.

*Neutral*

Noble, William C. "The Neutral Indians." In *Essays in Northeastern Anthropology in Memory of Marian E. White*, ed. William E. Engelbrecht and Donald K. Grayson, 152–62. Rindge, N.H.: Franklin Pierce College 1978
White, Marion E. "Neutral and Wenro." In *Handbook of North American Indians*, vol. 15: *Northeast*, ed. Bruce G. Trigger, 407–11. Washington: Smithsonian Institution 1978

*Ojibwa (also Mississauga and Ottawa, or Odawa)*

Bishop, Charles A. *The Northern Ojibwa and the Fur Trade: An Historical and Ecological Study*. Toronto: Holt, Rinehart and Winston 1974

Brown, Jennifer S.H. "Northern Algonquians from Lake Superior and Hudson Bay to Manitoba in the Historical Period." In *Native Peoples: The Canadian Experience*, ed. R. Bruce Morrison and C. Roderick Wilson, 208–36. Toronto: McClelland & Stewart 1986

Brown, Jennifer S.H., and Robert Brightman. *'The Orders of the Dreamed': George Nelson on Cree and Northern Ojibwa Religion and Myth, 1823.* Winnipeg: University of Manitoba Press, 1988

Désveaux, Emmanuel. *Sous le Signe de l'Ours. Mythes et temporalité chez les Ojibwa septentrionaux.* Paris: Fondation de la maison des Sciences de l'Homme 1988

Driben, Paul, and Robert S. Trudeau. *When Freedom Is Lost: The Dark Side of the Relationship between Government and the Fort Hope Band.* Toronto: University of Toronto Press 1983

Dunning, R.W. *Social and Economic Change among the Northern Ojibwa.* Toronto: University of Toronto Press 1959

Feest, Johanna E., and Christian F. Feest, "Ottawa." In *Handbook of North American Indians*, vol. 15: *Northeast*, ed. Bruce G. Trigger, 772–96. Washington, D.C.: Smithsonian Institution 1978

Hallowell, A. Irving. *The Ojibwa of Berens River, Manitoba: Ethnography into History*, ed. Jennifer S.H. Brown. Fort Worth, Tex.: Harcourt Brace Jovanovich 1992

Hodgins, Bruce, and Jamie Benedickson. *The Temagami Experience: Recreation, Resources and Aboriginal Rights in the Northern Ontario Wilderness.* Toronto: University of Toronto Press 1989

Jenness, Diamond. *The Ojibwa Indians of Parry Island Canada.* National Museum of Canada, Department of Mines Bulletin 7. Ottawa: King's Printer 1932

Jones, Peter (Kahkewaquonaby). *Life and Journals of Kah-ke-wa-quo-na-by (Rev. Peter Jones), Wesleyan Missionary.* Toronto: Wesleyan Printing Establishment 1860

———. *History of the Ojebway Indians; with especial reference to their Conversion to Christianity.* London: A.W. Bennett 1861

Kohl, Johann G. *Kitchi-Gami: Wanderings Around Lake Superior.* London: Chapman and Hall 1860; Minneapolis, Minn.: Ross and Haines 1956

Landes, Ruth. *The Ojibwa Woman.* New York: Columbia University Press 1938; reprint, New York: W.W. Norton and Company 1971

———. *Ojibwa Religion and the Midewiwin.* Madison: University of Wisconsin Press 1968

Macfie, John, and Basil Johnston. *Hudson Bay Watershed: A Photographic Memoir of the Ojibway, Cree and Oji-Cree.* Toronto: Dundurn Press 1991

Morrison, James (with Adolph M. Greenberg). "Group Identities in the Boreal Forest: The Origin of the Northern Ojibwa," *Ethnohistory* 29 (1982): 75–102

Odjig, Daphne, through R.M. Vanderburgh and M.E. Southcott. *A Paintbrush in My Hand.* Toronto: Natural Heritage/Natural History Inc. 1992

Rogers, Edward S. *The Round Lake Ojibwa.* Occasional Paper no. 5, Art and Archaeology Division, Royal Ontario Museum. Toronto 1962

Rogers, Edward S., and Flora Tobobondung. *Parry Island Farmers: A Period of Change in the Way of Life of the Algonkians of Southern Ontario in Contributions to Canadian Ethnology, 1975*, 247–366. Canadian Ethnology Service. Ottawa: National Museum of Man 1975

Ross, Rupert. *Dancing with a Ghost: Exploring Indian Reality.* Markham, Ont.: Octopus Publishing Group 1992

Schmalz, Peter. *The Ojibwa of Southern Ontario*. Toronto: University of Toronto Press 1991
Smith, Donald B. (with the assistance of Bryan La Forme). *The Mississauga of New Credit*. Canada's Visual History series, vol. 22. Ottawa: National Museum of Civilization and the National Film Board of Canada, n.d.
Southcott, Mary E. *The Sound of the Drum: The Sacred Art of the Anishnabec*. Erin, Ont.: Boston Mills Press 1984
Vanderburgh, R.M. *I am Nokomis, Too: The Biography of Verna Patronella Johnston*. Don Mills, Ont.: General Publishing 1977
Warren, William. *History of the Ojebway Nation*. Collections of the Minnesota Historical Society, vol. 5. 1885; reprint, Minneapolis, Minn.: Ross and Haines 1957

See also the sketches of Ojibwa, Ottawa, and Mississauga in the *Dictionary of Canadian Biography*: OJIBWA: vol. 3 (1741–1770), Minweweh, Wawatam; vol. 4 (1771–1800), Wasson; vol. 5 (1801–1820), Chejauk, Madjeckewiss, Zheewegonab; vol. 7 (1836–1850), Aisance (John), Bauzhi-geezhig-waeshikum; vol. 9 (1861–1870), Musquakie (William Yellowhead); vol. 11 (1881–1890), Steinhauer (Henry Bird); vol. 12 (1891–1900), Peemeecheekag, Ponekeosh; vol. 13 (1901–1910), McGregor (William Bruce), Migisi, Zhauwuno-geezhigo-gaubow; OJIBWA (Mississauga): vol. 3 (1741–1770), Wabbicom-micot; vol. 4 (1771–1800), Wabakinine; vol. 5 (1801–1820), Kineubenae; vol. 6 (1821–1835), Ogimauh-binaessih; vol. 7 (1836–1850), Jones (John); vol. 8 (1851–1860), Jones (Peter); vol. 9 (1861–1870), Kahgegagahbowh (George Copway), Nahnebahwequay (Catherine Sutton), Nawahjegezhegwabe (Joseph Sawyer); vol. 10 (1871–1880), Shah-wun-dais (John Sunday); vol. 11 (1881–1890), Kezhegowinninne (David Sawyer), Pahtahsega (Peter Jacobs); vol. 12 (1891–1900), Chase, (Henry); vol. 13 (1901–1910), Jones (Peter Edmund); OTTAWA: vol. 2 (1701–1740), Chingouessi, Koutaoiliboe, Kinongé, Le Pesant, Miscouaky, Outoutagan; vol. 3 (1741–1770), Kinousaki, Mikinak, Pontiac, Saguima; vol. 4 (1771–1800), Egushwa, Nissowaquet; vol. 5 (1801–1820), Chejauk; vol. 6 (1821–1835), Shawanakiskie; vol. 7 (1836–1850), Bauzhi-geezhig-waeshikum; and vol. 9 (1861–1870), Assiginack (Jean-Baptiste), Assikinack (Francis).

*Potawatomi*

Clifton, James A. *A Place of Refuge for All Time: Migration of the American Potawatomi into Upper Canada 1830 to 1850*. Ottawa: National Museum of Man 1975
Clifton, James A. "Potawatomi." In *Handbook of North American Indians*, vol. 15: *Northeast*, ed. Bruce G. Trigger, 725–48. Washington, D.C.: Smithsonian Institution, 1978

*Other Groups*

For any other group refer to *Handbook of North American Indians*, vol. 15: *Northeast*, ed. Bruce G. Trigger (Washington, D.C.: Smithsonian Institution, 1978).
    See also the following biographical sketches in the *Dictionary of Canadian Biography*: ERIE, vol. 1 (1000–1700), Gandeacteua; Fox, vol. 2 (1701–1740), Kiala, Noro, Ouachala, Pemoussa; SHAWNEE, vol. 5 (1801–1820), Tecumseh, Weyapiersenwah (Blue Jacket); vol. 7 (1836–1850), Tenskwatawa (The Prophet).

# Index

CPSIA information can be obtained at www.ICGtesting.com
Printed in the USA
LVOW031729240911

247611LV00006B/2/P